ROM

THIS

MOMENT

ON

FROM THIS MOMENT ON

America in 1940

JEFFREY HART

CROWN PUBLISHERS, INC.

NEW YORK

Published by Crown Publishers, Inc., 225 Park Avenue South, New York, New
York 10003 and represented in Canada by the Canadian MANDA Group
CROWN is a trademark of Crown Publishers, Inc.

Manufactured in the United States of America

Library of Congress Cataloging-in-Publication Data

Hart, Jeffrey Peter, 1930–
From this moment on.

Includes index.
1. United States—Social life and customs—1918–1945.
2. United States—Popular culture—History—20th century.
I. Title. II. Title: 1940.
E169.H288   1987   973.917   86-19853
ISBN 0-517-55741-X

Design by Jake Victor Thomas

10 9 8 7 6 5 4 3 2 1

First Edition

Acknowledgments

Grateful acknowledgment is given for the use of the following excerpted material in this book.

'Taint Right by Westbrook Pegler, copyright 1936 by Doubleday, Doran & Company, Inc.

Article by Richard Breitling from *Secret Conversations with Hitler*, edited by Edouard Calic, copyright © 1971 by Richard Breitling.

Genocide edited by Grobman & Landes, copyright © 1983 by Simon Wiesenthal Center. Reprinted by permission.

"Notes and Comment" from "The Talk of the Town," copyright © 1962 by The New Yorker Magazine, Inc. Reprinted by permission.

"On College Gridirons" by Allison Danzig and ". . . Enters Semi-Finals of U.S. Tennis—Misses Marble and Scott Continue Advance" by Allison Danzig, both copyright 1940 by The New York Times Company. Reprinted by permission.

The Red Blaik Story by Earl "Red" Blaik, copyright © 1960 by Earl H. Blaik and Tim Cohane. Reprinted by permission of Arlington House, Inc.

Joe Louis: My Life by Joe Louis with Edna and Art Rust, Jr., copyright © 1978 by Jeffrey Hoffman. Reprinted by permission of Harcourt Brace Jovanovich, Inc.

The Grapes of Wrath by John Steinbeck, copyright 1939, renewed copyright © 1967 by John Steinbeck. Reprinted by permission of Viking Penguin, Inc.

You Can't Go Home Again by Thomas Wolfe, copyright 1934, 1937, 1938, 1939, 1940, by Maxwell Perkins as Executor; renewed copyright © 1967 by Paul Gitlin, C.T.A. Administrator of the Estate of Thomas Wolfe. Reprinted by permission of Harper & Row Publishers, Inc.

To the Finland Station by Edmund Wilson, copyright 1940, renewed copyright © 1967 by Edmund Wilson. Reprinted by permission of Farrar, Straus, and Giroux, Inc.

The Hamlet by William Faulkner, copyright 1931, renewed copyright © 1958 by William Faulkner, copyright 1932, renewed copyright © 1959 by The Curtis Publishing Company, copyright 1936 by

For Nancy

CONTENTS

And fast by hanging in a Golden Chain
This pendant world, in bigness as a Star
Of smallest Magnitude close by the Moon.

John Milton,
Paradise Lost, Book II

It looked as if a night of dark intent
Was coming, and not only a night, an age.
Someone had better be prepared for rage.

Robert Frost,
"Once By the Pacific" (1928)

FROM THIS MOMENT ON

ROLOGUE

By the Sea

That summer, black men pushed the chairs along the boardwalk. The chairs were made of wicker, and there was a large wicker footboard in front of your feet. The chairs rolling lazily along the boardwalk had large wheels and red-white-and-blue-striped canopies. The men riding in them sometimes wore white trousers and hard straw hats with a regimental-striped hatband around them. The women in the chairs often had elaborate hairdos, though of course the expression hairdo was not used in those days. People moved down the boardwalk like crowded shoals of fish. The sun danced in small triangles on the ocean.

All the hotels along the beach had been built back in the eighties and nineties. They were wooden, and white or yellow or gray, and had turrets, verandas, dormer windows, gingerbread wood, and striped awnings; Grandmother stayed all summer at one called Ocean Vista.

Wearing bathing suits was restricted to the beach itself. Rules were strict because the town itself had been founded back in the nineteenth century as a Methodist summer camp meeting, and its huge, circular Methodist auditorium was an important religious center. So the bathers left their wooden hotels fully dressed and carrying their beach umbrellas, their suits, and their towels, and walked across Ocean Avenue to the Bathhouse, a white wooden structure that seemed to be partially underground and contained rows of white-doored and gloomy bath cubicles, within which it was permitted to change into your bathing suit. These cubicles smelled remotely of suntan lotion. And because the only light came from a six-inch slot below the door, they were always dank. You changed quickly, and it was wonderful to walk out through the dark, cement underground tunnel, chilly, into the amazing sunlight of the beach and its blazing sands.

All day long, if you were ten years old, you were among the bright striped children on that beach, while all day long, the ships crept by on the horizon, sometimes great ocean liners with their two or three smokestacks, sometimes the sleek, low profile of a destroyer, and always there was the grand eternal motion of the sea.

1

The older women, that summer before the war, still usually wore one-piece bathing suits, some of them still made of itchy, dark wool, though the boy's mother wore a one-piece Jantzen sharkskin. She had been an actress on Broadway. His father, when he came down from the city, wore dark blue woolen trunks with a white canvas belt fastened by two interlocking metal snakes that formed a buckle. There were bathing ropes attached to wooden piles, and the ropes stretched out into the surf. The women hung on them and screamed.

In front of all the hotels along the beach, there were American flags, either on a pole standing on the front lawn or hanging from a pole sticking out from the second-story veranda, and the flags had forty-eight stars. On most evenings during the summer, there were band concerts on the boardwalk, sometimes with fireworks, sometimes patriotic songs of the Sousa kind, and sometimes religious meetings with Methodist hymns.

The Jewish kids to the south in Bradley Beach called Ocean Grove "Ocean Grave." The next town north up the beach, Asbury Park, named for Francis Asbury, the great Methodist preacher, a disciple of the Wesley brothers, contained a large, and to a ten-year-old boy overwhelming, amusement park. You could pedal a Swan Boat lazily along Wesley Lake in the dusk, ride the huge Ferris wheel or the merry-go-round, which spun in a nineteenth-century, cast-iron building. You could sit on the boardwalk with an ice-cream cone and look out at the lights of the fishing boats winking on the horizon. The adults, the parents and grandparents, liked the auctions and the bingo games when they came down from New York, and they gave you a nickel for the man on the boardwalk with a big scale who "Guessed Your Weight." He was always right.

Back in the nineties, Stephen Crane had caught the flavor in his Jersey shore reports for the *New York Tribune*. "The Ferris wheel went up near the beach, its motor emitting sparks that disturbed the owners of the wooden hotels. There was a Baby Parade, with the infants in strollers along the boardwalk. There were the great crowds of the 'Nineties. James J. Corbett, the pugilist, who is preparing for his fight with John L. Sullivan in a handsome Loch Arbour cottage, is now down to hard training, and his admirers, who used to tramp the Asbury Park boardwalk in the evenings are somewhat at a loss. . . ." But those crowds of the nineties were not at a loss on the Jersey shore. Stephen Crane, for the *Tribune:* "The crowds here grow larger every day. . . . The number of people who take their daily promenade on the ocean plaza surpasses belief. . . . Down on the beach the famous boardwalk and the broad sandy beach are literally covered with people. . . . Daily excursion trains come here from all parts of New York, New Jersey and Pennsylvania, but the people who come here for a day are lost in the immense crowd of humanity which has come here for the season."

That was the way it was back in the nineties. But it was not so much different that summer. Grandfather came down weekends from New York. Sometimes he came on the excursion boat that docked nearby, and sometimes in his large new Huppmobile with its white-walled tires and spare tire in a chrome case. Though he had been an amateur bike racer back in the nineties, he was now cautious and never drove any faster than thirty miles an hour down the two-lane, blacktop roads of New Jersey. He was highly sensitive to the sun and never went down on the sand, but he liked to sit on the hotel veranda in a rocking chair and talk with the older people. Or, dressed in his white shoes, white trousers, white shirt, and Panama hat, he would stroll along the boardwalk in the dusk. He was not a Methodist, but he liked Methodist Ocean Grove because liquor was not sold there, there were no cars allowed in on Sundays, and the atmosphere was extremely peaceful.

Up in Brooklyn, he and Grandmother lived in a three-story town house with long, dark hallways, dark Victorian furniture, a dark cellar with a coal furnace, and a garden in the back with a cement birdbath. Grandfather made a good living as an executive and buyer in a wholesale blouse company up in Manhattan, and he liked to say that he was "the last gentile in the women's blouse business," which may have been true, but he got along very well with his Jewish partners. After he had his first heart attack and could work very little, they made sure that he did not suffer financially.

Besides the boy's mother, there were three uncles. Walter, a cripple, either stayed in his bed or sat in a wheelchair, a dark, brooding young man who had written several popular songs. When one came over the radio, the mother would say, "There's one of Walter's songs." Of the two other brothers, one was a golf pro out on Long Island, the other a college student in New York.

In those days, Italians sold fresh vegetables from horse-drawn wagons along the streets of the city, throwing water on the lettuce, the carrots, the spinach to keep it fresh-looking. The vegetables came from the Italian truck farms that covered much of Long Island in those days. Grandmother bought ice from an Italian off a horse-drawn ice truck. She did not see the need for a new electric refrigerator. An Italian, Fiorello LaGuardia, was mayor of New York, the Little Flower, who liked to don a fireman's hat and ride the screaming engine to the fire. An Italian, Joe DiMaggio, was the highest-paid player in baseball at $30,000. Often you saw an organ-grinder with courageous mustache and black eyes on the corner, with a monkey in uniform, who would doff his cap if you offered him a coin, and the organ-grinder was Italian too. The trolleys in Brooklyn were red and yellow and clanged along everywhere. You boarded for a nickel and sat on yellow rush seats.

By midafternoon down at the shore, you could see the heat waves rising off the sand, and Mother asked whether you might want to take a nap. The sand castle-building children played by the sea. Out beyond the breakers, four lifeguards lazily rowed a large, white, wooden boat. A man walked along the beach carrying a placard stating that a horse and rider would dive off the pier at Asbury Park at 8:00 P.M. The boy thought the breakers were fearful in those days, but later on they mysteriously diminished. Where had the great waves gone? He understood much later when he stood by the sea with one of his daughters and saw her shrink from a wave that hit him in the thigh.

One night, three years earlier, there had been a strange false sunset to the west when the *Hindenburg* blew up over at the airship landing field in Lakehurst, the glow lighting up the night sky as the hydrogen burned with a heat so intense that it melted the metal mooring tower as flaming passengers jumped to their deaths. One theory at the time was later found to be correct. A Communist crew member had fastened a time bomb to one of the girders of the huge airship. Everyone remembered the enormous red tail fins with the swastika inside the white circle as the *Hindenburg* circled the Empire State Building on its regular run from Germany.

Still earlier, back in 1934, the *Morro Castle* burned offshore one night, and the people on the verandas could see the distant blaze on the night horizon. The *Morro Castle* was a cruise ship of the latest design, with foolproof fire installations, and it was on its way from Havana to New York. The fire spread very rapidly through the ship. Many crew members panicked and seized lifeboats as the decks and walls grew red-hot. A passenger in a lifeboat remembers looking up and seeing passengers trapped in their cabins looking out through the portholes. One doomed man waved farewell. Bodies were washed up on the beach the next morning and put on the hotel verandas, which served as temporary morgues. That morning, the *Morro Castle* washed up on shore too, a huge blackened hulk beached just north of the new Asbury Park Convention Center. Everyone came down to the boardwalk to gape at the disaster. The investigators said it was arson and thought that Communists in Havana had planted incendiary material with timing devices.

The *Morro Castle* burned in the summer of 1934, the *Hindenburg* in the summer of 1937.

But this was the summer of 1940. France had fallen, and Hitler was at the English Channel.

THE WORLD
OF TOMORROW

The New York World's Fair of 1939–40 rose out of Flushing Meadow on Long Island as a luminous statement of American optimism, though everyone was aware that Europe and perhaps the rest of the world were sliding toward war. The lights of the fair were visible from Manhattan, ten miles away, and up close, they helped to create a magical world of tint and tone, but the skies were darkening dramatically across both oceans. "And at last," as Joseph Conrad wrote in the prophetic and symphonic opening of his story *Heart of Darkness,* "in its curved and imperceptible fall, the sun sank low, and from glowing white changed to dull red without rays and without heat, as if about to go out suddenly, stricken to death by the touch of that gloom brooding over a crowd of men." There have been many international expositions, beginning with the late eighteenth century, and they have always been expressions of progress and enlightenment, but the New York World's Fair, in those years on the threshold of the war, was intellectually and artistically the most successful of them all, at least since the Great Exhibition of 1851, the palace of glass and iron and art and technology that rose in London's Hyde Park as a reflection of Britain's empire and civilization.

For a ten-year-old boy whose parents had bought him a season ticket, and probably also for anyone else, the fair was an overwhelming experience. Everyone who went still speaks of it with awe. You got off the elevated IRT train at World's Fair Station—both train and station are still there, though it cost 5 cents to ride the train in those days, one dollar today—and you passed through the fair turnstiles. Then you walked down a broad, wooden boardwalk that is still there too. Today it takes you to Shea Stadium, where the Mets [professional] baseball team plays, and to the National Tennis Center, site of the United States Open Tennis Tournament. But in 1940, the boardwalk took you down to the fair and the optimistic vision of the World of Tomorrow.

The fair was built in what is called Flushing Meadow, which, so far as anyone knew, had always been a swamp. Back in the 1920s, the swamp had gradually been filled in with garbage and ashes from countless coal furnaces, hence its appearance in F. Scott Fitzgerald's *Great Gatsby* as the "valley of ashes," the wasteland where Daisy kills Myrtle. But at the end of that novel the moon rises again over a ghostly Long Island, transforming the scene, as that scene would literally be transformed again and again, now for the fair, later on for Shea Stadium and the Tennis Center. The immediate agent of transformation was New York's master builder of public beaches, bridges, parks, and roads, Robert Moses. He had long desired to build on the Flushing marshland a park site comparable to Manhattan's Central Park, and he saw the fair as a means to realize this. A complex reclamation scheme using state and federal funds was set in motion as Moses moved to transform the meandering Flushing Creek into an ordered parkland of lakes, canals, and horticulture.

The idea of the fair had originated in the spring of 1935, in the depths of the Great Depression, when a group of public-spirited businessmen and civic leaders, encouraged by the success of Chicago's "Century of Progress" exposition, adopted the idea of a World's Fair in New York that would raise morale and perhaps stimulate business in a grim economic climate. Three months after the formation of a World's Fair Corporation, one hundred "progressives in the arts" gathered at a dinner party in New York's Civic Club. A series of speakers called for a new kind of fair which, as Lewis Mumford put it, would "project a pattern that will fulfill itself in the future of the whole civilization." In Mumford's vision, "the story we have to tell . . . which will bring people from all over the world to New York, not merely from the United States, is the story of this planned environment, this planned industry, this planned civilization. If we can inject that notion as a basic notion of the Fair, if we can point it toward the future, toward something that is progressing and growing in every department of life and throughout civilization, not merely in the United States, not merely in New York City, but if we allow ourselves in a central position, as members of a great metropolis, to think for the world at large, we may lay the foundation for a pattern of life which would have an enormous impact in times to come." Much that Lewis Mumford and the other "progressives in the arts" envisioned in the planning stages came to pass. The fair did attempt, and to a great extent succeeded in projecting a future planned environment for enterprise and for living, as one formulation had it, "a unified whole which will represent all of the interrelated activities and interests of the American way of life." But the sheer vitality of the actual fair was something that could not be planned for, and the bursting life of the actual organism went far beyond any pedagogical purposes of the enlightened planners.

Briefly put, the fair's designers were concerned with three broad issues. First was the pervasive fact of the Great Depression. The assumption of the fair was that the means were available to create material abundance for all. Second, however, was the fact that the fair's planners were ideological democrats who wanted to assert democratic values against the looming challenges of fascism and communism. They believed that material abundance was vital to the preservation of the democratic system. And third, they were concerned with the psychological problem of alienation in an industrial society, and they sought ways to project a revitalized sense of community. In the first two of these aims, they were more successful than one might have expected, but the actuality of the fair went far beyond its intellectual rationale, and their prescription of a totally integrated planned environment as a cure for alienation was never very persuasive.

"It's a thing like a fair," says a character in Scott Fitzgerald's "Absolution," "only much more glittering. Go to one at night and stand a little way off from it in a dark place—under dark trees. You'll see a big wheel made of lights turning in the air, and a long slide shooting boats down into the water. A band playing somewhere and a smell of peanuts—and everything will twinkle. . . . It will all just hang out there in the night like a colored balloon—like a big yellow lantern on a pole." That was the way the World's Fair looked, especially at night, but in the daytime the first thing you saw as you came down the boardwalk and into the fair was its dominating symbol, the Trylon and Perisphere, the former a triangular, pointed tower 610 feet high, the latter a gigantic globe a block across, both gleaming white during the day and both illuminated at night by floodlights coloring them pastel hues of blue and yellow and pink. The Trylon and Perisphere remain with us today, not only in collective memory, but in the countless memorabilia that came down to us from the fair: saltshakers, plates, pencil sharpeners, scarves, glasses and bowls, rings and ashtrays. The Trylon and Perisphere were symbols so central that they possess a continuing imaginative life, severe modern geometrical symbols, but also an unforgettable visual experience and the signature of their era.

The Trylon and Perisphere did not spring newly from the brains of their designers, the architectural firm of Harrison and Fouilhoux. Their background was a continuous tradition in modern art and design. The master, modern painter Henri Matisse held that all spatial form could be resolved into three geometrical shapes—the triangle, the sphere, and the cube. Matisse himself was part of a tradition of radical, formal simplification. Visionary French architects of the late eighteenth century had imagined projects based upon the revolutionary and optimistic clarity of geometrical shapes. Descartes, Leibnitz, and Spinoza lurked in the background of all this. Globe-and-spire imagery was prominent in designs for the Columbian Exposition of 1893 and for the 700-foot Globe Tower projected for Coney Island's Steeplechase park. Architects and designers were aware of the visionary designs submitted in 1929 for the International Christopher Columbus Lighthouse Competition, in which a team of Russian architects—Krautikoff, Warentzoff, and Bounnie—submitted plans for a beacon tower beside a spherical structure that is strikingly prophetic of the Trylon and Perisphere. And of course, always present in the minds of modern designers was the Eiffel Tower, immensely controversial in Parisian circles when it was built, a symbol of modernism and the machine, its metallic and geometrical simplicity a calculated insult to tradition and to the Parisian mansard roofs and winding, cobbled streets upon which it looked down from a more-than-human scale. The Trylon and Perisphere represented a climactic moment in modern architectural design, and they established themselves in the popular consciousness as symbols of that enormous optimistic thrust.

The Trylon and Perisphere were, of course, male and female symbols, and inside the female globe the designers had gestated their vision of the World of Tomorrow. They called it Democracity. It was the most popular exhibit at the fair. The crowds approached it along a curving moving stairway called the Helicline that brought them to the entrance fifty feet in the air. Once inside the Perisphere, they stepped onto two revolving balconies that formed large rings apparently suspended in space. Standing on one of these rings, visitors saw a six-minute vision of the future.

PROGRAM NOTE

This book is intended not as a history of the year 1940 but rather as an evocation of it, and an attempt to capture the texture and tone of life in that pivotal year. In effect, it has two narrators—the author's ten-year-old self, who experienced many of the events of that year directly, though necessarily naively, and the author at the present time, who has reflected on that year a great deal and absorbed much of what has been written about it, including the books, articles, newspapers, and other material listed in the Selected Bibliography. The book makes direct use of such material for the process of evocation.

The book has a number of themes, but it might be useful to call attention here at the beginning to two of them. One theme is that the year 1940 marked the end of a distinctive era in American life. The war was on the horizon, a fact of daily consciousness, and it would work a great transformation in American life here at home as well as in America's position in the world. Another theme is the presence in America that year, to a degree not equaled after 1940, of individuals largely formed during the previous two decades who could be called champions, who succeeded, perhaps because of an undivided will, a will that remained intact, in being larger than life and in dominating their chosen activity, people like Franklin Roosevelt, Robert Moses, Joe Louis, Don Budge, Joe DiMaggio, Clark Gable, Ernest Hemingway, Alice Marble, Humphrey Bogart, Katharine Hepburn, and others. Despite the Great Depression, which was ending in 1940, these champions and others radiated a sense of possibility that did not afterwards appear in so pure and so concentrated a form. That sense of possibility, indeed, reached an apotheosis in the optimism and brilliance of the New York World's Fair of 1939–40, which is dealt with in chapter 1: The World of Tomorrow.

Abroad, perhaps related to the quality noted above, the principal world leaders of that year also possessed a special power and interest that went beyond their predecessors of the First World War, possibly because that war and its aftermath produced a universal sense of crisis that fostered a heroic attitude toward life. Thus Franklin Roosevelt is a more interesting and compelling figure than Woodrow Wilson, Winston Churchill than Lloyd George, Stalin than Czar Nicholas II, Mussolini than King Victor Emmanuel III. De Gaulle, the true leader of the French, is more interesting than Clemenceau, but unfortunately for the French, De Gaulle went into exile, and the actual French leaders strike us as tired, bewildered, and with Pétain, even senile.

Whatever the cultural and historical reasons, in the year 1940—to use Yeats—a terrible beauty was born, and after it, all would be changed, changed utterly.

It was meant to be a well-organized, futuristic community of a million people with a working population of 250,000. These jobholders lived in five satellite towns, Pleasantvilles, which were exclusively residential, or Millvilles, which accommodated some industry. Around these were green areas for agriculture and recreation. These various elements were linked by superhighways along which people traveled to their jobs at the Center, which was the business and cultural heart of Democracity. Electric power was generated by a giant hydroelectric dam, which alluded to the New Deal's Tennessee Valley Authority. Robert Kohn, a designer and the chairman of the fair's Board of Design, summed up the spirit of the model: "This is not a vague dream of a life that might be lived in the far future but one that could be lived tomorrow morning if we willed it so. The great, crushing all absorbing city of today . . . would no longer be a planless jumble of slum and chimney, built only for gain, but an effective instrument for human activities, to be used for the building of a better world of tomorrow. . . . The relation between these units of stone and steel, highway and green, is a symbol of the new life of tomorrow; that life will be based on an understanding of all elements to a new and living democracy."

As the crowd watched from the two circular and suspended balconies, the radio announcer H. V. Kaltenborn explained how Democracity functioned. After two minutes, daylight faded over the great dome, and as dusk slowly deepened, the concave dome gleamed with thousands of stars. To a musical accompaniment, a thousand-voice chorus sounded from the glittering heavens, while at ten locations on the dome you saw images of marching men—farmers in their work clothes, mechanics carrying tools—and as they came closer, you saw that they represented the various ethnic groups that make up an American metropolis, here presented as a vision of national unity. The music rose to a diapason, then subsided, and the marching men vanished behind drifting clouds. A blaze of polarized light climaxed the six-minute show. Ironically enough, the narrator of this optimistic panorama, H. V. Kaltenborn, became familiar to everyone with a radio after war broke out in Europe, and his nightly reports brought America the news of disaster after disaster. The superhighways and air travel and other features of Democracity, prophetic as they were, had to wait until after the war to achieve realization.

Nevertheless, this experience at the "theme center" was a powerful one. The designers intended that the show inside the Perisphere would provide a crystallization of the vision of the fair as a whole, divided as it was into seven sectors to accommodate the principal activities of modern life. The Trylon and Perisphere and the Democracity show also delivered an unmistakable message. American democracy had with it the possibility of creating a life of streamlined, modern abundance. There were, of course, other visions abroad of a possible world of tomorrow. The fascism of Hitler and Mussolini also offered integrated visions, in their case of a futuristic authoritarian state. There was no German pavilion at the fair, but the Italian pavilion provided a striking expression of fascist élan and futurism. The Soviets advanced a vision of their own: socialist man this time, in a pavilion of massive and heroic proportions, a symbol of collectivist power. The Trylon and Perisphere theme center asserted a competing vision and advanced it on the wave of optimism, generated by the movement of progressive reform that had roots in the nineteenth century and earlier, and it was reinforced by the modern movement in the arts. It was enthusiastic about the possibilities inherent in science and technology, but the controlling form was provided by the idea of democracy. Some sense of Whitman's American spirit was powerfully present at the fair, along with the more recent *The People, Yes* of Carl Sandburg. The fair meant to reject the dictators and the commissars and celebrate a futuristic, planned capitalism. No doubt this vision contained its contradictions, but it was potent stuff amid the surrounding international gloom. At the end of the fair's first summer, on September 1, 1939, Hitler, having signed a pact with Stalin a few days before, hurled his forces across the frontier and crushed Poland. England and France reluctantly went to war. Once again, as Lord Grey had said in 1914, "The lamps are going out all over Europe; we shall not see them lit again in our lifetime."

When the visitor finished looking at the Democracity show and made his way out of the Perisphere, he no doubt turned back to look at the vast structure. It was eighteen stories high, the largest globular structure ever built. Together with the Trylon, it seemed part of a luminous world, apparently suspended in air on jets of colored water—reds, greens, and blues—an arrangement of mirrors on which the water played, rendering the actual supporting columns invisible. At night, powerful lights projected moving cloud patterns on the surface of the sphere, creating the illusion that the building itself was revolving. Then the visitor launched forth into the rest of the fair.

Douglas Haskell, an architect, contributed an article about the architecture of the fair to the August 1940 number of the magazine *Architectural Record,* and though he modestly calls his essay merely "notes" on the fair, it remains one of the most interesting assessments of it. "Like a great city," writes Haskell, "the Fair set out to dramatize two things, the 'sights' and the crowds; by far its most decisive innovation lay in what it did with the crowds. . . .[The] greatest discovery in New York was the discovery of the crowd, both as actor and as decoration of great power. . . .[Often] the crowd took on a positive decorative pattern behind the recurrent guard rails. At General Motors the crowd was decoratively the making of the building, giving life, brilliant color and motion to the snaked ramps along the blank clifflike wall. Nothing of the inside was shown ahead of time; mysteriously the crowd moved into the blank 'future' through a deep narrow cleft; the conception was one of immense power. . . . In recent literature much has been made of the way in which the medieval town squares were planned so as to be at their best during those processions when all the ordinary citizens, actors for the day, created their own drama and most beautiful spectacle. Such opportunities still occur daily, unnoticed except by dictators, who have their own spectacular uses to make of crowds. Yet in democratic architecture *par excellence* the opportunity exists wherever crowds congregate in places made by architects. Even in public architecture, a large open place of assembly, with people at many levels, the crowd entertaining itself by watching the parts where it moves and the parts where it collects, a crowd held always loose and fluid and not in the rigid platoons of the dictators—such a place could exert an influence toward democracy more powerful than many a columned and porticoed public building. Was not the finest element in the World's Fair 'theme center' the 'helicline,' with that long line of *people* held confidently against the sky?"

In 1940 the word *people* and the idea of "the people" had a special power difficult to reimagine today. The New Deal's Works Projects Administration had projects dealing with Art for the People and the People's Theater, and of course Carl Sandburg wrote the volume of poetry called *The People, Yes*. In the 1980s this terminology is obsolete. We have the Public Theater and Shakespeare in the Park, but "the people" was an important symbol coming out of the 1930s and an important symbol for the fair. The idea of "the people" pervaded films by Frank Capra and John Ford. At the end of John Ford's movie version of John Steinbeck's *Grapes of Wrath,* Jane Darwell capped an Academy Award-winning performance as Ma Joad with a final defiant speech: "We're the people that live. Can't nobody wipe us out. Can't nobody lick us. We'll go on forever. We're the people." In his introduction to the fair's official guidebook, Grover Whalen, New York's official host and the president of the Fair Corporation, invoked the people symbol. "The Fair was built for and dedicated to the people. It was built to delight and instruct them." The gigantic TVA project in Tennessee—and the words were carved in stone—had been built "For the People of the United States." In 1935, the sophisticated literary critic Kenneth Burke shrewdly proposed that "the people" as a unifying symbol would be more useful to the political left than the older "class struggle" and the divisive "worker" symbols. He advised the American Writers' Congress: "In suggesting that 'the people,' rather than 'the worker,' rate highest in our hierarchy of symbols . . . I am suggesting fundamentally that one cannot extend the doctrine of revolutionary thought among the lower middle-class without using middle-class values. . . . The symbol of 'the people' also has the tactical advantage of pointing more definitely in the direction of unity. . . . It contains the ideal, the ultimate classless feature which the revolution would bring about—and for this reason seems richer as a symbol of allegiance. It can borrow the advantages of nationalistic conditioning and at the same time be used to combat the forces that hide their class prerogatives behind a communal ideology." In its general application, the idea of "the people" was more benign than in Burke's formulation. It was a myth that transcended the undoubted fact of competing political and social interests; it was an optimistic idea and a source of moral energy in the midst of the Great Depression; and it was a reassuring symbol in the face of dark threats from abroad. It was a powerful idea for Hitler and the Soviets as well, Hitler particularizing it as "the German people" in his rhetoric, *Ein Volk*. Indeed, *Ein Volkswagen*. In its more benign form, it was a central energizing idea of the fair.

Haskell also noted the architectural innovations at the fair, ideas that had the potentiality for future application elsewhere. "The notion of architecture as environmental control represents a great advance over older concepts built around the mere enclosing of space. Yet within this new notion the Fair seems to mark a certain turning point." He notices the way in which the Westinghouse exhibit made use of both natural and artificial light. "A walk around the building at either level carries the vistor through a subtle progression of light and dark, so modulated to a purpose that only a professional observer is aware of the subtleties. . . . It is worth noting, also, that even where the greatest dependence has been placed on artificial theater illumination, as in the Futurama, daylight played a subtle part at the start and finish: the sudden entrance into the pitch-black, eye-dilating hall at the start, the gradual brightening at the end, and the effect of seeing the final model of the sequence repeated full-size and true to Nature in daylight, an effect with great influence in making the drama seem 'real.'" Haskell analyzes how the architects created shade, either using structure or trees or some combination of the two, and the many creative uses of water—in pools, cascades, aquatic curtains, and so forth—and how the varied curvaceous shapes of the fair that "were not even buildings" nevertheless prefigured the building of tomorrow. Architecturally, the fair not only celebrated progress, but embodied it, and made important advances in design. Thinking of the previous exhibition in San Francisco, Haskell wryly expressed a certain sense of paradox. "The two exhibitions, one in New York and one in San Francisco, seem to have played paradoxical roles. It was the West that produced the rounded and harmonious achievement; it was the East that played the pioneer. Although New York's experimentalism sometimes went wide of producing a finished harmony, it did bring forth a wealth of new material."

If the fair did not achieve a "finished harmony," it is probably because the energies it released were too great for such an effect. The planners certainly produced a comprehensive design. In terms of spatial organization, it was a Beaux-Arts plan with the Trylon and Perisphere at the center and radiating avenues providing the spokes of the wheel, complicated by fanlike segments. The longitudinal central axis of Constitution Mall—and the name, of course, had political significance here—extended from the Trylon and Perisphere eastward to the oval Lagoon of Nations and then beyond it to the Court of Peace, where you found the pavilions of the foreign nations. At the Court of Peace you could visit, among others, the Italian, Japanese, Soviet, Polish, French, and British exhibitions, and by 1940 there were obvious ironies in this collocation. Extending at 45-degree angles from either side of the Trylon and Perisphere were the Avenue of Patriots and the Avenue of Pioneers, along which Greyhound operated specially constructed sight-seeing buses, ten cents a ride, with the seats facing outward and the horns playing the notes of "The Sidewalks of New York." At the Trylon and Perisphere, another axis running north and south connected the Court of Communications, with its great pylons, to the Plaza of Light, with its electrical utilities buildings. World's Fair Boulevard was a transverse axis, connecting the permanent aquatic amphitheater on Fountain Lake with the New York State exhibition building, and beyond it, across Grand Central Parkway, with the Transportation Zone. This geometrical arrangement accommodated the conceptual plan of the fair, a division into seven thematic zones with "focal" exhibits, supposed to represent the futuristic possibilities of modern life.

The planners included the nonideological Amusement Zone, to the east of Fountain Lake, and it proved to be so successful that they expanded it during the second year of the fair. As much as the democratic "crowd" liked the Perisphere and Democracity, they also liked the parachute jump, Billy Rose's Aquacade, and the dozens of other amusements. The other zones, more soberly, were Communications, Community, Food, Government, Medicine and Public Health, Production and Distribution, Science and Education, and Transportation. There was some sophisticated criticism of this geometrical organization. Some designers felt that true design need not be associated with a "neoclassic," geometrical clarity and logic. Others thought that the fair's geometrical design was at odds with the theme of growth and change. Against these criticisms, it was argued that the overall plan dramatized the emergence of the fair via a designer's drawing board out of the previously existing swamp, the very clarity of the plan making a creative statement. Those were interesting arguments, but the experienced fact was that the energy of the fair made them irrelevant. You could see the overall design on a blueprint, but you were not especially aware of it while strolling along the Avenue of Pioneers. People came for the general spectacle. Writing in the *Nation* magazine, Joseph Wood Krutch took an anarchic view of the whole thing and advised visitors to avoid "buildings given large inclusive titles like 'Food,' 'Communications,' 'Consumers,' and the like." Krutch preferred to immerse himself in the spectacle of the whole, the "showmanship . . . so good . . . that science and industry provide spectacles which could easily compete with the acrobats and trained seals of a conventional circus."

Nevertheless, the design was there, perhaps felt only marginally or subliminally. It was reinforced by an elaborate system of color-coding. "At the axis of the design," reported the *Herald Tribune,* "trylon and perisphere stand in pure dazzling white, flanked by a softer 'theme white' on the adjacent facades. From the theme center the colors undergo a gradual transition along the avenues which radiate from it like spokes from the hub of a wheel. Along the Avenue of Patriots a gamut of yellows shade from pale cadmium to deep gold at Bowling Green. Down Constitution Mall the progression is from rose to burgundy, and a series of blues on the Avenue of Patriots culminates in ultramarine at Lincoln Square. Connecting the ends of these vistas, Rainbow Avenue curves in an arc from gold through orange to red, and on through violet and blue. Within this frame of color lie the buildings, each related to its neighbor and to the whole."

lagoon. It all ended with a fireworks display, and then there was still time to cross Empire State Bridge to the Amusement Zone.

Grover Whalen, who had staged the monster ticker-tape parade and New York reception for Charles Lindbergh in 1927 and also put on a successful National Recovery Act parade, had a taste for fun and spectacle, and he knew instinctively that the fair could not be exclusively a matter of message and public enlightenment. He organized fireworks displays and light shows, and he had bands of strolling players—singers, dancers, musicians, acrobats, and clowns—moving along the many boulevards of the fair. They played banjos, sang popular songs, danced, and juggled, and they were invariably surrounded by crowds wherever they went. The 280-acre Amusement Zone over on the shores of Fountain Lake certainly was not high-minded either, but it also certainly was fun, colorful, and—above all—commercially successful. Indeed, during its second year, 1940, the fair endeavored to stress these successful aspects that many of the purists among the planners might well have viewed as frivolous. A formidable drink called the Zombie, sold in the amusement area, became a prime topic of social conversation at the time, and also of radio comedians' jokes. It consisted of several alcoholic potions, plus fruit juice, plus fruit, and was served in a glass about one foot tall—only one to a customer—for a dollar. It was supposed to turn you into a zombie, or at least put you in the mood suitable for a fling on the dominant ride of the amusement area (which was renamed The Great White Way for the 1940 season), the 250-foot parachute jump sponsored by a punning Life Savers candy company. This ride was actually a bit startling, especially the first time you tried it. You paid your 40 cents and sat in one of the double chairs that were suspended beneath eleven, gaily colored, cloth parachutes. In due course, the contraption rose in the air, lifted along a cable, and you relaxed as you enjoyed a fine panoramic view of the fair. In a short time, your chute hit the top, was released by a mechanism with a clank, and then suddenly dropped about 20 feet before the air pressure began to slow it down for the descent. Those first 20 feet of pure fall could be a disconcerting experience.

Another major attraction on The Great White Way—in fact, it was the first thing you saw when you walked over Empire State Bridge and into the amusement area—was Billy Rose's Aquacade, starring Eleanor Holm, the beautiful Olympic swimmer who had been kicked off the U.S. team by Avery Brundage when she drank a glass of champagne aboard the ocean liner taking them to the 1936 Berlin Olympics. The Aquacade structure is one of the few that still remain from the fair. It seated 10,000 people, who watched a precision

water ballet, fancy high-diving, clowns, fireworks, and a light show projected on a curtain of water.

Frank Buck's "Bring-'em-Back-Alive" Jungleland included a Monkey Island and 1,000 simians. At the Seminole Village, Indians danced, beat drums, and wrestled with live alligators. Unthinkable today because of the prevailing humanitarian sentiment in such things was a "tiny town" miniature village inhabited entirely by midgets. Birds in natural tuxedos strolled on Admiral Byrd's Penguin Island, and the stripper Gypsy Rose Lee regularly tantalized the crowds with her Dance of the Doves. There was a giant roller coaster, Whoosh; also a replica of an Elizabethan village and a replica of Old New York in the 1890s, a bobsled ride and bump-'em cars, and a woman lying on a bed who would be dumped into a tank of water if you hit a target with a baseball, and another woman who was frozen into a cake of ice but spoke to you through a microphone. In "Gang Busters" you could view personal items that had belonged to Dillinger, Pretty Boy Floyd, Baby Face Nelson, and other gunmen, as well as demonstrations of the latest FBI equipment and techniques. There was a penny arcade and a "Strange as It Seems" freak show, including a man who was "turning to stone" and a boy with "alligator skin" (apparently some sort of extreme eczema). The Museum of Natural History put you in a simulated rocket and, using planetarium techniques, took you on a simulated trip to the moon, Mars, Venus, and other features of the solar system. There were replicas of Washington's Valley Forge encampment and of Victoria Falls in Rhodesia and an African rain forest. In The Great White Way, one observer wrote, the theme "drops its Harvard accent and lapses into pure unadulterated circus." But no ten-year-old boy considered the amusement area any sort of lapse, and, judging by the attendance records set there, neither did the adults of the year 1940, contentedly sipping their Zombies.

Nazi Germany did not have a pavilion at the fair, but Mussolini's Italy put up an especially brilliant one, and you did not have to be an admirer of his new fascist Italian system to be impressed by it. Nor is there any doubt that its design, very successful aesthetically, was expressive of the best aspirations of Italian fascism, and indeed, it had National Socialist stylistic counterparts.

The Italian Pavilion amounted to a synthesis of the classical architecture of ancient Rome and the modernism of twentieth-century Italy, which indeed possessed many of the principal figures of the modernist movement in the arts, including the great F. T. Marinetti, whose Futurist Manifesto of 1909 is one of the prime documents of the movement. Rising above the colonnaded front of

the Italian Pavilion was a huge tower that formed the pedestal for a statue of the mythological Roma. From a point 200 feet high on this tower, a cascade of water flowed down an arrangement of steps, tumbling into a pool at the base of a monument to the inventor Marconi. On the ground floor inside, the visitor saw a series of exhibits designed to present contemporary Italy in terms of a second Renaissance, including science, technology, naval and aeronautical accomplishments, and a shimmering array of Italian products— silks, cottons, cosmetics, synthetic fibers. The overall impression was one of elegance and extreme modernity. This was reinforced by the Italian contribution to the Transportation exhibit, several cars from a super passenger train designed to achieve speeds of 100 miles per hour between Rome and principal Italian cities. Red metal, ultra-streamlined, and with red leather upholstery inside, this train was as impressive an example of industrial modernism as anything at the fair. It was also a political metaphor: Mussolini's fascism had its face toward the future and was speeding into the second Roman Empire. This story was set forth in the Italian Pavilion by exhibits portraying seventeen years of fascist advance in social welfare, land reclamation, science and technology, and even sports.

One feature of the Italian Pavilion embodied, it might be thought, a large contradiction in Mussolini's stern fascist dream. There was a fine restaurant and nightclub operated by the Italian Line and featuring its famous chefs and maîtres d'hôtel, with music, flowers, fountains, and exquisite cuisine, a perfect expression of Italian lyricism and love of the elegant good life. But the Hall of Honor in the Italian Pavilion contained a large statue of the Duce himself, with the Italian empire indicated in huge maps made of copper and black marble.

To a ten-year-old boy at least, the Italian Pavilion was much more attractive than the Soviet Pavilion not far away. This was larger, heavier. The Italian Pavilion expressed lightness, speed, a sense of brio. The Soviets attempted a massive, heroic statement designed not to charm, but to impress and intimidate. The building was topped by a huge statue of a "worker" who held aloft a large red star that gleamed in the night sky. This made the Soviet Pavilion the tallest structure at the fair, with the single exception of the Trylon, the national and ideological aspirations being expressed obvious enough to all. The facade of the building swept around the worker-pylon in a semicircle terminating in majestic sculptured wings, and the whole facade was divided into eleven sections, each ornamented to represent one of the eleven Soviet republics. Inside the building, painting, sculpture, and bas-reliefs proclaimed the achievements of the Soviet system, and there was even a life-sized reproduction of a station on the famous Moscow subway, cleverly designed with mirrors so that it looked longer and larger than it actually was, the tracks disappearing in the distance. You could see prize-winning Soviet films and eat Soviet food in an attractive restaurant. One exhibit showed the structure of the Soviet government, with photographs of the leading figures. But, in comparison with the Italian building, it was all a bit boy-meets-tractor. The heroic worker-figure atop the tower was designed in one of the styles of the period, with thick limbs and thick neck, and he looked unintelligent—though, to be reasonable here, there were other examples of that style, Thirties Heroic, visible elsewhere at the fair.

The Soviet Pavilion did not survive the Hitler-Stalin Pact and the Soviet-Nazi invasion of Poland. The structure was pulled down and carted away, and by the summer of 1940 it had been replaced by a bandstand.

There was a peculiar quality about the Japanese Pavilion over on Congress Street. It advanced no aeronautical or scientific claims of any sort, and there were no Italian-style claims to empire. Nor was there anything at all modernistic about the Japanese building. Since the late 1920s, Japan had had imperial designs on China; it occupied Manchuria and set up a client state there; and on July 7, 1937, it engineered an incident at the Marco Polo Bridge outside Peking which led to a full-scale attack on China itself. Japan had built a navy and air force; it had sunk an American gunboat on the Yangtse and engaged in shooting incidents with the British. Its best troops had fought a sharp engagement with Soviet Siberian forces. Americans remembered the "rape of Nanking," when Japanese soldiers ran amok.

The Japanese, in fact, showed considerable nerve in coming to the fair at all. Perhaps not surprisingly, their pavilion was modeled after an ancient Shinto shrine. It consisted of a long, wooden building with a slanted roof, and its color motifs were red, white, and gold. You crossed over a tiny arching wooden bridge which spanned a miniature river in which characteristic Japanese bonsai shrubbery was artfully arranged. You approached the building through a red-lacquered entrance with gold designs, and you saw walls decorated in the varying modes of the best periods in Japanese art and culture. The pavilion contained one of the strangest objects at the entire fair, a large U.S. Liberty Bell made entirely of Japanese cultured pearls. There were Japanese prints, dolls, paintings, fabrics, and Japanese women in silken garb, who explained and extolled Japanese culture. Periodically these women guides went through the elaborate rituals of the Japanese tea ceremony. This was not the World of Tomorrow, certainly not in the American sense, and not even in the Italian or Soviet sense. It was an effort on the part of the Japanese designers to contradict the widespread belief that the Japanese were barbarians who were probably going to shoot us up with the scrap metal they had purchased in the form of the Second Avenue elevated train. The pavilion also sought to root modern Japanese claims to power and empire in the ancient—and, one was invited to think, superior—cultural traditions of that mysterious island. In the year 1940, it is doubtful that many visitors to the fair found those claims impressive or the culture charming.

One of the most admired pavilions when the fair opened had been Poland's, with its rectangular golden tower, modern and light, rising above the main entrance on Continental Avenue. Inside you learned about the history of Poland and saw original documents and other memorabilia of the old Polish kings. Polish science and technology and the arts were represented, and there was even a Polish fashion show featuring clothes designed in Warsaw. Much was made of Polish democratic traditions (though Poland actually had a dictator) and of the important role Poland would play in the Europe of the future. The Polish Pavilion was gone by the second year of the fair, and so was the Finnish Pavilion. The theme of this had been "the land of the forests," and there had been a model of Helsinki Stadium, where the Olympic Games were to be held during the summer of 1940. There was a Finnish restaurant. But Stalin invaded Finland at the end of November 1939, and when Finland eventually lost the war, despite the tough performance through the winter of its white-clad troops, the Finnish Pavilion closed to the notes of *Finlandia*.

Against the gloom, the optimism of the fair burned brightly, even during that fateful summer of 1940. But at the beginning of the year, in early January, President Roosevelt had sat at his desk in the Oval Office, drafting his eighth State of the Union address. A cigarette smoked in his ashtray. The battle flags hung limp on their poles along the wall. From his window the president could see the Washington Monument illuminated by floodlights against the night sky. "It becomes clearer and clearer," the president wrote in pen with his strong, vertical strokes, "that the future world will be a shabby and dangerous place to live in—yes, even for Americans to live in—if it is ruled by force in the hands of a few."

The Last Winter Olympics

The 1936 Winter Olympics were held in the Bavarian town of Garmisch-Partenkirchen. There would be no 1940 Winter Olympics. The great American columnist Westbrook Pegler, on the scene in Germany, filed the following report.

GARMISCH-PARTENKIRCHEN—It is going to be pretty hard to do this, but right is right, as President Harding said, and I feel that I have done the Nazis a serious injustice, so this is my apology.

Two days ago these dispatches reported that the quaint little Bavarian town of Garmisch-Partenkirchen has the appearance of an army headquarters a few miles behind the Western Front during an important troop movement. That was wrong, and I can only plead that I was honestly mistaken and the victim of my own ignorance.

Those weren't troops at all, but merely peace-loving German workmen in their native dress, and those weren't army lorries which went growling through the streets squirting the slush onto the sidewalks, but delivery wagons carrying beer and wieners and kraut to the humble homes of the mountaineers in the folds of the hills. It is a relief to know this and a pleasure to be able to report that, after all, the Germans did not conduct their Winter Olympics in an atmosphere of war, which would have been very injurious to the Olympic ideal of peace through sporting competition.

My information comes from a kindly Bavarian cobbler in a long black overcoat who was standing in a cordon of cobblers along the main street Sunday afternoon during Adolf Hitler's visit to town to pronounce over the closing ceremonies the benison of a great protector of the world's peace.

"Are you a soldier?" I inquired, for I had been told that in Germany strangers often mistake for soldiers people who have nothing to do with the military establishment.

"Who, me?" he asked. "No, I'm a cobbler. All of us in the black costume are cobblers."

"Then why do you dress in military uniform?" I persisted.

"That's where you are wrong," said my cobbler friend. "This isn't a military uniform. It's a shoe-maker's uniform, and this big toad stabber in the scabbard at my side, which may look like a bayonet to you, is merely a little knife which we use when we cobble."

"But," I asked, "why do you march in military formation through the scenes of international friendship?" The answer was that they don't really march at all. They just walk in step in columns of fours, because they like to walk that way. And it is an old custom of theirs to form cordons of military appearance along the curbs and just stand there by the hour for pleasure.

"But what about those other troops in the brown uniforms?"

"Troops?" said my friend. "Those are not troops. Those are gardeners who have always worn brown suits, which seem to be

transplants, artificial hearts, and other futuristic medical developments. In 1940, Lindbergh was notable also as a leader of those Americans who wanted the United States to stay out of the European war, and he was a bitterly controversial figure because of this stand.

The World of Tomorrow was not anyone's tomorrow—certainly not the tomorrow of the dictators. It was to be an American, democratic, and streamlined tomorrow. The fair was an expression of American nationalism. It commemorated the 150th anniversary of George Washington's inauguration in New York City. On June 30, 1938, President Franklin Roosevelt presided over the laying of the cornerstone of the United States Government Building. The president of the World's Fair Corporation was the exuberant Grover Whalen, a former police chief who had become a symbol, along with Mayor Fiorello LaGuardia, of the dynamism of New York. In the vicinity of the Dupont exhibition—"Better things for better living through chemistry"—surrounded by low stone benches and identified by a round granite marker, there were two time capsules, sunk into their subterranean vaults on September 23, 1938, to be raised on September 23, 6938. They contained artifacts representative of American civilization at the time—cameras, radios, books, combs, thread, medical instruments, documents, a telephone, and so on. The time capsules, in a way, were the optimistic heart of the fair, assuming, as they did, that American civilization would matter five thousand years from now—assuming, indeed, that American civilization (this was the message inside the Perisphere) would be the basis for the world of tomorrow. The fair's optimism transcended depression and war. The pavilions of the other nations were far off at the Lagoon of Nations and around the Court of Peace, while the fair implicitly proposed a new American World Order, America as the world's future, in all but explicit opposition to the fading British Empire and the assertive new orders of Hitler, Japan, and the Soviet Union.

When night came to this vision of an American world order, the visual effect was extraordinary. The walls of the buildings became washed in pastel shades of color, the Perisphere a soft blue. The leaves of the trees along the avenues were rendered luminous by means of mercury-vapor lighting. At 9:30 P.M. the lights near the Lagoon of Nations were dimmed. For fifteen minutes the spectators around the lagoon or sitting in the restaurants of the French or Belgian Pavilions saw an elaborate light and water show. It depicted the life of George Washington, the creation of the world, or other epic themes, flashing the images on a curtain of water hurled into the air—40 tons of water thrown up by 1,400 water jets in the

The buildings themselves represented a variety of styles within the general lines laid down by the fair's design board. They included Art Deco, the modern International Style, Beaux-Arts Moderne, and variations. That a building should immediately announce its intended function was an idea that had come down from the *architecture parlante* of late eighteenth-century France. Thus the Marine Transportation Building declared itself by means of a huge pair of ocean-liner bows and a 150-foot mast. The Aviation Building consisted of a conically shaped hall that suggested a wind tunnel or a vast hangar. The Cosmetics Building looked like a powder box. A giant igloo housed the Carrier Corporation air-conditioning exhibit. The RCA Building looked like a giant radio tube, and the Gas Building had 90-foot pylons representing gas burners. The National Cash Register Pavilion was surmounted by a huge cash register on which the total daily attendance at the fair was continually rung up. Towers, domes, and spirals spread down the avenues. To symbolize electrical energy, there was a 150-foot tower of steel girders. A 105-foot tower demonstrated the uses of glass block. The Heinz Building had a beehive dome constructed of a thin shell of timber, and since the exhibitors gave away free samples of hot dogs, soup, and pickles, it was especially popular with ten-year-old boys around lunchtime. Heinz also gave out those souvenir, green plastic, pickle pins you still run across sometimes today. The cumulative messages of the design were unmistakable. Art and architecture were combined to celebrate a new age of technology and the machine—not this time the heavy power of the age of iron and coal, but the lighter and more mobile forms of the age of electricity and flight.

It was impossible in 1940 to foresee the eventual effect upon American life of much that was first introduced there to the wider public. But visitors to the General Motors Futurama show sat in 600 slowly moving chairs equipped with sound equipment and got a guided tour through a vast miniature conception of what America might look like in twenty years. Much there envisioned has come to pass: superhighways and streamlined, economical cars, mass air travel, television. In the Kodak Building, the coming of inexpensive, high-tech, color photography was foreseen, and also three-dimensional polaroid photography. Westinghouse exhibited, among other things, a voice-activated robot named Elektro. Much comment arose out of a chicken heart kept alive and pumping inside a device designed by Dr. Alexis Carrel and Charles Lindbergh. Carrel was a French scientific genius with fascist sympathies; Lindbergh was not only the lone eagle hero of 1927, but a self-taught, technological genius, and the Lindbergh-Carrel device looked ahead to organ

PROLOGUE

By the Sea

That summer, black men pushed the chairs along the boardwalk. The chairs were made of wicker, and there was a large wicker footboard in front of your feet. The chairs rolling lazily along the boardwalk had large wheels and red-white-and-blue-striped canopies. The men riding in them sometimes wore white trousers and hard straw hats with a regimental-striped hatband around them. The women in the chairs often had elaborate hairdos, though of course the expression hairdo was not used in those days. People moved down the boardwalk like crowded shoals of fish. The sun danced in small triangles on the ocean.

All the hotels along the beach had been built back in the eighties and nineties. They were wooden, and white or yellow or gray, and had turrets, verandas, dormer windows, gingerbread wood, and striped awnings; Grandmother stayed all summer at one called Ocean Vista.

Wearing bathing suits was restricted to the beach itself. Rules were strict because the town itself had been founded back in the nineteenth century as a Methodist summer camp meeting, and its huge, circular Methodist auditorium was an important religious center. So the bathers left their wooden hotels fully dressed and carrying their beach umbrellas, their suits, and their towels, and walked across Ocean Avenue to the Bathhouse, a white wooden structure that seemed to be partially underground and contained rows of white-doored and gloomy bath cubicles, within which it was permitted to change into your bathing suit. These cubicles smelled remotely of suntan lotion. And because the only light came from a six-inch slot below the door, they were always dank. You changed quickly, and it was wonderful to walk out through the dark, cement underground tunnel, chilly, into the amazing sunlight of the beach and its blazing sands.

All day long, if you were ten years old, you were among the bright striped children on that beach, while all day long, the ships crept by on the horizon, sometimes great ocean liners with their two or three smokestacks, sometimes the sleek, low profile of a destroyer, and always there was the grand eternal motion of the sea.

The older women, that summer before the war, still usually wore one-piece bathing suits, some of them still made of itchy, dark wool, though the boy's mother wore a one-piece Jantzen sharkskin. She had been an actress on Broadway. His father, when he came down from the city, wore dark blue woolen trunks with a white canvas belt fastened by two interlocking metal snakes that formed a buckle. There were bathing ropes attached to wooden piles, and the ropes stretched out into the surf. The women hung on them and screamed.

In front of all the hotels along the beach, there were American flags, either on a pole standing on the front lawn or hanging from a pole sticking out from the second-story veranda, and the flags had forty-eight stars. On most evenings during the summer, there were band concerts on the boardwalk, sometimes with fireworks, sometimes patriotic songs of the Sousa kind, and sometimes religious meetings with Methodist hymns.

The Jewish kids to the south in Bradley Beach called Ocean Grove "Ocean Grave." The next town north up the beach, Asbury Park, named for Francis Asbury, the great Methodist preacher, a disciple of the Wesley brothers, contained a large, and to a ten-year-old boy overwhelming, amusement park. You could pedal a Swan Boat lazily along Wesley Lake in the dusk, ride the huge Ferris wheel or the merry-go-round, which spun in a nineteenth-century, cast-iron building. You could sit on the boardwalk with an ice-cream cone and look out at the lights of the fishing boats winking on the horizon. The adults, the parents and grandparents, liked the auctions and the bingo games when they came down from New York, and they gave you a nickel for the man on the boardwalk with a big scale who "Guessed Your Weight." He was always right.

Back in the nineties, Stephen Crane had caught the flavor in his Jersey shore reports for the *New York Tribune*. "The Ferris wheel went up near the beach, its motor emitting sparks that disturbed the owners of the wooden hotels. There was a Baby Parade, with the infants in strollers along the boardwalk. There were the great crowds of the 'Nineties. James J. Corbett, the pugilist, who is preparing for his fight with John L. Sullivan in a handsome Loch Arbour cottage, is now down to hard training, and his admirers, who used to tramp the Asbury Park boardwalk in the evenings are somewhat at a loss. . . ." But those crowds of the nineties were not at a loss on the Jersey shore. Stephen Crane, for the *Tribune:* "The crowds here grow larger every day. . . . The number of people who take their daily promenade on the ocean plaza surpasses belief. . . . Down on the beach the famous boardwalk and the broad sandy beach are literally covered with people. . . . Daily excursion trains come here from all parts of New York, New Jersey and Pennsylva-

military but aren't. Just peace loving gardeners is what they are, and those blades which you see hanging from their belts are not bayonets, either, but pruning knives. It is an old Bavarian tradition.

"They too like to go for long walks in columns of fours and make gestures with spades, as soldiers sometimes drill with rifles, but they are not soldiers, I assure you, my friend. They are just kind-hearted gardeners who wouldn't hurt a potato bug. It is interesting to see them stack spades when they come to the end of a stroll in columns of fours. To some people unacquainted with our local customs they may seem to be performing a military drill with their spades, but nothing could be further from the truth." Thus far two of my military corps had been explained away as harmless and altogether peaceful workmen, but I thought I had him when I mentioned the men in gray uniforms, also with scabbards at their sides, who seemed to be regular infantry. He laughed uproariously at this.

"Oh, those!" he said. "Those aren't infantry. How could you make that mistake? Those are plasterers, and the tin hats which you undoubtedly mistook for shrapnel helmets are an ancient tradition of Bavarian plasterers. Sometimes the plaster falls down, and it would knock them for a lot of loops if they didn't wear something for protection. Wait till I tell the foreman of the plasterers—I suppose you have been calling him the general—that you mistook his boys for soldiers. He will laugh himself dizzy."

Still, there were other men all dressed alike in blue-gray, with wings embroidered on their clothing. Undoubtedly those would be soldiers of the aviation branch, wouldn't they? But my friend the peace-loving cobbler in the black suit, which looked very military but wasn't, enjoyed another pleasant hysteric over that one too. Those, he said, were Bavarian white wings in native dress.

It is not easy to be proven wrong in a serious matter. I had seen as many as five thousand, perhaps even ten thousand, men in apparel which seemed to be that of soldiers, and had recklessly accused the peace-loving Nazi regime of converting the Winter Olympics into a military demonstration, which would have been a grave breach of manners. My troops had been explained into gentle civilians, and the marching to which I had referred had turned out to be nothing but a habitual method of going for nice long walks.

The motor trucks still seemed questionable, however, for they were painted in camouflage like the lorries used in the war.

"Yes, I know," my friend the cobbler explained, "but we have painted our motor trucks in eccentric designs and colors for hundreds of years. It makes them look nicer."

A foreman of the cobblers came by at the moment, and my friend put his hand to his cap in a gesture which resembled a military salute. I asked him about this, but he said he was only shading his eyes.

The Nazi press bureau released a quotation from a dispatch to the *New York Times* intimating that anyone reporting the presence of troops at the Olympic Games was a liar. I guess that's me, but the mistake was natural, as you can see. When thousands of men seem to march but don't in clothing and tin hats which seem to be military uniforms but aren't, and carry harmless utensils which appear to be bayonets but ain't, any stranger is likely to make the same mistake.

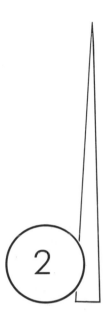

THE MAN OF 1918

I

As the decade of the 1930s drew to a close, a grade-school boy in suburban Queens, New York, would stroll home from P.S. 52 for lunch, past the neat rows of two-story brick houses with their porches and modest lawns. On a warm spring day, some of these homes had radios playing, and you could hear them as you walked past, often strange guttural accents, angry, from Berlin. At regular intervals there came the smooth, flatly unemotional tones of the BBC translator. "Herr Hitler says that there can be no solution to the Sudeten problem unless. . . ." The boy was familiar with the dark music of these speeches because he had heard so many of them, and he anticipated the inevitably approaching climax of the speech as the deeper guttural tones gave way to rising and apparently hysterical shrieks that blended with an oceanic roar of *Sieg Heil, Sieg Heil, Sieg Heil* from the crowd. The boy was not really aware of the particular issues—the Sudeten matter, the Jews, the Polish corridor—but he knew that these speeches were not Fireside Chats. When Czechoslovakia fell, his third-grade teacher, a beautiful brunette named Miss Furtena, a Czech refugee, wept openly in class and said that the Czechs had a good army and would have fought, but that now Hitler had changed the military balance in Europe and that war was inevitable. Hitler had eliminated the Czech military presence on his southern flank. France had committed suicide. Had the boy known the poem at the time, he would have applied the lines of Robert Frost:

> *It looked as if a night of dark intent*
> *Was coming, and not only a night, an age.*
> *Someone had better be prepared for rage.*

Adolf Hitler loomed over the emotional landscape of the year 1940, utterly dominating it, the power of his personal identity surpassing by far that of every political leader since Napoleon—and, in 1940, there did not appear to be any William Pitt or Duke of Wellington in Europe to stand in his way. William L. Shirer describes one of his entrances to the city of Nuremburg, sacred citadel of the Nazi Party:

> Like a Roman emperor Hitler rode into this medieval town at
> sundown today past solid phalanxes of wildly cheering Nazis
> who packed the narrow streets that once saw Hans Sachs, the
> *Meistersinger.* Tens of thousands of Swastika flags blot out the
> Gothic beauties of the place, the facades of the old houses,
> the gable roofs. . . . About ten o'clock tonight I got caught in
> a mob in front of Hitler's hotel shouting "We want our
> Führer." I was a little shocked at the faces, especially those of
> the women. . . . They reminded me of the crazed expression I
> once saw in the back country of Louisiana on the faces of
> some Holy Rollers who were about to hit the trail. They
> looked at him as if he were a Messiah, their faces
> transformed. . . ."

David Lloyd George, who had led Great Britain to its fateful victory over Germany in the First World War, viewed Hitler as one of the great men of history: "The old trust him, the young idolize him. It is not the admiration accorded to a popular leader. It is the worship of a national hero who has saved his country from utter despondency and degradation. . . . He is as immune from criticism as a king in a monarchical country. He is something more. He is the George Washington of Germany—the man who won for his country independence from all her oppressors. To those who have not actually seen and sensed the way Hitler reigns over the heart and mind of

Germany, this description may appear extravagant. All the same it is the bare truth."

Winston Churchill, his great antagonist, earlier described Hitler's achievements as "among the most remarkable in the history of the world." Had Hitler died suddenly in the late summer of 1940, he would be remembered as one of the greatest men in German history, easily comparable to Frederick the Great or Bismarck. His regime had stimulated the economy and reduced unemployment by 80 percent, while the democracies remained sunk in the Depression. The first Reich *autobahn* was authorized under a law of June 27, 1933, along with a system of savings that would allow ordinary Germans to buy the new *Volkswagen* automobile. The *Kraft durch Freude* (Strength through Joy) program transformed the leisure of the masses and sent them on undreamed-of trips through the Alps and cruises in the Mediterranean. As one historian sums up his achievements, "Hitler's rise had indeed been one of history's great political success stories. The unknown and uneducated common soldier of World War I, who had been a failure in all of his undertakings, had come to power in 1933 in a country that despaired of solving its social and political problems. Within five years he had given his nation stability and hope. A grateful people hailed him as the leader and savior who had eliminated unemployment, stabilized their currency, provided them with effective social legislation, and given millions of workers attractive vacations. He had sent the youth of the land singing and marching down sunlit roads; he had forged a new community of the German people; he had built magnificent freeways and promised automobiles to every laboring man; he had humbled the victors of Versailles and wiped out their treaty, which all Germans called the Treaty of Shame. In a series of brilliant and bloodless coups he had created a triumphant Greater Germany, proud and strong, remilitarized the Rhineland, and annexed Austria and Czechoslovakia." By the end of 1940, he had taken most of Poland, opening the way to an invasion of Russia. The destruction of Bolshevism and the seizure of the resources of the East had always been his prime political goal. He had overrun Denmark, Norway, the Low Countries, and defeated France in a few weeks. He had thrown the British army into the English Channel at Dunkirk and could gaze through his field glasses at the chalky cliffs of Dover, twenty miles away.

II

Hitler's physical characteristics, with the single exception of his eyes, were unimpressive. His 5-foot-9 frame tended to dumpiness, and his legs were too short. His nose was coarse and broad, a defect he attempted to cover with the famous toothbrush mustache. He parted his brown-black hair on the right and combed a shock of it over his left temple. His gait was often mincing, and his Nazi salute oddly effeminate. All of his personal charisma came from his eyes and from his voice. A boyhood friend, August Kubizek, remembered that in Hitler's countenance

> the eyes were so outstanding that one didn't notice anything else. Never in my life have I seen any other person whose appearance—how shall I put it?—was so completely dominated by the eyes. They were the light eyes of his mother but her somewhat staring, penetrating gaze was even more marked in the son and had even more force and expressiveness. It was uncanny how those eyes could change their expression, especially when Adolf was speaking. . . . In fact, Adolf spoke with his eyes, and even when his lips were silent one knew what he wanted to say. When he first came to our house and I introduced him to my mother she said to me in the evening, "What eyes your friend has!" And I remember quite distinctly there was more fear than admiration in her words. If I am asked where one could perceive, in his youth, this man's exceptional qualities, I can only answer, "In the eyes."

Nietzsche's sister was, typically, drawn to Hitler's eyes and also made uncomfortable by them: "They searched me through and through."

Not surprisingly, many biographers and historians have sought to explain Hitler by means of psychoanalytical theories. They have sought to reassure us by locating him outside the realm of the "normal"—in effect, explaining him away, a freak. He may indeed have loathed his bureaucratic and authoritarian father, and he may well have loved his mother, Klara, to a point of psychological excess. He may have worried about the possibility that his maternal grandfather was a Jew. He became a vegetarian as an adult, after the suicide of a mistress (the events seem to be connected), and he was obsessed with cleanliness. But the search for Hitler's possible aberrations misses the larger historical point. Whether or not he had an Oedipus complex or whatever, the fact remains that he articulated the feelings and beliefs of millions of Germans who cannot be regarded as pathological in any clinical sense of the word. Nor do we have to wander into psychobiography to grasp the essence of Hitler as a man. Hitler had three fundamentally decisive aspects, and his adult career was obviously shaped by them. He was a decorated war hero who was traumatized—indeed, the word is too weak here—by the German defeat in 1918. He was an intense aesthete and had been intoxicated by aesthetic emotions since boyhood. And he was a dogmatic and fanatical anti-Semite. These three unmistakable elements are sufficient to account for the nature of his spectacular career without recourse to dubious psychologizing.

Hitler shared with many of his European contemporaries the feeling that the outbreak of World War I in August 1914 was a spiritual deliverance. "To me personally," he wrote, "those hours appeared like a deliverance from the vexatious moods of my youth. I am not ashamed even today to say that, overwhelmed by passionate enthusiasm, I had fallen on my knees and thanked Heaven out of my overflowing heart that it had been granted to me the good fortune of being allowed to live in these times." We have, of course, the famous photograph of the crowd in Munich as war was declared, with an identifiable Hitler beaming with unmistakable ecstasy. In view of all that was to happen, such emotions seem to us preposterous, but other sensitive young men shared them. Rupert Brooke wrote at about the same time:

> *Now, God be thanked Who has matched us with*
> *   His hour*
> *And caught our youth, and wakened us from sleeping,*
> *   With hand made sure, clear eye, and sharpened*
> *   power,*
> *To turn, as swimmers into cleanness leaping.*

Herbert Asquith, son of the prime minister, wrote a famous poem about the war as a glorious dawn which relieved a clerk from the dreary routine of peace.

Hitler fought through all of the war's four years on the Western Front. He disliked leave among the civilian population, a reaction common to many frontline soldiers, and volunteered to stay in the lines during Christmas leave. His duty was dangerous. When artillery fire knocked out telephone communications, Hitler carried messages from regimental headquarters to the units in active combat, and the evidence is that he enjoyed the sense of playing a role in the ongoing tactical decisions that would have been virtually impossible for an ordinary corporal. Later on, sometimes, when asked where he came from, he would not answer "Austria," but "the Sixteenth Regiment." In the early postwar years, as a beer-hall and street orator, his use of the rough language of the trenches helped to create a sense of recognition and communion with other veterans.

His rhetoric was full of words like steel, mud, blood, wire, gas, muck, and machine guns. At the front, his bravery won him the Iron Cross, second class, in December 1914. He was wounded for the first time on October 7, 1916, at 5:00 A.M. near LeBarque when shrapnel hit him in the thigh. He was in the catastrophic Third Battle of Ypres in 1917 and in the great, failed Ludendorff offensive of 1918, that carried once again to within sight of the Eiffel Tower. On August 4, 1918, he received his second Iron Cross, first class this time, almost unprecedented for an enlisted man, and then was blinded by a British gas attack of October 14. He recovered his eyesight at the Pasewalk military hospital near Berlin, but he appears to have experienced psychosomatic blindness on November 9 when a chaplain brought to the men at the hospital the news of Germany's surrender. "Everything began to go black again before my eyes. Stumbling, I groped my way back to the ward, threw myself on my bed, and buried my burning head in the covers and pillows. I had not cried since the day I had stood at the grave of my mother."

It may be significant in light of the association he makes in that last sentence that he always referred to Germany as the "Motherland," rather than the more usual "Fatherland." He later claimed that in the Pasewalk hospital he had "heard voices" and knew his destiny. He could not rescue the beloved but dead Klara, but he could rescue the violated "Motherland," and his emotions toward Klara may indeed have attached themselves to Germany. Throughout his life he returned again and again to that moment in 1918. "When I began my political work in 1919 I based it [on the surrender]. . . . The first resolution was made in 1919 when after long internal struggles I became a politician and took up the battle against my enemy." He sometimes saw himself as a modern Joan of Arc, an instrument of the "voices" of 1918. "I go the way that Providence dictates for me with all the assurance of a sleepwalker." "I believe that it was God's will that from here [Austria] a boy was sent into the Reich and that he grew up to become the leader of the nation." "God has created this people and it has grown according to *His* will. And according to *our* will it shall remain and never pass away."

Though Hitler came from Protestant roots, he had been profoundly moved as a boy by Catholic ritual and Catholic hierarchy (he had briefly thought of becoming a priest), and his vision of politics was influenced by the theory of papal infallibility. As he announced to a closed meeting at the Brown House in 1930: "I hereby set forth for myself and my successors in the leadership of the Party the claim of political infallibility. I hope the world will grow as accustomed to that claim as it has to the claim of the Holy Father." He had heard the voices in 1918, and he had secularized the apostolic succession. It is not surprising that he had Albert Speer create for the Nuremburg party rallies a "cathedral" composed of intersecting searchlight beams. Or that on March 16, 1934, all German schoolchildren wrote the following on the orders of the Ministry of Enlightenment and Propaganda: "Jesus and Hitler. As Jesus freed men from sin and Hell, so Hitler freed the German people from destruction. Jesus and Hitler were persecuted, but while Jesus was crucified Hitler was raised to the Chancellorship. . . . Jesus strove for Heaven, Hitler for the German earth."

Hitler's oratorical performances were often resurrection scenes. I have it on the authority of a naturalized American who was a member of the Hitler Youth during the 1930s and as such was given a position of honor on the platform during several Hitler speeches. He has no adult sympathy with National Socialism, but he recalls the effect as emotionally overwhelming. Hitler would begin in a monotone. He would stumble and emit broken phrases. But gradually he would seem possessed by extraordinary powers, and the speech would become an operatic aria, its rhythms discernibly Wagnerian as it grew in power. He himself had come back from the abyss of 1918—the audience could see it enacted before their eyes. So could Germany. It is also clear that Hitler's voice had for him sexual meanings. "Someone who does not understand the intrinsically feminine character of the masses will never be an effective speaker." "By feeling the reaction of the audience, one must know exactly when to throw the last flaming javelin which sets the crowd afire." His biographers attest that Hitler never felt more content or fulfilled than after a successful speech.

III

The trauma of 1918 was thus one important component of the mature Hitler. It was added to another that had been present since his earliest years. Hitler possessed a powerful aesthetic sense and was an artist not altogether *manqué*. His very emotional and aesthetic receptiveness may have deepened the 1918 trauma, in contrast to the experiences of many other soldiers, who were able to put it behind them. His artistic sensibility certainly shaped the panache of his political movement.

Richard Breiting, a German journalist, recalls visiting Hitler in May 1931 at party headquarters in Munich. The style of the political operation was impressive. The Nazis had their toughs and street-fighters, who were an important aspect of the early movement, but the Brown House was a visual metaphor which brought together the themes of tradition, efficiency, and modernization. "Hitler's headquarters," writes Breiting,

> is in the Brienner Strasse, Munich, in the ex-"Barlow Palace" where the Italian Legation was housed until the 1890s. Immediately opposite is the palace of the Papal Nuncio. The Brienner Strasse is one of the smartest streets in Munich. Hitler paid 500,000 marks for the Barlow Palace and spent as much again on alterations. The swastika flag flying from the roof can be seen a long way off. There are sentries on the door who check the papers of everyone entering; they give the impression of extremely strict martial discipline. All of them are fine large military figures, hard-faced, and one can well imagine them giving their lives for the movement. Dr. Alfred Detig and I were received at the door by Rudolf Hess, Hitler's private secretary and one of his oldest comrades in arms. Hess had taken part in the 1923 Feldherrnhalle *putsch;* a glance at him showed that he was an ex-officer; traces of mental turmoil showed in his face and undoubtedly he had a streak of fanaticism. Hess led us into the marble entrance hall. A plaque bore the names of the thirteen National Socialists who fell in front of the Feldherrnhalle; one wall was lined with standards and Hess explained that another was reserved for a memorial which would carry the names of the three hundred National Socialists murdered or fallen in the cause of the Movement. The whole hall gave an impression of great solemnity and gravity. Swastika signs were everywhere, carved into the stucco ceiling, and even introduced into the valuable glass of the windows. Since Hitler was not yet there, Hess took us on a tour of the place. Innumerable offices occupied the ground floor and the basement. Everything was brand-new and showed first-class organization. We were taken into the records office in the basement lined with fire-and-burglar-proof steel cupboards containing the personal files of 500,000 members of the NSDAP (Nazi Party). The records were designed to deal with a million names and Hess explained to us that when the NSDAP had a million members they would accept no more. "Either we can do it with a million or we can't do it at all. . . . " Hitler's study and the offices of his immediate staff were on the first floor. The offices were fitted out in really exquisite artistic taste; everything was in genuine oak with valuable antique

cupboards; some of the lights were chandeliers of old
Venetian glass.

Hess took us into the "Hall of Senators," a large, ornate,
artistically furnished room containing 61 red leather chairs.
The marble ceiling included a Party badge in mosaic; the
floor was covered with vast priceless carpets into which were
woven innumerable swastikas. . . . Our astonishment grew as
we toured the great building. This palace, furnished with
antiques and in exquisite artistic taste, was in glaring contrast
to the offices of a "workers" party. . . . Hitler was sitting at
a vast ambassadorial desk next to the "Hall of Senators"; a
picture of Mussolini stood on the desk; on the wall was an
enormous oil painting of Frederick the Great. . . . Hitler
shook my hand and said in a friendly, almost genial voice: "I
am pleased to meet you; I know the part which you and your
paper play among the German intelligentsia and
bourgeoisie."

At the age of sixteen, in the year 1905, Hitler looked like a young
aesthete of the period. He had unruly hair, the beginnings of a
mustache, and a dreamy expression that was caught in a pen-and-ink
drawing by a classmate. It could have been called "A Portrait of the
Artist as a Young Man." He usually dressed immaculately in a white
shirt, a flowing cravat with a stickpin, and good tweed suits. For his
frequent attendance at the opera he wore a silk-lined black coat,
black kid gloves, and a top hat, and he carried an ivory-handled
cane.

In the spring of 1906 his mother Klara allowed him to visit
Vienna, then in its golden era as a center of art and music. "Tomorrow," he wrote to his friend August Kubizek back in Linz, "I go to
the opera to see *Tristan,* the day after to *Flying Dutchman.* . . . "
The young connoisseur found the interior of the Royal Opera House
mediocre. "Only when the mighty waves of sound roll through space
and the whistling of the wind yields to the frightful rushing billows
of sound does one feel nobility and forget the gold and velvet with
which the interior is overloaded."

There can be no doubt about the power of Hitler's feeling for
Wagner or about the effect upon him of Wagner's ideas. On a stormy
day in November 1906 a performance of *Rienzi* apparently had a
decisive effect upon him. The performance lasted until well past
midnight. Hitler was captivated by the story of Rienzi's rise and fall,
a champion of his people who had been stung into action by the
murder of his brother by the plebeians of Rome. As he walked home
with Kubizek through the blustery autumn darkness, Hitler was

uncharacteristically silent. When Kubizek tried to start a conversation, Hitler cut him off. When they reached the top of a hill, Hitler gazed silently at the sky, then suddenly grabbed Kubizek's hands. "Never before," writes Kubizek, "and never again have I heard Adolf Hitler speak as he did in that hour as we stood there alone under the stars as though we were the only creatures in the world. It was as if another creature spoke out of his body, and moved him as much as it did me. It wasn't at all a case of a speaker being carried away by his own words. On the contrary; I rather felt as though he himself listened with astonishment and emotion to what burst forth from him with elementary force. I will not attempt to interpret this phenomenon, but it was a state of complete ecstasy and rapture." The two young men did not get home that night until three in the morning, and years later Hitler would order that his huge Nazi Party rallies open with the overture to *Rienzi*.

Hitler regarded himself as "perhaps the most musical of all Germans," and he made regular pilgrimages to the Wagner festivals at Bayreuth. Sometimes this passion took an amusing turn. In 1925 Hitler ruled out General Ludendorff as a political leader because he had no ear for music. In 1945 he rejected Heinrich Himmler as a possible successor for the same reason. He believed that only the musically attuned could be aware of the deeper movements of the German soul and could find the right words and rhythms to move and lead the people. "When he listened to Wagner's music," recalls Kubizek, "he was a changed man; his violence left him, he became quiet, yielding and tractable. . . . He was intoxicated and bewitched." He was indifferent to Bach, Handel, and Mozart, favoring, after Wagner, Grieg and Bruckner. Though he was twice rejected early in his career by the Academy of Fine Arts in Vienna, his drawings and paintings demonstrate a far from inconsiderable talent, and in the architect Albert Speer and the moviemaker Leni Riefenstahl, he had the taste to discern artistic talent of the highest order.

IV

At Treblinka, deception began as the train arrived at the sham railway station. The Nazis erected this fake depot, complete with a large clock, baggage-check windows, waiting rooms and posted train-schedules. They created the illusion that this was a transit camp, a place en route to a final destination.

But deception to prevent resistance was used only when unsuspecting Jews from the West arrived at the camps. The transports from the East, carrying Jews who suspected their fate, were met with brute force, designed to induce shock and thus make revolt impossible. When those transports arrived, SS and Ukranian police lashed out at the Jews with whips to hasten their departure from the trains. Those who fell behind were immediately shot. As they passed the large number of piles of clothing scattered everywhere, they became suspicious. They were never given time to think, discuss, or plan a response. Within hours of their arrival, the selection for extermination, the separation of men from women, and the marching or running to their deaths was completed. . . .

In the so-called changing rooms at Auschwitz there were signs in several languages reading TO THE BATHS and DISINFECTING ROOMS. In addition, there were slogans on the wall, such as ONE LOUSE CAN KILL YOU, or CLEANLINESS BRINGS FREEDOM. Moreover, numbered clothes hooks and wooden benches urging people to hang up their clothes and to remember their numbers for after their showers, created an aura of normality. At Chelmno, the signs read TO THE PHYSICIAN and TO THE WASHROOM; at Belsce, the entrance to the gas chambers had signs reading WASHING and INHALA-TION EQUIPMENT. At some camps people were given soap and a towel as they entered the gas chamber; at Maidanek, children were given candy.

If the SS guards sensed that the deceptions were not working, they responded with brute force. They beat the Jews and yelled at them to undress. At Auschwitz, a group from the Sosnovitz ghetto who had undoubtedly heard rumors about the camp was handled this way. This "brutal action . . . completely unnerved [them]. They were confused, frightened, unable to communicate with each other and incapable of anything." As the SS continued their abusive behavior the group quickly undressed. They were then chased into the crematorium. Once inside, the same procedure was repeated with another group until about 600 people were crammed into the gas chamber. . . .

On another occasion, the SS dispensed with the deception when they realized that the Jews knew they were about to be murdered. As the SS surrounded the yard of the crematorium, the Jews understood there was no escape. Resigned to their fate they began undressing, trying not to cry in order to avoid upsetting their children. After undressing, someone in the

crowd led them in the *Viddui* (death bed confession). A Jew
who witnessed this scene recalls that as they finished this
prayer almost everyone wept. . . . Strangely . . . the SS did
not intervene, but let the people be (*Genocide,* edited by Alex
Grobman and Daniel Landes).

Hitler's anti-Semitism was radical and absolutely fundamental to
his view of reality. It was so much the essence of his politics that he
diverted scarce resources from the war effort in order to expedite his
final solution. At the same time, it is difficult— for this writer, at any
rate—to penetrate his state of mind imaginatively. Much as one
might affirm without hesitation the truth of the Law of Gravity,
Hitler believed unshakably that the Jews were a lethal source of both
biological and cultural corruption. There is no doubt that, if Hitler
could speak to us today, he would concede that he had lost his war
for a Germanic empire in the East, but he would certainly insist that
he had won the more important war, his war against the Jews.
Various psychoanalytical causes for Hitler's radical anti-Semitism
have been suggested, but the core of the ideology itself remains
opaque.

August Kubizek recalls that Hitler expressed anti-Semitic views
as early as 1904 or 1905, but the evidence seems persuasive that
these views became fully formulated only during his Viennese
phase, around 1908, and further, that they were reinforced and
deepened in intent by the chaos and leftist revolutionism that followed the collapse of 1918. Kubizek recalls that one day in 1908
Hitler burst into the room they shared and shouted, "Today I
became a member of the Anti-Semitic Union and I enrolled you
too." It was in 1908 also that he devoured the anti-Semitic literature
of Lanz von Liebenfels and other fanatical anti-Semites, along with
Richard Wagner's scathing attacks on the Jews. For Hitler, Wagner
may have been the decisive intellectual influence in this regard,
given the authority of his music for the young aesthete. Hitler
himself regarded the year 1908 as pivotal in his intellectual development, the time when "the greatest change I was ever to experience"
occurred—that is, when he became a "fanatical anti-Semite."

"The race question," said Hitler, "not only furnishes the key to
world history, but also to human culture as a whole." "There is
absolutely no other revolution but a racial revolution. There is no
economic, no political, no social revolution. There is only the
struggle of the lower races against the dominant, higher races." In
his view, there was only one people or *Volk,* one racial community,
that had to be purified in order to realize its true racial identity. To

him, race was much more important than the Hegelian idea of the
state. As he told a Nuremburg rally in 1934,

> To others it seems a riddle, a mystery—this force that ever
> unites these hundreds of thousands, that gives them the
> strength to endure distress, pain and privation. They can
> conceive of this only as the result of an order issued by the
> State. They are wrong! It is not the State which gives its
> orders to us; but we who give orders to the State! It is not the
> State which has created us; but we fashion for ourselves our
> State. For one we may appear to be a Party; to another an
> organization; to a third, something else. But in truth we are
> the German *Volk*. . . . Let us pledge ourselves at every hour,
> on every day, only to think of Germany, of *Volk* and *Reich,* of
> our great nation, our German *Volk*. Sieg Heil!

Hitler apparently was so overcome with emotion during this speech
that he temporarily could not go on, yet his idea of the *Volk*—like his
conception of the *Führer,* who embodies the spirit of the *Volk*—
remains a mystery. About all that can be said about it was that it
constituted a powerful myth or idea that he was able to make real for
the masses, who screamed back at him the terms of his new Trinity:
"Ein Volk! Ein Reich! Ein Führer!" This cheer, which makes little
sense analytically, is really a sort of mantra or prayer, an affirmation
of Oneness; after all, everyone *knew* there was only *one Führer.*

In the earliest piece of writing of his political career, a letter dated
September 16, 1919, Hitler stated his goals as "ruthless intervention" against the Jews and their "removal" from Europe. In this
early statement Hitler is careful to state that his anti-Semitism is not
based on emotion, but is coldly rational. "Anti-Semitism based on
purely emotional grounds will always find its ultimate expression in
the form of pogroms. A rational anti-Semitism, however, must lead
to the systematic legal fight. . . . Its ultimate goal, however, must
unalterably be the elimination of the Jews altogether." He never
wavered from this conviction. The Jews would be stripped of their
legal status as a prelude to stripping them of their lives.

Hitler's anti-Semitism may have been reinforced by events that
followed upon the collapse of Imperial Germany in 1918. The
Munich to which he returned in the spring of 1918 had been proclaimed the capital of Socialist Bavaria by Kurt Eisner, a Jewish
journalist, who, along with a bizarre collection of leftists, had risen
to the top of the chaos. Beyond Eisner, a substantial number of the
newly prominent leftists and Communists were Jewish—Rosa Lux-
emburg, Max Levien, Eugen Leviné, Béla Kun (who had seized

power in Hungary), and so on. Hitler later remarked that he had returned from the war to find "Israel king of Bavaria."

It is doubtful that many Germans or other Europeans shared Hitler's systematic and radical anti-Semitism. On the other hand, his program would not have exercised the appeal it did unless many were at least susceptible to a generally anti-Semitic appeal. In an important and unsettling article that appeared in *Commentary* magazine (March 1985), Professor Theodore S. Hamerow, a historian at the University of Wisconsin, argues that the anti-Semitic program was surprisingly popular in occupied Europe and enlisted the willing cooperation of many non-Germans. "That such collaboration was widespread," he writes, "is clear. Any consideration of the Holocaust as simply an organizational problem, as an exercise in logistics, suggests that the Germans must have had many highly efficient assistants. How else could some six million people, who knew or suspected what fate awaited them, and who therefore sought in every possible way to avoid capture, be rounded up, confined, deported, and killed? A task of such magnitude required a considerable commitment of manpower and equipment. Yet the documentary evidence shows that the number of Germans available to carry out the policies of the Third Reich in occupied Europe was surprisingly small." Professor Hamerow concludes persuasively that the Germans gained the decisive cooperation of local anti-Semites in Poland, the Balkans, the Ukraine, and elsewhere. Without it, there could have been no Holocaust.

Professor Gordon Craig of Stanford agrees with much of that analysis. Writing in the *New York Review of Books,* he reflects on the irony that Hitler's program took hold in Germany, where the Jewish population was highly assimilated, considered itself German, and had rallied patriotically to the colors in 1914. "The fact that the more the Jews came to resemble the Germans, the more they were rejected by them," writes Professor Craig,

> is the theme of George L. Mosse's book, *German Jews Beyond Judaism.* . . .[Mosse] finds the key to this tragic situation in the fact that the German Jews, to an extent that was never true of most Germans, dedicated themselves to the ideals of the Enlightenment—faith in reason, love of humanity, cosmopolitanism, belief in progress, willingness to be modern at the expense of the traditional and the orthodox—and remained faithful to them long after they had been replaced in the German consciousness by romantic notions of Germanness that were based upon a distortion of Herder's cultural ideas and by an increasingly xenophobic nationalism.

Much of the recent discussion of Dr. Josef Mengele, for example, foundered on a failure to understand his own "scientific" and radical anti-Semitism. Like Hitler and the other top anti-Semitic ideologues, Mengele, who possessed advanced scientific degrees, believed completely in a whole range of eugenic theories, among which was the tenet that it was a crime and corruption to mix German and Jewish racial strains. Like Hitler, Mengele had a passion for cleanliness and order and for precision of formulation. There is no doubt that at Auschwitz he presided over the extermination of tens of thousands of Jews and others, but he thought he was doing no less than his duty as a "scientist." Reports of conversations during his last years in Brazil indicate that he believed his racial theories to the end.

The Holocaust is only explicable by a complex set of converging circumstances. At the top of the Nazi state, the anti-Semitic ideology in its most radical form was dominant among the hierarchy. Below the leadership, the entire state was organized in a hierarchical way. And the government had total domination over the media and other means of communication. This was the necessary mechanism. But it also required, as Professors Hamerow, Mosse and others have shown, the existence of a widespread anti-Semitism of a more general and less radical kind within the Nazi empire. The radical doctrine fell on ears that were at least partially willing.

V

These then are the three key elements in the Hitler phenomenon: his descent into the abyss at the time of the German defeat in 1918, his intense aestheticism and dramatic flair, and his radical and obsessive anti-Semitism. Fused into an amalgam, they energized a policy that was revolutionary domestically and global in scope.

Hitler's instrument of totalitarian power was the Enabling Law, passed under intense pressure by the Reichstag on March 23, 1933, which conferred on Hitler's new regime the right to enact laws without the consent of the Reichstag or the Reichsrat. All constitutional restraints were thus removed at a stroke, and the regime was enabled to do whatever it wished to terrorize the opposition, gag the press, regiment the bureaucracy and the legal profession, and abolish independent labor unions. Where the latter are concerned, the events of May 2, 1933, possess a certain sardonic humor. Initially, the Nazi leadership had avoided a direct confrontation with the large unions, alternating friendly gestures with acts of random violence by the ever-present street fighters. May Day was proclaimed a national holiday in honor of labor, with the Nazi regime and the unions cooperating to organize mass demonstrations in celebration of the German workingman. Theodore Leiphart, the leading union official, declared that the unions would refrain from political activity and confine themselves to the social sphere, no doubt believing that this would satisfy the Nazis. Such a hope seemed plausible on May 1, as the mass demonstrations took place as planned. The next day, as had been prearranged, the union leaders were arrested and union offices seized by the police, and the unions were reorganized as part of the German Labor Front under Robert Ley, chief of staff of the political organization of the Nazi Party.

Eight days later, Josef Goebbels, the propaganda minister, organized the burning of "un-German" books by Nazi students in the Berlin Opernplatz. The *Gleichschaltung,* or national coordination, stripped the states of political power and centralized it in Berlin. The Nuremburg Laws of 1935 would begin the process of isolating the Jews and stripping them of legal status. Field Marshal von Hindenberg would die in 1934 a revered national hero. At a solemn ceremony held in the Garrison Church at Potsdam on March 21, 1933, Chancellor Hitler paid homage to the old war hero. Goebbels remarked privately that this was a "sentimental comedy." Two days later the Enabling Law was passed. Meanwhile, the Nazis busily honeycombed society with party associations and institutions. At first they competed with existing organizations, but gradually they got the upper hand. There were the SA and the SS, the Hitler Youth, women's organizations, Nazi associations for students, professors, physicians, civil servants, technicians, even a new Nazified Protestant church organization. For many Germans, this all represented a new, and not unwelcome, sense of social order, especially when compared with the recent past.

The elements of Hitler's radical foreign policy went into place just as rapidly and were carried out with great consistency right up to the catastrophe of 1945. Unlike the traditional German leadership of the postwar period, Hitler was not content with restoring the frontiers of 1914 and returning Germany to its position as one of the important European powers. Hitler's radical grand design never changed from the time he set it forth in *Mein Kampf.* On February 3, 1933, in a speech to senior army officers, Hitler declared that the aim of German foreign policy must be to conquer "fresh *lebensraum*" in the East, and that to consolidate this eastern empire, the entire region must be "ruthlessly Germanized." Thus Hitler intended to advance step by step beyond revision of the Versailles Treaty to establish German power in Central and Eastern Europe as a prelude to the final annihilation of Soviet Bolshevism and the colonization of

European Russia as a German breadbasket and inexhaustible source of needed resources. The Nazis would thus establish a continental European empire within which France would be, at best, a junior partner.

Prior to 1939, Hitler continually hoped for a deal with England that would free him for his eastward thrust. In November 1934 he indicated to Sir Eric Phipps, the British ambassador in Berlin, that Germany was willing to conclude an agreement that would limit her naval forces to 35 percent of the British total—that is, that Germany did not intend, for the time being at least, to challenge the island empire on the world's oceans. Significantly, though England tried to reach a similar agreement regarding air power, Berlin showed no interest in it. The Luftwaffe, however, lacked a long-range bombing force adequate for the Battle of Britain, and it lacked a long-range fighter to protect what bombers it had. It was largely a tactical bombing force and was largely intended to support the ground forces in a land struggle to the east.

Though Hitler never desired war with England and preferred an alliance with England to one with Italy, he was not willing to avoid war at the cost of his designs in Central and Eastern Europe and his ultimate conquest of Russia. The British goal, in contrast, was accommodation within the general framework of the status quo. The men in Whitehall would let Hitler have the Rhineland, Austria, Czechoslovakia, and probably a land corridor to Danzig. They were not prepared to allow Hitler to redraw the map of Europe and radically change the balance of power on the continent. On September 1, 1939, the British stake in the status quo finally and inevitably collided with Hitler's revolutionary policy of *lebensraum*.

There are some indications that Hitler may have had still more radical designs in store. At the end of January 1939, he approved the navy's "Z Plan" and gave orders for the construction of a large surface fleet. His toleration for England's oceanic hegemony may have been strictly provisional. During the summer of 1940, President Roosevelt became profoundly worried about German penetration of Latin America—politically, culturally, and perhaps militarily. Argentina's political elite contained many Nazi sympathizers, and German enterprises were spreading throughout the southern hemisphere. FDR told his secretary of the navy, the Republican Frank Knox, that as soon as Germany consolidated its gains in Europe, it would proceed to penetrate South America and that "then we will have our work cut out for us in this country." Roosevelt knew that Uruguay had become the headquarters for a German effort to fuse all of Latin America into a German-dominated trading bloc. Though the idea far outran his available assets in

1940, there is evidence that Hitler at least mused on the idea of an eventual struggle for world domination against a "mongrel" United States.

By the last day of the year 1940, such a prospect would not have seemed irrational to Hitler. He had in effect conquered power in Germany. He had seized the Rhineland and defied all of the Versailles powers. He had seized Austria and Czechoslovakia, smashed Poland, Denmark, Norway, Luxembourg, Belgium, and Holland with a new mode of revolutionary mobile warfare. His *blitzkrieg* had rolled over France, which had a large and well-equipped modern army, in a few weeks. He had humiliated the British at Dunkirk.

On that last night of 1940, Hitler celebrated the New Year at his Berghof, a white-painted chalet high in the Bavarian Alps. Those around him were impressed by his sense of inner serenity. The Christmas card he had selected, sent only to a few intimates such as Göring and Goebbels and Mussolini, had on it a photograph of the Winged Victory of Samothrace. The piece of ancient sculpture had been removed from the Louvre and now stood in Hitler's office. The Christmas card was decorated by a frieze of German aircraft and carried the message "Our Winged Victory."

That night Hitler, who never drank, permitted himself a glass of champagne. His guests followed him to a large picture window in the main room of the chalet. "For some time," writes historian Richard Collier, "the Führer stood with his glass raised, looking out into the night, staring eastward toward invisible sights: the snow-capped Carpathian mountains and the territory of the Ukraine. The most triumphant year of his life was behind him. Beyond lay the unknown."

Through genuine brilliance, however perverse, and through the sheer power of his personal will, Hitler by the end of 1940 had changed Europe and the world. Things would never be the same again. But he was at that moment also raising against him men of at least equal determination. His opponents now would be not Neville Chamberlain and Édouard Daladier, but Winston Churchill and Franklin Roosevelt, men of great personal will, who had experienced personal and political resurrections of their own, and who were orators of force equal to Hitler. By the end of 1940, the old world was gone forever.

Coney

In 1940 Coney Island was not the rusting, black-street-gang-infested ruin it is today. Ordinary people actually went there for a good time and a couple of Nathan's hot dogs. You did not go to the beach, which was so crowded that you had to step over people to get to the water, but you did go to the amusement park, the greatest amusement park ever built, which was still continuous with the golden era that began in 1897 when George C. Tillyou opened Steeplechase Park.

Tillyou had discovered in England a ride that simulated a horse race, with wooden horses running up and down grades and around curves on railroad tracks. He installed it at Coney Island in rivalry to Captain Paul Boynton's Shoot-the-Chutes. Boynton, who had become famous for floating across the English Channel in a rubber suit, opened a Sea Lion Park near a hotel actually shaped like a gigantic elephant, and Boynton's chief attraction was a ride in which you scudded down watery ramps into an artificial lagoon. Tillyou, however, had bigger things in mind. In addition to the English Steeplechase, he installed the largest Ferris wheel in the world.

In 1903 a couple of showmen, Fred Thompson and Elmer Dundy, bought out Boynton and redesigned Sea Lion Park as Luna Park, which was still there in 1940. It featured a simulated Jules Verne Trip to the Moon, live elephants, midgets, cannibals, a simulated Boer War battle with actual Boers brought over from the losing side, including General Piet Cronje, who had surrendered to Lord Roberts at Paardeberg. In Thompson and Dundy's Naval Spectatorium, the new American imperial impulses received fictitious gratification. The audience, sitting in a simulated coast gun emplacement, saw the great navies of the world—German, British, French, and Spanish—coming over the horizon and advancing upon Manhattan. Nothing doing. The American fleet swung out in battle order and sank every foreign ship.

That same year, 1903, Coney Island was electrified. Luna Park had 250,000 lights, but the new Dreamland, an architectural fantasia, had one million. The buildings of Dreamland were pure white and were inspired by the white classical vistas of the World's Columbian Exposition at Chicago in 1893. Albert Bigelow Paine watched dusk fall on Luna Park and wrote: "Tall towers that had grown dim suddenly broke forth in electric outlines and gay rosettes of color, as the living spark of light travelled hither and thither, until the place was transformed into an enchanted garden, of such a sort as Aladdin never dreamed." James Gibbons Huneker wrote about the same scene: "The view of Luna Park . . . suggests a cemetery of fire, the tombs, turrets and towers illuminated, and mortuary shafts of flame. . . . Dreamland . . . stands a dazzling apparition for men on ships and steamers out at sea. Everything is fretted with fire. Fire delicately etches some fairy structure; fire outlines an oriental gateway, fire runs like a musical scale through many octaves."

Everyone came to Coney Island—socialites, prostitutes, the Union League Club with permanent hotel suites for the use of its members in the summer, the Mafia, the Jewish mobsters. When Abe Reles, a mobster turned informer, was thrown out of a window of the Half Moon Hotel in Coney Island, one of his old friends in Murder, Inc., raised his wine glass with this toast: "To a great canary—who could sing, only he couldn't fly."

Coney Island, while it lived, was also raunchy, with a frisson of sexuality and transient abandonment running through it and heightening its pleasure. This was a relatively innocent pre-World War II sexuality. You hugged the girl on the Steeplechase ride and in the fun house and on the roller coaster. "Will she throw her arms around your neck and yell?" read the come-on for a ride called the Cannon Coaster. A historian of Coney Island, Richard Snow, tells of a charming old romantic moment in which a writer named

> Elmer Blaney Harris, out to spend a Sunday at Coney, was
> making his way across the beach when he came upon "a little
> maid in wet, diaphanous green, combing her hair, her nether
> limbs buried in the sand with which she had dried them."
> Harris stopped and stared down at her—something he
> probably wouldn't have done to a girl on a park bench back in
> the everyday city. "My shadow fell upon her and she, with a
> question on her tongue, looked up as if . . . to demand by
> what right I had obstructed her sunshine. I doffed my hat and
> apologized. She, smiling faintly, arched her head in ever so
> slight an inclination and went on with her combing. Her eyes
> were blue as the cloudless summer sky above us."

Later in the evening, Elmer Blaney Harris ran into the girl having dinner at Feltman's vast seafood restaurant, the

> "maid of the golden hair and sea-green bathing suit. She was
> sitting alone, entirely preoccupied with eating a bit of
> sandwich, and I had ample time to note the faded roses on her
> last year's hat and the characteristic grace of her hands before
> she looked up and saw me. . . . I caught Dora's eye (her
> name was Dora, if I may announce it without being anti-
> climatic) and in the freemasonry of the crowd we laughed
> simultaneously. At her table was the only unoccupied chair in
> the garden, and I asked her if I might sit there.
> "'Sure, you can sit there!' she said, still smiling. 'Anyone
> can sit here with a laugh like that. I'm never afraid of a man
> if he laughs loud.'

" 'Are you alone?'

" 'Of course I'm alone! . . . Oh, you needn't think I'm alone because I have to be, or because I like it. I s'pose there's thousands of men in this crowd I'd like, but—well, most of 'em—you know how it is—always the third rail—see?'

"I told her I saw perfectly, and that, if she pleased, we'd walk between the tracks."

Harris took Dora on some of the rides and then to the big dance in the Dreamland Ballroom, out at the end of the Iron Pier.

"Although prepared for much, I was surprised at the grace with which she danced. She didn't wish to be held in the prevailing fashion, tight and affectionately; nor was the slow half-time at all to her liking. She gave me but the tips of her fingers. . . . Imagine my surprise, therefore, when, at the close of the encore, she suddenly, with a little purr, flung both arms around my neck and kissed me lightly on the cheek.

" 'Oh, look!' she cried, pointing over my shoulder.

"I looked. And when I turned back—she was gone—swallowed up in that impenetrable crowd."

After the close of the 1939–40 World's Fair, the Parachute Jump was moved to Coney Island, much in the tradition of George C. Tillyou and his Steeplechase. In 1940 Coney Island was still alive, but in the mid-1950s it became unsafe to go there, with urban-renewal projects beginning to destroy the old neighborhoods, the streets perilous, and year by year, the paint peeling and the amusement park buildings failing to reopen. Steeplechase Park closed in 1964. On the nearest standing wall there is a new mural, placed there by an organization called the Coney Island Historical Society. It shows the old Steeplechase grinning man in front of a rendering of the old building itself, and the message:

Steeplechase Park. . . .
Come back. . . .
Come back. . . .

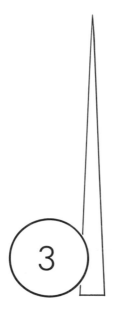

WENDELL WILLKIE VERSUS THE CHAMP

③

I

Nothing like the 1940 Republican convention had been seen in American politics for exactly eighty years. In the summer of 1860, supporters of front-runner William Seward had been locked out of the Chicago Republican convention, and the emotional turmoil caused by the supporters of Abraham Lincoln had influenced enough delegates to give the tall, melancholy, Illinois lawyer an upset victory on the third ballot. At some level of awareness, that 1860 convention was voting against slavery and for war. The 1940 Republican convention was also administering a historic shock, rejecting its isolationist and ambivalent candidates and, responding to a fast-developing national emotion, voting for Wendell Willkie and, implicitly perhaps, for war if absolutely necessary.

One week before the Republicans assembled at Convention Hall in Philadelphia, Hitler conquered France. During the weeks before the delegates voted, war news dominated the front pages of our newspapers. The papers were reporting an emerging deal between the Japanese and the Nazis to divide up the British, French, and

Dutch possessions in the Pacific. The French fleet was still intact and refusing to surrender in Casablanca, but if the Germans could take over that fleet, they would soon be sailing the Atlantic. A cartoonist for a Brooklyn newspaper summed up the situation that was developing in Philadelphia. H. E. Homan drew the menacing figure of Adolf Hitler standing in the middle of Convention Hall, and the title of his cartoon was *The Uninvited Guest.*

In September 1939, the American people as a whole had been determined to keep out of the new European war. They were not neutral: the vast majority despised and hated the Nazi regime in Germany, and most Americans were sympathetic to England and France. A Gallup poll published in the *New York Times* of September 20, 1938, asked this question: "Should we send our Army and Navy abroad to fight Germany?" The answers were as follows:

	Yes	No
Democrats	18%	82%
Republicans	13%	87%

Moreover, in that first fall of the new war—and indeed, up until April or May of 1940—the great majority of Americans were sure that Britain and France would defeat Germany without having to call upon our aid. Another question, asked in the same poll, demonstrated clearly that the prospect of an Allied defeat would have a signal effect upon American opinion: "If it looks within the next few months as if England and France might be defeated, should the United States declare war on Germany and send our troops abroad?"

	Yes	No
Democrats	46%	54%
Republicans	42%	58%

But this contingency seemed remote. Secure in their belief in the French army and the British navy, the people of the United States felt they well might stay out.

Almost every man in American public life faithfully reflected this sentiment. President Roosevelt declared that he hoped and believed we could stay neutral in the conflict, but he would not ask the people of the country (as Wilson had) to remain neutral in thought as well as in deed. Other members of the administration echoed his sentiments. It is neither unnatural nor sinister, therefore, that almost all Republican leaders of consequence declared their conviction that America should stay clear of the struggle.

Republicans generally felt that there was a good chance of defeating the president, if he should decide to run for a third term, and they were downright positive they could beat any New Dealer nominated to succeed him. In September 1939, a *Fortune* survey had reported the following question and answers:

> "Which of the following statements most nearly represents your idea of the Republican Party?"
>
> a. The election of the Republican Party in 1940 provides the only hope of saving this country 10.3%
>
> b. If elected in 1940, the Republicans could serve the country well, provided they find new liberal leaders who are in tune with the times 28.7%
>
> c. The Republicans and conservative Democrats are about alike, and it does not matter which elects a President, so long as there is a change from the present Administration 27.5%
>
> d. If the Republican party comes to power in 1940, it will be a calamity for the country 16.7%
>
> e. Don't know 16.8%

The Republican nomination in 1940, unlike that of 1936, might be a very important matter indeed.

Wendell Willkie won an amazing upset victory at the convention for several reasons. He was the only committed Republican internationalist, and the catastrophic events in Europe had overtaken the more traditional Republican candidates. During that astonishing summer of 1940, while Hitler rampaged in Europe and Japan loomed ever larger across the Pacific, American opinion was moving slowly and reluctantly, but ever more powerfully, in the direction of Willkie's internationalism—that is, fighting Germany and Japan if necessary. Second, Willkie came to Philadelphia with powerful support in the Republican media, and he had built up a sophisticated, though unorthodox, political organization. But perhaps most important of all, and not stressed in ordinary historical accounts, was the fact that Willkie was the first major Republican since Theodore Roosevelt with sex appeal.

That may sound frivolous, but you had to be alive in that summer of 1940 to understand what Wendell Willkie was doing to the American educated classes, and especially to women. It was a sort of middle-class convulsion. He was the barefoot boy from Wall Street. At six-two and slightly overweight he had a bearlike quality and a physical presence that, along with his intelligence and wit, impressed men as well as women. In Philadelphia, Broadway columnist Damon Runyon spotted Willkie at a hotel bar. In the July heat, Willkie was wearing a rumpled seersucker suit and a straw boater.

"Lots of us followed him into the bar to get a close peek at him," wrote Runyon. "Everybody that could get near him had something. He was so big and tough that he never budged an inch from his place at the bar when everybody was scrimming and scrounging trying to have something and somebody said it was a good thing they were not the fellows we were thinking of picking our ticket from or they would have got lost in the shuffle or knocked down and crippled." In the White House, FDR and his aides mused on the fact that Willkie, though married, was almost openly sleeping with Irita Van Doren, the powerful book editor of the *New York Herald Tribune,* the most important Republican newspaper in the country. Not surprisingly, just before the balloting in Philadelphia, the *Herald Tribune* endorsed Willkie. Willkie had an almost electric physical presence. With his shock of unruly, dark hair and deep voice, his ability to make an expensive suit five minutes after he put it on look as if he had slept in it, his intellectual aggressiveness and utter candor, his sense of America's danger and global mission, he created a sort of political orgasm among people who now would be called Yuppies—the educated, the rising, the articulate. Willkie Clubs had sprung up all across the nation, outside of and often opposed to the local Republican organization.

The other Republican contenders were formidable and, yes, admirable men. It is seldom that a political party has such richness of talent to choose from. Willkie's chief rivals that July, amidst an array of favorite-son and vanity candidates, were former President Herbert Hoover, who was trying for a comeback; the thirty-nine-year-old district attorney from New York, Thomas E. Dewey; and Senator Robert Alonso Taft from Ohio.

Tom Dewey was a small, precise, and cold man who had become a hero for his racket-busting activities. He was most certainly a hero nationally and the inspiration for the radio serial "Gang Busters." His personal organization was the best until Reagan's California mafia of the 1970s. Its core consisted of tough and ambitious young lawyers who modeled themselves on the cold and meticulous Dewey. Even today, some survivors of that circle can give you a chilly sense of the Young Master. Tom Dewey, someone said, could strut sitting down. His idea of a campaign photograph was to milk a cow in white shirt, tie, and vest. Alice Longworth Roosevelt said that he looked like the little groom on a wedding cake. A fanatic about cleanliness, he would wipe his palm with a handkerchief after touching a doorknob. It was said that to really hate him, you had to get to know him. He always had a clean desk, with a pitcher of icewater on it, and in his pursuit of gangsters he was devastating. often bending the law to achieve convictions. The gangsters—Jews, Italians, Irish (no doubt, all of them Democrats)—knew that Tom Dewey could send you to the electric chair with a memorandum. In the midst of the New Deal era, the young district attorney had come within one pecentage point of upsetting Herbert Lehman, the popular Democratic governor of New York. In the summer of 1940, Dewey was absolutely certain that he would be the next president of the United States.

Robert Alonso Taft was an authentic American aristocrat from Ohio who had been raised with the understanding that it was his natural destiny to be president of the country, and he was a dominant intellectual force in the Senate. His father had been both president and chief justice of the Supreme Court. Bob Taft had been first in his class at Yale and first in his class at Harvard Law School. He was a man of austere principle and ruthless intellect who gazed at the world through rimless eyeglasses. He expected to receive the 1940 Republican nomination almost as a matter of proprietary right.

The first of many remarkable events at the Philadelphia convention was the comeback attempt of former President Herbert Hoover, who believed that the faltering economy under the New Deal had justified him intellectually, and who was seeking political vindication. Correctly, Hoover could claim that many of the popular New Deal programs had their origin in his administration. He had been demolished by Franklin Roosevelt during the depths of the Depression in 1932, but he believed that he had a chance to reverse that verdict in 1940. Hoover walked down the aisle toward the podium with his son Allan and the governor of Pennsylvania flanking him, while the band played "California, Here I Come." The crowd of 15,000 in Convention Hall gave him a seven-minute, emotional, standing ovation, and delegates waving their state banners paraded through the hall. There stood Herbert Hoover, the very image of the old Republican party, wearing a double-breasted suit and the old-fashioned, high, starched collar that had become his trademark. Hoover, who had a formidable intellect, had worked on his speech for months, and he believed that it was the best he had ever delivered. "We are here faced with the task of saving America for free men. . . ." The speech came over the radio very well, serious and even brilliant. No one in the convention center heard it. Delegates chanted "Louder! Louder!" As Hoover spoke, people began to mill about or leave for a hot dog. A Willkie strategist named Samuel Pryor, later a judge, had bribed an electrician to provide Hoover with a dead mike. There would be no Hoover comeback.

With the old president out of the way, the real political fight could begin, and the 1940 convention had everything any historian or political buff could desire. It, too, was part of an older America, but an America on the threshold of something new and mysterious. In that older America, presidential candidates were really chosen at such conventions, rather than ceremonially anointed after a successful struggle through the primaries. At Philadelphia in 1940, if you listened closely, you could hear old and distant chants: "Tippecanoe and Tyler Too" and "Blaine, Blaine, James G. Blaine, / The Continental Liar from the State of Maine." At Philadelphia in 1940, there were tough tactics and dirty tricks, issues at stake that would affect the entire world, crushed personal ambitions, and a sawdust, Barnum-and-Bailey atmosphere that Europeans always mistake as a sign of American frivolity. The millionaire newspaper publisher Frank Gannett, a vanity candidate, hired a parade of "Gannett Elephants" and also bribed Philadelphia taxi drivers to boost his candidacy to their passengers. The cabbies made an unheard-of $500 apiece. H. L. Mencken, our best between-the-wars journalist, summed up the wild, quasi-corrupt essence of the whole thing when he wrote after Willkie's sixth-ballot "miracle nomination": "At the moment the sixth ballot was being counted I saw an angel in the gallery. It wore a Palm Beach suit and was smoking a five-cent cigar, but nevertheless it was palpably an angel."

The Dewey team, going into the convention, exuded a smooth arrogance that accurately represented the personality of the thirty-nine-year-old prosecutor himself. He had beaten all other candidates in the Republican primaries; he had led all year in the opinion polls; for two years he had been considered the most likely Republican to beat Roosevelt, should the president seek an unprecedented third term; and he and his efficient professionals calculated that he was within one hundred votes of the nomination. With a score of favorite-son and vanity candidates in the contest, those one hundred votes could surely be shaken loose somewhere. The Dewey descent upon Philadelphia resembled a coronation procession.

But there were tiny dark clouds. Dewey's pollster, Gerald Lambert, knew that Dewey had been sinking—in small increments, but nevertheless sinking—since June. Lambert advised the candidate and his professional handlers that they should hold back fifty votes on the first ballot and then put them into the second ballot to give Dewey the appearance of momentum. Dewey treated this advice with imperial disdain. He would roar forward at full strength and use that strength to make some deals. The nomination was within his grasp.

But Dewey and his professionals had overrated his first-ballot strength and not understood the history of their craft, one theorem of which is that no one who has lost delegate strength at a convention has ever won the nomination. Nor did they understand the dynamics of public opinion in that catastrophic summer of 1940. Dewey's youth and uncertain views in foreign affairs were handicaps after the fall of France, and he knew it. "Good health," he quipped at a press conference, was his only asset in being young. Conceivably, at the final hour, Dewey could have made a statement indicating that he realized the gravity of things abroad, but he remained ambiguous. Later people said that his candidacy was the first American casualty of World War II. Sensing the swing in public opinion, CBS had recently canceled the radio show "Gang Busters." After the fall of France, the show seemed beside the point, as did Dewey himself.

Robert Alonso Taft of Ohio came to Philadelphia with a conviction of his presidential legitimacy that had been nurtured since birth. He appeared to trail Dewey in first-ballot strength, but he was the Republican tactical and theoretical power in the United States Senate, and he had the support of the most influential Republican politicians across the country. He possessed all of the academic, intellectual, and political credentials. He believed that his solid support would weather the Dewey storm, pick up strength as the ballotting went on, and deliver the nomination. Most newspaper reporters in Philadelphia were picking Bob Taft on the fourth ballot. Still, with his actual delegate strength concentrated in his home state of Ohio, plus Texas and the South, Taft had serious problems. That is, even if he won the nomination, he could not defeat Roosevelt. Whatever Republican delegates from Texas and the South were going to do in Philadelphia, Franklin Roosevelt would sweep 100 percent of their electoral votes in the election. Gazing at this situation through his rimless glasses, Taft decided to go for the delegates and worry about Roosevelt later. Studying all of this with his inner circle, Roosevelt decided that Willkie would be his most formidable opponent.

Within the convention, the Taft forces faced a number of options and necessities. They could fight Dewey for the Illinois delegation, but they knew that Dewey had considerable strength there. They had a chance for the Pennsylvania delegation, once millionaire boss Joseph Pew pulled back the favorite-son candidacy of Governor Arthur James. Herbert Hoover's forty-four California delegates might well be pulled to Taft; after all, he had been one of Hoover's brightest young aides during World War I. Taft arrived in Philadelphia feeling not only that he deserved the nomination, but that he probably would get it, and there was not an ounce of Barnum-and-Bailey in his being. When he arrived at his suite in the Benjamin Franklin Hotel, he was outraged to find a pygmy elephant named Blossom, who had been rented by his staff, in his bedroom. "Get that damned Blossom out of my bedroom,'' he shouted. Bob Taft was a serious man.

Taft had problems of temperament, inspiring respect but not much love, and problems of image, to use a modern term. He had been an effective critic of New Deal centralization and a formidable debater in the Senate, but he seemed cold and academic. Most damaging of all, after France fell that summer, Taft was the most isolationist of the three leading Republican candidates. He had been an academic star at Yale and at Harvard, but his intellect reflected the heartland views of Ohio, of the Midwest, and Taft wanted no part of European wars. But with Hitler's May *blitzkrieg* through the Ardennes and his march to Paris and the British collapse at Dunkirk, the whole world balance of power was changing. For all of his cold intellectual brilliance, Bob Taft did not seem to realize that everything had changed politically.

Nevertheless, antiwar sentiment remained powerful in the United States and very powerful in the Republican party, and it included, as a kind of footnote, a murky little plot in Philadelphia. As the convention got under way, forty Republican congressmen and five senators published a manifesto demanding that the convention choose ''a leader with a past record consistently supporting Republican policies and principles and whose recognized position and recent pronouncements are a guarantee to the American people that he would not lead the people into a foreign war.'' This statement was aimed directly at Willkie, who had only recently changed his registration to Republican and who was the most interventionist of the leading candidates. It may have reflected a majority Republican isolationist sentiment, even after the fall of France. The only problem with it was that it had been organized by the German embassy, and German cash had paid some of the expenses of the signatories in Philadelphia. In the summer of 1940, things were not as simple as they once had been.

When Governor Harold Stassen of Wisconsin, at thirty-three the boy wonder of the Republican party and obviously a future president, delivered his Monday-night keynote address, the celebrities present in Convention Hall represented the apotheosis of American fame and a metaphor for one version of America. They were the gods and goddesses of the middle class, evocative of the twenties and thirties and even earlier, but standing for specific political and social content: the splendor and purity of the American past, distrust and even hatred of Roosevelt and the New Deal, and a widespread nervousness about the European war and about the darkening future. Former heavyweight champion Gene Tunney was there, and no doubt, most Republicans much preferred him to the current champion, Joe Louis; the sexy baritone Rudy Vallee came, with his Ivy League charm; and the familiar radio celebrities Lowell Thomas, H. V. Kaltenborn, and Grantland Rice, the last familiar not only from Kentucky Derby broadcasts— "Weep No More, My Lady"—but as the author of the greatest lead in the history of sportswriting. He began his account of the Army–Notre Dame game of 1927: "Against a cold blue November sky, the four horsemen rode again. In mythology, their names are hunger, disease, famine and death. In reality, their names are Leyden, Murphy, Stuhldreyer, Crowley." These gathering celebrities legitimated a Republican party that had been discredited by the Great Depression and by Roosevelt's landslide defeat of Alf Landon four years before. They embodied a pre-Depression and pre-Roosevelt America. Two widows of former presidents were there that summer as well—Helen Herren Taft, who had come to see the son of the president placed in nomination, and astonishingly, Mary Scott Lord Dimmick Harrison, widow of Benjamin Harrison, dressed in black. Charles Lindbergh, the Lone Eagle, perhaps the greatest of all American heroes and celebrities of the 1920s, did not attend the convention, but he was an unseen presence there. He had emerged from the bitterness and seclusion of the kidnapping to become a public figure once again and had led the antiwar movement in America with courage and eloquence. He had told the truth about German military superiority in Europe, especially its air force, but he had been subject to savage attacks, including the charge of treason, and Lindbergh stayed away from Philadelphia in 1940.

The emerging new world of political violence intruded upon the resurgent Republicanism of 1940 when Philadelphia police uncovered a terrorist plot designed to interrupt and perhaps discredit the convention. The detectives had infiltrated the terrorist circle. Several bombs filled with explosives and scrap metal were found in Convention Hall and other places where they could do the most damage. As the convention opened, it was reported in the newspapers that terrorists planned to assassinate Republican leaders in the hall itself. Two men were subsequently indicted for the plot, but after a long legal struggle, the state dropped the case, and the motives for the plot have never been made clear.

Unknown to everyone outside the Willkie inner circle, including Dewey and Taft, Willkie's team had managed to pack the galleries of the two-tiered Convention Hall with Willkie supporters. When Ralph E. Williams, a Taft man and chairman of the Committee on Arrangements, died of a stroke at the Bellevue-Stratford, a Willkie lieutenant from Connecticut, Samuel F. Pryor, took over and gained control of the tickets available to the public. In a move that may actually have changed the history of the world, Pryor slashed the tickets available to friends and relatives of Dewey and Taft delegates, doubled those for Willkie delegates, and issued special standing-room tickets to Willkie enthusiasts at Gate 23, now famous in political arcana. Pryor was certainly pulling "dirty tricks," just as when he had engineered a dead mike for Herbert Hoover. But another view is possible. Public opinion was shifting rapidly—literally on a daily basis—and Pryor's ticket tricks were opening up the convention and the arrangements that had been made weeks and months before to emotions that were boiling outside the walls of Convention Hall. The thundering "We Want Willkie" chants from the galleries no doubt played an important role in the nominating process in 1940. The emotion from the galleries, demanding not only intervention abroad but a Republican winner in Willkie, could not have failed to sway an undetermined number of delegates, who shared to some degree such emotions themselves.

The delegates were also subjected to a paper blizzard generated by Willkie's professionals and his hundreds of thousands of "Willkie Club" volunteers across the country. The New Jersey delegation alone received 100,000 letters and telegrams. Later some of the paper blizzard was found to be bogus, but most of it represented a genuine wave of popular feeling. In the last Gallup poll taken before Thursday's final ballot, Willkie had surged past Dewey among Republican voters and led by 44 to 29, with Taft trailing badly at 13. Besieged by hate mail from isolationists, Charles Halleck, a young congressman from Indiana, was to put Willkie's name in nomination. He fortified himself with "two or three good slugs" from a pint bottle and stepped to the podium. "I nominate Wendell Willkie," he began, "because, better than any man I know, he can build this country back to prosperity." *Boo, hiss.* Later Halleck said that he was "stunned" by the animosity that flowed up at him from the Dewey and Taft people on the convention floor. But as soon as the catcalls started, they were overwhelmed by thunderous chants from the galleries of *"We Want Willkie! We Want Willkie! We Want Willkie!"* Nothing remotely like this had happened in the Republican Party since the wild, rebellious days of Theodore Roosevelt.

On the first ballot, Tom Dewey led as expected, but at 360 votes, well short of his claimed 400. Taft came in at 189, another shortfall. International events and Willkie's personal appeal as a potential winner against Roosevelt were melting down the Republican establishment before the eyes of the nation. Willkie scored a sensational 105 on the first ballot, which meant that no one else was going to seize an early victory. Six other candidates accounted for the rest of the 1,000 votes, with Herbert Hoover coming in a humiliating last with 17. Dewey, from his hotel suite, grimly announced that he was confident of a gain on the second ballot.

In fact, he lost 22 votes and came in at 338, a loss that was like the razor blade of the iceberg quietly slicing the hull of the *Titanic*. The sense became widespread that the young prosecutor was not going to be nominated for president in 1940. Willkie's shrewd political chief, Halleck, had held back small pockets of delegate votes in various states, and he threw them in on the second ballot. Willkie picked up 5 in Maryland, 7 in Missouri, 5 in New York, and in a shock to all the professionals, 9 in Maine. Taft rose to 203 on that second ballot, up from 189 on the first, but Willkie, coming from far back was close behind him at 131. Throughout the proceedings, the galleries thundered *"We Want Willkie."* At 6:50 P.M. the convention adjourned for dinner, and the candidates began a furious scramble for votes.

Stassen, supporting Willkie, lobbied Alf Landon in an elevator for the Kansas votes, but the former candidate stuck with Dewey. Willkie himself refused Stassen's request for permission to approach millionaire Pennsylvania boss Joseph Pew for Pennsylvania's 72 votes. "Pew be damned," said Willkie. Taft thought he had the Pennsylvania votes, but Pew refused his phone calls, being at the time in the bathtub. Halleck believed that, with Dewey sinking and Taft merely holding steady, there were Willkie votes to be shaken loose in the New York delegation. Willkie was doubtful, but Halleck was correct. Incredibly, Herbert Hoover was refusing to release the California delegation, believing that he could still be the nominee of a deadlocked convention.

On the third ballot, Willkie picked up 27 from New York and gathered strength elsewhere, as the favorite-son candidacies expired: Massachusetts switched to Willkie, half of New Hampshire abandoned Senator Styles Bridges and went to Willkie, and Pew or no Pew, Willkie got 15 from Pennsylvania. When the clerk announced the total, Dewey still led with 315, Willkie was a strong second with 259, and Taft had dropped to third with 212. Back at his hotel suite, surrounded by staff and reporters, Willkie exuded confidence. "Boys, I think I am in." Listening to the radio roar of *"We Want Willkie,"* he joked, "There goes that paid-for gallery again."

On the fourth ballot the galleries became a scene of carnival and riot as Willkie surged into the lead and Dewey fell to third place, but these celebrations were premature. The regular Republican establishment was not dead yet, and as Dewey fell back and it became a Willkie-Taft contest, the scholarly senator from Ohio made his move. He picked up 20 delegates in Illinois and 42 overall. He was widely believed to have husbanded reserve strength in Iowa, Wisconsin, California, and Oregon, as many Republicans confronted the awful prospect of an interventionist and perhaps even a *war* candidate. Would Vandenberg release Michigan to Taft? As Taft's strength rose on the fourth and fifth ballots, Willkie's spirits began to sink in his hotel suite. "Well, I scared them," he said.

But as the historic sixth ballot got underway at twenty minutes past midnight, it became clear that Willkie's gloom had been premature. The lead changed several times, as Taft gained votes in California, only to be overtaken by Willkie votes in Florida and Illinois. "I don't see how they can pass me up," Willkie joked, and poured himself a highball. As the ballotting approached the finish line, Senator Arthur Vandenberg's campaign manager, Howard Lawrence, approached the podium and announced that the powerful senator had released his delegates. A hush fell over Convention Hall as Lawrence announced the Michigan results: Hoover, 1; Taft, 2; Willkie, 35. The galleries exploded, showering the convention floor with newspapers, paper cups, straw hats, shoes. Willkie now stood at 499, needing only 2 more votes. A few minutes later, former Senator David Reed announced a revised vote from Pennsylvania: "Pennsylvania casts 72 votes for Wendell Willkie."

Wendell Willkie's nomination in that summer of 1940 meant that the center of political gravity in the Republican party had dropped its opposition to Franklin Roosevelt's foreign policy—that is, serious aid to beleaguered England as our first line of defense, and perhaps less overtly, a stiffening line against Japanese expansionism in the Pacific and Asia. The clouds of war, coming in across both oceans, had defeated Dewey and Taft and changed the heartland–East Coast political balance of power within the Republican party. But Willkie's victory, described then and since as a "miracle," was a miracle that had been carefully engineered.

The Willkie who came to Philadelphia in 1940 was a remarkable man, who had lately been recognized by the most powerful Republican publicists in the country as the man of the hour, the one Republican contender who could bring the party to confront the international realities as they saw them, the one man—enormously attractive and no provincial—who stood a chance of beating Roosevelt, should he choose to run for a widely disliked third term. Willkie came to Philadelphia with the accelerating support of the most powerful magazines and newspapers in the country, and in a pretelevision period, this was a powerful asset. Henry Luce's *Time, Life,* and *Fortune* had become virtual Willkie campaign organs, and

top Luce staffers worked full-time for Willkie. His rugged hand-
someness gazed from their front pages. David Lawrence's *U.S. News*
printed a cover photo of Willkie in a World War I uniform and
endorsed him. Willkie dominated *Look* magazine and *Saturday Evening Post* coverage. He had the support of the powerful Scripps-
Howard newspaper chain and also the Whitneys' *New York Herald
Tribune*. Hundreds of other editors followed suit.

The editors and publicists who played a crucial role in Willkie's
nomination were far removed from the instinctive isolationism and
even pacifism of the small Republican towns of the Midwest and the
farm belt—Taft country. The vision of those powerful men in their
editorial offices was entirely different. With their international con-
tacts and their hordes of foreign correspondents, they were sharply
aware of the brutalities and the intentions of the Nazis and the
Japanese. But as a group, these men shared a powerful, positive
vision. They had been to Harvard, Yale, and Princeton, and some of
them had been to Oxford as Rhodes Scholars. Educated, civilized,
they believed as a group that Europe—and within Europe, England,
but in addition America—represented the present peak of civilization: democratic, progressive, hardworking, idealistic. They believed that these values should prevail around the world—in Europe,
of course, but also in China, where Henry Luce had grown up as the
son of a missionary. They were the confident progressive heirs of
William McKinley, Teddy Roosevelt, Woodrow Wilson, and behind
them were the great Whig statesmen of Victorian England. They
viewed Hitler's New Order and Japan's Co-Prosperity Sphere as
standing athwart the civilized future as they imagined it, and they
not only feared them, but viewed them with cultural disdain. It
would be fair to call the pro-Willkie editors and publicists Liberal
Imperialists. It was far from an ignoble vision, and Willkie was
their man.

On a steamy August afternoon, Willkie returned from his Philadelphia triumph to his hometown of Elwood, Indiana, where he
would ceremonially accept the Republican nomination. What was
estimated as the largest political crowd in American history turned
up in Elwood to catch a glimpse of the candidate, 200,000 people.
The barefoot boy from Wall Street had, temporarily, come home.

All of the Willkies, parents and children, had been overachievers,
as we now say. His father's parents had been German radicals who
had fled to the United States after the failure of the 1848 revolution.
Herman and Henrietta Willkie had both been community leaders in
Elwood, progressives in the older American sense. Herman, a lawyer and school superintendent, had cleaned up the Elwood saloon

and red-light district and transformed the old one-room-school system into modern grade schools. Herman had a home library of 6,000 books, and he would wake his children in the morning by shouting lines from Shakespeare or Thackeray from the bottom of the stairs. Henrietta would take nothing but success from her children, hated cooking, and was the first woman in Elwood to smoke cigarettes publicly. In 1890, after winning the Democratic nomination, William Jennings Bryan had spent a night at the Willkie home and became a permanent hero for the seven-year-old Wendell.

Willkie was a rebellious and erratic student in secondary school, and his parents, standing for no nonsense, sent him to Culver Military Academy to learn some discipline. His grades improved spectacularly, and then it was four years at the University of Indiana in Bloomington, where he was a campus leader and a student radical who denounced the fraternities and the college administration in a student magazine called *Bogus*. He set himself a schedule of reading one book a day. Discovering European socialism in Marx, Spargo, and others, he demanded that the university institute a course on socialism. Moving on to Indiana Law School, he graduated with prizes and performed as Class Orator. In one of his first cases as a young practicing lawyer, he was defeated by his father Herman, who commented, "I believe my son will make a very great lawyer. He can make so much out of so little."

Willkie enlisted when America declared war and got to France when it was all but over, and then, like many other men, returned to America and what he hoped was a golden destiny. His abilities as an Indiana lawyer attracted the attention of powerful men—Harvey Firestone, Governor James M. Cox, Newton Baker, William O'Neill of General Tire and Rubber. During the summer of the catastrophic year 1929, the utility tycoon, Bernard Cobb, offered him a big New York job as a lawyer representing Commonwealth and Southern, a utilities holding company that produced nothing itself but controlled eleven major electric-power producers. By 1934 Willkie's energy and ability had made him chief executive officer at Commonwealth and Southern and the major national critic of Franklin Roosevelt's public power enterprises. Willkie pronounced the TVA a "death sentence" for private power. By 1939 Willkie was being touted in a *Time* magazine cover story as "the only businessman in the U.S. who is mentioned as a presidential possibility."

When Willkie moved to New York, he also moved up rapidly, socially and culturally. Though married to his Indiana sweetheart, he had always been a womanizer, on the lookout for sexual opportunities from secretaries to celebrities, and in New York he fell seriously in love with Irita Van Doren. Van Doren, part of the

literary Van Doren clan, was married to Carl Van Doren, the
Columbia historian, but the marriage had withered. She was southern, beautiful, soft-spoken, and witty, and she presided over the
New York version of a Parisian salon. At Irita's gatherings, Willkie
fell in with Sinclair Lewis, James Thurber, Dorothy Thompson,
William L. Shirer, Mark Van Doren, John Erskine, and Joseph
Barnes. Willkie undoubtedly felt great social and intellectual doors
opening before him. One reason he resisted for a while running for
the presidency is that he knew it would change the nature of his
almost open relationship with Irita Van Doren. Indeed, during the
campaign, his Indiana sweetheart, Edith, got off one of its best
lines. Asked to pose for a husband-and-wife photograph with Wendell Willkie, she quipped, "Politics makes strange bedfellows." The
publisher Gardner Cowles, a close Willkie friend, commented that
"he was not at all discreet. I thought it was careless and stupid." But
after he won the nomination, Irita Van Doren and Willkie kept a
prudent distance, though he phoned her daily.

During the campaign, Franklin Roosevelt hungered to use
Willkie's adulterous affair against him. The Democrats had inter-
cepted some of Willkie's letters to Van Doren, which they referred
to as "dolly notes," but Roosevelt's hands were tied by a weird
development. Roosevelt knew that the Republicans had discovered
that his own vice-presidential candidate, Henry Wallace, was a
disciple of a bizarre white-Russian guru named Nicholas Roerich,
who was running a temple on the Upper West Side of New York. The
Republicans had off-the-wall letters from Wallace, the prospective
vice president, to the religious mystic. It would not help the ticket if
people got the idea that Wallace was nuts. Therefore, none of the
letters on either side was leaked to the press during the campaign. It
was pure deterrence, both candidates statesmanlike, campaigning on
the issues.

But this is getting ahead of the story. Let us go back to 1938 and
the rise of Willkie. One of the most popular radio shows of the
1930s was called "America's Town Meeting of the Air," where
opposing spokesmen debated current issues in a serious and often
influential way. On the night of January 6, 1938, Wendell Willkie
skinned alive one of the brightest rising stars of the New Deal,
Assistant Attorney General Robert H. Jackson. Jackson had been
widely talked about as a possible Democratic presidential candidate,
should FDR choose not to run for a third term in 1940. After Willkie
finished with Jackson on the radio show, Roosevelt and his advisers
scratched him as presidential material, and Roosevelt later named
him to the Supreme Court. A couple of months later, at the Harvard
Club in New York, Willkie took on New Deal superstar Supreme

Court Justice Felix Frankfurter before an elite audience of bankers, business executives, lawyers, and publishers. Willkie played very rough, charging that Frankfurter's Harvard Law School students— Tommy "The Cork" Corcoran, Ben Cohen, and David Lilienthal, all now New Dealers—were subverting private property and also the United States Constitution. Willkie was a bull of a debater, and he was calling one of the most brilliant men ever to teach at Harvard—or serve on the court—an intellectual subversive, and he was doing it at the *Harvard* Club.

The energy of Willkie's ascent in elite capitalist circles was enormous. This was no provincial from the prairies. This was a man who could more than hold his own with Bob Jackson and Felix Frankfurter, a man who combined broad, humane views with a spirited championship of American business. *Fortune* magazine published its Willkie profile, all but nominating him for president. The *Herald Tribune* printed a letter on its editorial page endorsing a Willkie nomination in 1940. The *Saturday Evening Post* printed a feature about Willkie called "The Man Who Talked Back." *Fortune* editor John Knox Jessup summed up the collective impression of the eastern Republican elite: "Willkie was exactly the hero [*Fortune*] had been looking for: the American businessman at his candid, articulate best, large-minded, earthy, brave, wholly committed to a bigger and better America and a bolder and more confident foreign policy." Yes, interventionism—and in other words, war if necessary.

When Joseph Alsop told Alice Longworth Roosevelt, Teddy's daughter and the heroine of the song "Alice Blue Gown," that Willkie was a grass-roots candidate, that brilliant and cynical aristocrat got off one of her many immortal lines: "From the grass-roots of ten thousand country clubs." But in 1940, Willkie really was a grass-roots candidate in a way, swept into candidacy by a powerful national emotion about events in Europe, even though, yes, he was also the overwhelming favorite of the educated middle class, the business and professional people. He was the only Republican contender Franklin Roosevelt feared.

II

The champ had no legs that he could feel and, since that terrible attack in 1921, had lived in pain and dependency. He feared fire obsessively. Yet in 1940 he was certainly the most powerful man in the world. Until now, historians have discussed Franklin Roosevelt in terms of issues and the workings of politics; they have debated his successes and failures; and they have made discoveries about his romantic personal side. But the overwhelming fact about him is that he was horribly crippled, and yet, through sheer courage and will, rose above his devastated lower body. In doing so, he became a half-consciously perceived metaphor for an America shattered and "paralyzed" by the Great Depression. In rising above his crippled body and seeming to walk again, though with difficulty, in his smile and vanity, cigarette holder and the intonations of his voice, Roosevelt told everyone that America would rise again and walk too. We "have nothing to fear but fear itself." Whatever that strange and famous sentence means, it surely implies a celebration of pure will. It is true that Adolf Hitler had somehow reinvented himself and raised himself to world-historic stature after his trauma of 1918, his psychosomatic blindness and sense of personal shame over Germany's defeat. But at virtually the same time, his future antagonist across the Atlantic was enacting what was, if anything, an even greater triumph of the will.

Focus for a moment on the old Madison Square Garden in New York City, site of the 1924 Democratic National Convention. The leading contenders at the outset were William McAdoo, former secretary of the treasury under Wilson, and New York's popular governor, Al Smith. Smith wanted Roosevelt, who had lost to Harding-Coolidge as Governor James Cox's running mate in 1920, to place his name in nomination. The big-city, Catholic product of the Tammany machine needed the symbolism of an upstate, patrician WASP. Roosevelt, a popular New Yorker who had been Wilson's assistant secretary of the navy, fitted the role perfectly. But this would be Roosevelt's first public appearance since his polio attack three years before.

Roosevelt had worked out elaborate strategies for minimizing the visual impression of his severely crippled condition. He refused to be seen in public in a wheelchair—indeed, there seem to exist only two photographs of Roosevelt in his wheelchair. Nor would he be lifted up stairs in public view. At Madison Square Garden, he and his son James arrived early for every session of the convention in order to be seated before the other delegates, reporters, and spectators arrived. James would wheel his father to the entrance nearest the seats of the New York delegation. At the door, he would pull Roosevelt to a standing position and lock his leg braces into rigid position. Though Roosevelt lacked all feeling and muscle control in his legs, he had been able, through months of practice, to develop a technique of swinging first one leg forward, then the other, to produce a slow, laborious, simulated walk. With James holding one arm and the other shoulder braced on a crutch, Roosevelt would slowly make his way down the aisle to their seats. Sometimes the powerful man gripped James's arm so hard that it required an effort for the son not to cry out in pain. Once they reached the seats of the New York delegation, Roosevelt took his place in a large, oak armchair which provided him with the necessary stability. He never left the hall until the session was over and the hall cleared, sitting there as long as necessary, greeting well-wishers and talking politics. When he finally struggled back up the aisle with James and his crutch, the people remaining in the galleries cheered and applauded him, understanding his courage.

On the day of his speech nominating Smith, June 27, Roosevelt made his way to the speaker's platform, leaning on James and his crutch, swinging one leg forward, then the other. During the introduction, James passed him a second crutch. Roosevelt was determined to get to the lectern by himself. "Let's go," he said. It was 15 feet to the lectern. Roosevelt would put one crutch forward, shift his weight, and swing the leg that had been freed up. Then he would push the other crutch forward, shift his weight to it, and swing the leg opposite. He concentrated on the floor, measuring each "step" in an athletic performance he had perfected in a thousand practice sessions. In the intense heat of the hall, he perspired profusely. A step behind him, James watched his father intensely, prepared to catch him if he lost his always precarious balance. A crash to the floor of the speaker's platform would remind everyone how severely crippled Roosevelt actually was.

When the introduction had ended, Roosevelt's name had been cheered and applauded. He had long been a popular figure in New York politics, and many of the delegates and other politicians had known him in the Wilson administration. He had always possessed a handsome, jaunty glamor. But the cheers gave way to a hush as Roosevelt made his slow way to the lectern.

At last he reached it. He looked out over the packed hall. Then he threw his head back in that gesture of triumph and joy that would become his visual signature, and the vast encompassing Roosevelt smile delivered its unmistakable message. The hall exploded in cheers. An oceanic roar filled Madison Square Garden, a moment always remembered by those who had been there. Roosevelt took hold of the lectern, steadied himself on his rigid leg braces, and handed his crutches to James. When he began to speak on behalf of Smith, he had the total attention of the audience, as he delivered, in that silvery and precise tenor that soon would be familiar around the world, one of the greatest speeches of his career. Four years ago

at San Francisco you who were there came to know him as
one greatly loved by his state, whose personality and
picturesque rise to high office produced, as you will

remember, a spontaneous wave of good feeling among the
delegates from every section of our land. Today he has
become more than a favorite son. . . . The masses of labor
look to him as a protector and good friend. The honest
businessman knows that he has never sought personal
preferment by demagogic attack on honest business. . . . He
has a personality that carries to every hearer not only the
sincerity but the righteousness of what he says. He is the
Happy Warrior of the political battlefield. . . . If you will
render your verdict in that sacred mood, it can only be for the
nomination of the man whom I present to you—the one above
all others who has demonstrated his power, his ability to
govern; this leader whose whole career gives convincing
proof of his power to lead; this warrior whose record shows
him invincible in defense of right and in attack on wrong; this
man, beloved by all, trusted by all, respected by all; this man
who all admit can bring us an overwhelming victory this
year—this man of destiny whom our state proudly dedicates to
the nation—our own Alfred E. Smith.

When Roosevelt concluded this peroration, the hall was silent for
a moment and then erupted with an ovation that lasted longer than
any in the recorded history of political conventions—one hour and
fifteen minutes. They were cheering Al Smith, of course, but even
more the courage of the crippled Roosevelt, himself a "happy
warrior."

At the conclusion of the speech Roosevelt was completely exhausted. He asked James to bring the wheelchair and, in view of all,
allowed himself to be wheeled from the hall. "We made it, James,"
he said. "We made it."

Four years later, at the 1928 convention in Houston, Roosevelt was
determined to appear, not as a man who had struggled bravely with a
crippling disease, but as a man who triumphed over it. For more
than a month he had practiced a new technique he had worked out
with his son Elliott. Holding his right arm rigidly at a 90-degree
angle, Elliott provided support for his father on one side. But there
would be no crutches this time. In his other hand Roosevelt held a
cane, with his index finger pressed rigidly down the barrel to
provide extra leverage. With this arrangement, again shifting his
weight and swinging his dead legs in their braces, he was able to
produce a toddling sort of "walk." He wanted to convince not only
the Houston delegates but the nation and perhaps himself that he was
cured, well again, not a cripple. That same year, 1928, running for
governor of New York and carrying the state despite Smith's cata-

strophic loss to Herbert Hoover, Roosevelt made a rare reference to his disease in a campaign speech: "I myself furnish a perfectly good example of what can be done with the right kind of care. . . . Seven years ago . . . I came down with infantile paralysis. . . . By personal good fortune I was able to get the best kind of care, and the result of having the best kind of care is that today I am on my feet." Perhaps he even believed it.

At the Houston convention Roosevelt "walked" slowly across the platform, moving between Elliott's rigid arm and the expertly manipulated cane, laughing, joking with the politicians, throwing his head back, flashing the famous grin. As he stood behind the lectern, he grasped its sides with his hands and spread his legs apart for stability. Again, the silvery voice went out over the hall and the airwaves, again nominating Al Smith, "one who has the will to win—who not only deserves success but commands it. Victory is his habit—the happy warrior, Alfred E. Smith."

Again, Roosevelt's words about Smith could have applied at least as much to himself. Will Durant was covering the convention for the *New York World* and wrote: "On the stage is Franklin Roosevelt, beyond comparison the finest man that has appeared at either convention. . . . A figure tall and proud even in suffering; a face of classic profile; pale with years of struggle against paralysis; a frame nervous and yet self-controlled with that tense, taut unity of spirit which lifts the complex soul above those whose calmness is only a stolidity; most obviously a gentleman and a scholar. A man softened and cleansed and illuminated by pain. . . . This is a civilized man."

In his winning 1928 campaign for governor, Roosevelt developed many of the techniques that permitted him to simultaneously minimize and exploit his crippled condition, techniques he would use to powerful effect as president. To refute Republican charges that he was too sick to be governor, he campaigned relentlessly all over New York State. Riding in the back seat of an open touring car, he led his retinue of aides and reporters from one town to another. He had ordered that a steel bar be installed above the back of the front seat, and when the car stopped for a speech to a gathered crowd, he would pull himself erect by using the bar. Most of the speeches followed a set pattern: praise for Smith, a description of himself as "an upstate farmer too," a description of the contest as one between progress and reaction, and an invitation to the crowd to judge for itself the state of his health. This last he did with withering sarcasm. He would list the places he had visted during the last few days: "Herkimer, Fonda, Gloversville, Amsterdam . . . and then, for good measure, we just dropped into Schenectady and spoke there early in the evening, and now here we are in Troy." Here he would pause. "Too bad about this unfortunate sick man, isn't it?" The famous grin. The crowds burst into laughter and applause.

Years later, writing in the *New Yorker,* Philip Hamburger would recall how skillfully Eleanor Roosevelt worked to ease the burden of her husband's condition:

> But what we remember most about that far-off afternoon—the depression lay ahead, and the Presidency, and the war—was the departure of the Governor and his wife from the hall. The only way out was down a narrow aisle running the length of the hall, past the camp chairs on which the audience had been sitting. The distance from desk to street could not have been more than a hundred feet, but it took the Governor an agonizingly long time to traverse it. His legs were in heavy braces, and he walked with the aid of two canes—first one foot and one cane forward, then the other. The audience, as though hypnotized, did not leave. It stood and watched the Roosevelts depart. Mrs. Roosevelt, walking alongside her husband, adapted her pace to his. The Governor was intent upon the task before him: to reach the street and the sanctuary of his limousine without help. Occasionally, she leaned over to whisper something in his ear, and he smiled and put the other foot forward. The slow procession became extremely impressive. Mrs. Roosevelt seemed to sense that we knew we should not stay but that we could not leave. Moving slowly along, she thanked many of us for coming, and expressed the hope that we had enjoyed the Governor's remarks. She greeted many of us with a wave of her hand. She turned again to say something to her husband, who smiled again, and moved forward. She never took his arm, and yet we knew that he was leaning as heavily upon her as upon his canes. Finally, the Roosevelts reached the street. The audience, still hypnotized, followed them outside. Mrs. Roosevelt and a chauffeur helped the Governor into his car. He put his head back against the cushions with the expression of a man who has accomplished his mission. Mrs. Roosevelt opened a window of the car and waved again. An audience of strangers had become a group of friends. "Goodbye!" she called out. "Goodbye!"

Roosevelt's 1921 attack of polio had been far worse than any but the members of a small inner circle realized. After swimming in very cold water at Campobello during August, he came down with the symptoms of what he first thought was lumbago. "The next morning when I swung out of bed my left leg lagged. . . . I tried to persuade myself that the trouble with my leg was muscular, that it would disappear as I used it. But presently it refused to work and then the other." The deepening paralysis was accompanied by a temperature of 102 degrees. By the third day, all the chest muscles and those below were involved, and Roosevelt experienced great and continuing pain throughout his body. Two days after that he was completely paralyzed from the chest down, his arms and shoulders were severely weakened, and his skin was so sensitized that the bedclothes, and even the movement of breezes, were painful. His bowels and urinary tract were affected, and he had to be nursed night and day. Though both Roosevelt and Eleanor were experts at concealing their actual feelings, there is evidence that Roosevelt experienced extreme despair during the most intense phases of his illness. His confidant, Louis Howe, recalls that Roosevelt would moan, "I don't know what is the matter with me, Louis, I just don't know." After his death, Eleanor revealed, "I know that he had real fear when he was first taken ill." In the draft of her autobiography, written during the 1930s, she wrote of his illness: "One night he was out of his head." The president blue-penciled the observation from the text. James Roosevelt recalls that Roosevelt had times of "great discouragement."

When the fever abated and Roosevelt began his convalescence, great pain nevertheless remained with him. The paralyzed muscles in his legs tightened, bending his heels backward toward his hips, and to halt this, his legs were placed in plaster casts and forced straight by hammering wooden wedges into the casts behind the knees. That winter, his convalescence completed, Roosevelt began the long effort to rehabilitate himself. His arms regained normal strength, the trunk muscles were strengthening, and he was determined to walk again without braces or crutches. He worked out on parallel bars, tried massages, saltwater baths, ultraviolet light, hot and cold baths, horseback riding. His daughter Anna recalled what it was like: "I think it's a bit traumatic, when you're fifteen years of age and you look up and see your father, whom you have regarded as a wonderful playmate, who took long walks with you, sailed with you, could out-jump you, and do a lot of things, suddenly, you look up and you see him walking on crutches—trying, struggling in heavy steel braces. And you see the sweat pouring down his face, and hear him saying, 'I must get down the driveway today—all the way down the driveway.'" Roosevelt worked to walk virtually every day for seven years and never made it to the end of the driveway.

In his first inaugural address, Roosevelt, in perhaps his most famous lines, told the nation that "the only thing we have to fear is fear itself—nameless, unreasoning, unjustified terror which para-

lyzes needed efforts to convert retreat into advance." Taken literally
and applied to the United States in 1933, those words came close to
being nonsensical. America had plenty to fear besides the emotion
of fear: it faced massive unemployment, closing banks and factories, world recession, and the rise of dictators. But it is plausible that
Roosevelt was drawing upon his own experience of the abyss and of
dread when he was first stricken by the disease: "nameless, unreasoning, unjustified terror." In the famous sentence he even uses the
word "paralyzes." He was making his own disease a metaphor for
the nation's condition and suggesting by implication that, as he had
triumphed, so could we.

Not all of those who knew Roosevelt or worked with him liked
him. Joseph Alsop, who was distantly related to Roosevelt and
treated as part of the family, greatly admired him as a politician and
statesman, but recalls that "from afar, he was always charming,
always impressive, always more than life-size; but at close hand, he
could too easily seem artificially genial, less than forthright, and
more than a little superficial." Dean Acheson, among others, found
something irritating in the unrelenting cordiality and courtesy, the
impenetrable aristocratic demeanor: "The President could relax
over his poker parties and enjoy Tom Corcoran's accordion; he could
and did call everyone from his valet to the Secretary of State by his
first name and often made up Damon Runyon nicknames for them
. . . he could charm an individual or a nation. But he condescended.
Many reveled in apparent admission to an inner circle. I did
not. . . . To me it was patronizing and humiliating. To accord the
President the greatest deference and respect should be a gratification to any citizen. It is not gratifying to receive the easy greeting
which milord might give a promising stable boy and pull one's
forelock in return."

In 1940 the Republicans were only too aware of the fact that in
Roosevelt they faced a man who had humiliated them in 1936,
rolling over Alf Landon and his running mate Frank Knox in one of
the largest landslides in the history of presidential politics. For the
Republicans, 1936 had been especially bitter, because in the spring
of that year, prospects did not seem all that dim. They might not win
the presidential election in November, but at least they could make
up some lost ground. Ousted from power in the Roosevelt landslide
of 1932, they had suffered another crushing defeat in the congres-
sional elections two years later. If Roosevelt seemed likely to be
returned for a second term, at least it could be by a reduced margin,
and the balance in Congress might be at least partially restored.

Buoyed by these modest but reasonable hopes, the party had nominated a mild-mannered, well-to-do, progressive governor from the Midwest and launched a campaign of fault-finding against the confident, smiling Democrat in the White House. If Alfred M. Landon lacked charisma, at least his faults apppeared to be few. Based upon a telephone poll, the *Literary Digest* had actually picked Landon to win. Then came Tuesday, November 3, 1936. Satisfied, generally speaking, with the first four years of the New Deal and widely unimpressed with Landon's criticisms, the voters trooped to the polls and returned Franklin Roosevelt to office by a margin that made 1932 look close. Roosevelt came in with 27 million votes to Landon's 17 million. The electoral vote was worse. Roosevelt amassed 523 electoral votes to 8 for Landon, who carried only Maine and Vermont, rock-ribbed and electorally insignificant states nestled against the Canadian border. The newspapers carried maps of the country with all of it colored a solid black, except for an almost invisible sliver up in the northeast corner, which remained white to designate "Republican." The slogan "As Maine goes, so goes Vermont" summed up the Republican disaster. On a bridge crossing from New Hampshire into Vermont, New Hampshire police found a sign nailed to a post: "You are now leaving the United States."

In Congress and in the 48 state houses, the Republican situation was just as dismal. Of the governorships at stake, the Democrats had taken 33, the Farmer Labor and the Progressives 1 apiece, and the Republicans 4. Out of the whole 48, the Republicans held 7, third parties 3, and the Democrats 38. In Congress, the Republicans were scarcely any longer a major party. The new Senate would contain 76 Democrats, 4 third-party senators, and 16 Republicans. The House had 332 Democrats and 88 Republicans. William Allen White called it "a political Johnstown flood." Worse, the party was bereft of new talent. Only the shrewd and sarcastic Styles Bridges of New Hampshire and young Henry Cabot Lodge, Jr., of Massachusetts had been added to their Senate ranks.

The Republicans began to stir with new life, however, in 1938. In New York the young prosecutor Tom Dewey came close to upsetting the popular Democratic governor Herbert Lehman. Robert Taft, a rising star, won a Senate seat in Ohio. In the House, the Republicans climbed from 88 to 170. The party quadrupled the number of statehouses it controlled, among them Wisconsin, where *wunderkind* Harold Stassen at thirty-one was the nation's youngest governor. Ohio's new governor, John W. Bricker, was thought to be of presidential quality. But for all these tentative signs of recovery, the Republicans knew that they would probably face the champ, one of the greatest vote-getters and instinctive politicians in the nation's history.

On New Year's Eve 1940, the president and his wife had a few friends in for a quiet evening at the White House after a hectic, event-filled, Christmas season. As midnight approached, the president turned on the radio, and the small group listened to descriptions of Times Square in New York, where a million festive people had gathered to cheer the New Year in. At the stroke of midnight, the president and the others raised glasses of eggnog. With a decided note of seriousness, the president said: "To the United States of America." He no doubt sensed that the year 1940 might well be momentous and difficult. In Europe, both sides had used the "Phony War" period to greatly strengthen their forces, and vast modern armies were poised for battle. The outcome was unforeseeable. In Asia, Japan had grown more menacing and increasingly intransigent.

No one knows when Roosevelt made the decision to run for an unprecedented third term. It is possible, but unlikely, that he had made up his mind to run a year or more before, but if so, absolutely no one around him was aware of that fact. At the annual Gridiron Club dinner, where newspapermen make jokes at the expense of national leaders, there was a large papier-mâché sphinx, out of the grinning mouth of which protruded a long cigarette holder. When pressed by reporters, the president brushed aside or kidded questions about his intentions and often talked with associates about his desire to return to Hyde Park, where his new library and hilltop house were nearing completion. He was also deeply involved with the polio rehabilitation center in Warm Springs, Georgia, which he had purchased with two thirds of his fortune in 1926 and built into a facility of world importance. His private conversation turned with increasing frequency toward Dutchess County, its history and its people. In addition, Roosevelt was showing signs of weariness after almost two presidential terms, and in early 1940 it had taken him weeks to get over a case of the flu. "I have to have a rest," he told President Dan Tobin of the Teamsters. "I want to go home to Hyde Park. I want to take care of my trees. I have a big planting there, Dan. I want to make the farm pay. I want to finish my little house on the hill. I want to write history." "The weariness of his last years," writes historian James MacGregor Burns, "had already begun." The decision to run almost surely shortened his life.

At the same time, and probably without making a final decision, Roosevelt did everything tactically required for a third-term candidacy. His political problem was clear enough: the issue would be precisely that third term. The founders had been hopelessly divided over the matter of limiting the president's tenure, and the Constitution was thus silent on the matter, but tradition was not silent. It weighed heavily against a third term. At the root of the tradition was the first president, George Washington, who had gone home to Mount Vernon after his second term. Did Roosevelt think he was more important or more necessary than George Washington? All polls indicated a heavy majority opposed on principle to a third term, which many people felt smacked of a personal dictatorship.

Roosevelt's control of the party was so firm that he could easily have engineered his own nomination, but that would not be good enough. He could not be perceived as *seeking* a third term. It had to be thrust upon him in the form of a spontaneous draft at the convention, which would take place in Chicago. And such a draft required that no powerful rival emerge around whom a substantial bloc of delegates might form. There were many Democrats critical of the New Deal, and among them were ambitious men who wanted to be president. This exactly suited Roosevelt's need for a multiplicity of candidates.

As early as 1938 he encouraged his close adviser, Harry Hopkins, to run in 1940 and even coached him on campaign strategy. In 1939 he appointed the handsome governor of Indiana, Paul V. McNutt, as chief of the Federal Security Agency and encouraged McNutt to try for the presidency. *Life* and other publications pumped up a McNutt boomlet, and McNutt himself felt that Roosevelt had more or less conferred the succession upon him. But so did Secretary of State Cordell Hull, the courtly, white-haired Tennessean. On several occasions Roosevelt told Hull flatly that he should be the next president. In early 1940 he told Senator Alben Barkley that "some of the folks here at the White House" favored a Barkley candidacy. He encouraged Henry Wallace and Robert Jackson, and he told Governor Herbert Lehman of New York that Lehman deserved the votes of the New York delegation. Vice President John Nance Garner, a conservative Texan whom Roosevelt loathed (they were scarcely on speaking terms), was mounting an anti-New Deal candidacy and passionately desired to block a third term.

The greatest potential danger lay in the direction of Postmaster General James Farley of New York, who had masterminded Roosevelt's two winning presidential campaigns. Farley now wanted the presidency for himself. A political genius in his own right, Farley had observed the Al Smith disaster of 1938 and now saw himself as the first Catholic president. But Roosevelt's plans remained wrapped in obscurity as the convention steadily approached.

The first evidence we have that Roosevelt had decided to go for a third term comes from Cordell Hull, and as late as July 3, when Hull had a luncheon meeting with the president. While still dismissing the idea of a third term, Roosevelt talked in a "sort of impatient, incredulous tone" about the pressure the party was putting on him to run. That is certainly plausible. After Roosevelt, the Democrats would drop far off in vote-getting potential. Hull decided that Roosevelt was going to run.

Jim Farley was less reconcilable. Visiting Hyde Park in early July, he urged the president to make a Shermanesque refusal to run or serve. The atmosphere became chilly. "Jim," said Roosevelt, "if nominated and elected, I could not in these times refuse to take the inaugural oath, even if I knew I would be dead within thirty days." From Roosevelt's earnest tones, Farley inferred that he was running but required a draft. Roosevelt gathered that Farley intended to go to Chicago, have his own name placed in nomination, and attempt to deny the president the draft his third-term plans required.

There are two expressions in the conversation quoted that bear some reflection. There is the suggestion, offhand, but perhaps indicating some half-conscious apprehensions, that Roosevelt might die in office. There is also the important phrase "in these times," which probably indicates Roosevelt's motivation. He genuinely enjoyed the presidency and was a masterful politician, but he also had a powerful pull toward Dutchess County. The international situation and the catastrophic events of the spring and summer in Europe almost certainly tipped the balance toward running.

III

Early in the morning of April 9, motorized German infantry struck across the undefended Danish border and occupied the country. A few minutes later, a dozen German destroyers materialized out of a snowstorm off the Norwegian port of Narvik, torpedoed the Norwegian gunboats, and landed 2,000 soldiers. At other Norwegian ports the Wehrmacht was landing, and within two days the Germans had secured all Norwegian ports. The British had themselves been planning to occupy parts of Norway, but the Germans had moved first and with impressive organization. In their first, large-scale use of parachute troops, they gave a foretaste of the adventurous panache and inventiveness that would soon stun France, thought to be a major military power. The British landed an expeditionary force in Norway, but it was badly mauled and withdrew. A new word entered the political vocabulary—*Quisling*. A Norwegian fascist named Vidkun Quisling simply seized power in the wake of the German victory. Hitler had not planned on a government headed by Quisling, but he let it go at that and turned to more important matters.

Discredited by his failed appeasement policy and humiliated by the British performance in Norway, Prime Minister Neville Chamberlain resigned. The maverick Winston Churchill moved into Number 10 Downing Street. He had been correct all along about the Hitler threat, but his judgment was suspect. He had been the architect of the Gallipoli disaster in World War I, and his adventurous mind led him to embrace other ingenious but suspect schemes. At least he seemed prepared to fight.

On May 10, 1940, an avalanche of German fire and steel began rolling across the Dutch and Belgian frontiers with all of the Poland-tested trademarks of the Nazi lightning war. Parachutists seized airfields and supposedly untakable fortresses. Every detail seemed to have been thought of: the undersides of the parachutes were colored blue to make them less visible, and the parachutists' faces were painted blue. The Stuka dive-bombers carried sirens that screamed as they dove, a morale-breaking weapon. Behind the first wave of assault troops, Hitler had amassed 120 infantry divisions and 6,000 attack airplanes. A half-million British and French troops moved up into Belgium to meet the attack. Then the plan of panzer genius Field Marshal von Manstein went into operation. German motorized divisions slashed through the lightly defended Ardennes Forest and began their lightning dash across northern France.

On May 15, Prime Minister Winston Churchill, calling himself a "Former Naval Person," sent an urgent message to President Roosevelt: "The scene has darkened swiftly. . . . The small countries are simply smashed up, one by one like matchwood. . . . Mussolini will hurry in to share the loot. . . . We expect to be attacked here ourselves." Disaster followed disaster, and huge crowds stood silently in Times Square as the appalling news bulletins flashed from the electric sign on the Times Tower. The day after he received Churchill's message, Roosevelt drove to Capitol Hill, where he addressed a cheering Congress, asked for a billion dollars for defense, and set the American production goal as 50,000 planes per year. Moving with public opinion, Congress voted more than Roosevelt had asked.

The German armored divisions slashed across northern France and pinned the Allies against the Channel coast. On June 16, Paul Reynaud resigned as premier, and Marshall Pétain, who had been demanding an armistice, took over and began to form a new cabinet. Five days later, in the forest of Compiègne, in the same railroad car in which the Germans had surrendered in 1918, the French capitulated. The correspondent William L. Shirer was on hand, and he recalls that Hitler exhibited a curious mixture of fury and joy. Nineteen eighteen had been avenged.

American presidential politics unfolded in the summer of 1940 against this lurid backdrop, with Roosevelt not yet a declared candidate and the Democratic Convention opening in Chicago on Monday, July 15. Roosevelt wanted the appearance of a spontaneous draft, but it did not work out that way, and the convention ended up looking rigged. With Roosevelt remaining at the White House, his man on the scene, Harry Hopkins, stayed in his suite at the Blackstone Hotel with a private line to the president in the hotel bathroom. The convention seemed paralyzed. The president's tactics had paid off, and no strong rival had emerged. Would Garner, Farley, and perhaps others form an alliance and mount a divisive challenge? Asked for guidance, Hopkins could give none. Key Roosevelt supporters asked for permission to take control of the convention and push the president's nomination through. Roosevelt vetoed the idea. Inside the hall, a huge, gray, sickly portrait of Roosevelt looked bleakly down at the candidates. "This convention is bleeding to death," Harold Ickes wired the president. "Your reputation and prestige may bleed with it." He implored the president to come to Chicago. There was no answer. Roosevelt awaited his "draft."

It occurred in a sort of parody of the "We Want Willkie" galleries in Philadelphia. On Tuesday night, Alben Barkley delivered an old-fashioned roaring political speech. At a passing reference to Roosevelt, a demonstration broke out on the floor. Then Barkley approached the climax of his speech, a message Roosevelt himself had sent him to deliver. The president had tried "in no way whatsoever" to influence the selection or the opinions of the delegates. "Tonight, at the specific request and authorization of the president, I am making this simple fact clear to the Convention. The President has never had, and has not today, any desire or purpose to continue in the office of President, to be a candidate for that office, or to be nominated by the Convention for that office. He wishes in all earnestness and sincerity to make it clear that all the delegates to this Convention are free to vote for any candidate. That is the message I bear to you from the President of the United States."

The delegates looked at one another in stunned silence. But almost immediately there came from the loudspeakers a single loud voice: "WE WANT ROOSEVELT." A few delegates seized their standards and started marching around the aisles. "EVERYBODY WANTS ROOSEVELT," thundered the man from the loudspeakers. The Chicago Democratic machine's superintendent of sewers was in a basement room with a microphone that plugged into the public address system. "THE WORLD WANTS ROOSEVELT," shouted the Voice from the Sewer, as the Republicans would call it. "ROOSEVELT . . . ROOSEVELT." The convention picked up the chant and became a screaming mob. Roosevelt had his "draft." When order was restored, the final vote was Roosevelt 946, Farley 72, Garner 61, Tydings 9, Hull 5. The mood of the convention, however, was sullen, and several vice-presidential boomlets reflected the restiveness: Harold Ickes, Jesse Jones, Paul McNutt, James Byrnes. Only by threatening to refuse the nomination was Roosevelt able to impose his choice, the eccentric and mystical Henry Wallace, on the convention.

It is possible that there was no way to gracefully circumvent the prescriptive prohibition on a third term, but the president might plausibly have pleaded the catastrophic situation in Europe and begged for the nation's indulgence. The way he played it, however, left a sour taste in the wake of the Chicago convention, and the master was perceived as stumbling politically for the first time.

The presidential campaign that year took place against the Wagnerian background of the Battle of Britain. On August 8, two hundred Stukas and Messerschmitts roared down over British convoys. Four days later, hundreds of German planes attacked British airfields and radar stations. The tempo escalated. On August 13, 1,400 Nazi planes swarmed over England. Two days later, 1,800. The next day, 1,700. The military issue was stark. In order to launch his Operation Sea Lion against England, Hitler needed complete control of the air over the Channel and over the English coastline where the Panzers would land. Without that air control, the Nazi invasion would be another Spanish Armada.

Day after day from their grassy airstrips, exhausted young Englishmen rose to engage the invaders in their Spitfires and Hurricanes. Those who lived did the same thing the next day, and the next. One pilot who fought in the battle and had a burned-off and rebuilt face told the author that, except for the airplanes, the British had "nothing." If he had landed, said the pilot, Hitler "could have walked to Scotland."

But Hitler made a mistake. By the end of August, the tide of battle had begun to turn against the English. Every evening, the news commentator Gabriel Heater would reassure his American listeners with the closing line, "And the sky over England is not in Hitler's hands yet." But a quarter of England's thousand pilots had been killed or seriously wounded. Its airstrips were pitted and its aircraft factories gutted. Hundreds of barges were moving down the rivers and the coastlines of Europe for the invasion. But Hitler shifted the attack from military targets to the city of London. The British had dropped a few bombs on Berlin. The Führer was outraged. In retaliation, he turned the Luftwaffe against London, which was militarily irrelevant. The battered RAF had a respite and gathered itself again. The Luftwaffe, after that, could never quite gain the necessary mastery of the air, and on September 12, Hitler's naval chiefs warned him that the British navy was still in control of the Channel. On September 17, Hitler called off Sea Lion.

From the beginning of the campaign, Wendell Willkie drew huge crowds. He was not a great orator, but his masculine intensity was charismatic, and his earthy Indiana accents contrasted favorably for many people with the aristocratic tones of the third-term candidate. "I will not talk in quibbling language," he vowed, as the twelve-car "Willkie Special" pulled out of Rushville. "I will talk in simple, direct Indiana speech."

The problem with Willkie's campaign was both organizational and conceptual. An inspired amateur, Willkie had never run a political drive for public office, and his staff operation was equally amateur. Letters and phone calls went unanswered, and the "Willkie Special" campaign train amounted to chaos on wheels. Political reporters, even those sympathetic to Willkie, wondered in print how the candidate would run a national administration when he and his aides could not manage an orderly campaign performance. Early in the nationwide tour, the candidate's voice began to crack, but he disdained microphones and the advice of speech coaches, with the result that his voice was soon reduced to a croak, and he had to take a respite from campaigning.

But the campaign also lacked a central theme. Willkie essentially agreed with Roosevelt's foreign policy. He had refused to attack the constitutionally suspect deal with the British, in which we exchanged fifty obsolete destroyers for bases off Canada and in the Caribbean, and he went along with Roosevelt on the draft. He tried attacking Roosevelt for neglecting America's defenses in perilous times, but the problem with that approach was that Republican isolationists in Congress had all along been opposed to preparedness measures. He foolishly charged that the administration was giving preference to Argentine beef, which was false. He charged that Roosevelt had phoned Hitler and Mussolini during the Munich crisis and urged the sellout of Czechoslovakia. False again. Willkie did have serious differences with Roosevelt on domestic matters, and he still held the free-enterprise views that had made him a chief opponent of the TVA. He called for a rollback of the New Deal regulations that he claimed were hobbling American enterprise. None of this, however, provided the thematic content necessary to push him ahead of Roosevelt, and the Willkie campaign came alive only at the last moment, in October, when he threw his principles off the rear platform of the "Willkie Special" and became an antiwar, anti-interventionist candidate. In late September, with France fallen and England under savage bombardment, a Gallup poll showed that a majority of Americans favored assisting England, even at the risk of war. Nevertheless, there existed a vast antiwar emotion, and Willkie tapped it in October.

In early September, a Gallup poll showed Willkie in a virtual dead heat with Roosevelt and even leading in projected electoral votes. By the middle of the month, however, with Willkie's campaign faltering and the war news bad, Roosevelt had moved ahead by 10 points and was leading in 38 states with 453 electoral votes. An opinion survey showed Willkie winning by 5.5 percent if the war ended, but losing by 18 percent if there seemed a likelihood that the U.S. would get involved. The direction of Willkie's polls was all downward. On October 6, the Gallup poll reported that his projected electoral vote had dropped from 78 to 32. Roosevelt was now ahead in 42 states.

In mid-October, at a speech in Philadelphia's Shibe Park, Willkie switched—in desperation—to the isolationist line. Roosevelt, he said, was responsible for a "drift toward war." We must, he bellowed, "stop that drift toward war. We must stop that incompetence. Fellow Americans, I want to lead the fight for peace. . . . We are being edged toward war by an administration that is careless in speech and action. We can have peace but we must know how to preserve it. To begin with, we shall not undertake to fight anybody else's war. Our boys shall stay out of Europe." Willkie thundered through the isolationist Midwest, repeating the formulation that, if Roosevelt's promises to keep out of war were worth as much as his 1932 promise to balance the budget, then the troops were "almost already on the transports." In St. Louis he declaimed, "We do not want to send our boys over there again. If you elect me president, they will not be sent. And by the same token, if you reelect the third-term candidate, I believe they will be sent." And Willkie generalized his message to include that third term: "One-man rule always leads down the road to war."

Antiwar sentiment was so widespread and profound in the country that Willkie's strategy began to work. Within two weeks of the thematic shift, the Gallup poll showed that he had cut in half the president's projected, popular-vote margin. He had surged ahead in five midwestern states and was moving up rapidly in the industrial Northeast. A *New York Daily News* poll announced that the Empire State was a toss-up. In the family of the ten-year-old boy in Queens, antiwar feeling was strong. His mother especially was a sure Willkie vote, and there were millions who felt the same way.

The White House panicked in the face of the Willkie surge, and Roosevelt's advisors urged him to abandon the statesman role and fight for reelection. He did so with characteristic zest. On October 23, his ten-car "Presidential Special" pulled into Philadelphia, and Roosevelt took the gloves off. "I will not pretend that I find this an unpleasant duty," said the silvery voice. "I am an old campaigner and I love a good fight." Even though Roosevelt firmly believed that America would probably have to enter the war, he challenged Willkie for the role of peace candidate. "We will not participate in any foreign wars," he said in Philadelphia, "and we will not send our army, naval or air forces to fight in foreign lands outside of the Americas except in the case of attack." A week later he returned to the theme in a speech in Boston Garden. "I have said this before, but I shall say it again and again and again. Your boys are not going to be sent into any foreign wars." In this controversial speech, Roosevelt omitted "except in the case of attack." If we are attacked, he told speech writer Sam Rosenman, it's not a "foreign war."

The campaign had a sour aspect of class warfare, which Roosevelt also fanned. Willkie and his wife were showered with eggs and rotten fruit in working-class neighborhoods, which Roosevelt denounced as reprehensible, but Roosevelt's own rhetoric played on the themes of envy and resentment. Stung by Willkie's charges that the New Deal had not put one additional man into a job and riding on a wave of war production, Roosevelt swung from the floor:

> I say that those statements are false. I say that the figures of employment, of production, of earnings, of general business activity—all prove that they are false.
>
> The tears, the crocodile tears, for the laboring man and laboring woman now being shed in this campaign come from those same Republican leaders who had their chance to prove their love for labor in 1932—and missed it.
>
> Back in 1932, those leaders were willing to let the workers starve if they could not get a job.
>
> Back in 1932, they were not willing to guarantee collective bargaining.
>
> Back in 1932, they met the demands of unemployed veterans with troops and tanks.
>
> Back in 1932, they raised their hands in horror at the thought of fixing a minimum wage or maximum hours for labor. They never gave one thought to such things as pensions for old age or insurance for the unemployed.

In 1940, eight years later, what a different tune is played by them! It is a tune played against a sounding board of election day. It is a tune with overtones that whisper: "Votes, votes, votes."

The champ could not walk, but he certainly could hit, and he was expert at playing upon envy and class feeling. An undertow of hatred tugged at the contest. Today political strategists would call it "negative polarization."

The campaign had its high and its low notes, but one low one deserves to be recalled—and indeed, is a political collector's item. The "Colored Division" of the Democratic National Committee issued a document charging in effect that Willkie was a Nazi. Here is the opening blast, part of the first page:

DEMOCRATIC CAMPAIGN FACTS—1940
SPEAKERS' BUREAU, COLORED DIVISION
HOTEL BILTMORE, NEW YORK CITY

Willkie

Wendell Willkie's father was born in Germany. Willkie's grandfather was born in Germany. Willkie's mother's parents were born in Germany. Willkie's wife was born in Kentucky of German parentage. His whole background is German.

Hitler in his book "Mein Kampf" states that "NEGROES ARE LOWER THAN APES." HE SAYS THAT FRANCE MUST BE DESTROYED BECAUSE IT IS POLLUTED WITH NEGRO BLOOD. No Negroes are allowed now to entertain in that part of France occupied by Germany.

Willkie was never a candidate for public office until the present international situation arose. He had no ambition for public office. He had no desire to devote himself to Public Service. He was too busy squeezing a large personal fortune from the pocketbooks of the poor.

Willkie was nominated in Philadelphia by the Hitler formula, otherwise known as the blitzkrieg method. Hitler grabbed power and control of Germany in this manner. (Fifth columns, bribery, trickery and false propaganda.) Senator Vandenberg was the only presidential candidate at the Republican Convention to release his delegates to Willkie or to any other candidate. Vandenberg is the leading obstructionist to preparedness in the Senate. He leads the interference to all things that would prepare us against the invasion of Hitler.

Willkie was nominated by Congressman Halleck of
Indiana. Halleck leads the opposition to the New Deal in the
lower branch of Congress. He, too, leads the interference
against all things which would prepare us against invasion.
The Floor Leader and spokesman for Willkie at the
Republican National Convention was Governor Stassen, the
Governor of the "German" State of the Union—Minnesota.

The heavyweight champion, Joe Louis, however, was for Willkie.
"This is almost as bad as fighting five men in one night," he said,
after addressing his fifth Willkie rally on September 30 in Harlem.
Louis argued that New Deal welfare "made his people lazy after pay
rises took their jobs." Willkie sent Louis the following telegram:

> IN COMPLETING MY TOUR NOTHING HAS GIVEN ME
> GREATER GRATIFICATION THAN TO RECEIVE THE NEWS
> OF YOUR SUPPORT. THIS WILL BE OF THE GREATEST
> POSSIBLE VALUE AND I CAN ASSURE YOU THAT MY AD-
> MINISTRATION WILL BRING ABOUT A NEW ERA IN IN-
> TERRACIAL RELATIONS.

The final Gallup poll before the voting showed a narrowing race,
and most political analysts predicted the closest contest since Woodrow Wilson won in the three-way 1916 election. Gallup had Roosevelt at 52 percent, Willkie at 48, but reported a "strong trend" for
the Republican, who was therefore "within easy striking distance"
of victory. Willkie, according to Gallup, had pulled ahead in New
York, Pennsylvania, Ohio, Illinois, Indiana, and Missouri and was
moving up in Massachusetts, New Jersey, and Minnesota. Nineteen
states with 274 electoral votes were doubtful.

The night of the election, Roosevelt listened to the returns at Hyde
Park, and when the early returns proved to be unfavorable, he
excluded everyone, even his family, from his study. But as the
evening wore on, the strength of the New Deal coalition, buoyed by
war-contract prosperity, carried the master politician to a third
term. By eleven o'clock, radio commentator Elmer Davis declared
that Roosevelt had won his third term. Roosevelt received 27.3
million votes to Willkie's 22.3 million, and 449 electoral votes to
Willkie's 82, but Willkie had received a record number of Republican votes, a total that would not be surpassed until
Eisenhower's 1952 landslide. The Willkie enthusiasm had carried
five new Republicans to the Senate, and the party had picked up two
governorships. "The collapse of the Allies made Roosevelt's election a certainty no matter what Willkie did," said Republican leader

Joe Martin. "The fall of France and the imminent danger of Britain filled the American people with a fear of switching administrations. 'Don't change horses in the middle of the stream' was never a more potent argument in American history than it was then."

In that election of the fall of 1940, both Willkie and Roosevelt were interventionists who campaigned as peace candidates, such was the reluctance of the electorate about war. "I felt that the country was on the verge of a profound change," wrote Marquis W. Childs, who covered Willkie for the *St. Louis Post-Dispatch*. "I think the people sensed it, too, that fall. Much in America we had known was to go. A greater, stronger America might come out of the ordeal ahead of us. Or we might forfeit our birthright, the wonderful heritage of spirit, of earth, of people. But nothing would be quite the same again. The high wind of change was in the air."

After he had knocked Willkie out of the ring, the champ was magnanimous. He actually liked the fellow, and later he would send him around the world on wartime diplomatic assignments. "I'm happy I've won," Roosevelt told his son James, "but I'm sorry Wendell lost."

At first glance, it seems strange that there is no monument to Franklin Roosevelt in Washington today. We have the three great monuments to Washington, Jefferson, and Lincoln. There is even a memorial to the late Senator Robert Alonso Taft, but nothing for FDR. Our only four-term president, he redefined the office and greatly expanded its powers. He led America in its greatest war. Surely as much as Abraham Lincoln, he was president at a time of great national crisis—in fact, multiple crises. In *The Politics of Recovery,* the best analysis of the economic policy—or policies—of the New Deal, Professor Albert U. Romasco of New York University recalls the national condition in 1933. "The complete collapse of the nation's banking system coincided exactly with Roosevelt's coming to power. The spectacle of commercial America with all its banks shut down symbolized the demonstrated failure of the old order not only to restore the nation's business prosperity but even to preserve its own vital institutions." Joseph Alsop writes:

> During FDR's second term as Governor of New York, the
> Depression became ever more severe: national income
> dropped from $85 to $37 billion, banks closed their doors,
> unemployment rose to 14 million. Indigent men lived in
> communities of temporary shacks, known derisively as
> Hoovervilles. There was even one in New York's Central
> Park. Breadlines proliferated. Worst of all was the feeling of

hopelessness that spread across the country. In a speech on
May 22, 1932, FDR proclaimed: "The country needs and,
unless I mistake its temper, the country demands, bold,
persistent experimentation. . . . The millions who are in
want will not stand by silently forever while the things to
satisfy their needs are within easy reach."

It is Professor Romasco's persuasive conclusion that Roosevelt
failed to bring about economic recovery because neither he nor his
many advisers understood the causes of the Depression. Thus the
administration shifted in an erratic way between traditional economic internationalists, with their stress on free trade and a sound
dollar, and nationalists, who favored protection from foreign competition and easy credit at home. The fact is that, despite all of the
public-works programs, there was no recovery from the Depression
until the buildup of war orders in 1940. Indeed, the country slid into
a deep economic trough in 1938. Professor Romasco thus believes
that the New Deal, economically speaking, was far from the "creative confusion" celebrated by many historians. It was merely
confusion.

But if the success of the New Deal in ameliorating the Great
Depression was unimpressive, a case for Roosevelt's greatness as a
president may be made on broader political grounds. Professor
Romasco argues that Roosevelt was adept at moving just far enough
to defuse the potentially disruptive forces of radical protest, whether
they boiled up from the farmers, the labor movement, or the unem-
ployed. If he had no real cures, he at least managed to govern.
Indeed, a far wilder spirit than either Roosevelt or Willkie had
planned, not at all irrationally, to win the presidency in the year
1940, on a radical left–populist platform. Louisiana's governor,
senator, and political boss Huey Long is now widely regarded as a
mere blip in the course of American history, but he was not a blip in
the early thirties, amid farm foreclosures, bank failures, breadlines,
and silent factories. He was anything but a blip when he was gunned
down under circumstances that are still mysterious in the halls of the
state capitol at Baton Rouge on September 8, 1935.

President Roosevelt faced reelection in 1936. He and his closest
lieutenants believed, correctly, that Long possessed the potential to
run as a third candidate and pull enough votes to throw the election
to a Republican. Postmaster General and top political pro Jim Farley
conducted a poll that proved ominous. Long's appeal was not confined to Louisiana, and he could expect to get 11–15 percent of the
vote in 1936. Long's own analysis coincided precisely with that of
the White House. He would run in 1936 and throw the election to the

Republicans. The ensuing four years under a Republican administration would be a disaster. Then Long would run and win in 1940. "If it weren't for being part of the United States," said Long, "Louisiana would never have known a Depression." In the spring of 1935 before he was shot in the halls of the capitol in Baton Rouge, he published a best-seller called *My First Days in the White House,* in which he said that in a Long administration, Roosevelt would be Secretary of the Navy, while Hoover could be Secretary of Commerce.

Huey Long was not a political joke, though he was content to be regarded as one by his rivals and by respectable editorialists. If they underrated him, that suited his purpose and ambitions. On the basis of his solid achievements in Louisiana, historians today rank Long among the most effective governors in American history, up there with Woodrow Wilson, Robert La Follette, Al Smith, and Earl Warren, and Long achieved his distinction in only one gubernatorial term. When Long was elected governor in 1928, Louisiana was one of the poorest states in the nation, with, for example, only 300 miles of hard-surfaced roads. Long built 2,300 miles more and 6,000 miles of gravel roads. He began 120 new bridges across Louisiana rivers, gave schoolchildren free textbooks (Louisiana ranked last in literacy), and established free night schools for adults. He built a new campus for Louisiana State University, a new medical school in New Orleans, a new system of charity hospitals, a new state capitol, and a new governor's mansion. He used patronage to control jobs and votes and restructured the tax system so that business, corporations, and the utilities would foot much of the bill.

Long openly avowed his presidential ambition. He often referred to "when I am in the White House," not whether. When former President Calvin Coolidge passed through New Orleans in 1930, Long asked Coolidge whether the Hoovers, then resident in the executive mansion, were good housekeepers. Informed that they were, Long replied, "Good. When I was elected, I found the governor's mansion in such rotten shape that I had to tear it down and rebuild. It started a hell of a row. When I'm elected president, I don't want to have to rebuild the White House."

Long's political message consisted of all-out, wealth-redistributing, left populism, demagogically delivered. His slogan was "Every Man a King," and he himself wrote a ballad to that effect and often sang it. He fulminated against the Morgans, Mellons, Rockefellers, and Baruchs; but he would allow a millionaire to retain $10 million, and redistribute the rest. No American would have less than a home, a job, an education, and a radio. Share-Our-Wealth clubs spread across the nation and would be useful for the 1936 Long candidacy.

Long was not the only radical demagogue appealing to the millions
of Americans who had been hard hit by the Depression. Father
Charles Coughlin, the Detroit radio priest, preached Social Justice
and published a tabloid with that title. Coughlin had a large following, as did Dr. Francis Townsend, who demanded a federal pension
for everybody over sixty. In this rich Depression growth of demagogues and potential Mussolinis, Long was by far the most intelligent and skillful.

He regarded Franklin Roosevelt with a contempt he did not
bother to conceal, savaging the New Deal in the Senate and over the
radio as a sham, not nearly enough. He regarded Roosevelt as a
genteel amateur whom he would take into camp and easily defeat.
Roosevelt was the creature of the Mellons and the rest. Long would
lead the Louisiana delegation to the 1936 Democratic Convention
and declare himself a candidate for the presidency. He would lose
the nomination, but he would leave the convention on a wave of
national publicity as the leader who had a vision that went beyond
the two major Tweedle-Dum, Tweedle-Dee parties. His national
presidential campaign would be financed by the big banks and
corporations, not because they liked Long—they despised him—but
because they saw in his national candidacy a way to defeat the
detested Roosevelt. The country would be ready for Long's strong
medicine in 1940.

Roosevelt, however, was not the genteel amateur Long considered
him. He and Farley used all the resources of the federal government
to destroy Long in his Louisiana base. He ordered tax investigations
of Long and his political allies. Farley, FDR's patronage chief,
ordered all federal patronage in Louisiana to be channeled through
anti-Long Democrats. Customs posts, U.S. attorneys and marshalls,
post-office contracts and postmasterships, public-works appropriations, and all the rest of the rapidly expanding federal capacity for
intervention in state politics were employed to strengthen the forces
hostile to Long and his machine. "Anyone working for Huey Long is
not working for us," commanded the president, and he brought into
being what amounted to an anti-Long political army. The New
Orleans police and the village vigilantes belonged to the anti-Longs.
The state police and his own large, armed bodyguard represented
Long's private army.

Both Roosevelt and Long played very hard ball. Long forced
from office judges, mayors, and any other official who spoke out
against him. He withdrew state advertising from opposition newspapers. Hodding Carter, Jr., who later would win a Pulitzer Prize,
was savage in his attacks on Long in a local Hammond paper. It is a
measure of the intensity of feeling surrounding the Kingfish that

Carter compared him with Hitler and said that "there remain only the ancient methods of righting wrongs." Long abolished the poll tax, thus adding hundreds of thousands of poor whites to the rolls, virtually all of them Long supporters. He pushed through legislation empowering the governor to appoint local officials. He was shot with a single thirty-eight caliber bullet on September 8, 1935, the gun wielded, supposedly, by a Dr. Carl Austin Weiss, Jr., a surgeon and the son-in-law of an anti-Long judge whom Long was trying to gerrymander out of office. The bullets of Long's bodyguard cut Weiss down, and their nicks can still be seen in the marble walls of the capitol at Baton Rouge. Long was intensely mourned by the "little people" of Louisiana, and not only of Louisiana.

As we now realize, and perhaps we did then, there are unknown factors in such assassinations. The hatred of Long by his enemies was surely enough to raise the emotional temperature in Louisiana to the point where Long was likely to be assassinated. But, at the very least, the operations of Roosevelt's political lieutenants also played an important part in raising this emotional temperature. Roosevelt himself was the principal political beneficiary of Long's death, and he coasted to victory over Landon in the 1936 election. Whatever the undiscoverable ultimate truth about Long's assassination, Roosevelt had played a tough hand, and if he was the prinicpal beneficiary, another beneficiary was certainly American constitutional democracy.

If Long and the demagogues posed a threat to constitutional democracy, Roosevelt had to take into account other and potentially lethal threats from other quarters. The Communist Party was strong in organized labor, in some quarters of the universities, in Hollywood, and in some of the federal agencies. The new totalitarian models abroad had appeal and might increase in influence. Through a politics of maneuver, of giving each constituency just enough, Roosevelt warded off potentially dangerous challenges to the entire system. Professor Romasco quotes the following exchange between the president and Secretary of the Treasury Morgenthau as they discussed a speech to be given on November 15, 1938, as the nation slid back into the economic depths:

> Morgenthau: *What business wants to know is are we headed toward State Socialism or are we going to continue on a capitalistic basis?*
> Roosevelt: *I have told them that again and again.*
> Morgenthau: *All right, Mr. President, tell them for the fifteenth time on November 15, because . . . that's what they want to know.*

The businessmen had good reason to be concerned about the

amount of power Roosevelt was concentrating in Washington, but as
he saw it, the situation was dire: "I want to put a flea in your ear," he
said in a kind of rambling soliloquy to Morgenthau. "Have you ever
stopped to consider that Fascism is winning out in this world and
that Democracies are gradually becoming weaker?" That judgment
was far from absurd at the end of 1938, and though Roosevelt was
popular, his constituencies were demanding that he do something.
Professor Romasco thinks that he did just barely enough.

The truth about Roosevelt and the New Deal may really lie in the
difference between what actually was and what seemed to be at the
time. Professor Romasco's weighty book establishes that the New
Deal was, in economic terms, a failure. Indeed, the intellectual tide
today has turned sharply against the idea of a centralization of
economic and bureaucratic power in Washington, as adumbrated by
the New Deal and metastasized by Lyndon Johnson. More de-
centralized and free-flow models are currently in favor
intellectually.

But what *seemed* to be was different from the reality that con-
fronts us in Professor Romasco's footnotes. The New Deal programs
may, in the longer perspective, have accomplished little. But TVA,
AAA, CCC, the Wagner Act, Social Security, FDIC, stock-market
regulation, even the unconstitutional NRA, all created the impression—the illusion—that Roosevelt was *doing something*. He was *not*
Herbert Hoover. Roosevelt's personality was, of course, an enormous political factor. Professor Romasco finds, in retrospect, something excessively manipulative about the man, something distant,
aristocratic, and finally, cold, remembered until only yesterday by
those who worked intimately with him, and also something occasionally cruel, perhaps the cruelty of a man in pain and possible
humiliation from the effects of his polio. Many of those who worked
most closely with Roosevelt did not in fact really like him, even
when they worshipped him, and these whispers of something finally
unsatisfactory about him within the political establishment may be a
major reason why there is no monument to him in Washington.

But his silvery radio voice, his eloquence, his upturned cigarette
holder, his aristocratic scorn, and perhaps above all, his half-hidden
metaphor of his partial physical and triumphant psychological victory over paralysis lifted the American spirit in depression and war
and made him a great political champion.

The Queen of Ice

Sonja Henie did not care who won the war. By 1940 she was a
major Hollywood star, the best skater in the world, making another

movie, *Sun Valley Serenade,* at the ski resort in Idaho—blonde, athletic, attractive, sexually insatiable. She had a broad face, bright brown eyes, and liked earthy jokes, peasant humor. The bulging muscles in her thighs were unsightly, and she tried regular massage, but it did not do much good.

If the Allies won the war, fine, she would still be a star. But if the Nazis won the war, she might be a still greater star, glittering in the firmament of the New Order. Hitler, Goebbels, and Göring had adored her ever since she swept the gold medals at the 1936 Winter Olympics in Garmisch-Partenkirchen, and she was on excellent social terms with Goebbels. Her Norwegian blondness and her athleticism fulfilled the Nazi racial ideal. She openly admired Hitler and agreed with his racial theories, insofar as she grasped them. At a skating exhibition in Berlin, attended by the Führer and his entourage, she skated briskly to his box, snapped to attention, gave the Nazi salute, and yelled "Heil Hitler." "If there is anybody to fear," she constantly told friends, "it is the Bolsheviks." Throughout the later 1930s, many Norwegians disliked her Nazi sympathies and friendliness with the top Nazis, but she was a national heroine nonetheless.

She owned inscribed photographs of Hitler, Goebbels, and Mussolini, and she had a Hohenzollern crest stickpin given her by Crown Prince Wilhelm. Indeed, her personal jewelry collection was spectacular, and she took enormous pride in it. Much later, in 1969, when she knew that she was dying of leukemia, she wanted her jewelry exhibited under glass after her death, like the British crown jewels.

At the ski resort making *Sun Valley Serenade,* she had a fine time. Her affair with Tyrone Power had exhausted the actor, causing his friends to worry about his health, and at Sun Valley she fell in with a crowd of handsome young German ski instructors. With them, she groaned over the sinking of the battleship *Bismarck* by the British.

Her friends on the set recall that she ran through the German ski instructors one at a time, and those she left behind continued to speak enthusiastically about her. Her producer thought he could pick out her partner of the moment by the way he looked in the morning. It did not matter to her that Germany had invaded her country, Norway. After all, they were all Nordics and Aryans together, though she probably recalled the sexual efforts of Joe Louis during their affair with nonideological affection.

Soon after she finished *Sun Valley Serenade,* the United States Government interned all of the German ski instructors for the rest of the war.

4

The boy's turtle waddled through the grass outside his bedroom window in the housing project, a brown and orange turtle about a foot long, moving more quickly than you would think to get to the dime-sized balls of hamburger he held out toward it. It was not a turtle at all, as he well knew, since he considered himself an expert on reptiles, a herpetologist even, and had met Raymond L. Ditmars at the Bronx Zoo. It was a box tortoise. It went out into the garden at night, no doubt eating worms, and came back in the morning for the hamburger.

The boy's room was full of reptiles and fish. He had aerated fishing tanks with tetras, mollies, guppies, and angel fish, flashing silver, blue, orange, and black. The most exotic were four Siamese fighting fish with long drapery-like fins, so ferocious that they had to be kept solitary in small separate tanks. He bought the fish and equipment at a store on Fulton Street in Manhattan, an extraordinary store with three rows of fish tanks and all the pumps, filters, plants, fish food, and vitamins that a fish fancier might want.

The swamp a mile or so away provided many interesting reptiles and amphibians, and he had garter snakes, water snakes, toads, and frogs. From a mail-order house in Arizona, he had bought horned toads, desert snakes, and on one memorable occasion, a small but definitely poisonous copperhead. The cardboard tube with the snake in it arrived in the mail one Saturday morning. He took an empty tank out into the yard, opened the tube, and tried to lasso the snake the way they did at the Bronx Zoo with a cord tied into a noose. His father, hungover and still in bed, witnessed this scene through a bedroom window. Informed that, yes, the snake was poisonous, he demanded that it be chloroformed immediately. They boy stuffed the copperhead and mounted it.

He also collected stamps and knew that Franklin Roosevelt did too. He understood that history was embodied in the stamps. He understood the meaning of the thousand-mark increases on the Weimar stamps. He noticed that the most insignificant countries usually had gigantic stamps—the Cameroons, for example—while the stamps from England and America were modest. Russian stamps were large and always celebrating some Russian who had flown over the North Pole or something. You bought the stamps through the mail, "on approval," or else at stores in the city. Macy's and Gimbels were excellent. Macy's was also a source of English-made lead soldiers, far superior to the ones made in America and sold at Woolworth's. The English toy soldiers were made with careful attention to detail. He had Grenadiers, Zouaves, German soldiers with their coal-scuttle helmets.

It wasn't exactly a "housing project," but a "garden apartment," six five-story buildings around a large central garden, grass, bushes, trees, and walks. That is where the tortoise walked. The development was owned, for some reason, by the Metropolitan Life Insurance Company. The rent was $39 per month, and when his father was too hungover to deliver the check to the office around the corner, the boy took it there himself, sometimes also picking up a carton of Lucky Strikes and a quart of Budweiser for his father at the local deli.

If you stood out in front of the apartment house and looked across 64th Street, you saw a row of two-story brick homes with neatly fenced yards and leafy trees. His father was quarreling with Mr. Callahan across the street. Callahan did not like him washing his second-hand Buick at the curb outside the Callahan house. Up the street were more of the same two-story brick houses, and up toward the corner some stores. Old Cohen the tailor was a hooked-nose Jew who could have played Fagin. He worked amid incredible clutter, but he was kind, sentimental even, and nice to the kids, and he worked quickly and expertly at his sewing machine. The Chinese laundry next to Cohen's place was so alien as to be virtually meaningless. An indeterminate number of Chinese lived and worked there, and the place smelled like strange food. You picked up mother's bundle and got out as quickly as possible.

The neighborhood was mostly Irish and German and Catholic, but there was a sprinkling of southerners, such as Mr. Lord, who was a motorman for the new IND subway. The Irish were the more outgoing. They had Clancy's Bar at one end of the block and the Seaweed Tavern at the other. Anyone was welcome in these bars, but they were strongly Irish, no doubt about that, and they were sinks of iniquity to the staid Irish Catholic wives. Just past the Seaweed, the elevated IRT railroad clanged and clattered on the route between the World's Fair in Flushing and Manhattan.

The Germans were friendly enough, but gregarious mostly with each other. They had a beer garden a couple of blocks away, surrounded by a high, gray, wooden fence. On Saturdays they had big parties there, beginning in the middle of the afternoon. You heard accordions and oompah bands playing polkas and waltzes, and there was laughter and German songs. No one the boy knew ever blamed these Germans for Hitler or the war or objected to the German music. Anyone could buy a ticket to the Saturday parties, but hardly anyone except the Germans ever did. The Irish just did not sign up for pigs' knuckles and sauerkraut. After all, there were no German songs at Clancy's or the Seaweed either.

If you stood in front of the apartment house the first thing in the morning, you very likely would run into the milkman. He had a horse-drawn, white wagon with rubber-covered wheels. The milk came in heavy glass bottles with waxed cardboard tops. Mother wore a red-and-white-checked apron, washed the used milk bottles, and left them at the backdoor to be picked up. Mayor LaGuardia was on the radio every Sunday, and that year, with his excited, high-pitched voice, he had a furious campaign going against Grade A milk. It was a *fraud,* said the mayor. Why pay the higher price? "Don't *give* your money to the milk companies." But mother did not believe it and bought Grade A. No one remarked that this was a strange thing for Mayor LaGuardia to be preoccupying himself with, probably because almost everything the mayor did was a little strange.

The boy's father, an architect, had been forced to teach in the public high schools during the Depression. The father's own father had made several million in the wholesale, imported woolen business but had died, and then the Crash wrecked the business and wiped out the fortune. The boy's father had degrees from Dartmouth and Columbia and had studied at the Art Students' League and wore Brooks Brothers clothes and had a waxed mustache, but there was just not much architecture during the Depression, and he had to teach what he considered illiterates in the public high schools. Some of his architect friends were sleeping on their desks in their Manhattan offices, unable to pay the rent for an apartment. His father submitted a design for the World's Fair to the contest that was held. The Trylon and Perisphere, of course, won the contest. His father submitted a classical design—columns, architrave, and so on—that certainly had nothing to do with the stated World of Tomorrow theme, and of course the classical submission lost. Probably his father was a mediocre architect. He despised Frank Lloyd Wright and liked to joke about the practical flaws in Wright's buildings, and he thought the "Bauhaus Boys" were even more ridiculous than Wright. Though earning a small teacher's salary, he always voted Republican, voting for Harding, Coolidge, Hoover, Landon, Willkie, Dewey, Eisenhower, and Nixon. He said that he'd voted for only one bad candidate, Harding, and so the percentage was pretty good. He would sooner have gone swimming at Coney Island than vote Democratic. He viewed the Democratic Party as a collection of Tammany-Hall types, crooks who ran the big-city machines, plus corrupt Southerners of the "Senator Claghorne" variety, with a conspicious dusting of fast-talking Communists.

Down the street in the course of the day would come a variety of peripatetic merchants. There were, from time to time, the Fuller-Brush man, with his suitcases full of brushes of all kinds, and the knife grinder, with his cart and large pedal-worked whetstone that gave off sparks when he pressed a knife upon it. Horse-drawn, wooden trucks brought fresh vegetables, constantly doused with water to keep them fresh-looking. Once a week a large coal truck backed up over the sidewalk, and with a lot of clanking and growling, the entire back part of it slowly tipped up. The coal man placed a slide between the back of the truck and a trapdoor at the base of the apartment-house wall, opened a door in the back of the truck, and let the coal roar down the slide into the basement. The janitor looked on, a scrawny, bow-legged man named John who had grown up in the British coal mines. His son, also John, had just enlisted in the Royal Air Force, going to England by way of Canada. There were daily visits by the ice truck for people who did not have electric refrigerators, the Good Humor man on a tricycle vending vehicle, jingling his bells, and the green and white police car cruising very slowly down the street.

Several families in the apartment house had accepted British children who were here to get away from the air raids. They all seemed scrawny, small for their age, but they were nice enough, usually freckled. One of them wept uncontrollably whenever a commercial passenger plane flew overhead.

Mother spent a good part of the day buying, preparing, and cooking the day's dinner. When the "pressure cooker" became available, it seemed to her a revolutionary development, both a tenderizer and a timesaver. The boy was wary of the thing, with its round pressure gauge sticking up through the cover, aware from the newspapers that one had gone off like a bomb somewhere and filled someone's kitchen with shrapnel. He preferred to be taking a bath while the thing was hissing and vibrating on the stove. Mother was also a great fan of the radio food-prophet Carleton Frederick, who went on for fifteen minutes every morning. Wheat germ was therefore canonical, spread on just about everything. Vegetables of course were boiled, according to the prescriptions of Frederick, inside envelopes of a special paper so that they would retain their juices. She had a brother named Willard, a young businessman who had just been drafted into the army and was stationed at Camp Yapank out on Long Island. He showed up in his uniform when on leave and was loud in his amazement about how willing the women were when they met the soldiers and sailors in the bars. "Nothing to it," he said. "Nothing at all." Another of her brothers had just died, a cripple named Walter in a wheelchair, dark and brooding, a professional composer whose songs you sometimes heard on the radio. He died when his remaining kidney got infected and failed.

That year the ten-year-old boy changed from his detested short pants to the, if anything, more detestable knickers. Why not trousers? "You don't want to look like a *little man,*" his father explained, explaining nothing. The problem with the knickers was the socks that went with them, knee-length, and there was no way to keep them from sliding down your leg and wrinkling. Garters, rubber bands— nothing worked, short of cutting off your circulation. Knickers. There is a fading snapshot of the boy that year, a bit fat and wearing knickers and a corduroy zipper jacket covered with Willkie buttons.

He could easily walk the half-dozen blocks to P.S. 52 and in good weather even get home for lunch. If he took a sandwich to school, it was in a small tin lunchbox which held a thermos bottle for milk and had room also for an apple or a pear. The school had a go-ahead principal named Emma H. Austra and a fast track for the better students. On the fast track, in addition to the usual subjects, you also worked on Special Projects, and the Good Neighbor Policy was a great thing in those days. You wore a serape and a Mexican hat, made relief maps of the Andes out of plaster of paris, and you knew that Chile had copper, Bolivia tin, and that the continent was full of llamas. Mrs. Austra was friendly with Mrs. Roosevelt, who would come out to the school, pat the kids on the head, and tell them how wonderful and very important Latin America was and how the president himself was proud of the Good Neighbor Project at P.S. 52. A photograph of President Roosevelt hung in the classroom above the blackboard.

You sat at desks which were bolted to the floor. They had an inkwell in the upper-right corner, which was filled from a gallon bottle of ink kept in the closet, and you wrote with a straight pen that you dipped in the well. There were maps on the side walls, and below them shelves covered with jars of paste, piles of writing and drawing paper, spare felt erasers, and boxes of chalk. All of the boys had to wear red neckties and white shirts to school, and every school day began with the Pledge of Allegiance. On the fast track, the competition for grades and for the teachers' favor was intense. The bright students wanted to get into one of the three special selective high schools in the city, and after that, they intended to go to college. His principal rival was a fierce worker of a girl named Nancy Leininger, the daughter of a local Lutheran minister. The grades war with this girl was win, lose, and sometimes draw.

But you learned a lot of things outside of school as well. The cards that came wrapped with a flat slab of five-cent bubblegum were a populist form of history, both political and athletic. You traded these cards with other boys, or gambled for them, either flipping them, heads or tails, or scaling them against a wall. The card getting closest to the wall won. You practiced to achieve a "leaner." But you knew from the cards that the Japanese had invaded China and were machine-gunning people in the streets of Chinese cities. The Japanese always seemed to be bayoneting people on the cards. You knew about the Marco Polo Bridge and the sinking of our gunboat, the *Panay,* on the Yangtse. There were cards with Spitfires on them and Stukas and submarines. The cards told you that Joe DiMaggio was the great baseball player and Joe Louis and Billy Conn great fighters. You read books about Tom Swift, the Hardy Boys, and fighter pilots in *Wings of the Navy.* Every week he followed the Finnish war in *Life,* passionately rooting for the Finns, gallant ski troops in their white winter uniforms, who were humiliating but not finally or decisively defeating the much more numerous Russians.

He liked to build model airplanes—Spitfires, Messerschmitts, Grummans. You bought a kit at Woolworth's. There was a paper diagram of the plane on which you pinned the airy-light, balsa-wood parts, fastening them together with airplane glue that smelled like ether and gave you a headache. When the structure was complete, you covered it with special paper, affixed the insignia, and lacquered the whole thing.

He belonged to a YMCA that was a couple of stops away on the subway and went to it on Saturday mornings to swim or play gym sports. He also belonged to the camera club there, where he met his first Nazi sympathizer, a photography instructor who taught the kids how to develop film and use the enlarger, a very careful and scientifically gifted man who knew all about photography. He frequently scorned this or that as "bourgeois," and the boy's father thought the man was therefore very likely a Communist, but this turned out not to be true. The man liked Hitler and viewed the Nazis as scientific, modern, progressive, disciplined. He liked German Zeiss cameras and preferred the German Agfa film to anything made by Kodak. He was certain that the Germans would win the war in short order and teach the decadent "bourgeois" countries a richly deserved lesson.

On Saturday afternoons, when the boy did not spend them in the darkroom at the YMCA, there were of course the movies. You could spend four or five hours watching the double feature at the Deluxe, the Earl, or Loew's Woodside. In addition, there were the cartoons, the serial, the coming attractions, the newsreel. In the last, you saw scenes from the wars in Europe and Asia, searchlights probing the sky above London, guns firing, troops marching, worried-looking diplomats doing something. Many of the characters in the serials were familiar from the comic books—figures like Batman, Dick Tracy, the Shadow, the Invisible Man, Charlie Chan.

Then too there were all of those important radio shows. For several years he had owned a small plastic radio, which had cost ten dollars at the local radio store, and it stood on a shelf of his bedroom bookcase. Over the tiny set came the shows of 1940. There were fifteen-minute, serial-style adventures directed at kids and selling things like breakfast cereals. There was "Don Winslow of the Navy," about a derring-do American naval officer; "Jack Armstrong, the All-American Boy," from which show you could order a whistle ring just like the one Armstrong himself used. The sinister voice that was the trademark opening of "The Shadow" was famous, but no one knew that the voice was that of Orson Welles: "Who knows what evil lurks in the hearts of men?" Welles rumbled in a sinister way. "The Shadow knows. Ha, ha, ha." The Shadow, a detective who could render himself invisible, invariably got his evil man. "I Love a Mystery" was especially chilling, opening with a squeaking door and a mysterious organ playing in the background. If you were permitted to stay up fairly late, you could hear "Gang Busters" with Colonel H. Norman Schwartzkopf, a reassuring glorification of the FBI. "The Chase and Sanborn Hour" brought Edgar Bergen and Charlie McCarthy. Fred Allen and Jack Benny conducted their fictitious rivalry over their weekly half-hour comedy shows, and their humor was often of high quality. Allen had a whole stable of regional and ethnic caricatures, from Mrs. Nussbaum to Senator Claghorne, with assorted comic types in between, while Benny, besides his execrable violin and his Jewish-stinginess jokes, had fat announcer Don Wilson, who quivered the Jello ads, drunken bandleader Phil Harris, naive tenor Dennis O'Day. No one should leave out his wife Mary, whom he had met at the May Company, and his gravelly voiced and credulous Negro servant Rochester. Benny's humor, which was usually directed at his stinginess or cowardice, can be typified by the following example. The stinginess struggles with cowardice when a holdup man says to Benny, "Your money or your life." There is no answer at all from Benny, as audience laughter builds. Then the holdup man at length asks what about it. Benny: "I'm thinking. I'm *thinking.*" The opening of Benny's vault was always good for laughs, with sound-effect variations of bolts being thrown, chains clanking, and huge metal doors opening.

On a hot summer day, if there were no trips to the beach, you could go to the giant, public swimming pool over in Astoria, under the new Triboro Bridge. The great New York planner Robert Moses had built the bridge and, as a matter of fact, had built the pool too, back in 1936, when a new giant pool opened somewhere in the city every week, making a total of ten.

In the year 1940, your parents, of course, had period-piece anxieties. There were the childhood diseases. The kid next door, Douglas, a disagreeable brat, suddenly died of diphtheria, feverish and choking. There was also whooping cough, measles, chicken pox, mumps, and scarlet fever, and most children had their tonsils cut out, with ice cream as compensation for a burning throat. But the scariest disease was infantile paralysis. The president had it. Sometimes the beaches and swimming pools were closed when there was an outbreak of it. The March of Dimes, started by Roosevelt, was important at school: everyone gave a dime. During the summer of 1940, a chunky little girl down the block suddenly contracted polio and died within a few days. You can imagine the effect of that on the parents of the neighborhood. Contagion seemed to lurk everywhere.

Also, coming out of the 1930s, kidnapping seemed to be on everyone's mind, perhaps because of the Lindbergh kidnapping back in 1932. The boy himself was old enough to remember that case; everyone talked about it, and when they put Hauptmann on trial in Trenton, he had listened to Gabriel Heater's reports about the trial. All of the adults he knew were certain that Hauptmann was guilty, bitter over this outrage committed against the great Lindbergh and his beautiful wife, glad that Hauptmann was electrocuted, and sorry only that he could not be electrocuted twice. But there

may have been more to the kidnapping fear than the famous
Lindbergh case. The 1930s had been the great age of the child movie
stars—Shirley Temple, Dickie Moore, Freddy Bartholemew, Judy
Garland, and dozens of others. Perhaps children were at the center
of consciousness during the Depression because they symbolized
the future and hope, the possibility of rising socially, all of which
may be the same thing. Anyway, kidnapping was a big fear, and one
day when the boy reported at home that a man with a mustache and
an Irish setter dog had offered him a lollipop through the wire fence
at the schoolyard, the result was instant consternation. The police
were called, and the next day the schoolyard looked like a police
convention. Everyone was questioned. And yes, the man had indeed
given lollipops to a couple of other kids. Very, very sinister. But he
never came back.

Despite the disease fears and the kidnapping mania, there are
respects in which life was a bit more relaxed than it is now. For
example, up the street was the local drugstore, with its two big jars
standing in the window, one filled with a red liquid, one with blue,
the significance of which remained mysterious. The druggist was a
thin man, bald, with a mustache and a white coat, and if you got a
speck of dust in your eye, he would solve the problem free of charge,
deftly rolling back your eyelid and removing the speck with a cotton
swab. No druggist would do that today for fear of a lawsuit. He had a
ladder that rolled along a rail near the ceiling that enabled him to
reach medicines and medical equipment on the upper shelves, and in
a corner of the store he also had a rental library—*Grapes of Wrath,
Portrait of Jennie, Gone With the Wind*, the historical novels of
Kenneth Roberts.

During the warm months, there were pickup softball games in a
vacant lot a few blocks away, pretty serious games, and sometimes
stickball in the street outside the apartment house. You used a
broom handle for a bat and played with a smooth rubber ball. The
boy also acquired a cheap tennis racquet at Woolworth's and practiced hitting the ball against the wall in the schoolyard. Tennis,
however, was not looked upon by his friends as a suitable game for a
boy to be playing. It was felt to be a game that was at once sissy and
snobbish.

That neighborhood in 1940 had a lot of open space around it.
Queens was one of the five boroughs of New York City, but there
were empty fields for kite-flying or picnicking, even in Jackson
Heights, which today is completely built up and indistinguishable
from Manhattan or the Bronx. Out in the fields, there were hills on
which you could sled in the winter, and some people even skied.
There was a local tennis club with sixteen clay courts and a little

clubhouse. Most of the members were businessmen and their wives and children, and many spoke with Southern accents. The boy joined that club, but not until after the war.

When he got on his bike and rode northward toward what was then known as North Beach, but is now LaGuardia Airport, he passed first along a dirt path through a large swamp which extended for a couple of miles beyond the school and the railroad tracks, a magical swamp, full of flora and fauna, snakes, small fish, newts darting and red, toads, frogs, and of course tadpoles, rats and muskrats, and a dozen kinds of birds. There were revelations of all kinds in the swamp, including some human revelations. One afternoon, a slightly older and vastly more developed boy, an Italian named Benito who was for some reason known as Patsy, invited a group of school kids, rather mysteriously, into the swamp. Once there, Patsy produced a kind of white rubber tube, donned it, masturbated into it, and filled it. This astonishing feat provided subject matter for a week of schoolyard discussion.

If you continued on past the swamp toward North Beach, you next came to a golf driving range, a Depression institution patronized by golfers who were too broke to play on a regular course—there were caddy and green fees even on the public courses. For a quarter, a golfer could get a tin pail full of golf balls and drive them off a dirt tee into a meadow. There were markers out there: 100 yards, 150 yards, 200 yards. It was not much, but it was something.

Beyond the driving range was a place called Holmes Airport. Mr. Holmes himself existed, but he seemed to be in some sort of trouble with the law or something, because he seldom came to the airport, and when he did, he stayed only for a few minutes. Once he wore a handkerchief tied over his lower face like a mask. Maybe he was crazy. But on his oiled-dirt runways you could see close up the small planes of 1940, the lacquered canvas over the wooden frames, monoplanes and also biplanes with their struts, and of course the new pioneer of recreational flying, the Piper Club, price $500. There were parachute jumps on Sunday afternoons and visits by the Goodyear blimp, rides $5. Once his grandfather plunked down $10, and he rode in the blimp along with his mother. The cabin held a dozen or so people, and when the seat belts were fastened, the men outside on the ground let go of the lines, and the blimp rose slowly up into the air. At a couple of hundred feet, the pilots started the motors, and the blimp moved forward now, still rising. It crossed Queens and flew over the Queensboro Bridge and down Manhattan, higher than the Empire State Building now and out over New York Harbor past the Statue of Liberty. There was Brooklyn down there and Ebbetts Field and Prospect Park. Then it was over Sheepshead

Bay and the New York beaches, Breezy Point, Riis Park, the Rocka-
ways. People were tiny on the beach, the blue water breaking white
on the shore. There were ships on the horizon and the New Jersey
shore in the distance. Coney Island was off to the left, the roller
coaster curling its long structure, the Ferris wheel turning lazily.
Then you were back at Holmes Airport.

Beyond Holmes's modest establishment, a different kind of airport altogether was growing up along the shore of North Beach. It
was fun to bike over there, packing a couple of sandwiches, and
watch the steam shovels and earth movers and the great barges
coming in with landfill. Mayor LaGuardia had wanted to have the
airport ready by the time the World's Fair opened in the spring of
1939, and the mayor even operated the steam shovel that heaved the
first dirt on September 9, 1937. At the turn of the century, North
Beach had been an amusement park, a mini Coney Island. During
the 1920s, the Curtiss Wright Corporation operated it as a private
airport for wealthy Long Island sports fliers. During the early
Depression years, Curtiss Wright fell on hard times, and in 1935 the
City acquired the land. Mayor LaGuardia, a bundle of executive
energy, wanted to bring jobs and enterprise to New York, and he
began pushing the Works Progress Administration to build a major
international airport in North Beach. Numerous LaGuardia committees issued reports demonstrating the superiority of the location to
that of the already existing airport in Newark, New Jersey. North
Beach was closer to midtown Manhattan. Bowery Bay and Long
Island Sound were perfect for the great Boeing flying boats. A
master of publicity, LaGuardia dramatized his case by refusing to
disembark from a passenger plane in Newark, insisting on flying on
to New York, the sole remaining passenger on the flight. In September 1937, President Roosevelt gave his approval to the project, but
though 23,000 men worked triple shifts, the airport did not make it
in time for the World's Fair.

The buildings were designed by the architectural firm of Delano
and Aldrich, the design inspiration art deco. The boy saw them go
up. The three-story administration building had buff-colored face
brick and black brick trimming. The marquee in front was made of
stainless steel. The facade had tall, wrought-iron-framed windows
with stainless-steel grilles. Inside the marble-floored rotunda were
the ticket counters and the passenger waiting areas, flight-control
and weather offices, and the Kitty Hawk circular restaurant that
immediately became a fashionable place to go for lunch or dinner.
The french windows of the restaurant opened onto LaGuardia Terrace and open-air dining.

The airport finally opened on October 15, 1939, one of those perfect cool and crisp days of a New York autumn. Some 325,000 people were on hand, not only Americans but aviation and commercial people from Canada, Europe, and South America. Seven gleaming new DC-3s stood on the apron, and one of Pan Am's huge Clippership Flying Boats rocked gently at anchor in Bowery Bay. Squadrons of army and navy planes roared overhead, as the dignitaries made short speeches. Mayor LaGuardia bounced around everywhere, smiling and shaking hands. The president of American Airlines, C. R. Smith, said that the airport was "the world's greatest development in civil aviation since Lindbergh flew the Atlantic." The war in Europe was six weeks old, but both Mayor LaGuardia and Postmaster General James A. Farley declared firmly that this airport would be used only for peaceful purposes. "It is fortunate for us here in the United States," said Farley, "that we can gather to dedicate an airport of this character to the pursuits of peace without thought of war, of conquest, of the dread possibility of armed conflict." But Farley hinted that the airport might indeed have a military capacity. "This airport," he said, "is a strong guarantee of the nation's peace and safety." In short, it was a weapon. Mayor LaGuardia also stressed peace. The World War I fighter pilot declared in his piping little voice that "we are dedicating a giant airport to peace, to bring tidings of happiness to commerce, and friendly relations with all the countries whose planes will land at this airport."

At that moment, the airport was called New York City Municipal Airport. But as the diminutive mayor spoke, three planes flying above began to skywrite "Name It LaGuardia Airport." A tremendous cheer went up from the crowd. Two weeks later the New York Board of Estimate and the City Council unanimously added "LaGuardia Field" to the original title. LaGuardia, said the resolution, "conceived the idea of this great airport and . . . was solely responsible for its development." By 1940, LaGuardia Airport was the busiest in the world, an enormous commercial success and a prime tourist attraction. All that could be seen ahead were blue skies and limitless horizons.

The most glamorous installation at the airport was the low circular building at the western end called the Pan Am Terminal, today known as the Marine Air Terminal. This was where you boarded the most elegant passenger planes in the history of aviation, the great Pan Am flying boats. The terminal was the first major international air gateway, home of the giant Boeing B-314 planes, which were housed nearby in a hangar the size of two football fields.

They gave you guided tours, which were fun to take. As you approached the entrance of the terminal, you walked toward a marquee made of stainless steel. Inside the glass doors you could see a stainless-steel staircase. A frieze of flying fish encircled the exterior of the building. Within you found a circular ticket counter in the rotunda, passenger lounges, customs offices.

Circling the interior of the terminal near the ceiling were the twelve-foot murals of James Brooks, a superb period-piece of Depression-era optimism called *Flight*. It was the largest and last mural of the fine arts program of the WPA. *Flight* is divided into three large sections. In the first we see early, earthbound man, oppressed by natural disasters and dreaming of escape through a life after death in the heavens. The dream turns into Icarus, son of Daedalus, who is shown soaring in the air and then tumbling to earth, his waxed wings melted by the heat of the sun. Next, a large figure stands contemplating the mysteries of the heavens, a religious censer in one hand, the other hand indicating various early imaginary aircraft. At the right end of the first panel Leonardo da Vinci launches a model aircraft of his own design, while an apprentice studies the motions of a bird's wings. Next we see ancient towers and tall modern buildings, meant to represent man's skyward aspirations, and various shapes with air currents moving around them, culminating in the Pan Am flying boats. We see Wilbur and Orville Wright testing models of aircraft, then other scenes of the earliest manned flight. A large male and female welcome the flight of a flying boat as a group of flight engineers performs the calculations necessary for such modern aviation.

James Brooks's *Flight* is a magnificent work of art, evocative of its historical moment. The figures are Depression-heroic, with thick necks and limbs, oddly suggestive more of physical than of mental power, but with a Faustian sense of man's possibility. Some mystery surrounds the fact that, in a 1952 renovation, the murals were painted over, probably just an act of careless philistinism. More than half of all the thousands of murals painted by WPA artists in post offices, libraries, and schools have also been destroyed, perhaps because they were judged old-fashioned. In 1979, however, the Brooks murals were uncovered and restored through some large private donations, and today they can be viewed in their original splendor.

On March 31, 1940, the first of the great flying boats took off from LaGuardia, with the mayor on hand to read a message from President Roosevelt. Slowly gathering speed out in the bay, lifting on to its step as the four engines growled, the *Yankee Clipper* lifted off Long Island Sound, Captain Charles A. Lorber in command, with a crew of ten, nine passengers, and 5,000 pounds of mail, heading for Lisbon, where it would land in the harbor 21 hours and 56 minutes later.

These flying boats were not the mass-travel, tightly packed flights we know today. It was more like travel on an ocean liner. On a typical flight, as departure time approached in the terminal, passengers and crew readied themselves in the rotunda beneath the Brooks murals. Champagne corks popped. When it was time to leave for Lisbon, Miami, or Buenos Aires, two bells rang, and the crew marched down the dock to the waiting seaplane. A few minutes later, the bells rang again, this time for the passengers. The four engines coughed and started, gradually building to a roar as the mooring lines were cast off, and the plane, led by a speedboat, moved through the waters of the bay, under the Whitestone Bridge and out into Long Island Sound. Then, in a spray of white water, the great ship took off.

The passengers inhabited spacious accommodations on two decks. The forward passenger lounge held ten people in what amounted to a living room, complete with large, comfortable, upholstered chairs. The other four lounges were similar. Meals were served by waiters in white jackets on tables that had white tablecloths, crystal, and silver. The deluxe buffet was famous for its high quality. There were cocktails and a variety of wines with meals. You went to sleep in a Pullman-style, double-decker bed.

Now, if that did not quite come up to your notion of elegance, and if you were not fussy about price, you could travel in a completely appointed private suite located near the rear of the plane—lounge, bathroom, desk, chairs, bed, all meals served in the suite. Flying down to Rio, all the women felt like Rita Hayworth, all the men like Glenn Ford.

In 1940, everything changed for the boy's architect-father as the nation intensified its buildup for war. The architect had a college classmate who was a business associate of Joseph Kennedy, who was tightly wired in to the Roosevelt administration. Kennedy was up to his ears in defense contracts, including coastal defense installations along the New England coast—as if Hitler were going to land there. Millions of dollars were pouring into the economy, obliterating the Depression. The architect and a dozen others gathered with Joseph Kennedy in his suite at the Roosevelt Hotel in Manhattan. For some reason, the ten-year-old boy was along, and soon bored. Kennedy noticed this and instructed one of his numerous lieutenants to "take the kid down the street" to the Radio City Music Hall for whatever movie happened to be playing there. It turned out to be *Pinocchio*.

Of course, there was a huge line stretching along Sixth Avenue, around the corner, and down the side street. But the Kennedy lieutenant went right to the box office; the manager appeared and was told that "Mr. Kennedy" wanted the boy to go right into the theater. Which he did. That is when he learned about power.

His mother hated the whole idea of the war and tried not to think about it. Back in the 1920s, she had been on the Broadway stage, playing in the Music Box Revue, the Ziegfield Follies, and big musicals like *Poppy* and *Showboat*. She knew W. C. Fields, Irving Berlin, and Billy Gaxton, among others. After the First World War, she and the other theater people would entertain the men in the veterans' hospitals, and they were all—perhaps she especially— horrified with what they saw left over from the Argonne and Belleau Wood. There were men with faces shot away, men without limbs, men paralyzed, men trying to breathe with half a lung as a result of the gas. Nothing was worth that, she thought. She and her husband had known Lindbergh during the early thirties and had gone to parties at his Hopewell Place. He was known as "Slim" in those days. And later, she especially admired Lindbergh's efforts to keep America neutral in the European war. Of course, all that changed the next year on the day the boy was playing with his red scooter outside the house while his father was inside listening to a professional football game, the Giants playing the Brooklyn Dodgers, and the game was suddenly interrupted with the announcement that the Japanese had bombed Pearl Harbor.

Tennis Apollo

By 1940, no one any longer expected Frank Shields to win the National Championships. Don Budge had overtaken him, then Bobby Riggs and Don McNeill, but it was said on the verandas of Newport and Southampton that Shields could beat anyone on a given day. Shields had been the bad golden boy of the 1930s, the last years of the great grass-court tournaments and of the glittering world of Newport, Longwood, Spring Lake, Seabright, South Orange, South-ampton, and Forest Hills. In that part of the thirties, the Depression was an unpleasant rumor: the music would always play, and the booze and the money would always flow.

Frank Shields's father was an accountant, his grandfather a saloon keeper, but the boy was also of the magical tribe of Bevil Rudd, the legendary Oxford undergraduate of the 1890s who, strolling by the university track one afternoon, put down his derby and cigar, broke the world quarter-mile record, returned his derby and cigar to their former localities, and never ran again.

Shields was a similarly endowed natural athlete, astonishingly quick and strong, a schoolboy baseball and basketball player as well as a tennis player. At 6-foot-6, he was drop-dead handsome, a dark Apollo. Yale wanted him for a pass-catching end, but he was academically impossible, and even tutoring proved futile. By the time he was seventeen, in the late 1920s, he swept all before him at tennis and began to be called "the second Tilden" by the sportswriters. In 1933, he was ranked number one in the United States and may well have been the best in the world, with a serve that was virtually unreturnable and a forehand much like Boris Becker's current top-spin bludgeon.

Shields's startling good looks did not appeal only to women; the great Tilden seems to have been in love with him. When Shields was rising in tennis, his father warned him not to go near "that man." Once, during an interminable match with Tilden at Forest Hills, Shields fell to the turf with leg cramps. Tilden walked over to him, threw his sweater on Shields's legs, and said, "Come on, Frankie, get better," then walked back to his own end of the court. Tilden took the last two sets of that match, 14–12, 6–4.

The trouble with Shields was that, like Bevil Rudd, he did not take athletic success seriously. Perhaps it came too easily for him. Parties, women, booze, and hijinks were as important as tennis titles, as important even as Wimbledon and Forest Hills, and Shields was the heavyweight champion of the nightclub brawl: "SHIELDS SERVES BLACK EYE." The British designer, Teddy Tinling, recalls the atmosphere during the thirties at Newport, the tournament and the parties that led up to the climactic Forest Hills. It was the "complete Gatsby era," with three or four orchestras on the lawn of each of the great Newport mansions. "Everybody was wild. The only thing that mattered was to get smashed and laugh." One night Shields dove out of the crow's nest of a yacht into Newport Harbor. He had the constitution of a horse and could play a five-set match after an all-nighter, and at the end of a day's tennis, he usually changed straight into his tuxedo.

In 1931, Shields became the only player in history to fail to show up for a Wimbledon final, against his crony Sidney B. Wood. This was a murky episode, in which legend has it that Shields was busy investigating the attributes of a matched pair of French countesses; the truth is, probably, that he defaulted because he had badly twisted his leg the day before in a match against Jean Borotra, though the two explanations are not mutually exclusive. In June 1933, after losing unexpectedly in the quarter-finals of the French championships and scheduled to play in Germany, Shields disappeared: "SHIELDS DISAPPEARS. TENNIS PLAYER DROPS OUT OF SIGHT IN PARIS." He had accompanied some friends on the boat train to Le Havre, champagne all the way, and woke up at sea on the *Warren Harding* with no possessions and no money, only his tuxedo. But for all that, this great tennis dilettante was right up there with Ellsworth Vines, Wilmer Allison, Sidney Wood, John Doeg, Don Budge, and the leading players of the thirties.

When he played in Los Angeles, the screams of the schoolgirls every time he hit the ball attracted the attention of the Hollywood moguls, and he got a lucrative movie contract. He failed as a screen sex object but had a wild time in Hollywood with such natural allies as Errol Flynn, Johnny Weissmuller, and Charlie Chaplin. He made a fortune in business and of course spent it, but continued to play topflight tennis until the war intervened. After slugging an officer of the day, he could have been shot but got a less-than-honorable discharge, and after the war continued to star in men's singles, playing Pancho Segura, even beating the better players, and finally, in his last appearance at Forest Hills, carrying the rising star Fred Kovaleski to five sets amid the hosannas of the sportswriters.

He always preserved the older grand style—long white trousers—from his glory days of the 1930s and never succumbed to the practicality of shorts. When back pains forced him to give up serious tennis, he became court tennis champion at the exclusive Racquet and Tennis Club in New York, though he was once suspended by the club for throwing peanuts at a member, the offense a serious one only because the peanuts' heavy glass bowl accompanied them in flight.

His later years were not funny. When drunk, which was frequent, he became coldly destructive and bullying with his strength. During his third marriage, recalls his son William, "A local doctor who was a good friend gave Mum a bottle of chloral hydrate and said she should put it in Pop's drink whenever the tribal drums began to call him. The idea was to knock him out. Well, it had no effect in his first drink, nor in the second. Finally when he was halfway through the third, which should have worked on an elephant, he said, 'This drink tastes awful.' With that, he left the house to find someone who could make him a decent drink. The man was amazing."

Local police protected him and got him to bed from Southampton to Palm Beach, despite his brawls and car crashes. All three of his wives loved him but could not stand him. "Children and Frank had a natural affinity," writes Number Three in a fond preface to a recent biography of him, "and much the same point of view."

After two heart attacks and a stroke, Frank Shields was dead of a third heart attack at sixty-five in a Manhattan taxi. Not long before he died, he phoned his son Frank with the message "The kid is gone." What? "The kid is gone." Frank met his father, who took him to a Catholic church. Someone had stolen the Christ child out of a Nativity scene. The kid was gone. "Come on," said Shields, "let's go have a drink."

His story has recently been told artlessly and with love by his son William, who saw beyond the multiple outrages to the core of innocence within the great athlete they often called The Jolly Schoolboy.

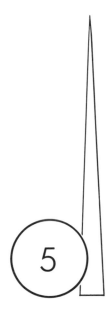

5

In 1940, people did not go to see a movie. They went to the movies, millions of people as a matter of habit and on a regular basis. That year some 80 million tickets were bought each week, 65 percent of the population. As the decade of the 1980s commenced, the statistics told the story of a change in our behavior. Each week about 20 million tickets were sold, about 10 percent of the population. With the spread of VHS and HBO and, of course, the ubiquity of television, there are plenty of explanations for the change. There may also be a further, simpler explanation. It is possible that movies were better then, before they became "films."

During the decade of the 1930s, the enormous demand for movies meant a vast number of neighborhood theaters, and this in turn meant the mass production of movies to keep pace with the demand. In Hollywood, this resulted in the "studio system," the vast and busy assembly lines of movie production that rolled out the movies to supply the voracious appetites of the theaters. Hollywood was the only major American industry that flourished throughout the Great Depression, that, indeed, seemed to wax and grow fat during those lean years. It provided the pictures, but it was also alert in the American way to the "bargain," the double feature, two pictures for the price of one, and often the theaters offered games—Keno, Bingo, Screeno—between the pictures. Adults could go home with a set of dishes or a vacuum cleaner.

On Saturday afternoons, the local Deluxe, Earle, Valencia, or Loews throbbed with children, admitted for a dime, barely controllable by the white-dressed matrons who patrolled the aisles with flashlights. Occasionally a matron would swoop down upon an urchin who had flung a wad of half-chewed bubblegum and expel the wretch from the theater. The hubbub usually continued through the shorts and previews; the cartoons like *Popeye, Woody Woodpecker, Bugs Bunny,* and *Tom and Jerry;* and the suspense serials like *Batman* or *Dick Tracy* or *The Revenge of the Mummy.* Then things calmed down for the main pictures, *Son of Frankenstein, Wings of the Navy, Behind the Rising Sun.* After about four hours in the magical dark, you emerged blinking into the hard glare of late Saturday afternoon.

Glittering off in the metropolis were movie emporia vastly different from the neighborhood theaters with their matrons and dishes and flung bubblegum, movie theaters like Moorish castles with fountains in the lobby and box seats like those in opera houses. It was in these that you saw first-run movies like *The Grapes of Wrath, For Whom the Bell Tolls, The Great Dictator, Fantasia, Pinocchio.* Perhaps the fanciest of the great movie houses were those built by Samuel L. Rothafel, whose nickname was Roxy. His ushers wore silk uniforms that matched the carpets and were a reflection of the theater's architectural motif. The walls of the theaters were decorated with ornate carvings in brass or wood. Gargoyles stared down from the balconies; plaster statues of Greek nudes gazed down from trellised cupolas. New York's Radio City Music Hall was the last and largest of Roxy's mammoth creations. Sid Grauman, the West Coast's version of Roxy, built a huge theater in the Chinese mode, complete with a pagoda roof and oriental carvings.

The great, urban movie palaces in 1940 were not only the scene of the first-run major pictures. Beginning in the late 1930s, they had also been the home of a new phenomenon, the Big Band and a new music called "swing." Long before dawn on a cold 1938 day, mobs of adolescents began lining up outside the Paramount Theater in Times Square, filling the streets, jostling with police, blocking traffic. Some 3,000 of them got into the cavernous theater, and when the early movie was over, a platform rose majestically out of the orchestra pit. As the band blazed away, the teenagers began dancing in the aisles. The interior of the theater became a riot, which spread to the sidewalks outside. Benny Goodman wielded his clarinet, and his big band was playing swing.

Actually, swing was a modified jazz revival and, in part, a reaction against the syrupy sweetness of bands like Guy Lombardo's. "Dangerously hypnotic," a psychologist informed alarmed parents, as little girls in towns across America in loose skirts and saddle shoes jitterbugged in high school gyms and ice-cream parlors and poured their nickels into jukeboxes. Goodman was the "King of Swing," always near the top of the *Hit Parade*'s weekly "top ten," but always challenged by Tommy Dorsey, with his slide trombone and brassier sound; by Harry James, who had broken with Goodman in 1939 and taken his trumpet solos to his own big band; by Count Basie and by Duke Ellington, with his sophisticated "jungle music" jazz; and of course by Glenn Miller and his famous unique "sound," the product of a fast tempo and lead clarinets.

To some, the hard-driving swing rhythms seemed menacing. The *New York Times* thought the craze was getting out of hand. The new rhythms may indeed have reflected the accelerating pace of history, a desperate sense of the need to live now, as the country—or at least its younger generation—danced away the night with the Lindy Hop, the Black Bottom, the Shag, the Big Apple, the Charleston. A swing devotee was an "alligator," a female singer a "canary," musicians "cats," a clarinet a "licorice stick," and a trumpet was usually played by a "liver lips." If you didn't dig it, you were "ickie" or maybe a "longhair." The year 1940 began to seem like a speeded-up film, as if with the foreknowledge that Glenn Miller would go down mysteriously over the English Channel in 1944. Apparently his small plane was hit when returning RAF bombers jettisoned their unused bombs.

It is one of the paradoxes of our culture that the mass-production "studio system" produced so many memorable artistic achievements between 1920 and 1945. Scott Fitzgerald, Aldous Huxley, Nathanael West, William Faulkner, and other talented writers hated the studio system, believing that it crushed all individual creativity, and from the perspective of the *writer,* they were undoubtedly correct. In the process of development, a movie traveled through an elaborate system, from department to department, from story idea to completed script, and often landed in finished form on the director's desk on the day of shooting. Many pictures were shot in a week and then went to the cutting department, which edited the movie into its final form, overseen by the producer. In fact and legend, many good things ended up on the cutting-room floor for artistic, moral, and other reasons. After the cutting was complete, the movie went to the distribution office, and from there to the chains of theaters across the country, which were owned by the studio. The great studios very much resembled their contemporary Ford River Rouge automobile assembly line outside Detroit.

Despite the obvious tension that existed between system and creativity under such circumstances, a number of factors made for great movies. Of the some 7,500 feature movies produced between 1930 and 1945, the most memorable 200 or so were shaped by about two dozen powerful and individualistic directors. Movie historians have also made a suggestive comparison between the "star system" of the great Hollywood studios and the repertory companies of the old theater. Shakespeare's and Marlowe's audiences came to see the plays, of course, but also Richard Burbage or Will Kemp, and later David Garrick. Such actors appeared over and over again, in a variety of roles, but within a broad framework of typecasting. The Hollywood studio similarly had a stable of regulars whose presence on the screen was at least as important as the movie they were in. People went to see Mickey Rooney, Errol Flynn, Ingrid Bergman, Humphrey Bogart, Rita Hayworth, Clark Gable, Judy Garland, Fred Astaire. Moviegoers also saw these distinctive stars frequently. They performed far more often than our contemporaries like Robert Redford or Meryl Streep and became much more constant presences in the lives of the audience. When Humphrey Bogart made *The Maltese Falcon* for Warner Brothers in 1941, he had already performed in 34 movies in a period of five years. He had played a convict in 9, had been electrocuted or hanged in 8, and had been riddled with bullets in 13. Part of the excitement of *The Maltese Falcon* was seeing Bogart move into new territory partially connected with the old, changing from small-time loser to private detective Sam Spade, tough but worldly, very much his own man, but possessed of a professional code of honor in an amoral criminal environment.

By the time Humphrey Bogart faced Ingrid Bergman on the set of *Casablanca,* he was an established screen presence. Born in New York in 1899, he was the son of one of the city's most eminent surgeons and an artistic mother. He went to the high-quality Trinity School and then the prestigious Phillips Academy in Andover, Massachusetts, but was expelled for bad behavior and joined the Marines in 1918. Mustered out after several months, he tried his hand at acting, initially without much success, but he persevered in minor roles on the Broadway stage and in inconsequential Hollywood movies. Things changed dramatically for the better in 1935 when he played the gangster Duke Mantee opposite Leslie Howard in Robert Sherwood's *The Petrified Forest,* which ran for more than seven months on Broadway. When Warner Brothers made the movie version of the play, Leslie Howard insisted that Bogart costar. For the next ten years he worked for Warner, typecast as a bad guy and a loser, usually in a supporting role under stars like Edward G. Robinson and George Raft. In *They Drive by Night* (1940), Bogart expanded a bit beyond his typecast loser roles and played a truck driver contending with the recognizable and sympathetic problems of fatigue and poverty. The next year, when George Raft turned down the lead role in *High Sierra,* Bogart was chosen, and in the role of Roy Earle, an aging and disillusioned gangster, revealed a pathos and complexity which went far beyond the requirements of the plot.

The full Bogartian character, however, emerged only with the Sam Spade of *The Maltese Falcon.* The private detective Spade is virile, independent, loyal to his own code, contemptuous of the police but disgusted by stupidity and evil, and he conceals his romantic vulnerability under a tough-guy exterior. The Bogartian hero owes much to the Hemingway ethos, either directly or transmitted through the hard-boiled fiction of Dashiell Hammett. Directed by John Huston, the movie surrounded Bogart with an ideal supporting cast: Sidney Greenstreet, the "fat man"; the Hungarian-born Peter Lorre, at sixty-two playing his first movie role as the oily Joel Cairo; and Mary Astor in her last major role as the psychotic murderer Brigid. "The trick is in the casting," Huston once said, and the chemistry worked here. Bogart, Lorre, and Greenstreet returned in *Casablanca,* with the stunning addition of Ingrid Bergman.

It is an interesting coincidence that Bogart and Bergman, forever linked in *Casablanca,* were also linked in death. Both died of cancer. By the time of *The Harder They Fall* (1956), Bogart exhibited the ravages of the disease, though it had not yet been diagnosed. His voice was huskier than usual, and his haggard face had to be touched up on the celluloid. He died two years later, emaciated, in a wheelchair, stoic and genial to the end, as Rick Blaine would have been. In 1974, Bergman dangerously postponed a needed mastectomy because of movie commitments, but finally had the operation in June at the London Clinic. The cancer slowly spread. She made *Autumn Sonata* and *A Woman Called Golda.* Knowing that she was dying, she intermittently considered suicide. On Saturday morning, August 28, 1982, getting out of her bath in her London townhouse, she felt a terrible pain in her back. The cancer had invaded her spine, collapsing the twelfth vertebra. By Sunday morning, her right lung had failed, and the left lung was only partially functional. She drank some champagne in bed, smiled at friends, and died that afternoon with tiny beads of blood on her lips.

After lunching with the young Ingrid Bergman, one of her friends remarked that it was like sitting across the table from a talking orchid. American audiences first became aware of her in 1940. She had been a popular young stage and screen star in Sweden, had starred in German movies, and was a friend of Josef Goebbels, who controlled the Nazi film industry. Even in the midst of making *Gone With the Wind*, twenty-six-year-old David O. Selznick was restlessly alert for new stars and fresh stories. He ordered his International Studios organization to be on the lookout for foreign talent. The Swedish version of *Intermezzo* had opened in 1937 at the Cinema de Paris in New York, and Ingrid Bergman had made a major impression on American critics. "It is poignant, full of pathos," observed *Variety*, "and above all has shown in Ingrid Bergman a talented, beautiful actress. Miss Bergman's star is destined for Hollywood." Selznick did not see *Intermezzo* for more than a year after it opened in the United States, but when he did see it, he instructed his organization that he wanted the story, the director, and "the girl."

As the war in Europe was breaking out, Selznick's representatives journeyed to Sweden and tried to sign Bergman. She was recalcitrant, explaining that she was still under contract to Goebbels's UFA studio. But Selznick, needing a major picture to fill the gap between *Gone With the Wind* and the projected *Rebecca*, was insistent. He needed *Intermezzo* for an American remake, and he needed a new star, someone fresh and different. Finally, Bergman signed a contract for $2,500 a week for eight weeks. She refused to change her name to something more glitzy. She took lessons in English. Beneath her demure manner, she was extremely tough and professional. She vetoed Charles Boyer for the male lead, insisted on Leslie Howard, and got him. When *Intermezzo* opened at the Radio City Music Hall in the fall of 1939, the critics were not especially enthusiastic about the picture, but Ingrid Bergman herself was a different matter altogether. Frank S. Nugent of the *New York Times* wrote that "there is that incandescence about Miss Bergman, that spiritual spark which makes us believe that Selznick has found another great lady of the screen." Nugent found her to be "beautiful; not in any stylistic sense, through perfection of feature or the soft-focus lens, but in her freshness, serenity, and (misused word) wholesomeness." Howard Barnes of the *New York Herald Tribune* called Bergman "the most gifted and attractive recruit the studios have enlisted abroad for many moons." In the *New York Daily News,* Wendy Hale commented that "it is extremely unfair to call her a second Garbo, just because she hails from Sweden. She has a combination of rare beauty, freshness, vitality and ability that is as uncommon as a century plant in bloom."

On January 2, 1940, Bergman sailed from Genoa on the ocean liner *Rex*, waving goodbye to her dentist husband, Peter Lindstrom, and carrying in her arms her infant daughter Pia. Ten days later she

arrived in New York amid a storm of publicity, interviewed by the
major papers, magazines, news services. What were her plans?
Would she play Joan of Arc? She did readings for the radio, appeared on the Broadway stage. Brooks Atkinson wrote about her
"luminous beauty." Christopher Isherwood, meeting her in Hollywood, sized her up as a tough professional: "She was absolutely
charming. In some ways she was the most beautiful woman I ever
met—not that women are my specialty. She wasn't a woman that
you'd spend time with unless you were involved with her. She had a
certain aspect of her that was almost masculine. She was so professional. When studio people would pinch her ass or something, she
would give them a dry smile as if they were men in a locker room."

Selznick thought Bergman would be perfect as Maria in the movie
of *For Whom the Bell Tolls,* which she read with the aid of a Swedish-
English dictionary. Hemingway later claimed that he had written the
novel with Bergman in mind as Maria and Gary Cooper as Robert
Jordan, and he mentioned Bergman as the actress to play Maria in
an article in *Life.* They had lunch together in Hollywood, and
Hemingway told her he would not work on the movie unless she got
the part. Selznick cast her as Maria, and the year 1940 saw the
emergence of Ingrid Bergman superstar.

America that year learned to adore her as wholesome and unspoiled, and Selznick fully understood the nature of her peculiar
appeal. Allegedly, he would not allow the makeup squad to touch
her, not even pluck her vigorous eyebrows. The perfection of her
complexion was beyond anything makeup could achieve. In fact, she
used special makeup to cover an uneven complexion and daily
shaved her hairline to create a larger, more intelligent forehead.
Bergman, however, was not virtuous in anything like the conventional sense. She was as complete a professional as Hemingway
himself. She believed that her movie love scenes would have greater
authenticity if she were sleeping with the male lead while making
the movie, and she usually did so. This had little or nothing to do
with love, only with acting. She even slept with Spencer Tracy, when
he was not sleeping with Katharine Hepburn. Soon after her marriage to upright, somewhat boring Peter Lindstrom, she casually
remarked to the startled bridegroom that she thought she would like
to sleep with a man from each of the many human races, no doubt
with some sort of investigation in mind connected with acting.

There was an odd detachment about her in other respects. She
was inclined to honor her German movie contracts, despite Hitler
and the war, until it was explained to her that . . . *this* . . . *was* . . .
impossible. When she left Peter Lindstrom for Rossellini in 1949,
pregnant by Rossellini and leaving Pia behind, she was probably not

(Peter M. Warner)

The Helicline at the Trylon and Perisphere. You walked up it into The World of Tomorrow.

Mayor LaGuardia looks at the future.

Notice the adoration in the crowd.

I'm sitting on top of the world.

FDR is a pretty tough character, too.

(King Features)

FDR on the way to his first of four inaugurals.

(King Features)

Scott Fitzgerald photographed by Carl Van Vechten outside New York City's Algonquin Hotel in 1937.

(King Features)

The sheer kinetic excitement Willkie generated was enormous.

The author and his parents in 1940.

Robert Larrimore "Bobby" Riggs, one of the great players of all time, Wimbledon champion and finalist against Don McNeill in 1940. His athleticism is obvious.

in love with the pudgy Italian roué, but rather professionally excited by the new mode of "Italian realism," of which Rossellini was then one of the masters. She had been overwhelmed by his *Roma: Open City* in 1946. Unfortunately for Bergman, the mode was largely exhausted and produced nothing much of merit after 1949. Rossellini's subsequent movies flopped, though they did influence important younger directors. Bergman dumped Rossellini in a 1957 divorce, returned to the stage, and then won an Academy Award for *Anastasia*. Rossellini made a movie in India and returned to Italy with the wife of an Indian director.

For Bergman, the performance was all. After she had a too-long-delayed mastectomy, Ingmar Bergman wrote her into *Autumn Sonata*, her last great role, as Charlotte, a concert pianist, a perfectionist whose devotion to her art has eliminated everything else from her life. Charlotte has left a chronically ill child in a home and has not visited her healthy child for seven years. She also discovers that she has cancer. In her last movie, *A Woman Called Golda*, she played a Golda Meir who was dying of leukemia. "How much longer do I have?" asked Ingrid-Golda of her doctor, understating the line in a whisper. The director was unable to watch her play the scene, finding it shattering. Bergman could exploit the theatrical potentialities even of her own fatal cancer.

One could argue with some confidence that among Bergman's great performances on the screen the greatest was as Ilsa Lund in *Casablanca*, a movie about the emotions of 1940 that appeared in 1942. She made other memorable movies, but this one somehow adheres to one's nervous system, perhaps because of its 1940 period resonance, perhaps because it engaged themes—in a sense prophetically—that were part of her emotional life. As Norwegian-born Ilsa Lund, she is torn between two differently impressive men, the high-minded, publicly committed, Czech anti-Nazi, played by Paul Henreid, who is her husband, and the tough-on-the-outside, romantic Rick Blaine, played by Humphrey Bogart. The tensions Ilsa Lund must deal with here have a universal quality— romance versus duty, the virtuous versus the fascinating, the public versus the private, principle versus passion. The movie also presents an accurate evocation of the atmosphere of 1940 as France fell and Europeans of many nationalities and purposes pour chaotically into the French colonial city. With its Nazis, Vichy French, Czechs, the Americans Rick and Sam, British, police, DeGaullists, secret police, and soldiers, the movie has the character of a microcosm.

As Hitler launches his *blitzkrieg* against France in the spring of 1940, Ilsa Lund believes that her husband Laszlo has been killed by the Nazis. She has an intense love affair with Rick Blaine in Paris. With the Gestapo in the streets, Rick arranges that they catch the last train to the south. Ilsa, having found that Laszlo is still alive, misses it. Blaine makes it to the enclave of Casablanca in French Morocco, a hotbed of international intrigue, which is run by the Vichy French and the Nazis. Rick becomes the proprietor of the town's hot-spot, the Café Américain, cynical—even devastated— because Ilsa has deserted him. One of the great scenes in the movie is when Ilsa and Laszlo walk into the Café Américain, she in white, her arm in his off-white suited arm. The color symbolism is obvious but effective. The Laszlos need letters of transit to get out of Casablanca on the plane to Lisbon, and the Nazi commander, Major Strasser, plans to prevent any such thing from happening. Of course, all of this is absurd. In real life, Strasser would have murdered Laszlo and probably Ilsa—there could have been no nonsense about that—or the Gestapo would have been told to get rid of Strasser. In the real world of 1940, the Nazis would not have fooled around with the likes of Victor Laszlo. But the powerful, romantic drama of the movie is the choice Ilsa Lund must make between her virtuous, but rather wooden, husband and Rick Blaine, the man she really loves and with whom she had spent her Paris idyll.

One of the strange things about this movie is that the writers and the director made it up as they went along. Paul Henreid and Humphrey Bogart both insisted that they "get the girl," the stereo-typed indication of who was in fact the hero of the picture. Henreid considered himself a romantic hero. Bogart also wanted to end up with the girl. He had created a macho sensation in a scene in *Now, Voyager,* when he had put two cigarettes in his mouth, lit both, and passed one to Bette Davis. Bogart worried that, after a series of strong masculine parts, including *The Maltese Falcon,* he would look too much like a man crying into his drinks over a lost love. Bergman worried about displaying adulterous emotions that her audience would consider immoral. After all, Ilsa Lund was married to Laszlo.

In the end, it all worked magnificently. Bogart, beneath the toughness, displayed a convincing romantic vulnerability. Berg-man's astonishing beauty and voice made it credible that the worldly-wise and alienated Rick would be overwhelmed by her. The two stars made the personal drama powerful, even as Victor Laszlo stood for the public world of invasion and murder and heroic re-sistance to it. When Ilsa Lund and Victor Laszlo first enter the smoky and noisy world of the Café Américain, she notices Rick's black piano player from Paris, Sam. She asks him to "Play it, Sam"—the song "As Time Goes By." Sam's voice registers his awareness of what is happening. He plays, and sings in a throaty way:

> *You must remember this,*
> *A kiss is just a kiss,*
> *A sigh is just a sigh.*
> *The fundamental things remain*
> *As time goes by.*

Bergman's eyes at this point express the entire meaning of the picture—pain, bewilderment, love, doubt. Her look was a metaphor for what millions of people in the real world were feeling at that point, the rending choice between the personal life and the public duty.

Though Bergman and Bogart had not been forced to make such a choice in the world of 1940–42, and Bergman herself was scarcely aware of events outside her acting career, others in the picture knew all about the external reality. Paul Henreid had fled Vienna after the Nazis took it over. Peter Lorre, a Jewish actor, had satirized the Nazis in Berlin and fled for his life. The German actor Conrad Veidt, who played Major Strasser, had fled one jump ahead of the Gestapo. The French technical director, Robert Aisner, had escaped from a German concentration camp.

At the end of *Casablanca,* this exigent public world triumphs over Ilsa's passion for Rick. The Laszlos get the papers and escape to Lisbon on the night flight. Rick and the French policeman, Captain Renault, go off to fight for the Free French. This represented a sharp reversal of the formula Hollywood ending, in which passion always prevails and Rick would have "gotten the girl." Standing there at the airport in a trenchcoat and felt hat, Bogart looks into Bergman's tear-filled eyes. "Look," he says, "I'm no good at being noble, but it doesn't take much to see that the problems of three little people don't amount to a hill of beans in this crazy world. Someday you'll understand that." The ending of *Casablanca* meant: the personal price is going to be terribly painful, but we're all in it for the duration. Bogart finally delivers the next most famous line of the picture: "Here's looking at you, kid."

Hitler's sudden victories in Europe during 1940 had serious implications for Hollywood. As his panzers smashed through the Low Countries that spring, 1,400 theaters immediately closed. This meant a loss of $2.5 million in annual income to Hollywood, which had already suffered serious income losses in Central Europe and

Scandinavia. Fearing the potential economic power of fascism, Louis B. Mayer and other moguls restrained Hollywood's antifascist impulses, though *The Mortal Storm* and *The Great Dictator* did attack fascism directly and *Mrs. Miniver* and other movies showed strong sympathy for the British. The famous *March of Time* newsreels, narrated in syrupy-rich tones by Westbrook Van Voorhees, brought the flash of artillery and the wail of air-raid sirens to the neighborhood screen. For a couple of hours of continuous newsreels, everything from the war to sports and high society, you could visit the Trans-Lux Theater.

If Hitler's advance cost Hollywood a lot of theater income, his rise had poured into Hollywood an extraordinary array of gifted European actors, writers, and directors. Often speaking no English at all, these Germans and Central Europeans ended up under the alien skies of Los Angeles, arriving in a trickle beginning in 1933, rising to a torrent in 1939 and 1940. For most of them, deeply rooted in the culture of the European continent, exile meant a wrenching break with their customary cultural environment, and many of them resisted the breakup to the point of extreme danger. On January 20, 1933, Thomas Mann, the great German novelist who was also a well-informed and sophisticated political intellectual, wrote to a friend: "Yes, things look bad in Germany, but, once again, they are surely not so bad as they look. . . . Germany is big and a love of freedom and rationality are basically more widespread and powerful than the screaming of the ruffians and the know-nothings allows one to think." Mann's Weimar liberal calm would be shattered by history.

He got out early. Traveling abroad as the Nazis consolidated their power, he did not bother to return to Germany for his books and personal effects and ended up in Los Angeles and Princeton. Billy Wilder, a leading German director, fled soon after the Reichstag fire, taking with him $1,000 in hundred-dollar bills. The great modern composer, Arnold Schoenberg, fled first to Paris, then to Hollywood and, shocked by what was happening in Europe, formally embraced Judaism. Close to Mann in Hollywood, Schoenberg would be an important model, along with Nietzsche and Wagner, for the composer Adrian Leverkuhn in Mann's great novel *Doctor Faustus.*

Some expatriated actors and actresses like Charles Boyer, Danielle Darrieux, Simone Simon, and Peter Lorre became successful by exploiting their exotic foreignness. Boyer entered the American consciousness, after a string of low-budget movies, with his 1938 role as the romantic gangster Pepe le Moko in *Algiers*. There entered into popular culture his line epitomizing illicit but widely admired romantic sex: "Come . . . with me . . . to the Casbah."

The composer Arnold Schoenberg, eking out a living in Hollywood by giving music lessons and, by the late thirties, working on avant-garde, twelve-tone-scale music, had a bizarre, but in its way classic, Hollywood-Europe encounter with the great American producer Irving Thalberg. At the end of 1935, Thalberg was working on MGM's movie version of Pearl Buck's *The Good Earth,* a novel about Chinese peasants. In typical Hollywood fashion, it starred Paul Muni, who had been an actor in New York's Yiddish theater, and Luise Rainer, a recent Viennese, in the lead roles. One evening in Hollywood, Thalberg attended a performance of *Verklärte Nacht,* which Schoenberg had written almost forty years earlier when he was still writing in conventional musical styles. Thalberg got the idea that Schoenberg would be just the man to write the background score for *The Good Earth.* His aide, Albert Lewin, broached the idea to Salka Viertel, who was working on an MGM script for Garbo about Marie Walewska, and she pointed out that Schoenberg's recent, atonal music was not what Thalberg could conceivably have in mind, but she arranged an appointment. For once in his life, Thalberg was on time, but the composer got lost in a studio tour. In the event, they got on well, and Schoenberg sketched out some tonal themes that pleased Thalberg. Schoenberg was not the musical purist that legend depicts. The deal foundered on money. Schoenberg demanded $50,000, which was twice what Thalberg was willing to pay, and the composer went back to his music teaching. Gradually Schoenberg made his way in Hollywood, and in 1936 had himself built a handsome house in turn-of-the-century style, lots of marble, in the manner of his Viennese architect friend Adolf Loos.

There had always been a sizable British colony in Hollywood, the jodphur set, but with the clear approach of war, the British arrived in droves. Aldous Huxley found the climate good for his health and went to work for MGM on the script of the movie about Madame Curie. He and his wife lived in Beverly Hills and West Hollywood and enjoyed a quiet social circle of an eclectic sort, including his mystical-spiritual adviser Gerald Heard, Anita Loos, Krishnamurti, and Christopher Isherwood, who arrived in 1939. The British actors and moviemakers who fled to Hollywood were widely condemned at home for not staying to endure the blitz, but one of the most disarming statements arising from the British diaspora was made by the playwright Frederick Lonsdale, who admitted that he was in Hollywood because he was terrified of the war and once announced that he was going to Japan because everyone there was so yellow that he could fade into the crowd.

Alexander Korda's "defection" to Hollywood in 1940 created a great commotion in England, though Korda was only a naturalized British subject and had sound business reasons for moving to the United States, including the presence there of his new wife, Merle Oberon. Korda transferred the production of *The Thief of Baghdad* to America and shot the remaining footage in the Grand Canyon. He proceeded to make *Lydia,* the *Jungle Book,* and *That Hamilton Woman,* the last a piece of rather too blatantly British propaganda about the love affair between Admiral Nelson and Lady Hamilton, which got Korda into trouble with isolationist congressmen in Washington. Admiral Nelson's long speech to the admiralty about the impossibility of making peace by appeasing Napoleon had plain contemporary relevance. Summoned before a succession of Senate committees suspicious of the "neutrality" of British moviemakers, and even suspected of being a British agent, Korda was swimming in deep waters. He was a close friend of Winston Churchill. Had Churchill asked him to go to America and make British propaganda films? He seems to have had connections with William Stephenson, the British spy-master in America. He received a knighthood for unspecified reasons in 1942. But in the event, he was saved by Pearl Harbor. Of course, the pro-British Korda was something of an exception on the Hollywood scene. There was a lot of sympathy for England in Hollywood and a good deal of leftist political feeling, but the controlling vector was succinctly expressed by Sam Goldwyn when he said that "messages are for Western Union."

At the outbreak of the war, Laurence Olivier was just beginning the shooting of *Rebecca,* while his English lover, Vivien Leigh, was finishing up another Selznick movie, *Gone With the Wind.* Encouraged by British officials to remain where they were, both went on to movies at MGM, Olivier to *Pride and Prejudice* (1940), costarring Greer Garson, a recent arrival from England, while Leigh starred in a remake of *Waterloo Bridge.* Then Alexander Korda put them into *That Hamilton Woman,* and, their divorces cleaned up, they married with the Englishman Ronald Colman as best man.

The war tended to consolidate the British colony in Hollywood, which welcomed a stream of fresh arrivals. It included, with comings and goings, Leslie Howard, Alfred Hitchcock, Charles Laughton, Victor McLaglen, Ian Hunter, Ray Milland, C. Aubrey Smith, Merle Oberon, Christopher Isherwood, Frederick Lonsdale, John Van Druten, and Dame May Whitty. The English arrived in Hollywood in a variety of moods. By 1940, Isherwood had given up his belief in Communism. He and Auden had arrived in New York and been celebrated in leftist circles for political beliefs they no longer held. Isherwood was even bored with the fight against fascism. He had been disillusioned by Spain, and one of his former boyfriends had been drafted into the German army. He worked on a variety of scripts for MGM, and his emotional void was soon filled by the mysticism of the Huxley circle and the teachings of the Swami.

The German expatriates in Hollywood formed what amounted to a little Weimar on the West Coast. "I believe," wrote Thomas Mann, "that for the duration of the present European dark age the center of Western culture will shift to America. It is my own intention to make my home in your country, and I am convinced that if Europe continues for a while to pursue the same course as in the last two decades, many good Europeans will meet again on American soil." In this 1938 prediction, Mann was correct. His brother Heinrich and the novelist Lion Feuchtwanger arrived in 1940. Franz Werfel got out of France by crossing the Pyrenees into Spain; on the way, he vowed that if he got out of Vichy France alive, he would write about St. Bernadette of Lourdes. He kept his promise with *The Song of Bernadette*. In Hollywood, where Mann was finishing his epic series of novels about the biblical Joseph (Franklin Roosevelt is in part the model for Mann's Joseph), the rapidly enlarging circle of Weimar Germans included the Werfels (everyone was made to understand that Alma Werfel had previously been married to the composer Gustav Mahler), Bertolt Brecht, Bruno Walter, Otto Klemperer, Otto Preminger, Billy Wilder, Lotte Lehmann, Max Reinhardt.

In the spring of 1940, the exiled Russian and current French citizen Igor Stravinsky settled permanently in Hollywood, joining Schoenberg there, the two greatest composers of the era. Stravinsky had the doubtful pleasure of seeing what Walt Disney had done with the *Rite of Spring* in the movie *Fantasia*.

Three movies released in 1939 remained topics of excited conversation among neighborhood children throughout 1940. Two were horror-thrillers and genuinely frightening to the child mind, and both were superbly cast: *Son of Frankenstein*, with Boris Karloff, perhaps the greatest sinister actor of all time, as the monster, and Basil Rathbone as Baron Frankenstein, and *The Hound of the Baskervilles*, with Rathbone as Sherlock Holmes and Nigel Bruce as the portly and bumbling Watson. The third of those movies has made a contribution to the language. When Saigon was falling in 1973, it was called Fort Zindenouf, after the undermanned Foreign Legion fort, by people who remembered *Beau Geste* from 1939 and 1940.

Coming out of the thirties, the big Hollywood musicals had been a staple. They had sagged briefly at the box office in 1933, but had been revitalized for the mid-thirties by the super-spectaculars in the Busby Berkeley mode, extravaganzas like *Gold Diggers of 1933* and *42nd Street*. As the decade drew to a close, however, the extravaganzas began to lose their appeal. Other thirties musical pictures also began to seem passé. The hit team of Ginger Rogers and Fred Astaire broke up in 1939, despite the brilliance of their last movie, *The Story of Vernon and Irene Castle*. Fading by the end of the decade were the suave elegance and deco chic of the earlier thirties. The singing team of Nelson Eddy and Jeannette MacDonald had sung at each other in a series of costume period-pieces, and they did outlast the decade, but that mode was exhausted too, and they broke up after the failure of *I Married an Angel* in 1942.

Hollywood needed to come up with a new formula and proceeded to do so: youth, plus popular, classic comedies. Deanna Durbin proved to be a teenage sensation with a strong voice of operatic quality in *Three Smart Girls* (1937), a low-budget movie that made millions and brought Universal Studios back from the brink of bankruptcy. The new formula proved successful well into the forties, with a string of hits often involving a struggle between the classics and low-brow "democratic" music, in which people like José Iturbi finally broke down and showed that they were good guys under it all by playing boogie-woogie or "cutting a rug," as people said then. The gimmick of "jazzing the classics" produced a number of box-office successes starring Mickey Rooney and Judy Garland, beginning with *Babes in Arms* (1939). One of the best was *Strike Up the Band* (1940), the "plot" of which revolved around Rooney's effort to get his high school band to a national contest. In "the sketches and musical numbers," wrote one New York critic, "the film goes into high gear and Mr. Rooney et al. are at the top of their form. Call him cocky and brash, but he has the sort of exuberant talent that keeps your eyes on the screen, whether he's banging the trap drums, prancing through a Conga, or hamming the old ham actors. The music is rollicking, especially 'Strike Up the Band,' and 'La Conga,' sung with a good deal of animal spirits by Miss Garland."

Other with-it teams, like Donald O'Connor and Peggy Ryan, were popular too. Eleanor Powell, considered by many the best tap dancer in the world, was not much as an actress, but her machine-gun, tap-dancing sequences held audiences through many weak vehicles. In 1940, MGM teamed her with Fred Astaire in *Broadway Melody,* in which they performed to Cole Porter music with a sense of style and a brilliant technical accomplishment rarely achieved in Hollywood. Their long "Begin the Beguine" sequence was one of the high points. In 1940's *Tin Pan Alley,* Betty Gable—soon to be G.I. Joe's favorite pinup—danced along with Alice Faye, and the two of them provided plenty of raw sex appeal.

The most famous movie comedy team of 1940 consisted of Bob Hope, Bing Crosby, and Dorothy Lamour in the famous "Road" series. Paramount had grabbed Crosby in 1932 after he had become an immediate success with his own radio program. Crosby's relaxed charm, and what at least appeared to be his completely effortless crooning, made him the star of a number of Paramount musicals, the most notable being *Rhythm on the River* (1940) and *The Birth of the Blues* (1941). Crosby and Hope were golfing cronies, and the idea of the "Road" movies was born on the golf course one day when the two made a foursome with Hollywood producer Harlan Thompson and director Victor Schertzinger. Crosby and Hope were so spontaneously funny on the golf course that the two along with them agreed that they would make a great movie comedy team. Sexy Dorothy Lamour completed the equation.

Paramount had an old, frequently doctored script of *The Road to Singapore,* and the virtuoso performance of the trio turned this dog-eared property into a $1.5 million money-maker in 1940 and led to the most successful comedy series in the history of Hollywood. Hope and Crosby had established a comic rivalry on their radio shows—as had Jack Benny and Fred Allen—and this fictitious rivalry provided many of the gag themes for the "Road" movies, as the two comics competed for the sexy affections of Lamour. They joked about waistlines, hairlines, ski-shoot noses, and big ears. Hope brought his own ace gag writers to Hollywood, the best in the business. He and Crosby would stroll onto the set as the cameras rolled and casually reel off a firecracker string of new jokes that were not in the script. These performances were often spoiled by the background laughter of cameramen and other technicians, but if so, they were redone and gave the movie audience the impression of being at a spontaneous live performance. Songs from the "Road" series made the hit parade—Crosby's "Too Romantic," for example—and Lamour's "Kaigoon" was a sultry favorite. An anticipated ploy with the audiences was the Hope-Crosby "patty-cake, patty-cake, baker's man" routine with which the two bewildered some menacing Oriental or African sucker before socking him in the jaw and escaping from a tight spot. "Professor" Jerry Colonna, from Hope's radio show, made brief pop-eyed appearances in the "Road" films.

There followed *The Road to Zanzibar* in 1941, in which Hope plays Fearless Frazier the Living Bullet and Crosby his con-man manager. The men patty-cake a slave trader and rescue Lamour from his clutches (her name in the movie is Dotty Latour). Making hilarious fun of the Hollywood jungle epic, Hope wrestles a gorilla. Then *The Road to Morocco* and on from there to *The Road to Hong Kong* in 1962, which failed, despite the help of Frank Sinatra, Joan Collins, Peter Sellers, Dean Martin, and Zsa Zsa Gabor. The gag had grown stale, but after all, it had been around for twenty-two years by then.

Western movies have always been popular, but they experienced a sharp upsurge between 1938 and 1940, partially at the expense of swashbucklers of the *Robin Hood* and *Count of Monte Cristo* type. With war on the horizon and the world full of strange political doctrines, audiences felt a psychological need to return to America, and in particular, to its heroic past of frontier and Indian war. Van Wyck Brooks was writing about the American literary past, Allan Nevins at Columbia about the great American entrepreneurs, and historians were debating the meaning of America and Americanness. The mass-movie audience, less intellectually, felt drawn to the Western. At Warner Brothers, Errol Flynn starred in a series of lavish Westerns—*Dodge City* (1939), *Virginia City* (1940), and *Santa Fe Trail* (1940). Cecil B. De Mille weighed in with *Union Pacific* (1939) and, shifting to Canada, *North West Mounted Police* (1940). Twentieth-Century Fox leaned to vast historical epics like *Brigham Young* (1940), about the founder of Mormonism. MGM's big 1940 Western was *Wyoming*. Even criminals were glamorized if they were Americans, as in *When the Daltons Rode* (1940). David O. Selznick contributed *Duel in the Sun* to the ride-and-shoot scene that year, a Technicolor apocalypse mostly directed by King Vidor. It amounted to pop Wagner with its blood-red sunsets, wild horse chases, abandoned dancing and lovemaking, with a background of lightning flashes and pealing bells. The love affair featured Jennifer Jones as the pouting and sexy half-breed Pearl Chavez and Gregory Peck as Lewt McCanless, macho and all bad, with a cigarette dangling out of the corner of his mouth. After a shoot-out, the two, mortally wounded, crawl across the blood-red rocks to die in each other's arms. There were, to be sure, hilarious takeoffs on the Western craze, like *Buck Benny Rides Again* (1939), starring Jack Benny and Rochester, and *Go West* with the Marx Brothers, a typical Marx Brothers farce in Western getup.

The "Andy Hardy" series with Mickey Rooney and Judy Garland combined comedy, Americana, and music in varying proportions. Garland sang and acted in three of them—*Love Finds Andy Hardy* (1938), *Andy Hardy Meets Debutante* (1940), and *Life Begins for Andy Hardy* (1941)—though the songs were cut from the final version of the last. The "Andy Hardy" series was interrupted in 1939 by the movie that firmly established Garland as a major star and provided her with the song which she used as her theme—and indeed, deepened with meaning—until the end of her life, "Over the Rainbow." Shirley Temple had been intended for the role, but when she proved to be unavailable, Garland was second choice. With Ray Bolger, Bert Lahr, and Jack Haley as the Scarecrow, the Cowardly Lion, and the Tin Man, *The Wizard of Oz* was the finest film fantasy ever made. With its superb sets and more-vivid-than-life color photography, the film's remarkable gallery of fairy-tale characters includes Margaret Hamilton as the Wicked Witch of the West, Billie Burke as the beautiful and lighthearted Good Witch, the Singer Midgets as the Munchkins, Frank Morgan as the all-too-human Wizard, and of course, Judy as the child Dorothy, all wistful longing on the prairie, all wonder and girlish American innocence when swept up into Oz.

At the beginning of 1940, *Gone With the Wind* had moved into the neighborhood theaters, as had Charles Laughton's *Hunchback of Notre Dame,* with Laughton turning in one of his best performances as Quasimodo, the grotesque, but sympathetic, bell-ringing hunchback of the great cathedral, ringing the great bells by swinging back and forth on them himself. Jimmy Stewart was starring in two pictures simultaneously, *Destry Rides Again,* with Marlene Dietrich, and *Mr. Smith Goes to Washington,* about a politically idealistic citizen.

Pinocchio was playing at the Radio City Music Hall, perhaps the best of all Walt Disney's animated movies. Disney had assembled a first-rate team of artists in 1938 and was himself an editor of genius. He launched a series of projects that proved to be stunningly successful. He selected stories that were ageless, from legend and fairy tale, and thus remained fresh for successive generations, beginning with *Snow White and the Seven Dwarfs* (1938) and triumphing technically and artistically with *Pinocchio* in 1940. It cost $2.5 million and contained such brilliant sequences as the opening multi-plane camera shot of Geppetto's village under the starry night, the underwater scenes, and the whale chase; inventive characterizations such as Stromboli, the volcanic puppet-master; the seedy villain, J. Worthington Foulfellow; and Jimminy Cricket, Pinocchio's conscience. Jimminy Cricket's song, "When You Wish Upon a Star," won an Oscar and became one of the big hits of 1940. "Mr. Disney and his men," wrote Frank M. Nugent in the *Times,*

> have been able to gaze into their crystal fantasy and see a world where innocence is not yet lost. The make-believe world they are seeing and letting us see in *Pinocchio* is that

curious part of it inhabited by Geppetto, the woodcarver;
Cleo, his goldfish; Figaro, his kitten; the little puppet who
comes to life; Jimminy Cricket, the puppet's chirping
conscience. . . . In such a world it is not at all strange to find
a cricket wearing spats, carrying an umbrella and sounding
very much like Cliff Edwards. In such a world there is
nothing odd about a coquettish goldfish with cupid-bow lips
and an affectionate nature. In such a world we can only grin a
little, and never would blink in disbelief, at the sight of old
Geppetto fishing for tuna from a ship's rail—Geppetto, the
tuna and the ship's rail all, we might add, being awash in the
belly of Monstro the whale.

Later that spring, Thornton Wilder's *Our Town,* more Americana
on the brink of war, opened in its movie version at Radio City Music
Hall. Enthusiastic audiences and critics alike found it to be not an
ordinary picture at all. The play had opened on Broadway in 1938,
and many found it to be almost unbearably moving in its depiction of
the joys, sorrows, and pathos of ordinary people in a small New
England town. The movie lost nothing of the play's remarkable
power. In the stage version, there was a character called the Stage
Manager who conducted the action of the play. In the movie, he was
replaced by a small-town local druggist who conducts us on a tour
through his rural New Hampshire town. He introduces characters
who speak directly into the camera, and he makes incidental remarks himself. On one occasion, he places his hand before the lens
to stop one sequence and introduce another. The story of a few
people in Grovers Corner, and chiefly of a boy and girl who fall in
love, get married, and have a child, the movie's power lies in its
simplicity. We feel we know these people in their entirety. We see
them in their ordinary daily tasks and sense the extraordinary
power of the ordinary. We see the dream of death and the survival of
the soul which is dreamed by the girl about to have the baby. As one
reviewer said, the movie, in Matthew Arnold's phrase, "brings the
eternal note of sadness in."

The great comedian W. C. Fields was still around in 1940, starring with Mae West in *My Little Chickadee* over at the Roxy. The plot
involves Flower Belle Lee, played by guess-who, a woman married
in name only, for legal reasons, to Cuthbert C. Twillie (Fields). The
two cut a wide swath in the Western gambling town of Greasewood
City, where absolutely every male develops an uncontrollable passion for My Little Chickadee. Fields's Twillie becomes sheriff, tends
bar, lies about his Injun fights and the time he swatted a female
barfly. Everyone enjoyed the boozy Fields, but some critics felt that

Mae West's kidding-of-sex routine had become so broad as to amount to self-parody, and one thought that she herself was getting pretty broad too. Mae West was nearing the end of a great and colorful career, always borderline risqué. Indeed, one of her best ad-libs in an earlier movie had ended up on the cutting-room floor. Confronted by two gunmen, one of whom had a pistol in his pocket, she quipped, "Is that a gun—or are you just glad to see me?"

Northwest Passage, based on a novel by Maine novelist Kenneth Roberts and starring Spencer Tracy, Robert Young, and Walter Brennan, opened at the Capitol early in the year. Tracy played the Indian-fighting hero, Major Robert Rogers of Rogers's Rangers. In 1759 Rogers's Rangers stealthily launched their whaleboats on Lake Champlain at Crown Point and rowed quietly away on a punitive expedition against the Indian village of St. Francis on the St. Lawrence River. They slipped past French ships at the mouth of the river, portaged over a bluff, struggled by foot through swamps and bogs, and then, having bashed the offending Indians severely, back again, fearful of ambush, running out of food, to a prearranged rendezvous at Fort Wentworth on the Connecticut River. Robert Young played a romantic young Harvard student who joins the expedition out of moral conviction, a taste for adventure, and too much hot buttered rum. There were stunning shots of redcoats on parade, Indians in their burning village fighting Rogers's men, silhouettes of boats gliding across the lake in the dark, and red-haired scalps drying on Indian tentpoles. Made long before the current "the Indians were right and we were imperialists" nonsense, the movie was a vigorous portrayal of the heroic and sometimes brutal tactics necessary to build this nation.

The winter months of 1940 also brought forth Edward G. Robinson in the fine biographical movie *Dr. Ehrlich's Magic Bullet.* Critics freely used the word "great" about the picture and compared it in achievement to *The Grapes of Wrath* and *Abe Lincoln in Illinois.* This was not the Edward G. Robinson of *Little Caesar* and other gangster movies, snarling out of the side of his mouth. As Dr. Paul Ehrlich, Robinson wore a beard "almost electric" in its attractiveness and turned in a subtle and powerful performance as the scientist whose formula 606 proved a cure for syphilis. The Hays Office and the Legion of Decency glared over every American director's shoulder in those days, and in this movie, the word for what medical writer Paul de Kruif in his Pecksniffian way described as "the reward of sin" is never mentioned. Most of the movie, in fact, deals with Ehrlich's important work on aniline dyes, his successful attempt to stain the tuberculosis bacillus, his formulation of the "side chain" theory of immunization, and his suspenseful experiments with human subjects that led to the diphtheria antitoxin. Ruth Gordon's Frau Ehrlich was so good that Frank Nugent publicly doubted that they had to "light" her on the set, she supplying her own light in her portrayal of the *hausfrau*. The syphilis cure comes at the end as the climax of a distinguished scientific career, but, Hays Office or no Hays Office, the producers knew where the public interest lay: *Dr. Ehrlich's Magic Bullet*.

In another movie biography, Mickey Rooney played the leading role in *Young Tom Edison,* his performance less Rooneyish than usual, as he made a—on the whole—successful attempt to subordinate himself to the role. The movie covers the early Port Huron years of the future Great Tinkerer. Young Tom, in fact, did dive before an onrushing train to save the life of a telegrapher's young son. He may or may not have prevented a freight train from going to catastrophe on a washed-out trestle, but he does in the movie. In young Tom's earlier years, his father and most of the neighbors thought there was something "addled" about the boy. He spent his money on chemicals. He almost blew up the school with one experiment, almost wrecked a train with a bottle of homemade nitroglycerine, but by sixteen he was clearly on his way to becoming the Sage of Menlo Park and inventor of the glories of the Kinetoscope, the electric light, the phonograph, and much else.

Contemporary history hit audiences hard that spring with the powerful anti-Nazi movie *The Mortal Storm,* based on the best-seller by Phyllis Bottome and starring Margaret Sullavan, Jimmy Stewart, and Robert Young. The story brings the terror into the heart of a peaceful German family. An established but "non-Aryan" professor lives comfortably with his family in a university city, probably Munich. Then Hitler comes to power. Because the professor refuses to deny a scientific fact about human blood, he is sent to a concentration camp. His two stepsons become Nazis, and his home breaks up. The mortal storm is the one raging outside the professor's comfortable bourgeois home and bound to destroy it. Robert Young plays the role of a fanatical Nazi with malignant dramatic power. The professor's daughter and a young man of the neighborhood, Jimmy Stewart, hold out against the madness, but the house, once filled with love and *gemutlich* living, is left desolate. The bookburning, window-shattering, *Götterdämmerung* of early Nazi Germany is powerfully here, and the picture is a bugle call to resist.

Today Pare Lorentz seems to be remembered only by specialists in the history of film, but there can be no doubt that he was a great artist. Oddly enough, his movies were sponsored by the federal government, and you might expect them to be heavy-handed, bureaucratic, figure-and-fact-laden productions. The Resettlement Administration had requested him to do a movie about soil erosion. The Farm Security Administration had requested one about floods. The former became a masterpiece of documentary called *The Plough That Broke the Plains*. The latter became another masterpiece, *The River*, which could be seen at the New York World's Fair. In *The Fight for Life* (1940), Lorentz addressed himself to medicine— telling the story of the life of a sensitive young doctor who has watched a woman die in childbirth—filming in a maternity clinic, consulting medical boards and statistics, bringing childbirth to the screen. We learn that 90 percent of the nation's babies are delivered by people without training and that childbirth kills more people than cancer. When the young mother dies in a great urban medical center, the young doctor wonders whether there was a "balanced second" when they could have saved her as her life ebbed. "Maybe there's a design," he wonders. "An eye for an eye, a tooth for a tooth, a life for a life." "Perhaps there is a design," an older doctor later replies, "but we don't know it. . . . Floods and erosion are normal in nature. Perhaps human erosion is normal. Too many still think so." On the basis of these three movies, Lorentz deserves a secure place in the history of film. He was able to endow his powerful visual imagination with genuine philosophical depth.

The newsreel staff of the March of Time prepared a unique movie that year called *The Ramparts We Watch* which, en route to its final version, went through a series of important changes which reflected events abroad and the changing mood of Americans. Begun in 1939 and intended as a full-length newsreel account of the events that had drawn the United States into World War I, it was shown around the country in successive versions. By the time it opened in its final version at the Radio City Music Hall in the fall of 1940, it had ceased to be an objective historical presentation of events in the past and had become an all-out call for Americans to defend their heritage against any threat from abroad. The story is one of America during the years 1914–18 as reflected in the lives of various people in a small American city. In 1914, life is peaceful and idyllic, consisting of picnics and churches, ice wagons, schoolrooms, and gay blades dancing the Hesitation. The war breaks out in Europe and gradually makes its presence felt. A foreign laborer departs to return to his homeland and the fighting. The *Lusitania* sinks, and ordinary Americans are outraged. Demonstrations for peace are countered by demonstrations for preparedness. Sabotage occurs in munitions factories. Finally, the United States is drawn in. The climax of the picture, which was highly controversial in the fall of 1940, meant to draw a parallel between 1916–17 and events then unfolding in the Europe of 1940. It makes effective use of a Nazi film called *Feuertaufe*, a brutal and hideous portrayal of the German invasion of Poland. The Nazis had shown it in Norway and the Low Countries to demoralize them and cow them into submission. This Polish footage was so powerful in its depiction of dive-bombing, firebombing, massed artillery, tanks, and summary execution of resisters that the movie was censored in Pennsylvania and other places in the United States.

Charlie Chaplin's *The Great Dictator* was an eagerly awaited fall picture. How would the comic genius of the great Chaplin adapt itself to the awful events abroad? Could Hitler be *funny*? When *The Great Dictator* had its world premiere at both the Astor and the Capitol Theaters in New York, the response to it was mixed. Many critics praised it, but a lot of rotten apples and dead cats flew through the air as well. Chaplin himself made appearances with his wife Paulette Goddard at both theaters, protected by a thirty-man police escort and visibly shaken by the tumult as Klieg lights penciled the air above Times Square. The premiere was a glittering social event, attended by Al Smith, Jim Farley, Franklin D. Roosevelt, Jr., John Raskob, Fannie Hurst, Charles Laughton, Elsa Lanchester, and countless other celebrities.

The plot is relatively simple. Chaplin plays a little Jewish barber who has returned from World War I after a prolonged period of mental dislocation. He does not know that the dictator Hynkel has taken control of the state, that storm troopers are everywhere, and that Hynkel—whom he uncannily resembles—is a megalomaniac who is persecuting the Jews. When the little barber tries to resist, he is beaten and forced to flee to a neighboring country. The little barber is the traditional comic Chaplin figure with baggy trousers, splay feet, cane, battered bowler, and trick mustache. As always, he is the comic-pathetic butt of cruel circumstances, beaten but always bouncing back. But in the foreign country to which he has fled, he is mistaken for Hynkel himself, who has just invaded the country and taken it over, and he is pushed out onto a platform to make a speech to a mass audience. Instead of the expected Hynkel rant, he delivers a passionate and eloquent appeal for reason, kindness, and brotherly love.

Chaplin, of course, also plays the role of the dictator Hynkel and achieves a devastating caricature of the Führer. He has the Hitler mincing walk and the feeble, affected hand salute down perfectly, and also the Hitler penchant for striking dramatic attitudes, the legendary fits of rage, the violent facial contortions. He is satirically powerful, with a wild burst of guttural oratory, a combination of German, Yiddish, and Katzenjammer double-talk. The most famous sequence in the movie consists of a kind of ballet which he performs with a large balloon painted to represent the globe. He bounces this prop around, pirouettes under it, and then weeps uncontrollably when it finally pops and collapses. In another outstanding performance, Jack Okie plays Napaloni, a neighboring dictator who is expansive, outgoing, and ridiculous, the opposite of the neurotic and tormented Hynkel. A fine comic scene occurs when Hynkel and Napaloni are seated in adjacent barber chairs, and each dictator tries to elevate his chair in order to be a bit higher than the other.

But joking about Hitler remained a problem for many. The movie was also felt to be overlong and repetitious, and there was general agreement that the barber's passionately humanitarian speech at the end was completely out of character for the little Jewish barber of the film. It was too transparently Chaplin himself, stepping out of the role and speaking directly to the theater audience. In an article that was widely discussed, Chaplin defended himself with considerable intelligence and force against these criticisms. "As to Hitler being funny," he wrote,

> I can only say that if we can't sometimes laugh at Hitler then
> we are further gone than we think. There is a healthy thing in
> laughter, laughter at the grimmest things in life, laughter at
> death even. *Shoulder Arms* was funny. It had to do with men
> marching off to war. *The Gold Rush* was first suggested by the
> Donner tragedy. Laughter is tonic, the relief, the surcease
> from pain. It is healthy, the healthiest thing in the world, and
> it is health-giving. . . . [As] to the ending. To me, it is a
> logical ending to the story. To me, it is the speech that the
> little barber would have made—even had to make. People
> have said that he steps out of character. What of it? The
> picture is two hours and seven minutes in length. If two hours
> and three minutes of it is comedy, may I not be excused for
> ending my comedy on a note that reflects honestly, and
> realistically, the world in which we live, and may I not be
> excused for pleading for a better world? Mind you, it is
> addressed to the soldiers, the very victims of a dictatorship. It
> was a difficult thing to do. It would have been easier to have
> the barber and Hannah disappear over the horizon, off to the
> promised land against the glowing sunset. But there is no
> promised land for the oppressed people of the world. There is

no place over the horizon to which they can go for sanctuary.
They must stand, and we must stand.

That represents an eloquent case for the defense here, but it
finally fails, it seems to me. Maybe Shakespeare could make Hitler
finally funny, transcend him through a supreme act of comic genius.
Chaplin could not, especially in the fall of 1940. The trouble then
and now is not only that Hitler was bringing about evils on a colossal
scale, but that he was indeed very impressive, if warped, as an
individual and a leader. And Chaplin as much as admits himself that
the final speech could not have been delivered by the barber, but is
entirely external to the movie itself. *The Great Dictator* was a flawed
movie with a great deal of comic invention nevertheless.

At about the same time *The Great Dictator* was released, John
Ford's *The Long Voyage Home* provided a grittier and psychologically more profound treatment of the war. *The Long Voyage Home*
was put together by Ford by combining four short plays by Eugene
O'Neill, *The Moon of the Caribbees, Bound East for Cardiff, In the
Zone,* and *The Long Voyage Home.* Originally, these plays were little
more than episodes, related only by the fact that they all take place
aboard the British freighter *Glencairn* and that the same characters
appear in all four. John Ford linked them by inventing a few incidents and achieved a loose structure which enabled him to tell the
story of several men without requiring any of the stories to be the
central one. The S.S. *Glencairn* and its crew make the long voyage
toward an ultimately elusive goal, an unattainable peace of soul. The
Glencairn sails from the West Indies to England via a stopover in an
American port, carrying munitions for the present war. The main
characters include Driscoll, a tough Irishman who is the leader of
the other toughs in the fo'c'sle; Olson, a big gentle Swede who wants
to return to his mother's farm; Smitty, a man of mystery with a dark
secret; and Cocky, the comic steward. The voyage they make is
more than the perilous one across the North Atlantic with a dangerous cargo. It is a voyage toward a land they desire and regard as
far better than the ocean on which they move slowly—but a land
which in every case, except perhaps that of Olson, receives them
harshly and disappointingly. The point is powerfully made that the
world is a forbidding place to the human spirit. En route, when
Yank, the big deckhand lies dying from a punctured lung, his last
words are, "I dreamed I was 'way in the middle of the land, where
yuh could never smell the sea or look at a ship." But as they
approach the desired land, an enemy plane attempts to bomb them,
and when they reach England, they fall victim to the drink and
knavery of London's lower depths and crawl back to their ship to put

to sea. The long voyage home becomes an ironic title: they do not get there. Ford's pictorial realism has a poetic power of its own. The iron of the ship, which rings as the men walk upon it, is virtually a character in the movie. When the body of the Yank is buried at sea, there is no sentimentality, merely a forlorn little group of men in the overwhelming and hostile vastness. The captain's reading of the burial service is lost in the sounds of the wind and heavy seas.

That year, Warner Brothers brought out *Knute Rockne: All American*, in which Pat O'Brien played the great coach, and the legendary George Gipp was played by a future president of the United States. Viewed today, *Rockne* remains an emotionally intense movie, much more than a period piece, with fine performances by O'Brien and Reagan, moving evocations of Notre Dame with the famous Notre Dame fight song always near at hand, and interesting shots of the old single-wing football. Real football sequences from the thirties were used in the picture. George Gipp's deathbed scene loses none of its power today. When the team is behind, and the breaks are going against the boys, Gipp tells Rockne from his hospital bed, "Just tell them, win one for the Gipper." The movie also possesses a good deal of historical interest. Its 1940 ethos precisely corresponds to that of President Reagan: the striving immigrant Rockne family makes good; the virtues of effort and integrity are extolled; there is a pervasive sense of America-the-beautiful, the shining city-on-the-hill; a high valuation of both independence and teamwork; a straightforward, un-Kierkegaardian Christianity. President Reagan could have wandered into the Oval Office, somewhat aged, straight from the film set; the 1940 emotions of *Rockne* are now a refreshing relief from ambiguity and *angst*.

As 1940 came to an end, W. C. Fields was excellent in *The Bank Dick* as Egbert Souse, a man who accidentally captures a holdup man and is rewarded with a job as a bank guard. The cowboy actor Tom Mix died at sixty in an Arizona car accident; he had served in the Spanish-American War. That December, in the waning days of 1940, the New York Film Critics picked *The Grapes of Wrath* as the best picture of the year; for the third time, John Ford captured the directors' award for that picture plus *The Long Voyage Home*; Katharine Hepburn was best actress in *The Philadelphia Story*; Walt Disney and Leopold Stokowski received a joint special award for *Fantasia*; and Charlie Chaplin won best actor for his dual role in *The Great Dictator*. The year had been an excellent one for the millions of Americans for whom Hollywood movies were an important part of their lives.

Trotsky Murdered

The famous defendants made preposterous confessions about working for Hitler, for Hirohito, for British intelligence. Andrei Vishinsky, the Moscow prosecutor, played it with a straight face, and much progressive opinion in the democratic nations went along with it. Most of the defendants were executed immediately in the basement of the Lubyanka prison, where workmen routinely hosed the brain tissue off the stone floor and walls. No one knows how many had been executed by 1938. Estimates hover around three million. Twelve million Russians were behind barbed wire, one out of every twenty in the population.

Lev Davidovich Bronstein, known to history as Trotsky, lived in exile in a fortified villa on the outskirts of Coyoacan, a suburb of Mexico City. The place was surrounded by a wall, patrolled by armed guards, and had a solid iron gate which opened only after a visitor had been examined through a spy hole. An American reporter who visited the former War Minister of the Soviet Union described him as "almost, but not quite, dapper in dark gray pin-striped suit without a vest, soft striped shirt with attached collar, dark tie. His mustache and goatee are gray, his pompadour white. He seems older than his fifty-seven years."

Trotsky and his wife Natalia lived with the certainty that Stalin would strike. With each new report of the slaughter in Russia, fresh ghosts haunted his sleep, familiar faces with a hole between the eyes. Oddly enough, though he knew that Stalin would try to kill him and though he loved Natalia, he was carrying on an affair with the Stalinist painter Frida Kahlo, mistress of the Stalinist painter Diego Rivera.

On the night of May 24, 1940, assassins gained entrance to the house and sprayed Trotsky's bedroom with bullets. He and Natalia survived by diving to the floor behind their bed. A red-haired American guard named Sheldon Harte, supposed to guard the iron gate, was found to be missing. A month later, police found his body buried in the dirt basement floor of a remote farmhouse. Harte's father was surprised to learn that he had been working for Trotsky, since he was an ardent Stalinist. The police believed Harte had been an accomplice in the assassination attempt and that the GPU had shot him to insure his silence. The Stalinist painter Alfaro Siqueiros was part of the assassination conspiracy, but was not punished. He said that the hundreds of bullets had been fired "for psychological purposes only," and the judge let him off.

Ramón Mercader was the son of a Spanish communist and GPU agent named Caridad who was the mistress of a senior GPU official.

He had been wounded in the Spanish Civil War and trained as an agent in both Spain and Moscow and, by 1938, was considered ready for his role in history. He traveled to Paris under the name Jacques Mornard and reached Mexico City in September 1939, travelling on a Canadian passport under the name Frank Jacson, forged by the GPU. No one noticed the spelling error in "Jacson." His mistress was doing some typing for Trotsky, and through her, Jacson became welcome at the fortified villa. He claimed to be a disciple of Trotsky.

On the night of August 19, Trotsky took a double dose of sleeping pills and awoke the next morning much refreshed. "I'll do a good day's work," he told Natalia. He tended to his rabbits and his garden, breakfasted, wrote some letters, worked on an article about the war in Europe and the inevitability of American involvement. He had theoretical difficulties over the question of whether this war was merely an extension of World War I or something different. Frank Jacson showed up around 5:00 P.M. wearing a hat and raincoat, though the sky was clear. He met Trotsky in the garden, asked him to read something he had written, and accompanied him into the study. Trotsky had two revolvers on his desk, but as he sat there reading Jacson's typescript, Jacson took an ice ax from under his raincoat and drove it with terrific force into Trotsky's brain. Trotsky let out a shriek Jacson-Mercader always remembered. He died in the hospital at 7:25 P.M. on August 21, 1940.

Jacson got twenty years in prison, where he was an exemplary inmate, studying electrical engineering. His cell was spacious and sunny, with a patio in front, and he had all the books and magazines he wanted, plus female visitors. Stalin personally awarded Caridad the Order of Lenin and, for her son, gave her a document making him a Hero of the Soviet Union. In 1960 Mercader, now using his real name, was released and went to the Soviet Union and then to Prague, where he worked as an electrical engineer. In 1977 he received a gold star on his Hero of the Soviet Union award from Brezhnev.

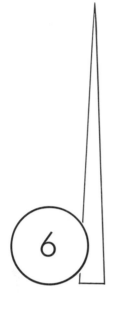

HE GAVE THE LION'S ROAR

6

What everyone heard during that summer was an entirely new voice, neither Hitler's hoarse imprecations rising to periodic screams nor Franklin Roosevelt's silvery baritone hauteur. Families heard this new voice from afar over their radios, often through a haze of static, the voice fading and returning. The new voice sometimes lisped its "s" sounds, threw its emphases in strange places, and halted for disconcerting pauses that served to heighten the effect of the next words. "This wath . . . their . . . finest . . . *hour.*" No one who did not hear Churchill's speeches over the radio in the summer of 1940, Big Ben booming over the BBC—bong, bong, bong—can begin to imagine how moving they were. When Clement Atlee was asked what Winston Churchill's contribution to winning the war had been, he replied, "Talk about it." That was far from the whole truth. Churchill as war leader was a demonic administrator, a hurricane of energy driving the vast war machine, pushing sometimes fantastic initiatives, devising grand strategy, sacking and promoting. But Atlee did have a large piece of the truth. The besieged British, the Americans with their ears to the radio, listened to Churchill and came to understand something important: that the German smash through France did not mean the final end of things, that there was will and poetry and nobility left in the West even in that dark summer of 1940, and that in challenging the presumed might of the British Empire, Hitler might really have overreached himself.

Americans first heard Churchill in the wake of the Norway disaster. On May 7, 1940, M. P. Leo Amery flung at the hapless prime minister, Neville Chamberlain, the words of Oliver Cromwell to the Long Parliament: "In the name of God, go." Three days later, Hitler launched his brilliant thrust through the Ardennes and the Low Countries. Neville Chamberlain tried to form an emergency national government including all parties, but failed to do so. Early in the evening of May 10, Winston Churchill, first lord of the admiralty, drove to Buckingham Palace in a limousine and accepted the charge of George VI to form a new government. On May 13 we heard the remarkable new voice. On June 4, after the Dunkirk evacuation, he delivered his famous oration of defiance, in its famous catalogue of resistance almost a magical invocation: "We shall fight in France, we shall fight on the seas and oceans, we shall fight with growing confidence and strength in the air, we shall defend our Island, whatever the cost may be, we shall fight on the beaches, we shall fight on the landing grounds, we shall fight in the fields and in the streets, we shall fight in the hills; we shall never surrender." When France finally surrendered, he declared that England would fight on alone and prevail: "Let us therefore brace ourselves to our duties, and so bear ourselves that, if the British Empire and its Commonwealth last for a thousand years, men will say: 'This was their finest hour.'" As the RAF fought the Luftwaffe to a standstill and then went over to the offensive, Churchill spoke past even this heroic moment to history itself: "Never in the field of human conflict was so much owed by so many to so few."

But Churchill was much more than a British Pericles. He was a cauldron of energy, a man of violent action. He knew that the climax of the aerial "Battle of Britain" was approaching that September, and he followed the war in the skies from his steel bunker at 10 Downing Street. On September 15 the RAF went for broke, and Churchill visited air bases where the red lights on the maps indicated that all reserve Hurricanes and Spitfires were in the air. In a tremendous engagement of air forces, the Luftwaffe lost. Hitler could not cross the Channel. Two days later, on September 17, he postponed the invasion of England indefinitely.

Hitler's will had collided with the deeply historical and civilized—but just as tough—will of Winston Churchill. Churchill did more than make speeches projecting the moment against the background of history. He was absolutely ruthless. Wars are not won with rhetoric alone. Churchill ordered that on the beaches of Dunkirk the wounded be taken off last—he wanted able-bodied men for the defense of the island. He gave orders to set oil on fire in the English Channel if the Germans came and orders to spray the landing beaches with poison gas. The Geneva Convention could go to hell. "We shall never surrender." If forced to do so, he was prepared to carry on the war from Canada. In the midst of the air war over England that July, he ruthlessly ordered the sinking of the French fleet at Oran—it would never fall into Hitler's hands. He ordered Bomber Command to carry out mass raids against German cities at night, of doubtful military value and killing civilians indiscriminately, killing babies. The planes might better have been used to search for U-boats over the Atlantic, but Churchill passionately wanted to "hit" Germany, as he said. In psychological terms, he was undoubtedly correct. He smashed the Germans' belief that Hitler was invincible. During one night raid, Foreign Minister von Ribbentrop and Soviet Foreign Minister Molotov scrambled into an air-raid shelter. Ribbentrop assured Molotov that the British were beaten. "Then why are we in this air-raid shelter?" Molotov asked.

As a matter of fact, Churchill and Hitler had many personal characteristics in common. Both were men of World War I and had been deeply wounded by it—Hitler when the German army surrendered in 1918, Churchill when he was savagely discredited as first lord of the admiralty by the disaster at Gallipoli. Each man, after the war, might have been thought to be finished. Both were military visionaries, and though Hitler achieved the earlier success with his Stukas, parachutists, and U-boats, Churchill was full of unorthodox schemes like the Q-boats and setting the Channel ablaze. Both were loners, contemptuous of the stodgily orthodox; both worked at night; both were monologuists; both were incandescent orators and champions of "race"—Churchill of the destiny of the "British race," Hitler of the "German race." Both were painters and amateur architects. Both could be charming or outrageous. Both were manic, perhaps somewhat mad: Churchill was followed all of his life by a dark depression which he called his "black dog," though usually his high animal spirits prevailed over it. Both preferred death to defeat. The difference between the two men, not to belabor the obvious, is that Churchill, though erratic, was also deeply civilized, his fanaticism kept under control by a sense of history, of responsibility to history, and he could not possibly have entertained the wild beliefs that Hitler held. Hitler once told the German people that he was the "hardest" man who had ever ruled them, and doubtless this was correct. But Churchill was very hard too, perhaps harder than any Western leader in 1940. He rose to the occasion because he knew that he had to be at least as tough as the barbarian. He rose out of the past, and as he would have put it, out of the "British race."

A day in the life of Prime Minister Winston Churchill must be something absolutely unique in the annals of civilized leadership at a time of acute national crisis. General Sir Alan Brooke, chief of staff, recalls Churchill this way: "As I look back on those five years of close contact with the greatest war leader of modern times I carry away in my memory deeply engraved impressions of unbounded genius, unrelenting energy, dogged determination, a refusal to accept defeat in any shape or form, vast personal courage, a deep sense of humour, and an uncanny facility for inspiring respect, admiration, loyalty and deep affection in the hearts of all those fortunate enough to work in close touch with him." Churchill's ability to sustain his hectic daily existence demonstrably came from a superb physical constitution, as well as a sense of having been chosen by history which Hegel would have understood. He had been visibly rejuvenated by the Norway and Dunkirk crises and the vast stage he now stalked. His body was like a tuning fork. When angered or dismayed, he seemed to contract physically, darken and withdraw. When in full cry, he expanded; his pink skin glowed; he seemed warm and plump, and his eyes sparkled. When exhausted, his speech thickened, but he had an extraordinary capacity to transcend fatigue and resume working at top speed.

He always awoke at 8:00 A.M., feeling supercharged, as if he had a bottle of champagne in him. His official boxes containing important papers were delivered to him at breakfast, which he took in bed, an amazing old-fashioned English meal of grouse, beef, cutlets, and so forth, washed down with white wine. "Carnivores will win this war," he chortled. He worked for most of the morning in bed, reading telegrams, smoking cigars (eight per day), seeing important people, sending messages, and issuing orders. He drank a large number of whiskey-and-waters. He used a hotel ice bucket as his ashtray. In late morning he bathed, groomed himself meticulously, and applied a scented handkerchief to his thinning hair. Then there was a sumptuous lunch, at which he discussed the war with high officials and selected guests, bottles of wine followed by champagne and brandy. Between 3:00 and 6:00 P.M. he took a nap, from which he rose entirely refreshed, issued more orders and heard more reports along with whiskey-and-sodas, which he took instead of the traditional tea. Then it was time for the real meal of the day, a multicourse feast with whiskey and gin and varied wines. He sometimes boasted that he could imbibe more than Stalin and Molotov combined, famous for their vodka toasts. "They only sip their liquor," he said contemptuously. But after dinner he was clear-headed and eager for serious work, conferring with ministers, chiefs of staff, and aides. As the evening deepened into night, efforts would be made to get him to go to bed, but usually to no avail. Sometimes, on the spur of the moment, he would have a movie shown, one of his favorites being *Lady Hamilton* with Vivien Leigh. He had it shown dozens of times, no doubt seeing himself as a player comparable to his heroes Nelson and Napoleon. His energies churned him forward into the small hours of the morning. When his exhausted colleagues asked him to postpone the morning meeting, he did so grudgingly—from 10:00 to 10:30. Before he went to sleep, he had the morning papers delivered to him, devoured them in bed, fell asleep, and slept like a stone.

Churchill looms so large in retrospect, casts so great a shadow in history, that we tend to lose sight of how odd a human being he really was. In the mid-1930s Churchill was generally regarded as a has-been, an erratic old man in his sixties, promising, no doubt at first, but undone by eccentricity and an uncontrollable ambition. In the devastating judgment of the British establishment, he was "brilliant" perhaps, but "unsound." Despite his great wartime—and indeed, historical—leadership, the establishment judgment might not have been entirely wrong.

Throughout his early years as a student and on into his years as a member of Parliament and young cabinet minister, few—including Hegel—would have identified Winston Churchill as a likely world-historical figure. In fact, he did not become one until 1940, at the age of sixty-five. The younger son of the also brilliant and unsound, but also syphilitic Randolph Churchill—scholars differ on whether he contracted the disease from a prostitute or a housemaid at Blenheim Palace—and his dazzling American wife Jennie, Winston Churchill was born at Blenheim, a vast eighteenth-century Baroque structure, larger than several football fields, erected by his ancestor, Jack Churchill, Duke of Marlborough, the only English general in history who never lost a battle and who became the eighteenth-century equivalent of a billionaire through his combined military and commercial exploits. Named after a famous Marlborough victory over the French, Blenheim had been designed by the architect-playwright John Vanbrugh, and its extravagant vastness was legendary.

Churchill was a rebellious and academically indifferent student at Harrow and at Sandhurst, the British West Point, but he enjoyed his tour of duty in India with its gin and tonic, polo, elephants, and maharajas. He enjoyed the fighting in Cuba as an observer in 1895. Out of the army and without a profession, he took up a career as a journalist and ultimately made a fortune as a writer and historian, but the writing—and here we are reminded of his contemporary, Theodore Roosevelt—was always rooted in action. He covered the Afghan War on the northwest frontier of India, the Dervish Rebellion in the Sudan which was summarily squashed by Kitchener, and, climactically for this phase of his career, the Boer War in South Africa. The Boers captured and imprisoned him. He soon escaped and, always in danger of capture, found his way, on foot and by train, to the coastal port of Lourenço Marques in Portuguese East Africa. Along the way, he said, his only companion was "a gigantic vulture, who manifested an extravagant interest in my condition, and made hideous and ominous gurglings from time to time."

Returning to England from Africa, he found himself a popular patriotic hero, called upon the major political leaders, stood for Parliament and won a seat, and went on a highly remunerative American lecture tour. A Tory, he switched to the Liberals—he thought the 1904 Tories were mossbacks—and became known to his former political colleagues as "the Blenheim rat."

His ambition was naked, overpowering, and to many repulsive. Under Sir Henry Campbell-Bannerman's Liberal government of 1905, he became undersecretary for the colonies and proved to be an office cyclone, issuing orders, leaving for far-flung expeditions, dictating into the night from a bathtub in Uganda. He married his Clementine, wrote, schemed, and rose. He became president of the Board of Trade, home secretary, then first lord of the Admiralty. Lord Esher noted, as did many others, that Churchill "wanted to push to the front of the Cabinet." The editor of the *Westminster Gazette* reported, correctly, that no other man lived "in such a perpetual state of mental excitement." His insults became famous. Attempting rapid naval rejuvenation among admirals who wished they were still under canvas, he was warned about naval tradition. "Don't talk to me about naval tradition," he replied. "It's nothing but rum, sodomy and the lash." Frustrated by the stalemate on the Western Front, he planned a Napoleonic masterstroke at Gallipoli: close the Dardanelles. But it turned into a disaster with enormous British casualties, and he left the Cabinet in disgrace, his political career apparently in ruins, brilliant but unsound. He went to the Western Front as an army colonel, loving the odor of cordite and the crash of shells. He was well supplied with brandy, but he also loved the intoxication of action. He addressed his letters to Clementine

"My Dearest Soul," the form in which the Duke of Marlborough had addressed his crazy red-haired duchess.

After the war Churchill's political fortunes ambiguously revived. Lloyd George wanted him inside the government and controllable, not outside as a loose cannon, and appointed him secretary of state for war in 1919. Churchill asked, "What is the use of being War Secretary if there is no war?" Bonar Law replied, "If we thought there was going to be a war, we wouldn't appoint you War Secretary."

Politically on the margin, Churchill became a rich man during the 1920s by writing. He wrote his six-volume *World Crisis* for a half crown per word, produced a great deal of high-priced journalism, and of course received his salary as a cabinet minister. The death of a distant relative brought him a large legacy, and he purchased and rebuilt Chartwell, his country estate in Kent. When Stanley Baldwin became prime minister in 1924, he made Churchill chancellor of the exchequer, his father's old post, and Churchill literally wept with emotion. "That fulfills my ambition. I still have my father's robe as Chancellor. I shall be proud to serve you in this splendid office." He fought the strikers in the bitter labor disputes of the later 1920s and generally moved to the right politically. He—though conspicuously not Clementine—delighted in ribald male company, such cronies as the brilliant F. E. Smith and the Oxford physicist Frederick Lindemann.

F. E. Smith, while at Oxford, had been a contemporary of Hilaire Belloc, and both had been such stellar performers in debate at the Oxford Union that they agreed not to get in one another's way afterwards. Upon graduation, they flipped a coin to decide who would become a Tory, who a Liberal. As a barrister, F. E. Smith was famous for his cutting wit. When a judge rebuked him in court by saying, "You are extremely offensive, young man," F. E. shot back, "As a matter of fact, we both are, but I am trying to be, and you can't help it." When he was an M.P., F. E. was blackballed in one of the big clubs in Pall Mall, but nevertheless stopped in every day to use its men's room after lunch. When a uniformed retainer accosted him one day with the information that "this is a private club, sir," F. E. replied, "Oh, I didn't know you had a club here too." The physicist Lindemann was famous for his academic feuds at Oxford and also had an acid wit. He once expressed the desire to castrate an Oxford colleague but added, "Not that it would make any difference."

Churchill was also strongly attracted to the Canadian press baron Max Aitken, Lord Beaverbrook, a wild mixture of Presbyterian righteousness and ribaldry who would sing Calvinist hymns while drunk and clamber up a bookcase like a monkey as he sang "Bound for Glory."

This was a swashbuckling, profane crew that liked to "pig it" at the Ritz, and during the grim 1930s they seemed increasingly obsolete. On the Labour Party victory in the General Election of 1929, Churchill's remarks to his political staff are entirely unprintable.

During the 1930s, the decade of social earnestness, the "Auden generation," when the culture moved left and many young men were Marxists or Communists, Churchill was an anachronism, no longer even on the margins of major-party politics. Beaverbrook called him a "busted flush." The writer Christopher Sykes thought him a "disastrous relic of the past, a dangerous has-been." Harold Nicolson observed that he appeared "incredibly aged." Nevertheless, his literary output was prodigious. He completed the sixth volume of his *World Crisis.* He wrote his magnificent four-volume life of the Duke of Marlborough. Newspaper and magazine articles poured forth, and the best were collected in the volume *Thoughts and Adventures.* His biographical essays appeared as *Great Contemporaries.* He contemplated writing a life of Napoleon and wrote much of his *History of the English-Speaking Peoples,* which appeared after the war.

It was Adolf Hitler who made possible the rebirth of Churchill as a British statesman. With the rise of Hitler, Churchill recovered a sense of mission, of destiny. His message, endlessly repeated—thought by many to be boring, but later remembered in sorrow—was as simple as it was correct. Only by being strong could Britain remain free and great. Only visible military strength could deter aggression, so clearly intended by Berlin. Disarmament would not bring peace but make war more likely.

In 1935, Prime Minister Stanley Baldwin made Churchill a member of a secret committee on air defense, and Churchill accepted the post on condition that he be allowed to speak out. He was not hostile to Mussolini's seizure of Ethiopia, and he supported the Japanese colonization of Manchuria, believing that the Japanese had stepped into a power vacuum which Communist Russia might otherwise exploit. When civil war broke out in Spain, he favored "nonintervention," which, since the Germans and Italians were aiding Franco's Nationalists, meant practical support for Franco. His consuming enmity was directed at the "Nazi beast," and he was only confirmed in his views, if that were possible, by Hitler's occupation of the demilitarized Rhineland in 1936.

While Hitler's progress rebuilt Churchill's stature to some extent, he himself dealt it a staggering blow by siding with Edward VIII in the political crisis over the king's desire to marry his mistress, the American divorcée Wallis Simpson. Stanley Baldwin, public opinion, the House of Commons, and much of the Empire were furiously and immovably opposed to the marriage, and when Churchill rose to defend Edward in the House, he was howled down. Churchill's morals were those of an older England, not middle-class and not censorious, Edwardian. He was absolutely faithful to Clementine, but he belonged to that relaxed earlier world in which newspapers could report that there was nothing between Edward (VII), Prince of Wales, and the actress Lily Langtry, "not even a sheet." Churchill was also a romantic as regards Edward and Mrs. Simpson and hoped that something, somehow, could be worked out. But the temper of the times was less forgiving, and once again Churchill found himself isolated, out of joint with public sentiment, an anachronism. When Neville Chamberlain succeeded Baldwin in May of 1937, the dour Birmingham businessman wanted nothing to do with Churchill and excluded him from the government. As far as Chamberlain was concerned, Churchill was a sort of gargoyle.

But Chamberlain, for all his good intentions and personal rectitude, was squashed flat by history. Everything that Churchill had prophesied was coming to pass. In March of 1938, Hitler seized Austria. Churchill demanded crisis-paced rearmament. All through the spring and summer, he warned that Hitler had immediate designs on Czechoslovakia. In September, he denounced the ceding of the Sudetenland as "the prostration of Europe before Nazi power." When Chamberlain returned from Munich proclaiming "peace with honour," Churchill declared that it had been a "total and unmitigated defeat." Hitler confirmed everything Churchill was saying by seizing the rest of Czechoslovakia in March, completely violating the agreement he had signed with Chamberlain in Munich. His foreign policy in tatters, his grip on the country slipping, Chamberlain in a panic made an impractical alliance with Poland, which everyone knew would be Hitler's next victim and which England could do nothing to defend. Hitler struck on September 1, and Chamberlain went reluctantly to war on September 3, bringing the prophetic Churchill back into government as first lord of the Admiralty, the post he had held in the First World War. "Winston's back," the Admiralty telegraphed the fleet at sea. Almost sixty-five, Churchill's great days lay ahead. He had been reborn, returned to history.

He complained that it was a dull war with only Germany to fight and hoped that Italy and Japan would come in and give his great fleet something interesting to do. Churchill speeded up destroyer production to counter the U-boat threat. He infused the navy with his own restless spirit and desire to "hit" the enemy. Because of his Cassandra warnings in the past and because of his visible aggressive and warlike temperament, he was the only Tory leader to emerge from the Norway humiliation unscathed. Chamberlain was obliged to resign, and the king called upon Churchill to form a government on May 10.

Churchill brought to bear upon a dispirited nation and a stunned world an extraordinary will and a remarkable rhetoric. He quite literally made the past live again in 1940, the forgotten spirit of Whig imperial greatness. The great William Pitt had told the Duke of Norfolk during an eighteenth-century European crisis, "I know that I can save this country, and that no one else can." A similar spirit drove Churchill, and in his speeches the past walked again. As John F. Kennedy remarked, he "mobilized the resources of the English language." When President Roosevelt's special emissary, Harry Hopkins, met him in London, he was overwhelmed by Churchill's vitality, his "rotund, smiling, red-faced" host with the clear and twinkling eye, his "mushy voice" and overpowering personality. "God, what force that man has!" Hopkins repeatedly exclaimed. "Jesus Christ! What a man!"

Churchill's oratory and his example may have won the war—mobilized the British war effort, brought the war vividly to the American public. If Britain had been defeated, it is plausible to believe that Churchill would have died in *his* bunker. But what was the specific strength of that great oratory?

Throughout most, or even all, of his prewar political career, Churchill's colleagues had regarded him with a mixture of awe and derision as entirely unpredictable and therefore potentially dangerous. After all, he had switched from Tory to Liberal and then back again and had talked seriously of starting a third party of his own. Sir Isaiah Berlin is surely correct, however, when he writes that Churchill's essential view of the world, his core of beliefs, never changed at all. These beliefs were there back in the 1890s; they were there in 1940 when he became prime minister; and they remained unchanged to the end. They informed everything he wrote or said throughout his career.

Churchill saw history as a great pageant, parti-colored and vivid, in which it was an easy matter to tell good from evil. Though he would have been outraged at the very suggestion, he was an instinctive Nietzschean. He loved the large, the noble, the beautiful, the active. He despised the gray and depleted, the ambiguous, the passive. In Marlowe's great phrase, Churchill saw nothing wrong in desiring to "ride in triumph through Persepolis." Like Theodore Roosevelt, he embodied vital and vibrant energy and was ever eager to deploy it in verbal, political, or military combat. "Whatever you may do," he told the bewildered and despairing French ministers as their world collapsed in 1940, "we shall fight on, forever and forever."

His sense of Europe had been shaped early by Gibbon and Macaulay, who—along with Burke and Johnson—also influenced his prose style, and this view of Europe was reinforced by his experience. It was a sense, as he himself would have said, that was "racial." There were the great nations, and Germany was one of them, anointed by history in the grand march of civilization. He hated the Nazis, but never the German race. He believed in the greatness of France, coming down through the centuries from the Gauls who had fought Caesar, from Charlemagne, from the Merovingian kings and the great Bourbons, from Napoleon and Clemenceau. The French too were a great race. He despised the Russians, even as Gibbon and Voltaire had, regarding them as a chaotic quasi-Asiatic horde beyond the borders of European civilization. This is not a world-view that has much intellectual or academic respectability these days, though it was commonplace in Victorian and Edwardian times. Today we are routinely expected to regard places like "Honduras" and "Yemen" as *nations*. But Churchill's view has much truth in it, and it shaped his finest hour.

He reimagined the British for themselves during that summer of 1940, conceived of them in heroic, world-historical terms, and such was the force of his personality that he was able to impose this vision on them and make them believe it and live within it. They had felt bewildered and diminished, but Churchill's imagination brought moral clarity and a sense of vast mission. The twenty-two-year-olds who took off in their Spitfires from those grassy runways that summer were also fighting at Agincourt. When Churchill flung 100 percent of his available fighters into the sky on September 15, a mighty all-or-nothing gamble that won the Battle of Britain, he was Nelson, Marlborough, Wellington. Sir Isaiah Berlin writes with great insight about Churchill's strange, archaic power, something premodern, as if Henry VIII or Oliver Cromwell had risen out of the ground and taken command. It "is doubtful how far he has ever been aware of what goes on in the heads and hearts of others. He does not react, he acts; he does not mirror, he affects others and alters them to his own powerful measure." History for Churchill was the equivalent of a cocaine high, as when he recalls the days of Dunkirk: "There is no doubt that had I at this juncture faltered at all in the leading of the nation I should have been hurled out of office. I was sure that every Minister was ready to be killed quite soon, and have all his family and possessions destroyed, rather than give in. In this they represented the House of Commons and almost all the people. It fell to me in those coming days and months to express their sentiments on suitable occasions. This I was able to do because they were mine also. There was a white glow, overpowering, sublime, which ran through our island from end to end."

How passé the Churchillian vision had previously been Sir Isaiah Berlin effectively demonstrates by citing Herbert Read's 1928 *English Prose Style,* a perfect reflection of the taste of its day. Churchill is the stylistic villain of the book—declamatory, ornate, public, unnuanced—everything a good style should *not* be, according to Read. The First World War and its corpses, and perhaps more broadly, democracy and egalitarianism, had killed that sort of thing. It was the style of mountebanks and impostors. "Such eloquence is false because it is artificial. . . . The images are stale, the metaphors violent, the whole passage exhales a false dramatic atmosphere." Read was writing from the perspective of the sensibility of the 1920s. Such a style and its puffed-up claims had led to the Somme and to Verdun. The truth that mattered was not public but personal. Personal relations, personal truth, personal destiny— these were the authentic reality. Nuance was all-important. Woolf, Fitzgerald, E. M. Forster. Churchill was not much interested in the nuances of individual feeling or in the gradations of personal relations (Clementine's life must have been something of a trial), but in the grand sweep of historical drama as it existed in his own imagination. When France fell to Hitler in 1940, everyone suddenly knew that there *was* a historical drama and that it was desperately important. Churchill was ready with the suddenly relevant style. He came stalking out of the political tomb, discarding his burial garments, and endowed the public fate with poetic meaning. He not only gave the lion's roar; he was the lion.

Years later, when then President Eisenhower talked world politics with Churchill in his last phase as prime minister, he frankly thought the old man a bit crazy. He records in his *Diary* that Churchill talked as if the British Empire still existed, as if England were still a great power and a major force in world affairs, with divisions at the ready and fleets of planes in the air. The unpoetic Eisenhower looked at his aides. Was Churchill putting him on? In truth, the same central vision of England that had always been there still burned in his brain, transcendent, beautiful, sacred, unaffected by external events. Had it not burned there in 1940, England might have gone under.

Neville Chamberlain died of stomach cancer on November 9 of that year, seven months after resigning as prime minister amid Hitler's triumphs on the Continent. It is not inconceivable that the stress of dealing with Hitler over a period of three years may have had something to do with his sickness. The new prime minister, Winston Churchill, did not want him in the reconstituted cabinet, but Chamberlain was still leader of the Conservative party, and with two hundred votes in the House of Commons, the Tories made it clear that there would be no new Churchill government unless Chamberlain was part of it. He received the largely honorary post of lord president of the council. During the summer and fall it became evident that he was ill, and in September he resigned from the cabinet, but the nature of his illness was not made public. Churchill was glad to be rid of him; the Germans were using Chamberlain's presence in the cabinet as evidence to support their spurious claims that the British were about to sue for peace.

On October 11, in his last public statement, Chamberlain spoke over the BBC to the thousands who had written to wish him well after his resignation from the War Cabinet. In a voice familiar and choked with emotion, he said: "Most of my correspondents are quite unknown to me, but they express their gratitude for what I have tried to do, and by their regard for me, with such transparent and sometimes passionate sincerity, they have indeed lightened my affliction and made up for many disappointments. From the bottom of my heart I thank them." Expressing the conviction that the British Empire would be victorious, Mr. Chamberlain repeated his famous broadcast the day the war began, saying: "It isn't conceivable that civilization should be permanently overcome by such evil men and evil things as we are fighting against."

Chamberlain was tall and gaunt, his black hair tinged with gray; he had a dark complexion and deep-set blue eyes. The son of the famous politician Joseph Chamberlain, who had been a vociferous opponent of the use of force in South Africa and Ireland, he belonged to what amounted to the first family of Birmingham. Like his father, Chamberlain was a social reformer, and he became a champion of municipalization, or city planning. A successful manufacturer, he also established the first municipal bank in England, served as the lord mayor of Birmingham, and was one of the few emerging leaders who understood the dimensions of the housing shortage. His plans led to the construction of some 900,000 dwellings in the Birmingham area.

During World War I, Lloyd George brought him into the administration. He won a seat in Parliament in 1918 and rose through a succession of increasingly important posts in which his performance was impressive. When Stanley Baldwin stepped down as prime minister on May 28, 1937, and became an earl, Chamberlain's succession was inevitable. There is no doubt that in normal times he would have been an enlightened reformer, concentrating on domestic policy, seeking the advice of experts, moving forward steadily and prudently. The world crisis dictated otherwise.

Europe smelled of gunpowder. The democratic countries and their allies had been pursuing a policy of "collective security"—really a policy of deterrence—directed against Hitler and very likely Mussolini. Hitler clearly had designs on Czechoslovakia, which could easily lead to general European war. The lineup of England, France, and Czechoslovakia against Germany was potentially explosive. Yet Chamberlain did not hold very high cards where deterrence was concerned. Hitler knew very well that the idea of another war horrified most people in England. Stanley Baldwin had deliberately misled the country during the general election of 1935 regarding German rearmament, fearing that to sound the alarm would cost him the election. During 1937 and 1938, England was woefully deficient in air power, and Chamberlain was in no position militarily to call Hitler's bluff over Czechoslovakia. Because they fully understood British weakness, even proponents of collective security like Churchill and Eden reluctantly accepted the Munich agreement, though regarding it as a catastrophic British defeat.

Chamberlain's perspective was quite different. He viewed the future peace of Europe as based not on collective security against Hitler, but on a negotiated settlement with him. If England and Germany could agree, Europe was safe. Churchill regarded Munich as buying time to build Spitfires. Chamberlain was seeking "peace in our time" and believed that he was achieving it.

"I had hoped in going to Munich," he later said, "to find out by personal contact what was in Herr Hitler's mind and whether it was likely that he would cooperate in a program of that kind. Well, the atmosphere in which our discussions was conducted was not a very favorable one, because we were in the midst of an acute crisis. But, nevertheless, in the interval between more official conversations, I had some opportunity of talking with him and of hearing his views; and I thought the results not altogether unsatisfactory." Back in Downing Street as a national hero, Chamberlain proclaimed that "I believe it is peace in our time."

That Chamberlain believed this sincerely is not open to question and is indicated by his shock and bewilderment less than six months later when, in flat violation of the Munich agreement, Hitler's armies moved out of the Sudetenland and occupied the rest of Czechoslovakia. Chamberlain expressed his shock in a major speech in Birmingham:

> When I came back [from Munich] I told the House of
> Commons of the conversation I had with Herr Hitler, of which

> I said that, speaking with great earnestness, he repeated what
> he had already said at Berchtesgaden—namely, that this [the
> Sudetenland] was the last of his territorial ambitions in
> Europe and that he had no wish to include in the Reich people
> of other race than Germans. Well, in view of those repeated
> assurances given voluntarily to me, I considered myself
> justified in founding the hope upon them that once this
> Czechoslovak problem was settled, as it seemed to be at
> Munich, it would be possible to carry further that policy of
> appeasement which I had described.
>
> I am convinced that, after Munich, the great majority of the
> British people shared my hope and ardently desired that that
> policy should be carried further, but today I share their
> disappointment, their indignation, that those hopes have been
> so wantonly shattered.
>
> What has become of this declaration of "no further
> territorial ambition"? What has become of Herr Hitler's
> assurance "We don't want Czechs in the Reich"?
>
> Doesn't the question inevitably remain in our minds: If it is
> so easy to discover good reasons for ignoring assurances so
> solemnly and repeatedly given, what reliance can be placed
> upon any other assurances that come from the same source?

Chamberlain could not fully understand that he had simply been
lied to by Hitler, that Hitler was a genuine radical, nor could he
understand the monstrous loss Munich represented. The Czechs had
a well-trained modern army on their border with Germany, a highly
fortified mountain defense line, a good air force, and the great
Skoda arms works, second only to Krupp. All of this was thrown
away, a strategic calamity. The Kremlin surely regarded this display
of British weakness with cold calculation. A straight line runs from
Munich to the Hitler-Stalin pact the next year and from that to war.
And, of course, Hitler now knew what sort of British opponent he
faced.

Shortly after the seizure of Czechoslovakia, Prime Minister
Chamberlain announced to the House of Commons that Great Britain had pledged its aid to Poland in the event of aggression and
called for emergency rearmament "to make good our deficiencies in
the shortest possible time." There were no loopholes in the commitment to Poland.

Chamberlain's hope that he could deal successfully with Hitler
persisted up to the outbreak of war, as is evident in the doleful
language with which he declared war on September 3, 1939. "You
can imagine what a bitter blow it is to me that all my long struggle to

win the peace has failed. *Up to the very last it should have been quite possible to arrange a peaceful settlement between Germany and Poland"* (italics added). Hope, and dismay over the prospect of war, had led to impenetrable illusion about Hitler. The result has been that Chamberlain has become a caricature in the lore of the twentieth century as the man with the umbrella, and the names "Chamberlain" and "Munich" have entered the English language as terms of condemnation. Yet it is fair to recall, as the *New York Times* did after his death, that the thousands "who cheered him on his return from Munich were cheering for one of themselves. If he had stooped to a general election in the immediate aftermath of Munich, there is little doubt that he would have won it by a triumphant landslide." And the *Times* concludes: "After all, Neville Chamberlain tried to bring peace to Europe. He tried boldly and bravely when other men had shrugged their shoulders. Was it not better to have tried and failed than never to have tried at all?" The worst that can be said of Chamberlain, perhaps, is that he lived within the civilized conventions of his background, while Hitler despised them and lived entirely outside them against some Wagnerian or Dostoyevskian backdrop.

It must have been due to the universal sense of Chamberlain's decency that his death that November produced an enormous outpouring of British emotion, even after the disasters of the summer and fall and the pounding Britain was taking from the air. Lying in a rambling farmhouse called Heckfield, surrounded by larches in the heart of Hampshire, Chamberlain slipped into a coma on Friday, November 8, and died at 5:30 P.M. the next day. The death was not announced until mid-morning Sunday, leading congregations throughout England to pray mistakenly for his recovery that morning. In the ancient Norman church of St. Michael's near Heckfield, the vicar, Rev. H. R. P. Tringham, asked the congregation to pray for Mr. Chamberlain, "who is very, very ill."

The funeral took place in Westminster Abbey. The time was not announced, lest the Germans bomb the building and wipe out the entire British leadership. Winston Churchill, looking grim and pale, was among the pallbearers, who included Viscount Halifax, Clement Atlee, and Sir Kingsley Wood. At the end of the simple Anglican service, a small oak urn containing Chamberlain's ashes was lifted from a catafalque and placed in a shallow cavity in the floor of the abbey, down the aisle from the tomb of the Unknown Soldier and not far from the statue of his famous father. As the morning light slanted through the tall gothic windows, Mrs. Chamberlain walked to the edge of the grave, took a single chrysanthemum from her handbag, and laid the crushed petals on the urn.

It was widely sensed that this also marked the end of an era, the collapse of Chamberlain's policies emphasized by the "all clear" siren that wailed just before the ceremony got underway and by the squadron of British planes that flew between London and the Channel coast in case the Germans suddenly attacked. There in the abbey were the principal opponents of his policies—Winston Churchill, of course, but also Anthony Eden, the war secretary; Viscount Cranborne, the dominion secretary; Alfred Duff Cooper, the minister of information; Herbert Morrison, home secretary; Ernest Bevin, minister of labor; Leo Amery, secretary for India; and many others. Chamberlain's former critics and enemies now constituted the government, and he belonged to history.

Göring's Bright Idea

As historian Walter Lord tells the story, everyone who was there remembered the moment when he knew that something had gone wrong.

On May 14, Group Captain R. C. M. Collard showed up for an appointment at the headquarters of General André-Georges Corap. The general and his staff had vanished. Two French officers were there alone, "waiting to surrender," they said.

Royal Engineer E. N. Grimmer, walking behind his lines in a French field, noticed preparations being made to blow up a bridge. "When you're advancing, you don't blow bridges," he thought.

Lance Corporal E. S. Wright, traveling into Arras to pick up his unit's mail, did a double take when a motorcycle sped past him on the road. The motorcycle was German.

At the River Dender, men in the 32nd Regiment were caught in a traffic jam at the crossing point. A number of motorcycles with sidecars pulled up to their left. The men of the 32nd were astonished when soldiers jumped out of the sidecars and began spraying them with machine guns.

Panic spread through the chaos. Rumors multiplied that Germans were moving along the roads disguised as refugees, nuns, monks, and in French uniforms.

As in Poland and then in Norway, the Stukas were in their element over the French roads and battlefields. The slow-moving, gull-winged dive-bombers would be obsolete flying coffins a year later and would be withdrawn, but here, diving with sirens wailing and bombs falling, they were magnificent morale destroyers.

The French commander, General Gamelin, unfortunately thought it was August 1914, Schlieffen Plan time, with a German attack through the Low Countries. When General Fedor von Bock's Army Group B crashed into the Low Countries, Gamelin knew exactly what to do. He moved the principal French forces, along with the BEF (British Expeditionary Force), northward to halt their expected thrust south to Paris. Too bad. That exposed his rear as General Gerd von Runstedt's Army Group A came slashing through the Ardennes Forest, spearheaded by 325 Stukas and 1,806 tanks. Racing across northern France toward the English Channel, Runstedt had the main Allied forces cut off and pinned against Army Group B, and he pushed them into a rapidly shrinking sack on the Channel coast. It had been a devastating maneuver, one of the great feats of military history—a Cannae, Blenheim, Sedan, Yorktown.

By May 20, some 400,000 exhausted Allied soldiers were trapped and short of supplies near the port of Dunkirk, virtually helpless before the onrushing panzers. On May 22, supreme headquarters, OKW, flashed the message "Abmarsch Nord." There were some doubts at the highest OKW levels about previous tank losses, fuel shortages, and the like, but this was traditional caution. Radical young tank soldiers like General Heinz Guderian and Field Marshal Erwin Rommel knew that Allied resistance would be feeble. Their tanks could crash through the British perimeter and either capture the Allied armies or make mincemeat of them. That is when Hermann Göring, head of the Luftwaffe, made his great contribution to the British cause. Göring may have lost the war with a phone call.

On the afternoon of May 23, Reichsmarschall Hermann Göring watched the situation with mounting outrage. He had flown with Richthofen, the Red Baron, in the last war and had been an authentic hero, an ace fighter pilot in the Flying Circus. That afternoon he was working at a large oak table set up for him beside his private train near the German-French border. He saw that the Wehrmacht was going to smash the British and French around Dunkirk. Not the Luftwaffe. Slamming his meaty fist on his desk, he demanded a direct line to Hitler himself. The conservative, even reactionary generals of the Wehrmacht would not seize the prize. No clanking armor and trench mortars for the Nazis, but air power. The twentieth century. When he got the Führer on the phone, Göring demanded that the tanks be stopped. The Luftwaffe would smash the Allies on the beaches, a cheap victory. A triumph for Hitler and revolutionary National Socialism.

Hilter liked the idea. He disliked the generals. He had other concerns as well, wanting to save his remaining armor in case the French stiffened their resistance before Paris. He remembered 1914, the Marne. Göring's easy solution appealed to him. He thought about the plan overnight and the next day, early in the afternoon, issued the order that "the forces advancing to the northwest of Arras are not to go beyond the general line of Lens-Bethune-Aire-St. Omer-Gravelines. On the west wing, all mobile units are to close up and let the enemy throw himself against the above-mentioned favorable defensive line."

It did not work. The Luftwaffe ran into fog, normal around the Channel coast, plus a furious resistance from Hurricanes and Spitfires, a fiery foretaste of the Battle of Britain. The slow Stukas blew up in the sky. Days passed without the victory Göring had promised, as fleets of small and large boats poured out of British rivers and estuaries to take virtually the entire trapped force off the shore. "The little ships," said Churchill, speaking in the Commons, "the unforgotten Homeric catalogue of *Mary Jane* and *Peggy IV,* of *Folkestone Belle, Boy Billy,* and *Ethel Maud,* of *Lady Haig* and *Skylark* . . . the little ships of England brought the army home." One of the little ships was owned and steered by Charles H. Lightoller, who made several trips across the Channel to Dunkirk. He had been second officer on the *Titanic* in 1912.

Oddly enough, a few weeks later, Göring sold Hitler on another idea. That the Luftwaffe, over the skies of England, would knock the island out of the war. It may be that Göring believed it. But Hitler, with not much of a navy, had nothing else that could get Germans across the Channel.

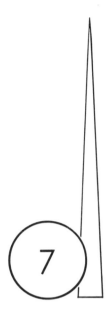

FIFTH DOWN AND SIX TO GO

7

When the 1940 college football season opened that fall, an older era was ending both on the campus and on its playing fields; 1940 had much in common with 1925. The great football trains carrying fans and alumni to Ann Arbor or to New Haven were major social events, and that year the ten-year-old boy boarded the "Dartmouth Football Special" at Penn Station with his father, wide-eyed at the hubbub, the drinking, the songs, the shouts, and the chatter, and wide-eyed in Palmer Stadium too at the passing exploits of Princeton's Dave Allerdice and the rubber-ball, deep reverses of Dartmouth's Ted Arico running out of the old single wing.

"Campus newspapers," recalls historian Jacques Barzun,

> gave news and views, those concerning the outer world being
> only a fraction of the whole and reasonable in tone. In
> curriculum matters, the Great Books and general education
> (Columbia offspring) had won wide acceptance. Chicago had
> accepted both and for the latter Harvard claimed credit
> without implementation in a useful and influential document.
> As the second depression (1932–36) grew less horrendous,
> the campus mood regained the contemplative tone of the late

1920s. The flight from teaching, the university as service
station, the arrogance of academic solutions to the world's
troubles, the administrative interference by the big founda-
tions and the government, the consequent shuffle, cake-walk,
really, of faculty people from place to place, the influx of
anti-college students, forced into academic work by parents
persuaded it was the path to high salaries, the credentials
mania and competition for grades, the need to adapt
programs to the needs of veterans brought in by the G.I.
Bill—all those things that gradually led to the destruction of
the 1960s were, in 1940, non-existent or as yet invisible. It
was a privilege, intellectual and spiritual, to earn a place in
the life of the mind, to be as student or teacher equally a
"member of the college or university." The duties were clear;
the rights were so obvious as never to be talked about.

True, and immensely moving as recollection, but at the same time
there were intimations of vast change, a gathering gloom on the
horizon. The presidents of Harvard, Princeton, and Yale called for a
military draft. President Nicholas Murray Butler of Columbia startled his faculty by announcing that their university was allied with
the government in a great effort of resistance to totalitarianism and
that therefore some undefined aspects of academic freedom had to
be temporarily suspended. Under pressure, Mr. Butler backed
down, but the war had begun to wash up on the shore where the boys
of 1940 played.

That fall, amid the mock Gothic or Georgian buildings of the
American campus, whether at the vast state universities or the older
and smaller Ivy League schools, there would as always be parties on
Friday night before The Game and on Saturday night after it. You
would find a four-piece band in the fraternity cellar or in the ground-
floor living room and a bass drum with a light bulb inside it shining
behind a picture of a windmill or an airplane. As the couples moved
to the rhythm in the darkened room or necked on the central
staircase, the band played "Stardust," "Little Brown Jug," "Chat-
tanooga Choo Choo," "Booglie Wooglie Piggy," "That Old Black
Magic," and "The White Cliffs of Dover." On Saturday afternoon,
after a milk-punch party at SAE or Phi Psi or Deke, the raccoon
coats marched as always under an azure sky to the stadium. The
girls wore chrysanthemums; the ivy on the walls of the college
buildings had begun to turn scarlet; and inside the stadium the
teams had begun to work out, throwing the ball—whump whump—
or kicking it—thwock. The raccoon coats made the stadium look
fur-lined; hip flasks and pint bottles circulated; and the band wore

sweaters and white trousers: "Going back, going back, going back to Nassau Hall. . . ." Above the din there could periodically be heard a whiskey bottle crashing on the concrete steps.

The sports fan of the 1980s, however, would be startled by an important feature of the 1940 season: the football teams of the Ivy League were big news, some of them national powers, the details even of their practice sessions covered by the press. Cornell defeated Ohio State that year, and Columbia beat Georgia. Four games into the 1940 season, the number one team in the national rankings was . . . Cornell, under its great coach Carl Snavely. Indeed, the Ivy League coaches were at the top of their profession: Fritz Crisler at Princeton, Earl "Red" Blaik at Dartmouth, Lou Little at Columbia, "Tuss" McLaughry at Brown, "Ducky" Pond and his assistant "Greasy" Neale at Yale, Dick Harlow at Harvard, and George Munger at Penn. Before their game with Syracuse, Lou Little felt obliged to warn his players not to take Syracuse too lightly. On a cold and rainy Saturday afternoon, Red Blaik outsmarted Snavely, and a mediocre Dartmouth team upset undefeated Cornell in what was considered the most startling event of the year in sports. It was indeed one of the most remarkable games in the history of football.

As the season of 1940 approached, the Columbia team, working out at Baker Field and short on numbers, but highly talented, looked forward to the approaching contests with guarded optimism. Much was expected of two backs, both sophomores and both triple-threat men, Paul Governalli and Ken Germann. Governalli would carry on the Columbia passing tradition begun by the great Sid Luckman, who was now playing for the Chicago Bears. "The Lions," you read on the sports page, were rehearsing "intricate spinner and reverse plays in preparation for a scrimmage with Army at West Point today. The West Point meeting will be closed to the public." Allison Danzig of the *New York Times* made his way up to Cambridge to assess Dick Harlow's Harvard squad and then went to New Haven and Hanover. He wrote that Dartmouth's hopes rested on new men: "First Eleven Powerful: Team Lacks Top-Notch Reserve Talent." "Despite its greenness," he observed,

> and even though there is the usual dearth of first-class
> reserves, Dartmouth should be a stronger team than it was a
> year ago, when the first six games were won and the last
> three were lost. It may not do as well in the percentage
> column, depending on the strength of the opposition, but the
> coaches, including Harry Ellinger, Andy Gustafson and Specs
> Moore, are pretty well convinced that the first team is a
> definite improvement over last year's. "We have a good

starting backfield," said Blaik, who is habitually on the cautious side, "and I can say that our line has more cohesion than a year ago. If we keep the first team together and do not have to make more than scattered substitutions, no one is going to push us around as they did in some of our games last Fall."

Princeton's hopes rested on the strong right arm of the remarkable Dave Allerdice, whose flat passes sports fans with long memories compare with those of Bob Waterfield. A flyer in the war, Allerdice was to be badly injured and die prematurely.

When the season opened, both Penn and Cornell gave fair warning of things to come. Headline: "Cornell Subdues Colgate 34 to 0 With Accurate Overhead Attack." News story:

> Cornell picked up today where it left off in 1939 and a strong scrappy Colgate team that tore into the Ithacans at the start was riddled and torpedoed by one of the deadliest aerial barrages ever laid down on Schoelkopf Field. Bigger and better and just as many of them is the red light that today's 34–0 stampede flashes to the opponents of Carl Snavely's 1940 streamlined varsity of seniors. The ease with which it handled the big, fast and aggressive Red Raiders and knocked everything out of them except their fight, as 15,000 looked on in baseball weather from the crescent, stamps Cornell as one of the football teams of the year to beat, a worthy foe for the scarlet scourge of Ohio State that will come here on the 26th. Cornell has everything that goes into the making of a team, including experience, savvy, size, speed.

But the University of Pennsylvania, that same Saturday, gave every indication that it was not going to yield dominance to Cornell without a fight. Penn beat Maryland 51–0, led by its great back Frank Reagan: "Crowd of 40,000 Sees Penn Overwhelm Maryland's Team on Franklin Field." "Gaining momentum as the game progressed," read the write-up, "Pennsylvania opened its fiftieth football season today with an overwhelming 51–0 victory over Maryland on Franklin Field before 40,000 spectators. . . . In the second [quarter] Frank Reagan and Jack Welsh crossed the Terrapin goal line. In the third, Reagan and John Dutcher made six-pointers, while in the last period, Harry Gifford, a sophomore, Bob Hartwig, another new player, and Welsh went over for touchdowns."

On the second Saturday of the season, Penn crushed Yale 50–7: "Defeat Is Worst in Elis' Football History—Reagan Bags Three

Touchdowns." But Cornell kept the pace: "Cornell Routs Army 45-0, Scoring Seven Touchdowns," an all-time record against the Cadets. The flashy deep reverses of Dartmouth's diminutive Ted Arico—he ran forty yards back and forth behind the line to gain five or ten in front of it—were not enough to hold off Columbia, as "Governalli Runs 75 Yards" in a 20-6 victory in Hanover. Yale was not having a good year, and to cap it all off, Handsome Dan IV, the bulldog mascot, died that fall: "Handsome Dan IV Goes Where All Good Bulldogs Go." The same day Handsome Dan died, however, Yale managed to defeat Dartmouth 13-7, while Columbia produced headlines inconceivable in the 1980s: "Columbia Downs Georgia 19-13." "In a rousing and spectacular affair," wrote Arthur Daley, "that almost seemed as if the boys had borrowed the script of the drama-laden, Columbia-Army football series, the Lions took the lead for the third and last time in the final quarter to defeat Georgia 19-13 before 23,000 fans at Baker Field."

Cornell and Penn continued to roll. "Cornell's Aerials Sink Syracuse 33-6." Against Penn, Princeton's great Dave Allerdice put on an aerial circus of his own, throwing forty passes for an amazing 350 yards, but to no avail, as Frank Reagan and George Munger's players thrust the Tigers aside 46-28.

By the time the fourth game of the season approached, with Cornell ranked first in the nation and Penn eighth, with Michigan and Tom Harmon in third place behind Notre Dame, football excitement reached a pitch of extraordinary intensity. "It's the Ivy League against the Big Ten this week," wrote Allison Danzig, "Pennsylvania against Michigan at Ann Arbor in the stand-out game on Saturday's football program and Cornell against Ohio State at Ithaca, where every seat in Schoelkopf Crescent, as well as all hotel and rooming-house accommodations, have long been reserved for the renewal of last year's memorable battle of Columbus." "Not in a number of Saturdays for some seasons back," wrote reporter Robert F. Kelley, "has college football had two games attracting the attention that will focus on Ithaca for Ohio State and Cornell and on Ann Arbor for Penn and Michigan."

The next day in the football column of the *New York Times*, Allison Danzig reached for his high-colored vocabulary:

> On Saturday, before the record crowd to see a game at Ithaca, Cornell will send out on Schoelkopf Field a team that may take its place high on the roll-call of the gridiron great. Possibly there is some flaw in it that has gone undetected and that will be exposed by a powerful Ohio State eleven with painful memories of 1939 and stung by the loss of two close decisions to North-

western and Michigan. But on the record of the Reds'
accomplishments and on its personnel, Cornell appears to be
qualified for any assignment it undertakes. It has every requisite
of a winner, and unless the human equation intervenes with
twists or quirks of fate—known as the breaks—only a foe of rare
skill and strength would seem to be a match for it. . . . The team
that Ohio State will tackle in Schoelkopf Crescent is the same
team, except for one regular, that got up off the floor of the
Columbus Stadium, after being trampled on two long touchdown marches, and scored 23 points against the Big Ten
champions last fall. Walter Scholl, who exploded the first
bombshell, a 79-yard touchdown run behind scythe-like blocking, and who immediately fired a second torpedo, a 68-yard
scoring pass, is still a substitute halfback. So is Swifty Bohr-
man, who caught the pass. The poise, intelligence and quick
reaction that characterized the 1939 team, particularly in its
pass defense, have been in evidence again. It is a more experienced team, with almost every man on the first two elevens a
tested veteran, whereas a year ago two of its mainstays, Landsberg at fullback and Finneran at center, were jayvee recruits.
The poise, intelligence and quick reaction that characterized the
1939 team, particularly in its pass defense, have been in evidence again. It has the same smart direction from Captain
Walter Matuszczak, who, according to Carl Snavely, did not call
a single bad play in 1939. It is still a team that strikes for home in
a single play or with a minimum of first downs, rather than
grinds out yards. It counts on no big line-smashing fullback of
the type of Piepul or Kimbrough, but a lot of whippets who lance
through the tackles, reverse the ends and throw on the run, and a
halfback bucker who spins and darts through the middle.

Defensively, Cornell has looked to be markedly stronger than
it was a year ago when Ohio State went 158 yards for its two
touchdowns and threw only one pass in the process, netting 37
yards. Colgate's fast backs ran into a stone wall. Syracuse
rushed the ball for 118 yards, but West and Hershey were both
out of the game at left tackle and left end and Dunbar, left guard,
made his exit with a broken nose in the second period.

Ohio State will present seven men who started against Cornell
last year and seven others who got into the game. Among these
are Don Scott, the versatile 213-pound quarterback, one of the
best in the country last year; Jim Langhurst, regarded as the
equal of any fullback in the Big Ten; the fast left halfback, Jim
Strausbaugh, and Charley Maag, the big tackle who won the

1939 Minnesota game and the Purdue game this year with field
goals and also kicked one against Pittsburgh and Northwestern.

On the big day, October 21, "Michigan Conquers Penn 14–0"
before a crowd of 60,000 at Ann Arbor as the great Tommy Harmon
had one of his best days. "Harmon played football of a type that few
individuals have played on any gridiron, and when it was over he
had to fight his tired way through a queue of clutching admirers to
reach the showers. It was Harmon's biggest test, talked of for days,
and it brought hundreds from miles away to this stadium. Harmon
met the test fully. There is no longer the slightest doubt that he is a
great football player. He punted, he passed, he ran, he tackled and
he blocked. Above all, he kept a steady, frightening threat over the
heads of the men in Red and Blue, and this threat, perhaps more
than anything else, weighted the scales."

But at Schoelkopf Field in Ithaca, the Big Ten fared less well as
Cornell trounced Ohio State 21–7: "Last Period Cornell Scores
Subdue Ohio State's Eleven—Bofalino Crashes Across Twice in
Closing Quarter After Scholl's Run Turns Tide—34,500 See Buck-
eyes Tally Early." Danzig covered the game: "The Battle of Columbus, one of football's red-letter melodramas of 1939, was duplicated
on Schoelkopf Field today as Cornell came back again from a
terrific battering in the opening period to administer the worst
defeat suffered by Ohio State in the seven years of Francis Schmidt's
tenure as head coach. . . . With this victory over the 1939 champions of the Big Ten, Cornell added appreciably to its prestige as the
top-ranked team of the country and extended its winning streak.
Going back to 1938, Carl Snavely's team has now won fifteen games
and tied one since it lost to Syracuse two years ago."

The great Cornell team appeared to be absolutely unbeatable,
easily defeating Columbia 27–0 at Ithaca despite the heroics of
Governalli, Germann, and the rest. "Cylinder or no cylinder," wrote
reporter William Richardson,

> this Cornell team can really move along the football
> highway. . . . It proved its greatness again today when it
> ground the Columbia Lions into the turf of Schoelkopf Field
> 27–0 before a slender, but fully convinced, crowd of 15,000.
> Not once, from the moment Len Will sent the initial kickoff
> booming down the field until the final tick of the clock, was
> there the slightest doubt that the Big Red would gain its fifth
> consecutive victory of the year and enlarge on its great record
> of twelve games without a single setback. Even the

acknowledged cunning of the wily Lou Little, Columbia's
great coach, was unable to stem the red tide that has already
surged over Colgate, Army, Syracuse and Ohio State this
season. It was simply an impossible task that the schedule
makers had assigned to Columbia's willing but powerless
warriors.

Though Cornell by this point in the season had done everything
required of it, it slipped from first to second place in the national
rankings because impressive performances by Minnesota had nar-
rowly moved the Golden Gophers into the top spot. Still Carl
Snavely and his three complete Cornell teams had little reason to
fear a mediocre Dartmouth team as they walked out onto Memorial
Field in Hanover on that chilly Saturday afternoon of November 16,
1940, but in fact, they were walking into the strangest and most
startling upset in the seventy-one-year history of football, a game
still talked about with awe in football circles. Dartmouth came into
the game with losses to Franklin and Marshall, Yale, and Columbia,
plus a win over St. Lawrence. The team's performance had been
sloppy all season, though with isolated flashes of brilliance. Cornell
was one of the best teams in the nation—perhaps *the* best—and was
undefeated. Cornell was a prohibitive favorite in the odds.

A small crowd of 8,000 was on hand in Dartmouth's Memorial
Field, almost filling the cement stands on the western edge of the
field. The wooden stands across the way had only the center section
filled. While the two teams warmed up on the field before the game,
a light snow fell, but tapered off before the kickoff. The field was
dry and firm because it had been covered overnight with a tarpaulin.
Dartmouth's Lou Young and Cornell's Walt Matuszczak, the rival
captains, walked to the center of the field and shook hands. Cornell
won the coin toss and elected to kick off. Dartmouth's sophomore
back, Ray Wolfe, received the ball and on the first play of the game
gave an indication of things to come. Taking the ball on his 10-yard
line, Wolfe dashed upfield, avoiding tacklers, and would have gone
all the way for an opening-seconds Cornell disaster except that the
last Cornell defender managed to tackle him on the Cornell forty-
five.

During the first quarter, the Dartmouth Indians smothered every
effort of the vaunted Cornell attack. The line outplayed Cornell so
decisively that the backfield was called upon for assistance on only
three plays. The second quarter resembled the first, with Cornell
unable to advance the ball beyond its own 33-yard line. In contrast,
drives through the Cornell line kept Dartmouth constantly threatening to score. Wolfe, Kast, Hall, and Krieger moved the ball steadily,

and quarterback Don Norton ran Coach Earl Blaik's offense with a precision that was marvelous to see. Dartmouth was controlling the ball so successfully that the Indians did not attempt a pass throughout the first half.

After the intermission, the crowd held its breath. The Dartmouth coaches had devised a defense that had never been used before in football. Twice they had seen the Dartmouth team line up a yard and a half behind the line of scrimmage, while the Cornell team registered its amazement and lost its timing. Would Cornell solve its running problem during the second half? The answer, immediately, was no. Desperate on the ground, Cornell took to the air with an explosive forward pass offense.

The next day the Sunday headline read: "Cornell Tops Dartmouth 7–3 at Finish." But that was not to be the end of the story. As William Richardson described it in the *Times*:

> With less than three seconds to play in today's Dartmouth game, Cornell's prayer for victory was answered when Bill Murphy, who had gone in at right half only a few minutes before, leaped high into the air to catch Walt Scholl's pass in the end zone. When the ball nestled in Murphy's arms it sealed the doom of one of the fightingest Dartmouth teams in history—a team that had outfought the famed Big Red almost from start to finish and was leading 3–0 as a result of a brilliant 27-yard field goal by Bob Krieger in the opening minutes of the last period of one of the most thrilling gridiron encounters that has ever been waged.
>
> Underdogs at something like 4 to 1 after one of the poorest seasons in Dartmouth history, the Indians had amazed the 10,000 spectators huddled in Memorial Stadium by their fight and determination. But that one do-or-die catch of Murphy's undid everything and left them on the losing end of a 7–3 score for which they will never have reason to be ashamed.
>
> For one-half of the game . . . the Indians had outplayed Cornell as completely as any team had ever been out-played. And in the third period they had stopped an awe-inspiring Cornell drive by intercepting a pass in the end zone and then had surged back on the attack once again, finally taking the lead on Krieger's perfect boot.
>
> Twice thereafter Cornell, driven to desperation at the thought of being dropped out of the unbeaten class, surged toward the Dartmouth goal, but on two occasions interceptions brought the march to a halt. Once Wolfe intercepted on the Dartmouth 43 and on the next Ed Kast hauled one in on

the 8 after the Big Red had moved from its own 23. Then, with two and a half minutes left, Cornell started its final march that led to victory and controversy. Relying chiefly on aerials, the Big Red moved steadily to first downs on the 41, then on the 31, then the 18 and finally the 6.

Mort Landsberg drove for 3, and he and Scholl to the one-yard stripe, fourth down. Here Cornell was penalized, making fourth and six, and then Scholl passed and Ray Hall [of Dartmouth], thinking it fourth down, as did almost everyone else, knocked the ball down instead of catching it as he might have done.

His amazement was the same as everyone else's when an official started to put the ball on the 20, meaning it was Dartmouth's on downs, changed his mind and replaced it on the 6, from where Scholl passed to Murphy in the extreme end of the end zone.

Except for the extra point, that was the last play of the game. But had Cornell scored on an illegal fifth down? Captain Lou Young of the Indians and other Dartmouth players insisted that this was the case. "We have the crisis of a lifetime in the making here," yelled the radio announcer. Most of the football writers' charts showed that Mort Landsberg had rushed twice and Scholl once before the latter threw the pass that Hall knocked down behind his goal line. That amounted to four plays. Carl Snavely at first assumed that on one of the plays both teams had been called offside, thus nullifying one play, but the officials assured him that this had not happened.

Just before the scoring pass to Murphy, Captain Lou Young of Dartmouth and other players demanded that Referee W. H. "Red" Friesell give Dartmouth the ball, but Friesell refused and declined to discuss the matter afterwards. The next day, Asa Bushnell, head of the Eastern Intercollegiate Football Association, announced that even if an error had occurred, he had no power to change the result. As far as he was concerned, the score was on the board and changes were up to Cornell and Dartmouth. Dartmouth announced that movies of the game were being processed and would be shown in Hanover on Monday. Some 1,500 Dartmouth students staged a tumultuous "victory" rally.

And then it *was* a victory. On Tuesday the headlines announced the decision made the day before: "Dartmouth 3, Cornell 0, Official Admits Error." Arthur Daley wrote up the unprecedented sequence of events:

Cornell beat Dartmouth 7–3 on an illegal extra play at Hanover last Saturday. William H. Red Friesell, the referee, yesterday publicly admitted he had been in error in giving the Big Red a "fifth down" on which it scored a touchdown. Cornell relinquished all claim to the victory and Dartmouth accepted the triumph, the score of which posterity will recall as 3–0.

This action is unprecedented in intercollegiate football. Friesell had the courage to admit he had been wrong and Cornell had the sportsmanship to yield a success it felt it had not rightfully earned. Only by this extraordinary combination of circumstances could the score be reversed, because the referee's jurisdiction ends with the game and there is no other authority beyond the colleges themselves to make amends for the error.

Thus did Cornell voluntarily remove itself from the list of unbeaten teams. It had gone through eighteen straight games without a setback, seventeen victories, and one scoreless tie. Ithaca authorities had said on Saturday night that they would refuse to accept the 7–3 triumph if the winning play was an illegal one.

Friesell confirmed yesterday that it was illegal in a special report sent to Asa S. Bushnell, commissioner of the Eastern Intercollegiate Football Association. It was as follows:

> Since the conclusion of Saturday's Cornell-Dartmouth football game at Hanover I have made careful and thorough study of all evidence having to do with the final series of plays which led to Cornell's touchdown and 7-to-3 victory just as time expired in the fourth quarter.
>
> On the basis of numerous charts kept by the press and motion pictures taken by both of the competing colleges, I am now convinced beyond shadow of doubt that I was in error in allowing Cornell possession of the ball for the play on which they scored.
>
> I find that, after a Cornell first down on the 6-yard line, there followed three line plays which gained five yards, then an extra time-out penalty which cost Cornell five yards, and then a forward pass into the end zone knocked down by Dartmouth.
>
> At this point Dartmouth was entitled to take the ball on their 20-yard line, first down, with about six seconds of play remaining. Unfortunately, however, thinking it was Cornell's ball, fourth down, on the 6-yard line, I awarded it to them for what was actually an illegal fifth-down play—a play which produced the winning score.
>
> This mistake was entirely mine as the game's referee, and not shaped in or contributed to by any of the three other officials. I realize, of course, that my jurisdiction ceased at the close of the game and that the football rules give me no authority to change even an incorrect decision such as the one described, but I do want to acknowledge my mistake to you as commissioner of the Eastern Intercollegiate Football Association and, if you see fit, to the football public as well.

"Cornell," continued Daley's account, "acted as soon as it learned of the Friesell report. James Lynah, Director of Athletics, and Carl Snavely, Coach, promptly wired to Graduate Manager William H. McCarter and Coach Earl Blaik of Dartmouth and conceded the victory to Dartmouth."

In Hanover of course, the jubilation was unrestrained. Captain Lou Young; the scat back, Ted Arico; the other backs, Wolfe and Hall, had outplayed far more celebrated men like Scholl, Landsberg, and Murphy. The heretofore lowly Indians had upset the team that had crushed Ohio State. Some 2,000 Dartmouth students rallied behind the Dartmouth band on Monday evening, and the band made the rounds of the dormitories, as students, faculty members, and townspeople gathered at the main intersection of the small town, and calls went up from the crowd for the appearance of the football heroes from within the senior society Casque and Gauntlet. One by one they did appear, to the accompaniment of ear-splitting cheers from the crowd. "I am tickled to death with the result," said Lou Young, the first to appear, "and the fellows deserve it. They are a grand bunch and by that I mean from the varsity through the jayvees to the freshmen. It was a squad victory and is a great tribute to Coach Blaik and the whole staff." Bob Krieger, who kicked the winning field goal, got a thunderous ovation, and Arico, Hall, and the others were not forgotten by the crowd. After the players had all appeared the band swung off down the main street playing "Far Above Cayuga's Waters." The band and a snake-dancing crowd then moved up and down the streets of the town as merchants and businessmen watched from doors and windows.

The next day, Cornell President Edmund Ezra Day, a Dartmouth graduate, told a rally in Ithaca that Cornell did not want any football victory through a "long count," a reference to the famous Dempsey-Tunney fight of 1927. He told the throng that the final scoring play, which had been disallowed, was still a great play. "At Hanover I saw the greatest football finish ever played out by a great team. The score may came off, but the play remains." He continued: "If we hadn't made that decision, we'd have been explaining that game as long as football has a place in intercollegiate atheletics—and I want no long count in Cornell's athletic history." As Cornell began practicing for its final game against Penn and Frank Reagan, Captain Walt Matuszczak reported to the infirmary with a stomach disorder.

Dartmouth's coach that year, Earl Blaik, a West Point graduate, had left the army after the First World War and prospered in real estate, but he was increasingly drawn to football and coaching. In 1927 he responded to the call to return to West Point as an assistant coach. The great success of the Army teams brought Blaik to the attention of Dartmouth's president, Ernest Martin Hopkins, who lured him to Hanover as head coach in 1934. With Blaik, who demanded 110 percent effort—"You have to pay the price" was his motto—Dartmouth became a serious contender in major football. He broke the long string of losses to Yale, the "Yale Jinx," and with players like Bill Hutchinson and Bob MacLeod running the ball—"As good as any backs anywhere," Blaik said—gave Dartmouth a taste of football glory during the 1930s. After the season of 1940, Blaik was prevailed upon to return to West Point, with mixed feelings about leaving Hanover, and there he coached the wartime powerhouses of Blanchard and Davis and the postwar national championship teams. In the history of modern football, he belongs in the pantheon along with men like Frank Leahy and Ara Parsegian of Notre Dame, Joe Paterno of Penn State, Columbia's Lou Little, and Vince Lombardi and Don Shula of the pro game.

But Blaik's career extended well beyond football brilliance. He was a man of intelligence and character, a friend and confidant of Dartmouth's president, Ernest Martin Hopkins, who was an educational leader of national and even world reputation. After Blaik retired from coaching at West Point, he had a major corporate career as vice president of AVCO. He was close to Douglas MacArthur, Dwight Eisenhower, Robert Kennedy. He believes firmly that MacArthur never intended to run for president in 1952. Leaving LaGuardia Airport by plane to die in Walter Reed Hospital in 1964, MacArthur ordered the plane halted on the runway to say goodbye to Blaik, who had been delayed by traffic.

The 3–0 Dartmouth victory over Cornell owed much, of course, to the determination of the players themselves, but it would not have been possible at all without some brilliant strategy on the part of Blaik, particularly on defense. Blaik has written two memoirs, *You Have to Pay the Price* (1960) and an expansion of this book entitled *The Red Blaik Story* (1974). His own account of the 1940 Cornell game is an important addition to football history. Here it is in Blaik's words:

> In 1940, we slipped a little more. Yale beat us, 13–7, for the first time since 1934. We had lost three other games and had no ranking whatsoever as we approached the next to the last game on our schedule: Cornell, at Memorial Field, November 16. Since midway in 1938, Cornell had won eighteen straight, was ranked No. 1 nationally and was at least a 4–1 favorite over us. Snavely himself told Allison Danzig, veteran expert of the *New York Times* and a Cornell alumnus, that of his three powerful teams of 1938 through '40, the '40 team was the best until weakened by injuries, especially on the left side of the line. All but one of these injuries were

incurred in the first quarter of our game due to the rugged
play.

In preparing for that game, I had two problems: the first
technical, the second psychological.

For two years, Cornell's running attack had featured tricky spins,
reverses, and traps, with relatively little reliance on straight-ahead
power. The year before, we had played into their hands by using a
hard-charging line and they had cut us to pieces.

This time, we put together an elaborate defensive pattern,
which may well have been as complicated as any devised up
until then. We played our ends normally on the line but
posted our tackles and guards a yard and a half off the ball.
The linebackers, playing shallow, approximated the same
depth as the tackles and guards. The plan was for these six
men to sit there, forgo early commitment, angle off in the
direction of the ball, and by quick reaction give up the short
gain and no more.

Now, part of the reason why Cornell seldom hit straight
ahead was that the fullback, or No. 3 back, in their single
wing, Mr. Landsberg, was speedy and nifty at darting through
a trap hole rather than powerful. On certain plays, however,
Landsberg exchanged places with Captain Walter
Matuszczak, Cornell's back No. 2 or blocking back. This gave
them more straight-ahead plunging power and also enabled
them to utilize Matuszczak's powerful blocking on sweeps.

They also had a dangerous counterplay from this series, on
which Walter Scholl, the tailback, faked a run to the strong
side, stepped and tossed a "back diagonal" pass to Landsberg
in the weak-side flat. With Landsberg's speed, it was a
potential long-gainer or game breaker if called at the right
time, and had proved effective. To cover it, Bob Crego, our
weak-side backer-up, who was later to give his life in World
War II, was instructed always to play Landsberg, come what
may, when he shifted to the No. 2 spot.

So much for the outline of our defensive plan.

We naturally worked at building our men psychologically
for a supreme effort. We did not have to sell Cornell's stature.
Their record, rank, reputation, and what they had done to us
the year before took care of that. There was no problem
getting our men keyed up for the game. But as Saturday
neared, I thought I detected signs that they might be wound a
little tight. This could be just as harmful as a casual
approach. To execute the complex defensive blueprint
assigned them and also put on their own offense smoothly,

they needed to be dedicated yet relaxed, a finely drawn fusion not always easily achieved.

On Friday afternoon, we repaired to our regular pre-game bivouac, the Bonnie Oaks Inn on Lake Fairlee outside Fairlee, Vermont, not too far from Hanover. Saturday morning, we went through our usual routine: an early walk and breakfast. The players were then ordered to rest in their rooms until called by Bevan to have their ankles taped. Any boisterousness was supposed to be out of order. They were supposed to relax.

After breakfast—I guess I had a cup of tea—I went to my room and lay down. I thought about the squad. They looked a little too tight. I thought it over and phoned Captain Lou Young to come up to my room.

When Lou arrived, I tried not to look as white as the bed sheets. I tried to joke with him about the game, but I didn't do a very good job at it. I asked him how he thought the players felt about it. He said he thought they were ready, real ready. I asked him if he understood fully the defense signals he was to handle, and he said he did.

"Well, Lou," I said, "I think the team is wound a little too tight. Now, there isn't any need for this. We are really a much better team than Cornell expects to meet. We are ready to take them. So, I want the players to relax. After Bevan finishes taping them, I want you to get down in the lobby and turn on the record player. Play some of that hot jazz which seems to be the order of the day. We want to go into the stadium relaxed."

Lou carried out my instructions and when we boarded the bus, the players seemed to be a little looser. During the ride, I walked up and down the aisle and actually did some clowning, the first time I had done any acting of that type since my role as "Buttons the Bellhop" back at Steele High. Maybe my act wasn't very good, but I believe the players were relaxed the way I wanted them to be when we got to Memorial Field.

I had written in our pre-season football brochure: "the mysterious Indians on one occasion will rise to great play." This was the day. Our defense did the job we wanted. In the first half, we stopped them cold. In the third period, they marched, but we stopped them by an end-zone interception. Then we marched ourselves, and early in the final period we got close enough for end Bob Krieger to place-kick a 27-yard field goal.

With only four and a half minutes to play and the ball on their 48-yard line, Cornell took to the air. Although a light snow had dampened the ball and the field, Scholl was connecting with his receivers. Perhaps they should have begun passing earlier.

One pass was allowed for interference on the 18-yard line, but we were of no mind to complain. It was the "back-diagonal" pass to Landsberg. For once, Crego forgot to pick him up right away. Our phone spotters, sensing it immediately, jumped up and yelled, although Crego couldn't possibly have heard them. Crego, however, realized his mistake as the play developed. He saw that Landsberg was sure to get to the ball before he could, and that would likely spell touchdown and game. But Crego also saw that he had enough of an angle to tackle Landsberg and take the penalty, which he did. It was quick thinking. In light of what followed, it probably saved the game.

From the 18, another pass from Scholl to right halfback Bill Murphy gave Cornell first down on our 5. There was less than a minute to play as Landsberg hit into the line for two. On second down, Scholl drove to the 1. On third down, Landsberg was piled up for scarcely any gain. The ball rested less than a yard away from our goal line. There was time for two more plays at the most.

Now began a series of events which proved to be a weird prelude to an emotional Donnybrook and an aftermath never duplicated in football history.

To stop the clock, Snavely called time out, so Cornell was penalized 5 yards for delaying the game. This placed the ball on our 6-yard line.

On fourth down, Scholl passed into the end zone. The ball was batted away from Murphy, the intended receiver. William H. (Red) Friesell, a referee of long-proved excellence, put the ball on the 20-yard line, apparently in our possession.

But then, after a consultation requested by Captain Matuszczak, Friesell changed his mind and returned the ball to our 6. For some reason, according to a subsequent quote from Snavely, Matuszczak and other Cornell players thought there had been a double-offside penalty called on the pass which had been batted down in the end zone.

Captain Young protested vigorously to Friesell that there had been no such penalty, and two of the officials backed him up. But Friesell, apparently confused, continued to allow Cornell possession on the 6-yard line and another down.

There were six seconds left—time for Cornell to get off one play. They huddled and decided to go for a touchdown and victory rather than a field goal and a tie. Two seconds remained on the clock when Scholl passed to Murphy in the end zone, and this time Murphy caught it. Nick Drahos, Cornell tackle, kicked the extra point. The game was over and Cornell had won, 7–3.

The coaches on both sides and the fans thought that was it. But our players, two of the officials, and the writers covering the game knew that Cornell had scored on a fifth down. The writers so reported it. The news swept down from the press box, through the crowd, out onto Memorial Field, into Davis Field House and on through Hanover like wildfire. Students began parading, proclaiming a Dartmouth victory. They paraded throughout the weekend, every hour on the hour. One of the parades ended up in front of our house.

When the situation was brought to the attention of Jim Lynah, Cornell's athletic director, he stated that if the officials discovered that there had been five downs, the score would be recorded as Dartmouth 3, Cornell 0. Dr. Ezra Day, president of Cornell, concurred.

President Hopkins and I drove Referee Friesell across the Connecticut River to the White River Junction station. He admitted to us he had apparently made a mistake.

On Monday, after Cornell officials had studied the films, which showed five downs and no evidence of a double-offside, they called Asa Bushnell, Executive Secretary of the Eastern Intercollegiate Association, who then forwarded the information to Friesell.

Friesell issued a statement, expressing his regret. Bushnell then stated that no official had jurisdiction to change the outcome of the game and that any further action would have to come from Dartmouth or Cornell.

When this was reported to Cornell, they sent us two wires. One from Jim Lynah read:

IN VIEW OF THE CONCLUSIONS REACHED BY THE OFFICIALS THAT THE CORNELL TOUCHDOWN WAS SCORED ON A FIFTH DOWN, CORNELL RELINQUISHES CLAIM TO THE VICTORY AND EXTENDS CONGRATULATIONS TO DARTMOUTH.

A second from Coach Snavely read:

> I ACCEPT THE FINAL CONCLUSIONS OF THE OFFI-
> CIALS AND WITHOUT RESERVATION CONCEDE THE
> VICTORY TO DARTMOUTH WITH HEARTY CON-
> GRATULATIONS TO YOU AND THE GALLANT
> DARTMOUTH TEAM.

And we wired Cornell:

> DARTMOUTH ACCEPTS THE VICTORY AND CON-
> GRATULATES AND SALUTES THE CORNELL TEAM,
> THE HONORABLE AND HONORED OPPONENT OF
> OUR LONGEST UNBROKEN RIVALRY.

As the year 1940 drew to a close, sports experts delivered a wide-ranging assessment of what had gone on in the various athletic seasons. One conclusion was: "Cornell Figured in Greatest Upset: Defeat by Dartmouth Voted Most Surprising Event in 1940. Tigers' Pennant Second. Bimelech's Setback in Derby and Stanford's Football Rise Next on Shock List."

Nothing in the remainder of the 1940 football season could compare with the "fifth down" game and the upset of the nation's number two team. Cornell was no doubt subsequently demoralized to an undeterminable degree. Earlier in the season, a delegation of Cornell players, led by center Bud Finneran, had approached athletic officials and demanded what response the school was going to make to charges in the press that the Cornell players were really pros. President Day indicated publicly that he resented the charges and compared himself to the suffering Job of the Old Testament. On the final Saturday of the season, Penn defeated Cornell before a crowd of nearly 80,000 at Franklin Field in Philadelphia. Wrote Allison Danzig:

> In one of the most thrilling see-saw battles in the forty-seven
> years' history of the rivalry, Pennsylvania yielded 13 points to
> Cornell in the first seven minutes of play today, then came on
> in a fighting fury to snatch victory midway in the final
> quarter as Francis X. Reagan turned in a dazzling, record
> breaking performance to close his varsity career on Franklin
> Field. . . . With this victory, Penn's first over Cornell since
> 1936, the team of captain Ray Frick, a dynamic leader and
> intercepting ball-hawk, ousted the Ithacans as champions of
> the Ivy League, and Halfback Reagan, in scoring three
> touchdowns besides setting up a field-goal by Gene Davis

from the 28-yard line with a 52-yard run from scrimmage,
brought his total points for the year to 103.

The final score was 22–20, and the great Cornell team, which had
earlier been ranked number one in the nation, must have ended the
season bitterly disappointed.

Elsewhere in The Game, Harvard crushed Yale 28–0, Columbia
beat Colgate 20–17, Princeton beat West Point 26–19 as Dave Allerdice threw eleven passes for 157 yards, and Dartmouth wrapped up
the game against Brown with early scores and won 20–6. The great
Tom Harmon had one of his biggest days against Ohio State, scoring
22 points and breaking Red Grange's record, winning the Heisman
Trophy, and being voted best male athlete of 1940, with slugger
Hank Greenberg of the Detroit Tigers second, and Cincinnati ace
pitcher Bucky Walters third. Notre Dame suffered its worst defeat in
four years, losing 20–0 to Northwestern. At the season's end, Minnesota led the nation, followed by Stanford and Michigan, while
Penn stood at 14 and Cornell had plummeted to 15. Today any Ivy
League team would be delighted to rank 15 in the nation and it is
unlikely that any will do so, but as the 1940 season ended, it is
unlikely that the Cornell players were particularly happy about the
idea.

Jim Agee

Out of Lexington, Kentucky, the Episcopal Church, Phillips Exe-
ter Academy, Harvard, and Henry Luce's new magazine *Fortune,*
plus the bottle, the bottle, searching through the small hours for
purity, for something crystalline and without taint, prose raptures,
women, rages, and suicide threats—that was James Agee. His editor
at *Time,* T. S. Matthews, found him touchy, irritable, difficult to
work with, but maybe some kind of saint. Once he stayed up all
night on his own hook, after a week of working late nights, and
completely rewrote a *Time* cover story on Laurence Olivier's movie
of *Hamlet.* It was astonishingly brilliant, but too late to get into the
magazine.

Matthews knew about his rages. Once he picked up his own office
phone and through some accident of crossed wires heard Agee, his
voice muddy with rage and alcohol, cursing a telephone operator as
if he hated and despised her. He told his wife he was going to kill
himself, and when she hurried up to his office, she found the
window open. She was relieved and then furious to find Agee hiding

behind the door. Was he just another Southern windbag conning the New Yorkers?

All through the year 1940, his supposed great book languished, rejected by Harper & Brothers, perhaps unprintable because of its obscenities and distended absence of form. One warm June afternoon in 1936, he and Walker Evans, the photographer, had headed south in a jalopy, hating capitalism, seeking the clean lines of . . . poverty. He had once felt cleansed after offering his shoes and socks to some starving factory workers in Knoxville. He hated Henry Luce and Time-Life, hated the Chrysler Building and Rockefeller Center, and he spent hours watching Charlie Chaplin movies. Faded, pressed blue jeans, clean and very pale, lined and weathered faces, outback drawls—*there* was purity, the purity of poverty.

But where were the sharecroppers; where was the true clean poverty? Perhaps they were to be found in Oklahoma. He and Walker Evans headed the jalopy toward Oklahoma in a kind of panic but found no sharecroppers, only poor people of the usual sort struggling to get along. Like prospectors, Agee and Evans pushed on to Alabama, hoping for a change in their luck, a nugget of pure poverty. Even in the midst of the Great Depression, what they wanted was hard to find. They did not just want poor people. They wanted a kind of holy poverty—poor people who nevertheless possessed greater natural dignity than the corrupt bourgeoisie back in New York. Thirty miles from Tuscaloosa, they thought they found it, a Klondike poverty strike, a moral Sutter's Mill. Walker Evans developed his photographs in a darkened hotel room. Yes, there they were, the lined and hopeless faces, the faded work clothes, the pitiful shacks.

Agee experienced a spiritual rebirth. He began to walk as the sharecroppers did, a little stiffly, and he began to talk softly and slowly, like a sharecropper. He wore sneakers without socks and rolled up the legs of his trousers as they did. "The odors of cooking," he wrote. "Among these most strongly, the odors of fried salt pork and of fried and boiled pork lard, and, second, the odor of cooked corn. The odors of sweat in many stages of age and freshness, this sweat being a distillation of pork, lard, corn, woodsmoke, pine and ammonia."

He labored over the manuscript and thought himself the artistic successor of Joyce. This would be something entirely new and would scorch the bourgeoisie. When Henry Luce sent him to cover a cruise to Havana, the sleek and vulgar passengers made him want to vomit. He considered himself a Communist.

He had a vision of universal brotherhood and communal love, and he goaded a reluctant Walker Evans into sexual intercourse with

Mrs. Agee while he sat at the foot of the bed watching. The sight of the writhing bodies devastated him, and he began to weep, but he felt also "post-Dostoyevskian." While writing about the advanced purity of the sharecroppers, he wore proletarian checked shirts to Time-Life and bullied the bourgeois secretaries. Weekends he visited friends like Wilder Hobson on the North Shore of Long Island. Hobson liked to march up and down of a Saturday night in the nude, blowing on a slide trombone. When a woman appeared naked from the waist up on his tennis court, Hobson had the aplomb to inquire, "Am I seeing double?"

Eunice Clark, a talent scout from Houghton Mifflin, heard Agee read sections from the manuscript at a party in New Jersey and brought it to the attention of the Boston publisher. They wanted to publish it, but Agee was difficult. He wanted the book done in newsprint, even though in that form it would turn to powder in a few years. Houghton Mifflin said no, but agreed to carefully nick the photographic plates to make them look fly-specked. Agee demanded that there be no promotion, no effort to "ingratiate it with the public."

When the book finally came out in the summer of 1941, Agee was on his third wife. Lionel Trilling, a rising star of the Columbia English Department, wrote that *Let Us Now Praise Famous Men* was "a great book" and "the most realistic and important moral event of our generation." But by the summer of 1941, war production had ended the Depression; attention was focused on Europe and Asia; no one wanted to read about the wonderful pure poverty of 1936 sharecroppers; and the book sold 600 copies.

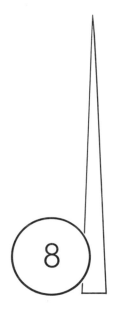

EVERYBODY'S FINNS, NOBODY'S JAPS

8

You followed the Finnish war with mounting excitement, in the newspapers, over the radio, in classroom discussions at P.S. 52, but especially in the pages of *Life* magazine. Unforgettable still today are those photographs of the Finnish ski troops, hundreds of white-clad soldiers on skis gliding through arctic villages and silent forests to achieve what seemed to be military successes of a Napoleonic character.

The Hitler-Stalin Pact of August 1939 had contained a secret protocol which came to light only in 1945, but which Soviet judges kept out of the Nuremburg trial. It divided Eastern Europe into spheres of influence but left open the question of an independent Polish state, and it looked forward to future cooperation between Germany and the Soviets. Of course all of this was nonsense. Hitler fully intended to carve out a vast empire in the East, including the grain-rich Ukraine, and there was no room in his future for Stalin. Nevertheless, as Paul Johnson writes, on the night of August 23–24, 1939, "there was a gruesome junket in the Kremlin. Ribbentrop reported: 'It felt like being among old party comrades.' He was much at ease in the Kremlin, he added, 'as among my old Nazi friends.' Stalin toasted Hitler and said 'he knew how much the

German people loved the Führer.' . . . As the tipsy killers lurched about the room, fumblingly hugging each other, they resembled nothing so much as a congregation of rival gangsters, who had fought each other before, and might do so again, but were essentially in the same racket.''

After Poland had been smashed by the Stukas and the panzers and had been divided between Hitler and Stalin, another agreement was sealed, the Soviet-German Frontier and Friendship Treaty of September 28, 1939. This gave Stalin a free hand in Latvia, Estonia, Lithuania, parts of Rumania—and Finland. Stalin made his move against Finland in early November, a bad time of year to begin arctic hostilities. He personally called Finnish diplomats into his Kremlin office and showed them a map of the Baltic. Three small Finnish islands and a sector of Finnish territory north of Leningrad were encircled in red. Stalin casually asked the Finns, "Do you need these islands?"

The Finns believed that any concessions would lead to more demands from Stalin. In Moscow, O. W. Kuusinen, leader of the exiled Finnish Communist Party, who was also Stalin's ghostwriter and a Comintern official, assured the credulous dictator that Finland was ripe for revolution. Andrei Zhdanov, Stalin's designated heir and the political boss of Leningrad, thought Finland would collapse before a few Red Army divisions. After all, Hitler's Wehrmacht had just shown what a great power could do to a small one.

On November 26, 1939, the Soviets handed the Finnish ambassador in Moscow a note that claimed Finnish artillery had killed Soviet troops in a suburb of Leningrad. On November 30, the Soviets severed diplomatic relations. The next morning, Soviet planes bombed Helsinki and Soviet troops attacked in strength at numerous points: on the Karelian Isthmus in the south between the Gulf of Finland and Lake Ladoga; north of the lake in a pincers movement; further north at the narrow waist of Finland; in the Arctic; and on the islands in the Finnish Gulf.

American opinion covered the spectrum from despondency to outrage. Apparently another small country was going to be crushed by a dictator. The Gallup poll showed 90 percent support for the Finns, 7 percent for the Soviets. In his diary, foreign correspondent William L. Shirer wrote: "The whole moral foundation which the Soviets have built up for themselves in international relations in the last ten years has collapsed like a house of cards. . . . Stalin reveals himself of the same stamp as Hitler, Mussolini and the Japs. . . . The Kremlin has betrayed the revolution." But sensationally, inspiringly, Finland did not collapse—and in resisting successfully, it became the intense focus of hope that brute force need not always prevail. After the opening battles, Major George Fielding Eliot analyzed the situation in the January 15, 1940, *Life* magazine: "The first phase of the Russo-Finnish war is now at an end, with the repulse of all the Russian attacks over the whole stretch of frontier between the Arctic Ocean and Lake Ladoga. Finland is thus temporarily freed from any further anxiety in the North, and the Russians appear likely for the present to confine their attention to attempts to break through in the South by sheer weight of numbers."

Major Eliot, a sophisticated military analyst, expressed a restrained professional delight in the Soviets' folly:

> The half-baked thinking behind the Russian plan of attack
> becomes clearly apparent when we look at map Number 3.
> Here is what appears to be a sort of *Blitzkrieg,* with a touch of
> Von Schlieffen about it. The Germans attacked Poland from
> six points. "Very well," one can hear the Russian staff
> officers saying, "we will attack Finland from six points too."
> But the German attacks were in force, and supported each
> other, while the excellent German air force blasted the Polish
> air force and the Polish railways, and thus prevented the Poles
> from concentrating on any one German column of invasion to
> its destruction. The Russian air force, because of poor
> training, poor command, lack of available bases and bad
> weather, proved incapable of doing the same thing to the
> Finns.

The Finns had become everyone's hope. In the fifth-grade home room at P.S. 52 there was a large map of the battle area and an intense student involvement with the unfolding situation. The industry and population of Finland is concentrated in the south, difficult for the Russians to attack. The Finnish commander, Field Marshal Mannerheim, had constructed a defensive line across the Karelian Isthmus, bordered on the north by the immense Lake Ladoga and on the south by the icy Gulf of Finland. The Karelian Isthmus itself was full of frozen lakes, swamps, and tundra—a defensive tactician's paradise. In addition, Mannerheim had constructed a sophisticated railway system—internal lines of communication, as the military strategists call it—which enabled him to shift his limited forces as the situation demanded. For once, a dictator—Stalin—was in deep trouble. The kids in the classroom studied the newspapers and *Life* and moved the red and blue pins on the map.

Much closer to the scene of action, a young Russian soldier, Vyaschlev Oreshin, wrote in his diary:

> For four days now we have tried to take Lounola Station. The
> men have lain in snow for three days and didn't dare lift their
> heads. Several of them are frostbitten. We are compelled to
> sleep with our clothes on, and can't even take our felt boots
> off. . . . Our casualties are heavy . . . more from frostbite
> than from enemy fire. The butchers are accustomed to fire
> carefully at our troops from the side of the road. We can't
> even put our noses out of the trenches. Our men have
> launched several attacks but have always been beaten back.
> The barbed wire is man-high. Tank obstacles are everywhere.
> The marshes and splendidly camouflaged posts around us
> make the Finns invulnerable.

Yes, the Finns were holding. As the Finnish epic, the *Kalevala,*
put it, "Let our contests be in the winter, / Let our wars be on the
snowfields." The Finnish soldiers owned the winter. They ate rein-
deer meat. They took boiling saunas and then rolled naked in the
snow. They moved swiftly and silently on their skis to attack half-
frozen Russians huddled around campfires. Finnish riflemen, at
thirty below zero, wore fur gloves with a specially tailored trigger-
finger. When the Russian soldier was hit, he froze where he stood.
The Finns invented the "Molotov Cocktail," derisively named after
the Soviet foreign minister. The Finnish Liquor Board released
70,000 empty bottles; these were filled with gasoline. With a rope
fuse, they were lit and flung against Russian tanks. The Finns called
Russian tanks "death boxes" and the Russian mass attacks "moving
zoos."

Yes, it could be done. There in the January 22 *Life:* "The Finns
Prove Themselves the Best Winter Soldiers in the World." Photographs of ski troops in white, smiling, armed, sliding in a column
through a snowy village. The wooden building on the left has a sign
on it: "Hattulike." It's a women's hat shop. The kids in the fifth
grade read *Life* and moved the pins on the map. "The soldiers of
Finland in six weeks of war," said *Life,*

> have made a brave beginning on the most glorious page in
> Finland's history. If they can fight off the Russian *Juggernaut*
> for a few months more, they will have made Finland's name
> forever. Never before has a large-scale war been fought under
> such conditions. Snowflakes fall almost without interruption
> in the North. The temperatures are such that few civilized
> men ever feel. . . . Often it drops to 40 degrees below zero.
> Men live and work and fight chilled to the marrow, their
> faces aching, their fingers and toes numb with pain. . . .

Finland in January, in fact, is no place to fight a war. Joseph
Stalin's imperative demand for a war there is characteristic of
the arrogant Czarist and Bolshevik practice of asking sub-
normal Russians to achieve superhuman feats on pain of
death.

In the opening phase of the war, the Soviet troops, if not "sub-
normal," were certainly not very good. Their performance undoubtedly led to the contempt Hitler felt for the Red Army and to his
confidence in the summer of 1941 that the Wehrmacht would be in
Moscow in a matter of weeks, invading without available winter
uniforms. In Finland, the Soviets were out of their depth militarily.
It is reasonable to speculate that the two dictators, Stalin and
Mussolini, were under increasing psychological and political pressure to produce spectacular results—cheaply—like those of the
magician in Berlin.

A full-page photo in *Life* shows a figure in white operating a
range finder. Caption: "White-robed Finn kneels like a priest to
sight Russian tanks with range-finder for the anti-tank crew in the
fox hole."

Day after day the news came in upbeat. "Finns Smash a Red
Division." You gleefully scanned the story. "As the old year goes
out, the Finns have inflicted two crushing and costly defeats on the
Russians. . . . Remnants of the division have taken refuge in the
forest." Dispatches appeared in the daily press from American
reporters "with the Finnish Arctic Army." Americans read:

> In the stillness of a dark Arctic morning, with the
> temperature 30 below zero, the only sound was that made by
> the runners of three supply sleds and one sled laden with a
> field kitchen carrying hot soup as we moved cautiously
> toward a Finnish patrol base an unknown distance ahead
> toward the Soviet lines. With the woods filled with Finnish
> and Russian patrols, every shadow spelled danger. . . .
> Fifteen minutes seemed like fifteen hours. Everything was
> quiet; there was no wind to disturb the fantastic blue shapes
> of the snow in the moonlight. Suddenly the stillness was
> broken by a sharp crack. The sled stopped and the driver
> grabbed his rifle. I piled out into a snow-filled ditch beside
> the road and lay there waiting. Looking up, I saw six white
> figures on skis come silently from the woods and approach
> the sled cautiously. . . . of the six men in this patrol, one had
> a submachine gun, with an extra ammunition drum around his
> neck; one had a telescope-sighted rifle captured from a

Russian patrol two days before; and the others had ordinary rifles.

During that winter of 1940 the good news from Finland was uninterrupted. The Finns could hold. The huge French army blocked Hitler in the west. Perhaps the worst was over. "The brilliant victory of the Finns over the 163rd Soviet division near Lake Kianta may go down in Russian history as a second, though smaller, Tannenberg." "Finns Hold Foe in Icy Death-Trap. Then Rout Half-Frozen Regiments." You read:

> There was frightful carnage. The Finns, hidden in the forest cover familiar to them, waited until the Russians were a scant twenty yards away and then released their fire. The freezing, bewildered Russians, advancing in great clumps, were shot down with hardly a chance to defend themselves. The Finns continued firing until all was quiet, for it was impossible to take prisoners. The place of carnage was marked by heaps of dead Russians, mostly lying as they had fallen, with the bare hands stuffed into their sleeves to keep warm. Many were pierced by several bullets and others were virtually blown to bits by Finnish shells. Finns detailed to collect Russian weapons were sickened by the dreadful sight.

In America, the Gallup poll indicated for the first time that the American people now regarded the Soviets—70 percent to 30 percent—as a greater threat than the Nazis. Congress debated aid to Finland. The Swedes and British sent artillery to Finland, and the French sent planes. Former President Herbert Hoover, who had headed Belgian Relief in the First World War, now headed Finnish relief, and Big Bill Tilden organized a professional tennis exhibition to help Finland. Big Bill, fifty, fought the 1938 champion Don Budge to 8–6 in the first set. In New York and other cities, socialites held fancy-dress balls for Finland, and the Finnish Olympic track star Paavo Nurmi, along with other Finnish athletes, toured America for Finland.

But on that map in the fifth-grade classroom, something was terribly clear that was not being stressed in the American press. The blue Finnish pins were where they always had been—but so were the red ones. Despite their brilliant defensive victories, the Finns faced unlimited Soviet manpower, and in a war of attrition, without decisive outside help, their outlook was bleak.

On May 4, 1940, four Japanese fishing-boat operators were arrested at Pearl Harbor and held for grand jury action. One sampan had penetrated into the key naval channel. Others had gotten into similarly prohibited areas. The violations were called "particularly startling" because the entrance to the harbor had been fitted with antisubmarine and antitorpedo nets. Taken into custody were Nasaichi Ishazaki, sixty-three; Kojiro Omura and his son Robert; and Yasaturu Yaji.

President Roosevelt had ordered special security on Oahu and around Pearl Harbor since ordering most of the American battle fleet to Pearl for maneuvers in the Pacific, at undisclosed locations. Only one aircraft carrier remained in the Atlantic, which was felt to be the province of the British and French fleets.

For a ten-year-old American in 1940, who knew next to nothing of Japan's history or culture, Japan was thoroughly contemptible. The toys the Japanese made were cheap and tinny, and the label "Made in Japan" was a joke, an absolute guarantee of poor quality. His bubblegum cards, the movies he saw, and his discussions at school reinforced this sense of Japan. He knew about the sudden murderous attack upon Manchuria in the fall of 1931 and that a Chinese commander in Manchuria had been made to cede Chinese territory to Japan with a gun at his head. In the first terror bombing of the period, Japanese planes on January 29, 1932, had leveled the Chinese quarter of Shanghai. "Operating from a fair height," wrote a reporter, "the Japanese aviators came in lower and lower until at the time they bombed the Railway Station they could have been little more than 300 feet up. They were so low that they leaned over the sides of their machines as they were maneuvering into position, waved their hands to the watching volunteers below, then banked, circled, flew over their targets, and could not possibly miss their objectives. Outer Chapei is ruined. Larger buildings, with few exceptions, last night were bare and gaunt walls, their interiors a seething mass of glowing embers, reflecting against the night sky. Houses by the hundreds are a wreck and a ruin." Perhaps 10,000 people died that day in Shanghai.

In the Movietone News and on the bubblegum cards there had been the Rape of Nanking, terror on the ground to match the spreading Japanese terror from the air. Japan was a sleazy gangster state, in the boy's view, the ruthless bully of East Asia, the Japanese an inferior people in every possible way. Chiang Kai-shek, forced out of Nanking by the Japanese, moved his government to Chungking. He was a hero, waging an uphill struggle against the invaders, and Madame Chiang was an international heroine, highly visible in the American media.

By the beginning of 1940, public opinion in America was, if possible, even more hostile to Japan than to the Soviets' invasion of

Finland. The Japanese performance in China was hated, as was her manifest ambition to seize the rubber, tin, and oil of the Dutch East Indies. At the same time, in early 1940, political opinion in Japan became increasingly hostile to the United States. The leading newspaper, *Asahi,* demanded editorially that Japan "liquidate her erstwhile dependence on the United States and prepare for the worst." These were brave words but impossible as policy, because in 1939 the United States had supplied 45 percent of Japan's imports.

At the same time in the United States, pressure mounted for an embargo on all exports to Japan that might support its war effort. Early in the year, numerous resolutions were under committee study in Congress, all of them having the goal of cutting the Japanese off. On February 14, the Gallup poll showed that Americans favored an embargo against Japan by 75 to 25 percent.

Professor John W. Dower has demonstrated in *War Without Mercy: Race and Power in the Pacific War* (1986) that exceptional racial antagonisms existed on both sides, with the result that when fighting did break out, it was especially savage in character. Americans widely regarded the Japanese as subhuman, and they were so represented in the respectable media, often as little yellow monkeys. No comparable animosity inflamed the fighting in Europe. Shooting Japanese prisoners was commonplace, as was collecting their gold teeth. "Your enemy is a curious race," General Thomas Blamey told his troops, "a cross between the human being and the ape. . . . You know that we have to exterminate these vermin if we and our famlies are to live. We must go on to the end if civilization is to survive. We must exterminate the Japanese." Charles A. Lindbergh, on a Pacific inspection tour, was appalled by the barbarousness of the fighting. Admiral William Halsey vowed that by the end of the war, Japanese would be spoken only in hell. In Europe, the enemy were "Nazis" and "Fascists," not Germans and Italians. In the Pacific, the enemy were "Japs."

Japan's policy in China and in the Western Pacific was on a collision course with what the Roosevelt administration, backed overwhelmingly by public opinion, regarded as American and Allied interests. In China, the Japanese wanted a vassal state, a regime subservient to Tokyo, and in March 1940, they set one up in Nanking under President Wang Ching-wei. American policy had historically demanded an independent China and an "open door" to trade there. The *New York Times* commented editorially:

> Yesterday a new "Chinese National Government" was
> proclaimed in historic Nanking, where Dr. Sun Yat-sen lies
> buried, where a progressive Chinese Republic functioned for
> so many fruitful years, and where thousands of offending
> Chinese were massacred two winters ago by Japanese troops

and bombing planes. The choice of Nanking for the ceremony is the last refinement of cynicism, for the new "President" who was inaugurated there is Wang Ching-wei, once a disciple of Dr. Sun, now a puppet in the hands of the Japanese Army. . . . The artificial rejoicing in Nanking should deceive nobody outside Japan; but it would be a mistake for outsiders to dismiss it as a hollow joke. The formal advent of Mr. Wang is an event of immense seriousness to the United States and to all nations with interests in China. However shady its origin, however weak its popular support, the Wang regime will be in nominal control of that vast central portion of China, the home of 200,000,000 people, the heart of China's commerce and industry.

It had become increasingly clear that Japan's goal was to carve out an empire in Asia, which might well include the Dutch East Indies as well as French Indo-China and even the Philippines, and calling it the Greater Asia Co-Prosperity Sphere, establish a commercial and military monopoly. It was therefore in Japan's interest, conceived of in this way, that Hitler defeat the European colonial powers, leaving the British, French, and Dutch colonies in East Asia vulnerable.

From the beginning of 1940, the United States and Japan moved inexorably toward a collision, which at the time, everyone sensed would occur, and yet, contradictorily, hoped that something might turn up to avert. Very few serious voices were raised to argue that Japan's policies in East Asia and Manchuria were intellectually defensible, and those few voices had no impact whatsoever.

That spring William R. Castle, a former undersecretary of state, addressed the annual meeting of the American Academy of Political and Social Science. Mr. Castle saw the weakness of China as the key to the entire situation in East Asia. China was a power vacuum, and the Japanese were moving into that vacuum at the expense of Soviet ambitions in Asia. He cautioned against ignoring "the faults of the Chinese" and against depicting the Japanese as "blacker than truth." He said that if China had to be under foreign influence, as seemed likely, he preferred, "as an American," Tokyo to Moscow, "which at the moment seems to be the alternative." Mr. Castle saw Wang Ching-wei's Nanking government—usually referred to as a Japanese "puppet"—in anti-Soviet terms. "Wang Ching-wei hates Communism and believes Chiang Kai-shek to be dominated by the Soviet." Mr. Castle argued that it would be better for China to come to terms with Japan than to fall under the domination of the Soviets. He contended, with a good deal of prescience, that a Western trade embargo against Japan would put Japan decisively on the side of Germany and would result in the loss of Hong Kong and Singapore.

These reflections met with little favor among the assembled American political scientists and were denounced, notably, by Professor Philip C. Jessup of Columbia, who hoped that the United States would take a strong diplomatic stand against any Western attempt to "appease Japan at the expense of China or the Netherlands." This debate, which engaged momentous choices in foreign policy, appeared on page 32 of the April 14 *New York Times* and caused practically no ripples. In fact, there was no consequential debate whatsoever about American policy in the Western Pacific. On the same day, April 14, the *Times* reported that because of a crash building program, the Japanese navy now possessed a 5 to 4 advantage over the United States.

That June a retired U.S. admiral, Yates Stirling, Jr., made an accurate assessment of events as they were then developing. In an article sent out by the United Press, he wrote in part:

> It is becoming increasingly clear, in my opinion, that our interests as well as those of Britain lie in reaching a friendly understanding with Japan, if one can be attained.
>
> Japan so far is following a policy of "non-belligerence" toward the war, but there are indications she may be leaning toward collaboration with the Axis powers. Obviously that collaboration is not in the interest of the British or ourselves.
>
> The question is not one of "appeasing" the Japanese. It is one of looking facts in the face.
>
> The Japanese foreign minister, in his address to the world Saturday, stated the situation we face. He asserted that Japan was the dominant power in East Asia and indicated that the Empire shares the view of the Axis powers that a new world order must be created in which the great military powers in the chief geographical divisions of the world will dominate groups of the smaller nations.
>
> The plan, as I understand it, is that Japan intends to become—as, indeed, she already is—the dominant power in East Asia and contiguous areas of the Pacific Ocean. This part of the world, if the Japanese can make good in their far-reaching plans, would be reorganized economically, and to an extent politically and militarily, so that it would constitute a unified whole of cooperating peoples. Japan would be the great armed power that would prevent encroachments by other great powers and would make East Asia a region primarily for "Asiatics."

If one looks at a map, it is apparent that the Japanese plan involves changes in the whole strategic and economic set-up that has prevailed in East Asia for more than a century. It means that British and French power in East Asia must be broken and that our own role in this part of the world, if peace is to be maintained, must be limited largely to fields in which we will not "challenge" the Japanese.

For the British and French the immediate problem is more serious than it is for us. Britain's naval station at Hong Kong already is menaced by Japanese forces, the British Concession in Tientsin has been rendered impotent.

Japanese "inspectors" are stationed in French Indo-China and the Japanese are exercising increasing "control" on the French Concession at Shanghai. The Japanese have obtained concessions from the Netherlands Indies and are demanding more, including a larger share of the trade of these rich islands.

Throughout the whole area they have chosen for themselves the Japanese are on the move. History would indicate they can be stopped only by superior military force. And there is no power now that can divert its force to this region. We have been forced by the developments in Europe to disperse our naval power. British, French and Netherland strength in the Orient is negligible.

The problem, as I see it, is to prevent Japan from adopting a policy of complete cooperation with the Axis powers. This can be done only by convincing Tokyo that Japanese interests, in the long-range view, lie in cooperating with us and with Britain. And I believe that is where they do lie, economically, culturally and strategically.

The great bulk of Japan's trade, outside her own immediate sphere, always has been with us and the British Empire. These economic interchanges are largely reciprocal and noncompetitive.

Strategically the Japanese position never will be secure in East Asia so long as we are a potential enemy. We have the resources to build a greater navy than Japan ever can hope to build. In the present expansion of armaments the Japanese are bound to fall behind very rapidly as soon as we hit our stride.

Culturally the Japanese always have leaned toward us and Britain rather than Germany and Italy.

Such sober arguments were entirely lost in an atmosphere of building tension and repeated crisis in the Pacific. Much public opinion regarded Japan as a paper dragon, essentially a have-not power. Early in 1940, a British financier, Sir Victor Sassoon, arrived in San Francisco from Shanghai on the liner *President Coolidge* with comforting words plus one insight. America, thought Sassoon, was "playing poker in Japan with five deuces," and America had got Japan "absolutely cold." "The business people in Japan and diplomats want peace in China," he said, "and friendliness with the United States. They say it is 'our only hope.' But there are other forces to be reckoned with. The navy favors peace, but figures it can run a bluff and get something for nothing, why not try it. However, the navy is not looking for trouble. It is the army, sitting in the middle of Manchuria, which wants to fight America, while the navy, which would have to do the fighting, does not."

Whether or not America was playing with five deuces, the Japanese a few days later introduced an enormous new armaments budget of over 1.6 billion yen (about $408 million). This was defended in the parliament on the basis of Soviet raids into Manchuria and the requirements of the Chinese war. General Shunroku Hata, the war minister, declared that the mission of the million Japanese soldiers in China was "to destroy Chiang Kai-shek's anti-Japanese, pro-Communist regime, to restore peace in East Asia, to fulfill the great ideal of universal brotherhood, to realize good neighborliness, for joint defense against communism, for economic cooperation between Japan, China and Manchukuo and the establishing of a New Order in East Asia, which has been the national policy of the Japanese empire since its formation."

As the weeks passed, the scope of the New Order in East Asia began to be defined in increasingly specific and alarming terms. In the magazine *Hinode,* for example, Admiral Sankichi Takahashi, former commander of Japan's combined fleet, wrote that the new Prosperity Sphere begins with Manchukuo in the north and extends to Australia in the south; in the east it extends to 180 degrees longitude, and in the west to Burma and the Bay of Bengal. "It will be constructed in several stages," wrote the admiral. "In the first stage, the sphere that Japan demands includes Manchukuo, China, Indo-China, Burma, Straits Settlements, Netherlands Indies, New Caledonia, many islands in the West Pacific, Japan's mandated islands and the Philippines. Australia and the rest of the East Indies can be included later. Greater East Asia will be built up in proportion to Japan's national strength. The greater our strength, the larger will be the sphere of Greater East Asia." On the question of war with America, the admiral was nothing if not forthright: "Statesmen will try to prevent such a calamity, but the circumstances are beyond their control. There can be no settlement until Japan and America have a showdown."

That spring, before Hitler's *blitzkrieg* against France and the Low Countries, the Western democracies stepped up the pressure against Tokyo. The French repaired bridges damaged by Japanese bombing and reopened the rail line between Hanoi and Yunnan Province in China, at the time a major link with the outside world. Gasoline and other war matériel began to flow to Chiang Kai-shek's government in Chungking. In Washington, Chief of Naval Operations Admiral Harold R. Stark appeared before the Senate Committee on Naval Affairs and testified in support of a $650 million naval appropriations bill. "We feel reasonably certain," said Stark, "that Japan has eight of these [superdreadnoughts] actually underway now. There is at the same time some thought that she may have twelve of these ships building or authorized. In addition, she has ten other battleships in commission."

At about the same time, Tokyo made protestations about respecting the status quo in the Pacific, which meant in concrete terms that Japan would not try to seize the Dutch East Indies, an important source of rubber and of 25 percent of Japan's oil. Holland was in no position to defend its Pacific empire against the Japanese fleet, but clearly, in the event of an oil embargo by the United States, all bets would be off. Secretary of State Cordell Hull warned the Japanese in diplomatic language that "any change in the status of the Netherlands Indies would directly affect the interests of many countries." This American statement was greeted with an outburst of anger in Tokyo.

With the Nazi continental triumph in the spring *blitzkrieg,* Tokyo immediately saw its options in a new light and stepped up its expansionist timetable. The erstwhile European colonies were now up for grabs. British, French, and Dutch possessions would be incorporated into the Japanese system. The East Asia Co-Prosperity Sphere was renamed the Greater East Asia Co-Prosperity Sphere. Japanese troops sealed off the access routes to China from French Tonkin (North Vietnam) and closed down Chinese ports. China would be starved into submission. As now envisioned from Tokyo, the new world order, succeeding the older order of the European empires, would have four powerful foci: Germany, Japan, Russia, and the United States. For the time being, Japan would not challenge the anachronistic American position in the Philippines. Military and political opinion in Japan was profoundly affected by Hitler's spectacular European victories, and Japan began to view the Nazi political model as the wave of the future.

In the United States, pressure for an embargo against Japan mounted relentlessly. Henry L. Stimson, a Republican who was soon to be named secretary of war by President Roosevelt, wrote a long and very serious letter to the *New York Times* analyzing the situation. It is a reasonable surmise that the letter was inspired at some level of the Roosevelt administration. Stimson demanded an embargo. "Those leaders desire strongly to subjugate China," he wrote, "but they also clearly recognize that a head-on quarrel with us would be fatal to that project. . . . On January 26, next, the six-months' notice given by our government of the abrogation of the trade treaty with Japan will have expired. Our government then will be morally free to act with respect to our commerce."

The *New York Times* thunderously supported this move to cut off the Japanese imperial design at the knees:

> Mr. Stimson's letter, published in the *Times* this morning, is a
> forceful argument for an American embargo on the shipment
> to Japan of supplies that enable that country to make war on
> China. We believe that the overwhelming mass of the
> American people have reached precisely the same conclusion
> about the war which Mr. Stimson himself has reached: that it
> is a crystal-clear case of unprovoked aggression by Japan; that
> Japanese tactics in the field have been particularly brutal; and
> that the plain objective of the Japanese campaign has been the
> spoliation of China and the subjugation of its people.
> American ore, American scrap iron and American gasoline
> are Japanese allies in this war. From no other country does
> Japan receive so much assistance. . . . Mr. Stimson calls it by
> its right name—a dirty business. . . . On this moral ground
> the case for an embargo is unanswerable.

Indeed, on the ground in China the entire Japanese enterprise looked shaky. A million better-trained and better-led Japanese troops faced a Chinese army of more than 2 million men and had achieved little more than a stalemate after three years of heavy fighting. Even in the areas they occupied, Japanese authority extended only as far as they could shoot. In the occupied areas, they were constantly harassed by guerrillas, and the forces of Chiang Kai-shek, supplied over the Burma Road, showed no signs of quitting. In heavy fighting throughout 1939 and 1940, both sides suffered heavy casualties. By 1940, moreover, Japan was suffering severely. Copper, rubber, metals, and gasoline were in short supply, and Tokyo itself was experiencing brown-outs because of a shortage of coal to generate electricity. Infant mortality was up sharply because of a decline in nutrition. Cotton cloth was scarce, so was rice, and milk and eggs were rare and expensive. Early in the year, a government edict ordered the chief Japanese industries to reduce their power consumption by one third. The Greater East Asian Co-Prosperity Sphere was, literally, running out of gas, along with much else.

Not surprisingly, Secretary of the Navy Charles Edison expressed public concern over the vulnerability of the Navy to air attack. The Pacific maneuvers, he thought, had demonstrated a "temporary" advantage now possessed by air power over sea power and showed the need for improved ship armor and the evolution of new tactics. The use of ships near enemy shores, he thought, might now be too dangerous.

On July 25, President Roosevelt suddenly pulled the plug on Japan. He halted all exports of American oil and scrap metal except for a small amount under special license. Japan was the nation most affected by the July 25 order, since 65 percent of its oil and 85 percent of its scrap metal were imported from the United States. German Economics Minister Funk responded with an Axis economic threat: after the war the United States faced the possibility of being locked out of the markets of a Nazi-dominated Europe, and furthermore, the United States could not compete with Europe for Latin American markets.

At the beginning of August, Japanese Premier Prince Konoye announced a plan for an entirely new Japanese state, based upon the totalitarian model and designed to implement expansion southwards to Indo-China and the Indies. It would be a "yen bloc" and would mean "a new order for Greater East Asia." General Kuniaki Koiso proclaimed that the rubber of the Dutch East Indies was vital for American industry and that "it is necessary to emancipate the oriental races and we are determined to solve this problem." The Foreign Office in Tokyo commented that the southern Pacific was definitely included in the Greater East Asia system, but declined to be specific about the Philippines.

The belief in Tokyo that a "new order" was emerging in the world, that there would be a reformulation of the global power equation in the wake of the collapse of the European empires, was certainly valid enough. The Japanese mistake was to believe that Hitler and Germany would dominate a Nazified Europe and that they could impose a new Japanese order on Asia by means of military force. The United States was powerful enough to prevent this, guarantee the defeat of both Japan and Germany, and emerge as the dominant postwar global power.

Early in August, the Japanese seized de facto control of French Indo-China, using regular troops and teams of "experts" to block further communication with China. The *New York Times* sized up the situation editorially:

Japan is the aptest and most faithful imitator of Western products, both good and bad. After announcing the other day that it has gone "totalitarian," the Government wastes no time or scruples in staking out claims to a vast "Lebensraum" in the Pacific.

Hardly had Tokyo coerced the hard-pressed British into closing the Burma road than it proceeded to turn the screws on the more helpless French. If the reports emanating from Vichy and Hanoi are true, the Japanese are taking advantage of the misfortunes of France to extend not only influence but actual control over the roads, ports and air bases in French Indo-China. Their ostensible purpose is the same as that behind the pressure to close the Burma road—to prevent supplies from going to China; but the real aim is clearly to attack Chiang Kai-shek's forces from the south, in the area where the new munitions plants are situated. And that is only the first step toward ousting the weakened French from their Asiatic possessions.

Even if the move did not coincide with measures to force "closer economic cooperation" with the Netherlands Indies to replace the oil and scrap iron hitherto received from the United States, it would be obvious that the imperial march is on. From both sides of the world the aggressors are joining up at a pace that will soon leave us little room for choice or argument.

Early in September, President Roosevelt extended the embargo to include equipment and formulas for manufacturing aviation-grade gasoline, as well as all things needed for the manufacture of aircraft. Henceforth the Japanese planes, like the Germans', would have to fly with inferior fuel reinforced by lead. The Japanese government responded furiously, and on September 25 concluded a pact with Germany and Italy. If the United States entered the European war, Japan was committed to an attack in the Pacific. On the other hand, if the United States moved against Japan, Hitler and Mussolini would do something or other in the Atlantic. No one could discern that Japan had gained anything at all through this new alliance. Germany and Italy could do nothing in the Atlantic beyond their present submarine strategy. They certainly could do nothing in the Pacific. There was much speculation at the time that Hitler had bullied the Japanese into signing the agreement by threatening to turn the Soviets against them in Manchuria.

On September 26, President Roosevelt rendered the embargo on war matériel absolute, excluding only Britain and the Western Hemisphere. Strategic analysts agreed that Japan could not now meet its minimum needs through resort to alternative sources of supply. At a press conference, Secretary of State Cordell Hull made it clear that the United States was not concerned over reports from Tokyo that the Japanese government was finally convinced that the United States government was irrevocably opposed to Japan's expansion in Asia.

The Export-Import Bank authorized another $25 million loan to China. The position of the United States was based upon strategic, economic, and political considerations. The "old order" in international relations had been based upon assumptions of free trade, however modified in various circumstances by tariff barriers. The "new order" would be entirely different, with a German continental cartel in Europe, a Japanese cartel in Asia, and a Soviet autarchy on the Euro-Asiatic land mass. If the British went under and the "new order" emerged around the globe, the United States would be isolated as a liberal, free-trading nation. Moreover, the kinds of societies that constituted the emerging "new order" were totalitarian and profoundly repugnant, the individual entirely subjugated by the state. The future of an America isolated in a totalitarian world would certainly be problematic.

Tokyo, however, had in fact embarked upon an enormous gamble, the shaky premise of which was that Hitler would win his war. The projected "new economic order" in the world absolutely required that. Without a Nazi victory, Japan's strategic position was built on sand, its traditional American and British economic ties now severed. Japan was still unable to win its war with China, and it was blocked to the south by Roosevelt's declared policy of defending the status quo in the southern Pacific. On October 5, Premier Konoye admitted that the plans for a Greater East Asia might well involve Japan in a war with the United States.

A substantial part of the Japanese political establishment regarded the developments of the summer and fall of 1940 with deep dismay. The whole policy, they saw, represented a wild and ill-considered gamble. Hitler had been unable to subdue the British, and the RAF had defeated the Luftwaffe in the Battle of Britain, destroying some 1,000 German planes in the process. Franco, meeting with Hitler in a railroad car at Hendaye in France, had politely but firmly refused to enlist Spain in the new order. Geographically, Japan seemed impregnable in a defensive sense, its home islands plus the related islands it had acquired making it a fortified breakwater along the coast of East Asia from the Bering Sea to the Gulf of Tonkin. Japan's military resources were formidable when concentrated around this geography. The United States could not and would not attack under such circumstances. But spread those Japanese forces south and east—that would be an enormous strategic gamble. Furthermore, England had not only fought off Hitler, but had reopened the Burma Road into China.

On advice from the State Department, American businessmen and their families were leaving Japan. The Canadian Pacific liner *Empress of Russia* left Tokyo on October 12 with one hundred Americans aboard, and bookings were heavy on all ships scheduled to leave soon.

Prince Konoye told a political meeting that Japan was "at a great turning point" that required "a new political structure" and that the country faced a situation equal in seriousness to anything faced by the emperors of the past. Washington, at about the same time, granted China credits of $85 million.

A Gallup poll taken in the middle of October indicated that 96 percent of the American public agreed with President Roosevelt's embargo against Japan, and almost that many felt that it should have been done sooner.

On October 15, two new squadrons of American fighter planes were dispatched to the Philippines, bringing U.S. air strength to 150 planes. U.S. naval matériel was being stored at Hong Kong. The Japanese opened talks with Moscow with a view to settling territorial differences in order to protect the Japanese flank in the event of a probable war with the United States, but the talks came to nothing. London advised all British subjects to leave Japan that fall.

But as 1940 drew to a close, the Japanese seemed to pull back from the brink. The appointment of Admiral Kichisaburo Nomura as ambassador to the United States was widely regarded as a conciliatory move. Admiral Nomura had been a prominent advocate of conciliation with Washington and was appreciative of Washington's concern about its prospective exclusion from trade with one quarter of the world's population. With Admiral Nomura on his way to Washington at the end of the year, there came a pause in the escalating crisis.

In an astonishing sequence of two days, Eleanor and Franklin Roosevelt took opposite positions before the 4,000-member meeting of the Communist-leaning American Youth Congress in Washington. The Youth Congress had refused to condemn the Soviet aggression against Finland, as might have been expected, given its Stalinist orientation. The president's wife, who had addressed the congress, refused to condemn this position, maintaining rather fatuously that the Communist group should not condemn the Soviets unless they believed in the condemnation. The next day, the president, on the White House lawn, gave it to the Youth Congress with the bark off. He dealt with their pro-Communist resolutions sarcastically, condemned the Soviet dictatorship, and told some 4,000 AYC members and other pro-Communists that 98 percent of the American people supported the Finns. To the AYC assertion that support for Finland would drag us into the war, the president replied witheringly that this was "about the silliest thing I have ever heard in my life." Implicitly, the president had rebuked his wife, and perhaps even condemned her mentality.

But all of a sudden the news from Finland turned sour. In the middle of February, even as the Senate approved a loan to Helsinki, a Soviet offensive on the Karelian Isthmus reached such intensity that the Finns began to give ground. The Soviets had brought up fresh divisions and massed artillery that poured 300,000 shells a day on the defenders. Soviet casualties were enormous, with officers carrying out battlefield executions to drive the men forward out of fear, but there was no mistaking the momentum the attack was building up. The House had not yet passed the Finnish loan, and key fortified points were reported falling. On March 13 there came the news of the Finnish surrender, and a chill fell over America as large chunks of Finland went to the Soviets. Said the *New York Times* editorially: "Russia once had friends. She was not only great and supposedly powerful but she could count on a measure of sympathy and understanding on every continent. A great body of liberals in most European countries and in our own were so friendly that they turned a blind eye to cruelties within Russia's boundaries." But now, thought the *Times,* all of that was finished.

No one, after all, had yet turned back the dictators, and it was characteristic of the year 1940 that each disaster, each shock to the collective nervous system, was followed by a still greater one. On April 9, Hitler invaded Denmark and Norway, the former falling immediately, Norway falling to a *blitzkrieg* involving the mass use of paratroops for the first time in history. A badly conceived British force was routed and had to flee to its ships as the Germans once again stunned the world with the brilliance and inventiveness of their military tactics. While still mopping up in Norway, Hitler sent his panzers into the Low Countries on May 10. The *sitzkrieg* or "Phony War" on the Western Front was over. In six weeks Hitler crushed the supposedly formidable French army. In magazine and newspaper articles, the military experts discussed the question of whether anyone could resist this new kind of warfare which had now exploded westward with unprecedented force.

Eliot

The great poet had undergone profound changes. He had left Harvard, where he had studied with Royce and taught philosophy, and where he and Santayana had developed a mutual dislike. He was drawn to the skeptical idealism of the philosopher F. H. Bradley and wrote his dissertation on it. The elective system supported at Harvard by President Eliot, a relative, earned his intellectual contempt. Western culture was not an elective; it possessed content. He studied in Germany, also at the Sorbonne, felt the reality of "the mind of Europe," decided to live in England, and became a British subject. He moved from a poetry of despair and emotional paralysis to a poetry of Christian affirmation.

He wrote poetry in twelve languages, including Sanskrit, and spoke in multiple voices: the French poets, Virgil, the Elizabethans and Jacobeans, the Provençal poets, Dante—above all, Dante . . . haunting, haunting. "What seas what shores what granite island towards my timbers / And woodthrush calling through the fog / My daughter. . . ."

He worked in a London bank and became expert at international finance, taking a pride in his expertise that derived from his Puritan ancestors, but sometimes he wore green face powder in the evening and a peculiar lipstick, no doubt a spoof of the gaslit nineties. He seemed to have multiple selves, and his friends did not know what to make of him, precise or weary, witty or ill, encyclopedically learned and a frequenter of music halls, practical joker and despairing melancholic. He seemed to be always in some complex inner dialogue with himself, the truth of which, if there was one, would be mainly dramatic. He possessed a profound religious sensibility and was a careful analyst of the states of the soul, but he declined to be forthright about the grounds of his religious conviction.

During the thirties and forties he grew to awe-inspiring artistic and intellectual standing. When he was a fellow at Princeton's Institute of Advanced Studies, along with Einstein and the rest, faculty members were afraid to approach him, and he ate dinner alone at the Nassau Inn. He signed his letters from Princeton "Advanced Student." After one of his readings in London, his mentally disturbed, ill, and rejected wife reproached him and tried to lure him back home with their dog, Polly. "I cannot," he said, "speak with you now." She continued to call herself "Mrs. T. S. Eliot" and died suddenly in confinement.

Eliot had the reputation of being a highly intellectual poet, but the actual effect of his words was primitive, mysterious, his witch-doctor rhythms reaching all the way back to some unnameable past, earlier than the cave paintings, earlier than Stonehenge or the runes: "April is the cruellest month," his sepulchral voice intoned, "breeding / Lilacs out of the dead land." He had remarked that he understood Dante even before he could read Italian, and people were captured by Eliot's rhythms even before they knew what he was talking about. He and Yeats were alone at the pinnacle of modern poetry in English.

At Easter in the year 1940, he published "East Coker," the second in a sequence of four difficult religious poems and named after the town from which his ancestors had left England for America in the seventeenth century. "East Coker" seemed to affirm, amidst the apocalypse of that 1940 spring, the enduring continuity of the English tradition, and it placed the suffering of the moment in the universal perspective of death and resurrection. "East Coker" sold 12,000 copies, *Mrs. Miniver* for highbrows.

Death is a powerful presence throughout the poem. "Houses rise and fall, crumble, are extended. . . . Old stone to new building, old timber to new fires, / Old fires to ashes, and ashes to the earth. . . . O dark dark dark." For those who read "East Coker" in 1940, that was familiar emotional territory.

But the poem also had a countermovement, the descent fusing with ascent: "I said to my soul, be still, and wait without hope. . . . So the darkness shall be the light, and the stillness the dancing." It had all happened before, after all, death and life, again and again and again, an Easter poem full of continuities, England and everywhere: "There is only the fight to recover what has been lost / And found and lost again and again." Yes, Milton, Dante, St. John of the Cross, Charles I, St. Augustine, T. S. Eliot speaking on Easter 1940. "In my end is my beginning."

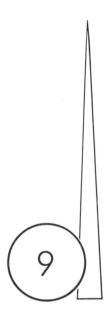

DIGNITY AND GREATNESS

9

That year Joe Louis was as completely the heavyweight champion as Franklin Roosevelt was president. There were few certainties, but surely two: that Roosevelt was president and probably always would be and that Louis could knock anybody out. In fact, Louis was so good that, with the partial exception of Billy Conn the next year, nobody could really fight him. At six feet one and a half inches, and trained down to 200 pounds, he was an astonishing athletic presence. On June 22, 1938, in their second fight, before 70,000 people in Yankee Stadium, Max Schmeling had lasted only two minutes and four seconds of the first round. During that brief time span, Louis threw more than fifty punches. As Schmeling twisted on the ropes trying to get away, punches by Louis fractured his vertebrae. The lethal power of Louis's punches resulted from hand speed and sheer kinetic force.

The champion's autobiography, *Joe Louis: My Life,* published in 1978, is insufficiently known. It is an American classic, a remarkable literary and historical document. Louis taped his recollections, and his coauthors shaped them into print. By some miracle, they managed to transmit to the printed page the authentic colloquial tones of the champion, and it is a marvelous voice. He is utterly realistic in his judgments of himself and others. His sense of fact is crystalline. His humor is rich. And for all the violence of his profession, he is essentially a gentle man. Here is his account of the second Schmeling fight:

> Before the bell rang, I felt like a racehorse in the starting gate. . . . The sweat was pouring but my body was warm. The muscles were dancing too. I was rarin' to go. In round one I came out of my corner and wasted no time in getting at Schmeling. It took me less than five seconds to get myself together. I hit him with two left hooks to the face that snapped his head back, then I banged a right to his jaw. He threw a right hand that I blocked and tried a left to my head that fell short. Those were the only punches that he threw. Then I drove him into the ropes with a lot of hooks and right hands. . . . He kept backing up into the ropes, trying to cover up the best he could. But he couldn't seem to lift his hands. Schmeling was completely helpless. He kept staggering backward like a drunken man. The crowd was in an uproar as I carefully measured him. Max was an open target. His jaw was not protected and it was very inviting. His stomach was wide open. It was time for the kill. I started hitting him with everything I had—about five or six lefts and a right to the chin—and his legs started shaking. He started sinking to the floor and he grabbed the upper strand of the rope and held on. He was sideways and his eyes were blinking, and his face looked like it was in great pain.
>
> As he hung on the ropes, I hit him with a right to the body. Trying to get away from the punch, Schmeling twisted and took the blow in his lower back. Referee Donovan stepped between us as if he wanted to stop the fight and waved me to a neutral corner. He gave Schmeling a count of one. Then Schmeling got off the ropes, ready for more. I came back as my corner shouted at me, and I hit Schmeling with a right to the jaw. He went down for a three count. When he got up I tore into him with lefts and rights. He went down again and got up at two. I followed with two hooks and a right to the jaw, and he fell onto the canvas again. His trainer Max Machan threw a towel in the ring, but Donovan tossed it on the ropes and continued to count. It was all over in two minutes and four seconds.

Joe Louis: My Life, remarkable as it is, nevertheless, to my knowledge, does not appear on the syllabus of Black Studies courses in colleges around the country. The reason seems mysterious. The book is extraordinary. Nor was Louis unaware of black-white relations in America and his own role in American history. Perhaps there is just too much joy and too little bitterness in the life he recounts for this book to enter the literature of resentment.

In that 1938 rematch with Max Schmeling, Louis had risen from an earlier knockout by the German to become himself a knockout machine. He eliminated a serious flaw in his style, a tendency to drop his left after a hook, and he developed a new competitive ferocity, a killer instinct. He fought all comers—Steve Ketchel, Bob Pastor, Natie Brown. The implacable athletic force could not be denied.

A year earlier in the 1937 championship bout in Chicago against Jimmy Braddock, Louis saw Braddock make the sign of the cross when the bell rang, and he himself said a silent prayer. Early in the first round, Braddock hit him with a right uppercut and knocked him down, but Louis sprang up and hit him with a left cross and a right at the bell, and Braddock went to his corner on shaky legs. Louis's corner people had told him to hold his big punches and box until the seventh round, but he punished Braddock, splitting his lip and raising welts over his eyes. By the eighth round, the champion was helpless, legs wobbly, unable to keep his hands up. "I knocked him out," Louis writes, "with a punch we called the D.O.A. (dead on his ass) in the gym when I was amateur. It was a left to the body and a right hand to the chin. The punch took him off his feet. He whirled in the air and fell on his face. I knew he couldn't get up."

The new champion could hardly get to his home on South Michigan Avenue, the crowds were so thick. It seemed to him that the entire city of Chicago was standing and yelling in the blocks around his house. He felt himself almost crying as he and his wife Marva came to the door again and again to wave to the crowds. The memory of old Jack Johnson was a lively presence, as some blacks shouted at Louis, "We got another chance. Don't be another Jack Johnson. We're depending on you." At least that is the way Louis remembers it, though perhaps those were his own thoughts on becoming the heavyweight champion of the world.

Jack Johnson had been a genuinely bad man, an outrage in any color. He won the heavyweight championship on December 26, 1908, by knocking out Tommy Burns in the fourteenth round in Sydney, Australia, and then returned to the United States determined to give offense. In the ring, Johnson kept up a stream of insulting chatter. Very fast on his feet, he mocked his opponents' attempts to hit him. He moved around the country accompanied by two or three white prostitutes. When he fought exhibition bouts, he would wrap his penis in cloth to make it look bigger. In 1909, he married a white woman who committed suicide three years later. In May 1913, Johnson was arrested by federal agents and charged with violating the Mann Act, transporting women across state boundaries for immoral purposes. Convicted, Johnson jumped bail and fled to Europe. He got $30,000 to fight the 250-pound Jess Willard in Havana on April 5, 1915. Willard knocked him out in the 26th round, but suspicion has always existed that Johnson threw the fight. Johnson returned to the United States and served a year in Leavenworth. After that, he worked in the flea circuses around Times Square. This was the grotesque legacy with which Joe Louis had to deal.

Louis fought everyone who was plausible—Tommy Farr, Nathan Mann, Schmeling again, John Henry Lewis, Jack Roper. There was "Two Ton" Tony Galento, the New Jersey bartender and brawler who succeeded in knocking him down before being knocked out, bloody, in the fourth round. There was another fight with the elusive Bob Pastor, knocked out in eleven. In these fights, the result was always the same as you listened to them on the radio: "The challenger circles to his left now; he tries a left jab. He moves to his left along the ropes and . . . oh! the champion lands a left to the jaw, a left and right to the body and a right to the head. . . . He's down. . . . One, two, three. . . ." That could happen in the first round or the eighth, but it always happened.

Louis first heard the wood *nigger* when his family moved to Detroit when he was twelve. That was in 1926. He never heard the word in the red-clay country of Alabama where he grew up in a sharecropper family, a seventh child. The Barrows tilled the soil and picked the cotton and scratched out a living. His mother was a strong farm woman, who weighed 170 pounds. His father had disappeared into mental hospitals and was presumed dead. Joe Louis Barrow was a shy and quiet boy who liked the farm work and also church, but simply did not participate in the lessons at the rural school, even when he was physically present in the classroom. He did not learn to read, write, or do arithmetic. He liked to play "Skin the Tree," a version of Hide and Seek in which you hid amid the branches of a tree. "Thinking back, I remember the white Langley family around Camp Hill. They owned most of the land around there. The father ran the country store and was very nice to us. His sons James and George and I would play around with each other. Generally I met them on the way to the Mt. Sinai School and we'd fool around chasing each other, or playing marbles or something.

They were on their way to their white school. Since none of us probably wanted to go to school, it was a good interruption."

Joe Louis would later play an enormous role in black-white relations, becoming a national as well as a racial hero, and erasing the offenses of Jack Johnson. He helped to integrate the U.S. Army and advanced the career of Jackie Robinson. He did all of this without a trace of rancor, no doubt because of his innate generosity of spirit, but perhaps also because of those tranquil early days in rural Alabama. "Pat and me would lay on the cotton and bounce up and down on those dirt roads. When we got the cotton to the cotton gin in Camp Hill, we'd love to watch the machine suck it off the wagon." He later became aware of the "angers and hurts and lynchings" that took place in the South, but he never saw anything of that kind when he was a boy.

In 1926, his mother, remarried to a man named Brooks, moved the family to Detroit in hopes of wider opportunities. Louis was wide-eyed. He had never seen so many people before, movie houses, trolley cars, brick buildings. His new overalls seemed out of place. But "Detroit looked awful good to me." The family was poor, and everyone worked at menial jobs when they could get them. Louis avoided school, as usual, and loved the movies, especially Tom Mix, and would get to the movie house before noon in order to get in for a nickel. He was not a tough kid, but after a few encounters in the street, the tough kids learned to respect him, and they left him alone. He did poorly at the violin lessons his mother made him take, and carrying the violin case around was an embarrassment to him, but characteristically, he has a warm feeling toward his adolescent years in the new environment of Detroit.

At the Bronson Vocational School, he had an older friend named Thurston McKinney, who had won the 147-pound Golden Gloves title and was one of the few people who did not kid him about the violin. McKinney lured him away from the violin lessons and introduced him to the life of the Brewster East Side Gymnasium. Watching the boxers spar, seeing the punching bags, the weights, hearing the laughter and the grunts, Louis fell in love with boxing at first sight. "One day Thurston asked me to be his sparring partner. That was a real honor to me. Well, he beat me all over the ring. He hit me with a right to the jaw that almost dropped me. I got mad. I let go my right. It caught him on the chin. His eyes got glassy and his knees buckled, and if I hadn't moved fast to hold him up, I would have knocked him out—and he was the Golden Gloves Welterweight Champion of Detroit. I remember Thurston shaking his head and then grinning at me and saying, 'Man, throw that violin away.'"

Louis chose his destiny, even as he hauled coal and sold vegetables to help the family out. "I'm going to be somebody." His reputation at Brewster's Gym spread, and the neighborhood children followed him around as he walked down the street. "There was one kid in particular who seemed to know my schedule. He'd be there, Johnny-on-the-spot, asking to carry my bag. I felt embarrassed and silly and proud, but anyway I let him carry it to Brewster's Gym for me. When he moved to New York I missed him. He was a real nice kid. His name was Walker Smith. Later they changed his name to 'Sugar' Ray Robinson."

Joe Louis Barrow also changed his name, fighting in the amateurs as "Joe Louis" so that his mother would not know that he was in the ring in a serious way. In his first amateur bout, held in the Detroit Naval Armory, an Olympic boxer named Johnny Miler made a fool of him. "I had seen a photograph of Miler, and there was something about the way he posed that convinced me that I could beat him. I knew it. This was going to be the start of a successful career. . . . It was scheduled for three rounds. Miler knocked me down seven times in two rounds. He won. I lost."

Humiliated but not discouraged, Louis went back to the gym to learn his craft. He had no weapons except that tremendous right-hand punch, so one day his trainer tied his right hand to the ring post so that he could fight only with his left and put Thurston McKinney in the ring with him. "Thurston beat the hell out of me. I yelled to Ellis, 'Tie me loose' but he just laughed and made me practice that way. I learned the importance of using my left hand—I had no choice. Holman got me a three-round amateur fight with Otis Thomas at the Forest Athletic Club in Detroit. When I climbed in the ring, I had Miler on my mind. Would this guy knock me all over the ring, too? I promised myself, 'Not this time.' I beat Thomas, K.O.'d him in round one with a left hook and a right to the jaw. I'd scored my first official knockout. I was on top of the world."

Louis attracted the attention of serious promoters, John Roxborough and Julian Black, the latter a numbers man who had a stable of black fighters in Chicago. Off a string of amateur victories, Louis turned pro. In his first professional fight, he knocked out a white man named Jack Kracken in the first round. There followed a two-year streak of twenty-six victories, most of them by early-round knockouts. His reputation and his income were growing, and talk about the heavyweight championship accompanied them.

Except for one thing. Jack Johnson had poisoned the well for black fighters. A great heavyweight champion, he had racialized the title, flamboyantly driving in a white car with a white chauffeur and his white mistress. Johnson had been so offensive that unspoken barriers existed to the idea that there could ever again be another black heavyweight champion. Before he could get a shot at the title, Louis had to prove himself again and again, and then once more.

On June 13, 1935, Jim Braddock took the title from Max Baer, and Louis, feeling that he was better than either of them, wondered why he was not fighting for that title himself. His managers advised him that he was still young, and also black, but they had a plan. By 1935 Louis was recognized by insiders as the best fighter in the world.

The early Louis was immensely impressive. His back and shoulders were massive, though his powerful muscles were deeply buried. In the ring he moved delicately, often herding his opponent toward the ropes or into a corner. His punching speed was electrically fast, and he used combinations—multiple hooks and jabs of devastating power. Louis had demolished a series of undistinguished fighters across the country when the New York promoter Mike Jacobs saw his chance to break the Madison Square Garden boxing monopoly by signing up Louis. The man who controlled the heavyweight champion of the world controlled boxing, and Jacobs's star would rise with that of Louis. He announced in the spring of 1935 that Louis would fight the Italian giant, Primo Carnera. The Italian was big but clumsy and not much of a puncher. Controlled by Owney Madden, who owned the famous Cotton Club in Harlem and was also a bootlegger, racketeer, and murderer, Carnera had won twenty-three fights in a row against nonentities. Insiders knew that Carnera would not have a chance against Louis, which suited Jacobs's plans precisely.

The sportswriters employed the overblown style of the day during the buildup for the Carnera fight and perhaps revealed in their hyperboles and alliterative tags some nervousness about writing about a black heavyweight contender. The alliteration was not at all new: Jack Dempsey had been the "Manassa Mauler." But with Louis they went overboard. He was the Brown Bomber, the Dark Destroyer, the Sepia Slugger, the Dark Dynamiter, the Dusky David from Detroit, the Sable Cyclone, the Tawny Tiger-Cat, the Saffron Sphinx, the Dusky Downer, Mike Jacobs's Pet Pickaninny, the Coffee-colored Kayo-King, the Chocolate Chopper, the Tan Tarzan of Thump. Jungle associations were much employed, absurdly for an American from Alabama who had grown up in Detroit. Grantland Rice, the dean of sportswriters, called him a "Bushmaster" and a "Brown Cobra" who had the speed of the jungle, the instinctive speed of the wild." Others rang the changes on the jungle mythology.

Puzzling to Louis, politics entered the picture. He was going to fight an Italian, and Mussolini was threatening Ethiopia. Much to his surprise, people told Louis that he was "representing" Ethiopia, which he knew nothing about and could not point to on the map. Someone mentioned Marcus Garvey to him, the Back-to-Africa movement. He had never heard of Garvey and felt no emotional pull toward Africa. He thought all of this symbolism was a bit heavy for a twenty-year-old fighter who was being asked not only to beat Primo Carnera, but represent his people and issues in global politics while he did it.

Mike Jacobs and Louis's handlers knew that Louis's public image would be important to his success, and they worked to create such an image—though without a genuine relationship to the inward nature of the man, it could not have been successful. With the infamous Jack Johnson always in mind, they told reporters that they had laid down seven commandments for Louis's public behavior: (1) he was never to have his picture taken along with a white woman; (2) he was never to go into a nightclub alone; (3) there would be no soft fights; (4) there would be no fixed fights; (5) he was never to gloat over a fallen opponent; (6) he was to keep a "dead pan" in front of the cameras; and (7) he was to live and fight clean.

These rules were never spelled out to Louis in the form in which they were issued to an approving press, but his handlers had inculcated their essence to the fighter. His principal vices later on were womanizing and financial extravagance, but he was discreet about both, and the seven "rules" did help to shape the way in which he was perceived. In his vices he would be discreet; the rest were natural to him. Before his great public exposure in the Carnera fight, his handlers even hired a tutor to teach him the elementary facts of grammar, history, and geography. Louis accepted the inevitability of his role. In *Joe Louis' Own Story,* a brief biography ghosted by Gene Kessler, he said: "I realize the Negro people have placed a big trust in me. I can't throw my race down by abusing my position as a heavyweight challenger. It is my duty to win the championship and prove to the world that, black or white, a man can become the best fighter and still be a gentleman."

On the night of June 25, when Louis climbed into the ring in Yankee Stadium, he looked out over 60,000 fans and 400 sportswriters, the biggest crowd to see a fight in New York since 1927, the Dempsey-Tunney "long count" fight. Louis was nervous waiting for the bell, but felt that this would disappear as soon as he landed the first punch. Carnera was 6 feet 5 inches tall and weighed 260 pounds, but Louis found that he could move him around. In a clinch, Louis picked the giant up and held him there in the air. Carnera whispered, "I should be doing this to you." All Carnera had was a good left jab, but it was nothing that could hurt Louis. In the sixth round, Louis hit him with a right, and blood spurted from his mouth. A right to the jaw knocked him down. Another right to the jaw put him down again. Then Louis finished off with a left-right combination. Carnera went down for the third and last time. Louis said Carnera had not hurt him, and he felt ready for any heavyweight in the world—Jimmy Braddock, Max Baer, anybody.

After the Carnera fight, Louis discovered high life. He had always been exuberantly sexual, but now he had made it in New York, at Yankee Stadium. He loved his girl, Marva Trotter, back in Detroit, but there were "those sweet, beautiful girls I had met. It was a round of Small's Paradise, the Memo Club, and some I can't remember the names of." He was thrilled to meet Duke Ellington, "dressed like a king," and it may have been Ellington who told him about the expensive Broadway tailor Billy Taub, who outfitted celebrities like Kid Chocolate, Babe Ruth, and Dizzy Dean. Louis ordered a dozen suits from Taub. Then he knocked out "King" Levinsky in the first round at Comisky Park. "When I looked around Levinsky was sitting on the bottom strand of the ropes yelling at the referee 'Don't let him hit me again. Don't let him hit me again.'" Louis's managers signed up Max Baer, the 6-foot-2-inch, 220-pound, former heavyweight champion.

At this point, strange interlude, the old former champion, Jack Johnson, who had fallen on bad times and was working in side shows and flea circuses around Times Square, emerged as a debunker of Louis. He told the newspapers that even at age fifty-seven he could have done as well against Carnera and Levinsky. Johnson said that Louis's stance was wrong and that he was a poor boxer. Louis had admired Johnson and was hurt. The best explanation is one offered by Louis's managers—that Louis was an immensely popular black fighter, while Johnson had been hated.

Louis married Marva in a Harlem apartment about two hours before the fight with Max Baer in Yankee Stadium, and he thinks the Baer fight was his best performance as a professional. There were 95,000 people in the stadium to see the rising black heavyweight. Marva was at ringside, and Louis wanted this to be a quick fight so that he could get home to his bride. It did not bother him that Jack Dempsey was in Baer's corner. Baer seemed in top condition, but scared, and Louis knew that he could beat him after he hit him with a left uppercut in the first round. At the end of the second round, Louis dropped his hands at the bell, and Baer hit him with a solid right to the jaw, enraging Louis. In the third round, a Louis right put Baer down for a count of nine, and then another right put him down for a count of four, interrupted by the bell. In the fourth round, a hard left hook and a right put Baer down again, and he was on one knee when referee Arthur Donovan counted him out. "I've never had better hand speed," writes Louis. "I felt so good I knew I could have fought for two or three days straight."

Here is the famous radio announcer Clem McCarthy broadcasting the Louis-Baer fight. For reasons that become obvious when you think about them, prizefights were *more* exciting over radio than over TV. Radio, in Marshall McLuhan's terms, is a "hot" medium, while TV is "cool." In every fight there are periods when nothing much is happening, but a great announcer like McCarthy makes it sound as if enormous things are happening all the time. Here is the master:

> Max straightened up, and Louis gives him another left. Now Louis is in close, and Baer ties him up. And Louis is backing away, but he comes in on Baer. They're right above me as I talk now, Baer with his back to me, and Louis gives him two left jabs. But Baer wants more. Louis leads with a left, and Baer has got his hands back close against him. Now and then he sticks out—he ducks his head back that time, and he got a left, ah, good stiff left jolt on the chin. And now he missed with a left that, ah, Louis ducked and went under. Louis gave him a left full in the face, a left over the eye. Louis another left, another left, and Louis is ready with that right at any instant. Now they are out there in the middle of the ring, fiddling; neither one has made a move for about five seconds, and then Louis jabbed him with a left. Now Louis is following up another left; aw, these lefts are like—but there came a fast right, a right swing right across that got Max high on the jaw, and Max went into a clinch. The referee orders them to break. They're over here against the rope. Max has got his back [oohhhhh!] and he took an awful right and then a left to the jaw, and he has gone to his knees. He's down, and the count is four . . . five . . . six. Baer's on one knee, seven, eight, nine. Baer is not up [booo!], and Baer is on his knee at the count of ten. Your fight is all over; your fight is all over. The boys are coming into the ring with the speed of a Buick. Of a new Buick, and I'm going up to see these fighters if I can.

The next step, clearly, was the heavyweight championship, now held by James J. Braddock, a tough Irish-American, and only a fight with Max Schmeling stood in the way. Louis, overconfident and overweight, prepared sloppily for Schmeling, for whom he had little regard. Louis had no doubt that he would annihilate Schmeling, who came into the ring a 10 to 1 underdog. Instead, Schmeling knocked him out and humiliated him, making him vow that he would never again take his professional duties so carelessly.

The loss was doubly painful because the sportswriters and publicists had politicized the fight, constantly identifying Schmeling as a German or a Nazi, the "Terrific Teuton," the "Nazi Nudger," and the "Heil Hitler Hero." Schmeling's training camp was picketed and there were pickets at the weigh-in. Louis was cast as the defender of democracy and the answer to Hitler's "master race" theories. All of this hype was cynical. Schmeling was not a Nazi. Most of the sportswriters liked him and found him to be polite, thoughtful, and gentlemanly. In addition, they sympathized with him as an underdog against a Louis who was considered unbeatable—indeed, dangerous. Dozens of times Schmeling was asked whether he was afraid, and he naturally replied no. The Nazi media themselves downplayed the fight, believing Schmeling likely to lose. In fact, both men, Louis and Schmeling, did not view themselves as symbols of international politics. Both saw themselves as professional fighters whose fame and bank accounts depended on success in the ring. The fight itself was the worst experience of Louis's life, at least before his last years, when he was old, poor, and ill.

Schmeling entered the ring first, wearing a gray-and-black robe, and Louis climbed through the ropes seconds later, wearing a blue robe with red trimming. Louis felt ready. When the bell rang, Schmeling came out looking off balance, bent backwards at the waist. His chin was tucked in his left shoulder, and his left arm was stuck up in the air to protect his chin. His right was steady. He did not come out punching or weaving. Louis felt he could jab Schmeling easily. He jabbed until Schmeling's eye was almost closed in the first round. "When I look at some of those old fight films," Louis later said, "I could kick myself. His left was so high that his body was wide open for a right hand."

In the second round, Louis hit him—boom, boom, boom—with jabs that did not seem to bother him. Then he did what his manager told him not to do, dropped in a left hook. Immediately, Schmeling came in with a right hand over that landed like a bomb to his chin. Louis thought he had swallowed his mouthpiece. He was dazed, everything clouding over. "I don't know how I stayed on my feet," he wrote. "I kept jabbing until my head cleared a little bit." In round three, Louis shook Schmeling up with some right uppercuts to the body, tried to hit him in the jaw, but was fended off by Schmeling's left. Schmeling was relatively passive, right hand always ready.

Louis opened a cut under his right eye with a left hook in the fourth round. Immediately, Schmeling landed a sharp right to Louis's jaw, and he went down for a two count. Louis was startled and felt as if his jaw was broken. This was his first knockdown as a professional. Just before the end of the sixth round, Schmeling hit Louis so hard with a right to the head that he could barely make it back to his corner. Everything was in a fog; he was fighting on pure instinct. He lost his poise to the extent that, when he tried to mount a body attack, he hit low twice. The referee warned him, and he lost those rounds, but the power had gone out of his punches and Schmeling bided his time.

In the eighth round, Louis's legs felt weak, and Schmeling started shooting right hands again, punishing Louis, landing three solid rights to the jaw as the round ended. In the ninth, he kept landing hard right-hand blows. In two minutes and twenty-nine seconds of the twelfth round, Schmeling finally put Louis away, making the challenger feel that he had been hit with about fifty right hands in that round.

When Louis recovered his senses and looked in the mirror after that fight, he saw that his features had been rearranged. His forehead was so swollen that he could not find his eyebrows. His cheeks were puffed up grotesquely. His lips were split and swollen.

In the black section of Chicago, people stoned streetcars in their fury over Schmeling's devastating victory. In New York, a black woman drank poison in a drugstore and had to be rushed to the hospital. Louis could not bring himself to go back to the Teresa Hotel in Harlem but stayed out of sight for three days with friends. His own comment in his autobiography sums it all up: "Shit!"

Louis came back strongly from the Schmeling humiliation and may have been a greater fighter because of it. The old conviction of his invincibility was certainly gone, and he paid more attention to technique. Above all, he learned not to drop his left after a hook. Schmeling had known about that flaw, and whenever Louis had done it, Schmeling would smash him with a right over the left. At age twenty-three, the presumptive successor to the title found himself making a comeback. He knocked out Jack Sharkey and ten other heavyweights and on June 22, 1937, knocked out James J. Braddock in eight rounds to become heavyweight champion.

The next year, while he fought all comers, there came the redemption in one savage round against Schmeling, and the flood of big money became a tidal wave. He bought his mother a house plus a farm. He took up horseback riding and bought a 400-acre horse ranch. He sent a sister through Howard University. He put up money for a Joe Louis Bar in Harlem. He bankrolled a Brown Bombers softball team. Marva learned to ride and competed in horse shows. In those heady days, you could see Louis and his friends on the public golf courses around New York—blacks were not allowed in the private golf clubs in those days. A large entourage always followed him around the course. He was always magnificently dressed in tailored golfing clothes. His golf was excellent, and of course he hit towering drives, but his game was not as good as he thought it was. Often he and a friend played a couple of pros, and at bets of $500 per hole, Louis dropped quite a bit of money.

Marva was still there, but Louis had always been enthusiastic about women. In Hollywood, "John Barrymore and me became good friends. And, oh, the women again. You know, there's something about women and men who can't resist each other. Now I'm older, I know it's just an ego trip. A big movie star would see me, the Heavyweight Champion of the World, and wonder how I am in bed. We would find out very easily. These were just one-night stands. Neither of us could afford to be found out in America in those days. However, some of those one-night stands went on for weeks. Marva got a lot of expensive presents."

According to his autobiography, he had a passionate affair with Lena Horne and wore a gold bracelet with her name on it. He also had an affair with Sonja Henie. *My Life*:

> I don't know where they get this idea that women are the
> weaker sex and that they're shy. My god, the women, the
> starlets, white and black, came jumping at me. I was the
> weaker sex. I didn't resist one pretty girl who had a sparkle in
> her eye. In particular, there was one of the cutest gals I ever
> met. Her name was Sonja Henie. She was from Norway, and
> she had won the Women's Figure Skating Gold Medal in three
> Olympics, one after the other. Now she had come to
> Hollywood to make pictures. She was a pug-nosed blonde
> with bright blue eyes, and one of the best sports I've ever
> known. We had a nice thing going, but she was a smart
> woman and so kept everything "undercover."

A recent biography of Sonja Henie casts some doubt upon Louis's account of his relations with her, and there is a peculiar aspect to the whole question. Henie was on good terms with Adolf Hitler and other leading Nazis, and she sympathized with their racial views. "When she was later reported to have had a romance with a black American prize-fighter," write her biographers, "she was infuriated by the allegation." I believe Louis. Her general racial attitudes gave way before the charm of a particular man. She was at least as sexual as Louis. "Sonja met [Tyrone Power]," according to her biographers, "when he came on the set of *One in a Million*. He invited her to lunch and they soon began a torrid affair. They saw each other before shooting in the mornings, at lunch, during breaks, and after work. Sonja felt no need to sit patiently through the preliminaries of courtship. When she saw something she wanted, she wanted it right away." Hitler or no Hitler, she liked Louis.

By the beginning of 1940, Louis had run out of domestic opponents both plausible and implausible, and so Mike Jacobs looked abroad and came up with a Chilean unknown, named Arturo Godoy. They met on February 9 in Madison Square Garden, and Godoy unexpectedly gave Louis one of the most frustrating evenings of his career. Godoy had a craggy face and dark, curly hair and fought from a position it would be an understatement to call a deep crouch. Godoy was like a turtle scuttling around the ring, bent at the knees and from the waist. Louis could not get at Godoy, who also clinched frequently. When in minimal trouble, Godoy would touch the canvas floor with one of his gloves, forcing Louis to a neutral corner as the referee's count began. The referee, Arthur Donovan, kept urging Godoy to mix it up, but that was not his plan of battle. Everyone was disgusted except Godoy, who lasted fifteen rounds and lost the unanimous decision. The Wild Bull of the Pampas, as Godoy was known, had not been so wild after all, but he had had a decent payday.

In June, Jacobs matched Louis with Godoy again. Godoy had been telling reporters that he would knock Louis out. Asked for a response, Louis said, "Any dog can wag his tail." The referee stopped the fight in the eighth round as a battered Godoy remained helpless on his knees in the middle of the ring.

That was the summer of 1940, and the astute Mike Jacobs feared that the United States might soon enter the war; he determined to make as much money out of Louis as he could before the champion faced a possible military draft. He decided that Louis would fight as often as possible. When he had announced the first Godoy fight he also said that Louis would fight Johnny Paycheck, a journeyman heavyweight. The *New York Post* referred to Louis's schedule as "The Bum of the Month," and the derisive slogan was picked up by sportswriters generally as Louis knocked out Paycheck (aptly named), Al McCoy in December, Red Burman shortly after the New Year, Gus Dorazio in February, Abe Simon in March, and Tony Musto in April.

Louis resented the bum-of-the-month slogan, since these were the best heavyweights available, and as a professional, he knew that a hard punch by a strong man could change the situation in seconds. He registered his irritation later in his autobiography: "Those guys I fought were not bums. They were hard-working professionals trying to make a dollar, too. I knew the training they went through, and I knew the dreams they had. No different from me. I respected every man I fought. It's no easy job getting up in that ring; you got to have a special kind of balls." Louis's innate decency, his chivalry even, shines through such a statement.

On May 23, 1941—to move a bit ahead of 1940—Louis knocked out Buddy Baer, Max's brother, at Washington's Griffith Stadium. Then came his fight against Billy Conn that everyone alive at the time remembers. The audience was riveted to the radio at the prospect of Louis losing to the handsome light-heavyweight from Pittsburgh, a gifted and courageous boxer and master of ring strategy. When reporters asked Louis whether he thought he could cope with Conn's speed, he made his famous reply: "He can run, but he can't hide." They fought on June 18 before 55,000 people at New York's Polo Grounds.

By round three, it began to be clear that the champion was in serious trouble. He was unable to hit Conn solidly, and Conn was repeatedly beating him to the punch and keeping him off balance. Cornerman Jack Blackburn told Louis to pick up the pace, and the champion outpointed Conn in rounds five and six, opening a cut on Conn's nose, but Conn sped away, and by round seven Louis seemed tired, and the balance began to tip against him, apparently decisively. Conn made Louis pursue him around the ring—he could indeed run, and he did not need to hide—and then he would suddenly dart in and out, hitting Louis with two or three punches before the champion could retaliate. By the twelfth round, Conn was toying with a weary and tactically bewildered Louis. Coming out of a clinch, Conn's left hook and a right-cross–left-hook combination staggered Louis, whereupon a Conn left threw Louis off balance and into the ropes. After the eleventh round, Louis's corner told him that he would have to knock Conn out in order to win.

In the thirteenth round, Conn abandoned his winning tactics and thought he could knock Louis out. With the two fighters slugging in the middle of the ring, Louis hit Conn with an overhand right that was enough to slow the boxer down. A solid right uppercut sent Conn's hair flying. Another hard overhand right had Conn out on his feet, still standing through habit. A barrage of rights and lefts put Conn on the canvas, but he managed to stagger to his feet at the count of ten with two minutes left in the round. Louis walked toward Conn for another barrage, but the referee, recognizing Conn's helplessness, stopped the fight. Louis was still champ after all.

Joe Louis admired President Roosevelt, but in 1940 he was swept away by the charisma of Wendell Willkie. When "I listened to

Willkie, I fell in love with him. He said things like 'Every American is going to have a place in this country.' Hell, a lot of people forget black people are Americans, too. We've been here for a long time. God bless Africa, but I never saw it. . . . I campaigned all over for Willkie, but he just couldn't beat Roosevelt. Roosevelt had that special charm. Never mind, though, I thought Willkie would have made one hell of a president." After the Buddy Baer fight in May 1941, Willkie visited Louis in his locker room. "I really liked that man," Louis said.

Then the war. Soon after Pearl Harbor, Louis, profoundly patriotic, enlisted in the Army as a private. "This is the best country I know of . . . and I'd gladly defend her." At the request of the White House, he fought dozens of exhibitions for the soldiers and sailors, and he also gave all of his ring earnings during the war to programs for the fighting men. In an article in *Liberty* magazine in early 1942, Paul Gallico summed up what many now thought of "Citizen Barrow":

> Years ago I wrote that Joe Louis was "mean." Then he was a primitive puncher just emerging from the pit. Somewhere on his long, hard climb Joe found his soul. It was this, almost more than his physical person, that he handed over to his country. "You can't think of yourself these days," Joe said. But I can think of him. I write of him now not especially as a hero—every unsung youth who has shouldered a gun made a similar sacrifice—but as a simple, good American Joe who has become one of the most popular of all champions, cheered by white and black alike. But he has won more than popularity. He has won respect. The simple, unlettered colored boy has brought to the championship a dignity it has too often lacked.

During the war, Louis fought many times, exhibitions and genuine bouts, and gave all of his earnings to Army and Navy Relief and similar causes, despite the fact that he was heavily in debt to both the IRS and Mike Jacobs from 1941 and before. He was imprudent financially. Yet it is with a sense of sadness and outright disgust that one reads about the relentless hounding the IRS subjected him to after the war, a persecution that saddened him but could not permanently extinguish his native good spirit. He won his battles with drugs and alcohol. It is ridiculous that neither Truman nor Eisenhower wiped out his tax debt, in view of the hundreds of thousands of dollars he had contributed voluntarily during the war. In his last years, friends got him a job as official host at Caesar's

Palace in Las Vegas, and he enjoyed the job, coming and going as he wished, socializing, playing golf with the customers. Marva had divorced him, remarried him, and then divorced him again, but they remained on good terms.

At his peak in 1940, Louis was the most convincing of all our heavyweight champions—Johnson, Dempsey, Ali, and the rest. The game of guessing who would have beaten whom is, in a sense, foolish but also fun. In the modern era of boxing, who could have beaten Louis? Dempsey was a terrific puncher, but he was twenty-five pounds lighter than Louis and could be hit. On one occasion in his later years, Louis was visited by Muhammad Ali, also of course a great champion. Ali told him that he had had a dream about fighting Louis and that he had won. "Muhammad," said Louis, "don't even dream about that." Ali would certainly have used his speed to stay away from Louis. But as Louis said memorably about Billy Conn, "He can run, but he can't hide."

Louis laid to rest the racial ghost of Jack Johnson. Virtually illiterate, Louis was naturally a gentleman. Some black chauvinists today condescend to him as the black who tried to be pleasing to whites, but the point is that it was natural to him to try to be pleasing to everyone, and he was. In the Army, he would not box before segregated audiences. When he saw an instance of racial injustice, he did not hesitate to call the White House. He forced the Army to let Jackie Robinson play football and baseball. He was principled and firm, but far above all show-off abrasiveness.

In October 1977 he suffered a serious heart attack and was flown to Houston, where Dr. Michael DeBakey, the eminent heart specialist, performed an arterial graft. While recuperating at the hospital, he had a cerebral hemorrhage that left him barely able to speak. Frank Sinatra paid all the expenses for Louis's extensive hospitalization. He returned to Caesar's Palace in a wheelchair, stricken but alert, and delighted with the attention paid to him. On April 12, 1981, he collapsed at home with another heart attack and was pronounced dead shortly after arriving at the hospital. His body— weirdly, but maybe not—was displayed at Caesar's Palace.

Under a special presidential decree signed by President Reagan, Joe Louis was buried in Arlington National Cemetery, the body carried from the service in Fort Meyers Chapel in a horse-drawn caisson. At Arlington, he was buried with military honors and a twenty-one-gun salute and finally the playing of taps. Caspar Weinberger, the secretary of defense, read a message from the president stating, correctly, that "all Americans share his loss."

A good epitaph for Louis—not the one on his tombstone at Arlington—was composed by Louis himself. His autobiography ends: "I almost always did exactly what I wanted to do. I've been in a whole lot of fights inside the ring and outside the ring, too. I like to think I won most of those battles. Well, like the man said, 'If you dance you got to pay the piper.' Believe me, I danced, I paid the piper, and left him a big fat tip."

Early Pacific Casualties

The Pacific, the blue and moving frontier of America, stretching westward under cloudless skies—Hawaii, Samoa, Tahiti, China. . . . The wagon trains and the railroads and the gold prospectors pushing westward, the energies of the continent moving always westward. Well might Cortez and his men have gazed upon the Pacific with a wild surmise, as in Keats's imagination. It had its islands with golden sands and blue lagoons, on which there was always landing one of those white Pan American flying boats. See the shower of spray as the hull touches the blue water. The pilot and copilot stepping off into the quay always wore starched, white cotton uniforms with gold braid and short white sleeves. Tanned. Salutes. This would not be the usual war in Europe when it came. Pearl Harbor, Coral Sea, Tarawa, Guadalcanal, Iwo Jima . . . the names would have a special poetry.

Everyone was thrilled with horror when Amelia Earhart disappeared somewhere out over the Pacific during the summer of 1937. She had been the first woman to fly the Atlantic, and now she and her navigator were trying to circle the globe at the equator. She rather disliked being called "Lady Lindy" by the press, because she wanted her own independent identity, but the odd thing was that she looked like Lindbergh, thin, with short hair and a wide grin, somehow quintessentially American. Even her name had a touch of poetry about it, Amelia Earhart, in Joycean terms lover of the air, somehow belonging there in the skies and not down here on earth.

On her last flight, she and her navigator, Fred Noonan, flew an advanced-model, twin-engined, aluminum Electra specially designed for the trip. It was known in the press as the "Flying Laboratory." On July 2, 1937, all contact with the plane was lost, and searches by U.S. ships and planes failed to turn up any trace of Earhart, Noonan, or the plane. As far as anyone at the time knew, they had simply disappeared into that vast blueness.

It turns out that Amelia Earhart and Fred Noonan were the first casualties of the coming Pacific war with the Japanese. Vincent Loomis, a former USAF pilot with extensive Pacific experience, became fascinated with the Earhart mystery and made it his business to solve it, which he has done. It is a remarkable, enormously romantic, and heartbreaking story. Loomis went to the Pacific, traveled around the relevant islands, and found natives who had seen the plane crash and had seen Earhart and Noonan. He interviewed the surviving Japanese who were involved, and photographed for his book the pertinent, and until now unknown, Japanese military and diplomatic documents. The mystery is a mystery no longer.

For all of her fame and accomplishments, Amelia Earhart was an innocent flying out over the Pacific. Unaware, she flew her plane right into the middle of the secret war plans of the Japanese Empire. She and Noonan were also incompetent navigators and did not know how to work their state-of-the-art equipment. They were thus more than one hundred miles off course when they ran out of fuel and had to ditch the Electra in the midst of a highly secret Japanese military buildup that had been going on for more than fifteen years.

By 1937, Tokyo had long since concluded that war with the United States for control of the western Pacific was inevitable. They were hatching plans with Hitler to divide up the British, French, and Dutch possessions that would be vulnerable as a result of the coming European war. The projected Japanese Empire, the Greater East Asia Co-Prosperity Sphere, would have its large mainland anchor in a China the Japanese were attempting to conquer, and they would use the Pacific islands as the first line of defense against the U.S. Navy. The Japanese knew that the United States was unlikely to tolerate their geopolitical plans and would be decidedly hostile to any monopolistic co-prosperity sphere run from Tokyo.

The Japanese had acquired control of the key Pacific islands at the end of World War I under a League of Nations mandate. In violation of international law, they were pouring military resources into them. All Japanese military personnel worked in civilian clothes. Newly paved airstrips were marked "farms" on the maps. Foreign visitors were absolutely excluded. If the local natives obeyed the Japanese rules, they were treated fairly, and the Japanese even married some of them. An infraction, however, could mean instant death.

On July 2, 1937, bewildered and lost, Amelia Earhart crash-landed into the middle of all this, putting the Electra down and running into an atoll near Mili Mili, a principal military position in the Japanese Marshall Islands chain. The Japanese took her and Noonan prisoner and tried to figure out what to do with them. They could hardly release them, not knowing what they had seen. Perhaps Earhart and Noonan could blow the cover on the whole secret operation. The Japanese thought they might even be spies. Actually, the American fliers had seen nothing.

The two Americans were shipped to Japanese military headquarters on Saipan and jailed. The conditions were miserable, but not unusual for that time and place. The jail was not set up to serve food to the prisoners, mostly natives, whose meals were brought to them by relatives. But they did provide the two Americans with soup, fish, and rice, though of very poor quality, and with medical treatment. When an exasperated Fred Noonan threw a foul bowl of soup at a Japanese jailer, he was forced to dig his own grave and was immediately beheaded. Japanese culture was not permissive.

After a while, Earhart was allowed a certain amount of freedom and made friends with local native families, some of whom Loomis interviewed. She was permitted local visits to friends, and her diet and spirits improved. In mid-1938, however, life in the tropics proved too much for her, and she came down with a severe case of dysentery, weakened rapidly, and died there on Saipan. She does not seem to have grasped the significance of the things she had stumbled upon and witnessed. Ironically enough, she was a philosophical pacificist. The Japanese military asked the natives to provide a wreath for her, and she was buried with Noonan.

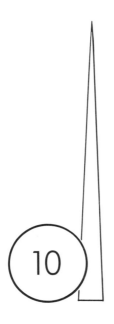

THE BOYS OF
AUGUST

10

You can make the case that the golden era of lawn tennis began with Big Bill Tilden, his dominance of Little Bill Johnson, and his famous duels with René Lacoste during the 1920s. But a stronger case can be made that the golden era began before World War I, with the rise of Maurice McLoughlin, the California Comet, and ended in 1940 with a burst of American tennis brilliance as the thunderheads of war rolled across the Atlantic.

McLoughlin ended the Victorian era in tennis, and he played two of his greatest matches during the summer of 1914 as Europe was going to war. The scene was the new West Side Tennis Club in Forest Hills, the Davis Cup match against England, with the Americans pitted against two of the greatest prewar English-Australian players, the startlingly handsome Anthony Wilding of England and the formidable Norman Brookes of Australia.

The reporter Al Laney, who has been, with the possible exception of Allison Danzig, our greatest tennis sportswriter, saw McLoughlin through the awestruck eyes of a young boy from the far provinces of Pensacola, Florida. Laney recalls it all with Proustian clarity, enriched but not softened by the pathos of time. To define that era in tennis that began back before the first war and ended in 1940, before the next war, let us look briefly over the shoulder of that small boy from Florida.

A relative had invited Al Laney up to New York for a few days, knowing that the boy was a sports enthusiast and that the league-leading New York Giants would be playing at the Polo Grounds. At the same time, the England–United States Davis Cup match would be underway at the West Side Tennis Club. In his hotel on West 86th Street, Laney was torn between the two events. The morning papers on a Tuesday were so full of the coming tennis matches that Laney decided to give up only one day to the Polo Grounds, despite the great Christy Mathewson. He saw the Giants beat the surging second-place Braves 8–2. The next day he got up early and took the Long Island Railroad out to Forest Hills. It was the day before the cup matches. He hoped to see the players practicing, hoped to catch a glimpse of the red-haired California Comet.

On that morning the new West Side Tennis Club clubhouse was recognizable as the structure we know today, a stucco-and-beam, Tudor building with its pointed gables, but then it stood in the middle of a meadow instead of the later, also Tudor, suburb of Forest Hills Gardens. From the Long Island Railroad station you walked along a country path for two blocks to the club. Laney arrived early that Wednesday morning and was afraid to enter. He was not a member. Instead, he circled the fence and through a gap in the canvas covering saw a couple of players strolling out onto the clay courts. Laney grasped the wire of the fence with his hands. He had never seen such well-kept clay courts. When the men began to play, he experienced a revelation. These were not the Davis Cup players, maybe only club members or college boys, but Laney saw a different game than he had been playing with his friends down in Florida. "Here I saw a method of striking the ball very different from the strokes my boyhood opponents and I employed. This, I thought, must be the real thing, the way the great ones do it, and every single detail of it must be carefully observed and stored in memory to take back home and practice." Right there exactly is the desire for technical knowledge that made Laney later on a great reporter, able to write about tennis in a way the best players respected.

As the morning wore on, Laney slid into the clubhouse in the midst of some students from Columbia who were arriving to practice for their tasks as ushers for tomorrow. Laney stood on the famous terrace and gazed out at the immaculate grass courts with their precise white lines. He had admired the club's clay from outside the fence, but this was something else altogether. It was, he recalled, "beautiful, this perfect-looking green grass with the white lines upon it. It was just about the most beautiful sight I had ever seen."

The next day he arrived early with his ticket and took his seat in the wooden grandstands that surrounded the two grass courts in front of the clubhouse. As the time of the matches approached, he watched the seats gradually fill up. He remembers the taste of the crisp bologna sandwich he had brought with him from the hotel, and also the oddity, as the stands filled, of looking down on a solid vista of stiff straw hats. "Looking down from the rim you could see nothing but the tops of those hats. Many of the women in the crowd wore larger versions with pins sticking out. . . . Every head among the fourteen thousand seemed to have one, except for the occasional soft Panama."

There was a burst of applause from the crowd when two white-clad figures emerged at the top of the stairs from the second-floor locker room and descended to the terrace and the grass court, R. Norris Williams, captain of the Harvard team, who had swum away from the *Titanic* and lived, and the great British player, Anthony Wilding.

R.N. Williams had an unusual conception of how to play tennis, always forward, taking the ball only inches after it had bounced, using the momentum of the ball to increase his own power and using a wrist motion, firing it back at his opponent. A decade later, old-timers say, R.N. Williams played the single best set of tennis ever played. Tilden was then totally dominant, but in a match at the Germantown Cricket Club in Pennsylvania, Williams won the first set from Tilden 6–0 in twenty minutes. After that, Williams's high-risk shot making cooled off, and Tilden pulled out the match. Nothing like that happened against Anthony Wilding, and Al Laney watched the Englishman with his impressive baseline strokes polish off the Harvard student in three straight sets. What Laney really wanted to see, however, was Maurice McLoughlin against the Australian champion, Norman Brookes, the second match of the day.

"I can well remember," writes Laney, "how these two looked as they came down the steps and stood for their pictures to be taken. Brookes, long of face and solemn, wore long sleeves and had in his hand a cap which he would wear throughout the match. McLoughlin's shirt was open at the neck and the sleeves were cut off at the elbows." McLoughlin's mop of red hair completed Laney's first glimpse of the American tennis hero from the West. "McLoughlin smiled a lot. Brookes seemed very dour. My confidence was shaken many times before that terribly long first set was over. Brookes gave the impression that he would never yield no matter how many thunderbolts our man might hurl at him, blows one never could have imagined possible with a tennis racket."

This match pitted Brookes's old-fashioned perfection and resolution against something that was utterly new in 1914. The California Comet hit a "Western"-style forehand, with the hand wholly behind the racket. With this grip he could hit with heavy topspin and blast a winner from anywhere on the court. But his major weapon was his remarkable serve, behind which he would run to the net and volley. Nothing like McLoughlin's serve had been seen before. He used three serves, with variations of them: a hard, flat cannonball, a slice that curved in, plus his specialty—an "American Twist," hit with terrific spin that curved out. During a crisis, Laney remembers, "McLoughlin served three balls that Brookes could not even touch with his queer-shaped racket." McLoughlin took the first set 17–15 over the Victorian, then ran out the match.

There was no going back now. A new way of playing tennis had come out of the American West. "One picture," writes Al Laney, "must be my very own. It is of McLoughlin, all fire and dash, leaping from the ground to smash a lob and, as the ball bit into the turf and bounced impossibly away, of Brookes dropping his racket, raising both hands above his head in despair and calling on high heaven to witness his despair." It was McLoughlin 17–15, 6–3, 6–3. The next day Laney saw the British take the doubles. On Saturday, McLoughlin blasted Anthony Wilding off the court to tie the match, but Brookes subdued R. N. Williams, and the British took the Davis Cup.

That was the last Davis Cup match for five years. By the next spring, Anthony Wilding was in a grave in Flanders, killed early in the war. The British stopped a passenger ship in the Atlantic and interned the German Davis Cup team. Something strange happened to the game of the California Comet. Two weeks after his stunning performance at the West Side Tennis Club, he lost in the National Championship finals to R.N. Williams, and McLoughlin never won another important match. "The shock of McLoughlin's defeat was great," writes Laney. "I wondered at first if there could be some mistake. It was as if something had gone wrong with natural law and it was difficult to forgive Williams when I knew it was true."

In 1940, as in 1914, things were ending with a glorious sunset glow. The wooden grandstand, from which Laney had gazed down upon the magnificent McLoughlin, was gone and had been replaced by the concrete horseshoe stadium required to accommodate the crowds who wanted to see Big Bill Tilden during the 1920s. Between that distant 1914 and 1940, there had come an amazing procession of players, Tilden and Johnson and Richards, the glory days of the French and Tilden's epic duels with René Lacoste (the

Crocodile), Ellsworth Vines, Frank Shields, the last great English
player Fred Perry, who took the ball on the rise in a modification of
R. N. Williams's stroke, and then the rise of the Californians Don
Budge and Bobby Riggs, the latter coming to Forest Hills as defend-
ing champion, Wimbledon champion, and odds-on favorite for the
American title.

By 1940, the West Side Tennis Club had the familiar contours of
today, with a perimeter of clay courts around a center of grass
courts, then as many as forty of them, the number varying to
accommodate wear and tear on the grass. The stadium had two more
grass courts. Alongside the stadium was a wooden grandstand for
the number two matches, and of course there were fresh flowers and
blue and yellow awnings everywhere, the colors of the West Side
Tennis Club.

Everyone knew that this 1940 National Championship would be
the last real tournament for a long time. It began against the background of the European catastrophe and the daily saturation bombing of London. The Willkie-Roosevelt election was coming to its
autumn climax. With the exception of Mary Hardwick, who led
a strong contingent of British women players, it was virtually an
American tournament: no German, no French, no British or Italian
or Japanese. Things were closing down, and everyone knew it. Most
of the Americans playing in the championships that year had a date
with the military draft. The next year, to be sure, there would be a
tournament, but it didn't seem to matter as much any more because
of the apocalypse abroad. The 1940 tournament was the end of an
era, a last island of light. Many of those who played in it and many
of those who watched it would not come back for five years, and
many of them would not come back at all.

In an ideal vision you think of those grass courts and those blue
and yellow awnings under a gleaming and cloudless sky, but torren-
tial rains delayed the start of the 1940 tournament by three days.
Each day tournament officials met, only to postpone the opening
matches. Newspaper accounts give you something of the social
flavor. Among the officials were Dr. Ellsworth Davenport, the
referee, along with P. Schuyler Van Bloem, Charles Hubbell, Fred
Pond, and Ben Dwight. When the sun shone on the morning of the
third day, the players began flocking into the clubhouse and out onto
the courts for morning practice: Robert Larrimore "Bobby" Riggs,
the defending champion; Alice Marble, another Californian and
perhaps the best woman player of all time; Pauline Betz, great speed
and great backhand, but weak forehand; Don McNeill, a young
Oklahoman whose game seemed to come into intense focus as the

season developed; and two players who could do more with a tennis ball than anyone else except win the last point in a championship match, Frank Kovacs and S. Welby Van Horne, Jr. There was also Bryan M. "Bitsy" Grant, the diminutive defensive specialist, Frank Parker, Bill Talbert, Ellwood Cooke, and the formidable Sarah Palfrey, who was given the best chance against Marble and would soon become Mrs. Ellwood Cooke. There were two explosive talents up out of the junior ranks, the Californians Ted Schroeder of La Jolla and Jack Kramer of Montebello. They would "bear watching," as the newspapers put it in those rhetorically chaster days of tennis writing. On the scene too was Frank Shields, the handsome grandfather of Brooke, with his tremendous serve and forehand, and Sidney Wood, the impeccable stylist and volleyer. They all came to Forest Hills in that summer of 1940.

"Kovacs is in the same half with the champion," wrote Allison Danzig in the *New York Times*.

> He defeated Riggs at Southampton and four times stood at match point against him at Seabright. The unpredictable Californian, who has played some of the most amazing tennis this observer has seen, is able to dictate the pace against the champion, but it has been a different story when he has met the hard-balling McNeill. In the final at Southampton and again at Newport, he played poorly against the Oklahoman. Riggs has had his troubles with McNeill too, losing to him in the clay-court championship and winning only after he had stood within a stroke of a deficit of 2 sets to one. But the champion would probably feel happier if Kovacs were in McNeill's half.

Frank Kovacs. Welby Van Horne. These two players are among the enigmas of tennis. Kovacs was a gentle and handsome giant with a good sense of humor who could produce any shot in the tennis repertory but who did not seem to know how, or even be interested in, the process of working toward winning a point. Kovacs liked to hit balls with the kids around the West Side Club. Jack Kramer, a nineteen-year-old who emerged spectacularly in that 1940 tournament, remembers this of Kovacs:

> Frankie never won anything, but he was a draw and everybody figured he was going to win everything tomorrow. He was a big attractive guy, 6'4", with a great smile—sort of a Nastase type, only harmless, not mean. There was one time Kovacs was playing a match at Forest Hills against Joe Hunt,

and Kovacs looked up at an airplane. Hunt mimicked him, so
Kovacs lay down for a clearer view, and Hunt did the same,
and there they were both soon lying flat out on the turf
watching an airplane while the fans watched them. Kovacs
had picture strokes, but the reason he could never win
anything is because he didn't have any idea how to go about
winning. He never had a set plan for a match. Hell, he never
had a set plan for a shot. He would sort of decide what to do
with it halfway through the stroke.

There may have been reasons other than temperament for the
genial Kovacs's loss of concentration. One of his opponents told the
author that in the midst of a match with Kovacs he had run out of
Cokes and asked Kovacs if he could have a drink of his. Kovacs had
several open Cokes at the umpire's stand. Kovacs said sure. The first
swallow nearly bowled the opponent over. Half gin.

At age twenty in 1940, S. Welby Van Horne had every quality for
tennis immortality except for his asthma. "Welby," says Kramer,
"had a super forehand crosscourt, and he could cream second
serves." He also had a tremendous twist serve and a forehand volley
that seldom permitted a return. He was lean and over 6 feet tall with
a profile that looked Aztec, and he came into the tournament in 1940
with a splendid 1939 record behind him.

In 1934, Frank Parker had been ranked number four in the
country, when he was only eighteen. At 5 feet 8 inches, he lacked the
power of the big hitters, but he had fine strokes and a sure instinct
for hitting the ball where it would most inconvenience an opponent.
But a terrible thing had happened to Parker. He was taken up by
Mercer Beasely, a tennis guru who was coaching at Lawrenceville
Academy. Beasely himself could barely hit a tennis ball over the net,
but he persuaded Parker to change his splendid topspin forehand
into a chop. "It was obscene," says Kramer; it was like painting a
mustache on the Mona Lisa. For some reason Beasely got it into his
head that Parker should hit with a forehand like Leo Durocher threw
the ball from shortstop to first base. That was what Beasely pat-
terned Parker's new forehand after. At last Frankie understood that
he simply could not get his new forehand past somebody at the net.
An opponent could step up to the net and slap it away. So late in
1938, Frankie came out to the Bel Air Tennis Club in Los Angeles.
He worked every day, eight hours a day, and developed a new
overspin forehand. He could never get his beautiful original stroke
back because the chop had been with him too long, and a little hitch
was ingrained. But he did develop a better forehand, a whole lot
better game, and he moved up to number two in the rankings in

1939. Parker had a certain revenge on the old fraud Beasely, running away with and marrying Beasely's wife, who was about twenty years older than Parker.

Bobby Riggs, the defending champion, is probably the most underrated of all the acknowledged great tennis players; at least, that is Kramer's opinion.

> It wasn't his fault that he didn't look like a champion. Tilden, Vines, Perry, Budge, myself: we were all big, tall, lean, powerful boomers, while Riggs was a scrawny little scrapper with a whiny voice. . . . Kovacs looked the part, and Kovacs couldn't win. Riggs looked like he came in out of the rain, but he won, and I guarantee you he is the most underrated champion in the history of tennis. . . . I'm sure he would have beaten Gonzales—Bobby was too quick, he had too much control for Pancho—and Laver and Rosewall and Hoad. . . . He didn't have the big serve, but he made up for it with some sneaky first serves and as fine a second serve as I had seen at that time. When you talk about depth and accuracy both, Riggs' second serve ranks with the three best that I ever saw: von Cramm's, Gonzales', and Newcombe's. He was aggressive naturally and he had superb anticipation. He could keep the ball in play, and he could find ways to control the bigger, more powerful opponent. He could pin you back by hitting long, down the lines, and then he'd run you ragged with chips and drop shots. He was outstanding with a volley from either side, and he could lob as well as any man. I had to learn to lob better myself just to stay on the court with him. He could also lob on the run. He could disguise it, and he could hit winning overheads. They weren't powerful, but they were always on target.

Well up in the all-time top ten, Riggs, with his jaunty, duck-footed walk, was expected to win in 1940.

Three days late, with crowds filling the stadium and the grandstand and milling around the field courts, and as glasses clinked amid the buzz of conversation on the clubhouse terrace, the National Championships of 1940 got under way. The atmosphere was still reminiscent of the 1930s and even the 1920s, with all-white clothes and some of the men still in long white trousers. Manners on the court were restrained, and there was a premium on sportsmanship after the historic, English, amateur model. "Fine shot" was heard on most courts as play started.

The first day produced at least three notable matches. Alice
Marble, the tall, blonde, wide-shouldered player from California,
unleashed her great twist serve and biting overheads against Bar-
bara Strobhar of Newtown Square, Pennsylvania, but met surprisingly stiff resistance in the opening match in the stadium. Then, on
the same stadium court, the nineteen-year-old Kramer, who had
recently won the National Doubles title with his friend Ted
Schroeder, gave another portent of future greatness, defeating Gil
Hunt in four sets. Kramer gave the impression of tremendous power
as yet under incomplete control. When he rushed to the net behind
an overpowering serve, he was virtually irresistible, but his backhand was erratic, and his play underwent cycles of failure. One
seeded player made an early exit, as Gardner Mulloy lost on the
grandstand court to the veteran Hal Surface.

The next day saw the Welby Van Horne disaster. The year before,
the young Californian had upset John Bromwich of Australia, one of
the best players in the world, and lost to Riggs in the final. Now he
was ranked number four in the United States and considered a
coming champion. Late on the afternoon of the second day, playing
on a wet and slippery field court, Van Horne met his waterloo at the
hands of an unranked student from the University of North Carolina, Harris Everett. "Only a few hundred spectators," wrote
Allison Danzig,

> standing four deep around the outside court, saw Van Horne
> go down after he had saved two match points in the fourteenth
> game of the final set and had stood within a stroke of victory
> himself in the twenty-sixth game. They looked on perplexed
> at the alternate brilliance and listlessness of the young
> Californian's play, as have galleries who have watched Van
> Horne in action all through the season.
>
> At times irresistible with the fury of his hitting, Van Horne
> would lapse into painfully slip-shod tennis, as he did all
> through the fourth set, in which he got only six points, and as
> he did after pulling up from 3–5 in the final set. Not until he
> stood with his back to the wall could he summon the
> willpower and concentration to play the tennis of which he is
> capable, and finally they failed him in the pinch as he lost
> five successive points in the concluding game after leading
> 40–0.

Everett played a careful, accurate game, but Van Horne was fighting
his asthma as well as his opponent.

The rise of Kramer, however, stood in stark contrast to the fall of Van Horne. Danzig wrote of

> the amazingly fine performance of the youth who came East with Van Horne in 1939, when they won recognition as the country's two leading hopefuls. In defeating Edward Alloo of Berkeley by the crushing margin of 6–0, 6–3, 6–3, John Kramer of Montebello played the highest grade of tennis to come from his racket on turf. From the opening game, in which he knocked back three serves so fast that Alloo could scarcely move out of his tracks. Until he ended the play with one of his score of service aces, the rangy 19-year-old Californian played like a Budge or a Vines. His forehand was murderous in its speed and depth, and the regularity with which he scored with it in coming in fast on a short ball was definitely first class.

The shocker on the third day came when a seventeen-year-old schoolboy from Philadelphia took the first two sets from Frank Kovacs before losing in five sets. Vic Seixas, playing Kovacs on the grandstand court, drew the fans out of the stadium to witness his challenge. This

> mere stripling of medium height showed the poise and determination of a veteran and the strokes of a finished player that stamped him as one of the likeliest hopefuls the East has brought forth in more than a decade. He has no one-shot game but a splendidly rounded repertoire that bespeaks both sound, thorough coaching and pronounced natural ability. No one could teach him to volley so expertly from the backhand or to swing with such rhythmic flowing power overhead. His service was so good that in the fifteenth game of the second set he exploded three clean aces to win it at love. From the forehand he was nailing the ball with beautiful hard, flat drives, and he was firm and penetrating from the backhand.
>
> Kovacs took his early adversity good-naturedly with pantomimic effects that added to the crowd's enjoyment of the match, but he wasn't shirking the issue even though his forehand was bad. He got much better, making the gallery gasp with his exploits from the backhand and attacking mercilessly, but even in winning the last set 6–1 he was challenged to show his dazzling virtuosity until Seixas's control finally deserted him near the end.

The same day, Riggs eliminated the rising young star William Talbert, a superb stylist, in straight sets: 6–3, 6–4, 6–3. In the women's matches, Helen Jacobs, Pauline Betz, and Dorothy Bundy moved into the quarterfinals, while two Englishwomen, Mary Hardwick and Rita Jervis, and two Americans, Patricia Canning and Helen Bernhard, reached the third round.

On Friday, things got serious in the men's singles. At the end of the day, as the setting sun sent its slanting rays over the stadium, young Jack Kramer came from behind to upset Frank Parker in five sets, 1–6, 6–4, 2–6, 6–3, 6–4. No one could remember louder or more frequent cheers in the historic stadium, as the long-legged blonde youth from Montebello upset the number-two-ranked player and moved into the semifinals. In the opening set, Kramer sprayed errors all over the place, while Parker was in his usual machinelike form, and Kramer could manage only one game in the set. With the cocktail and dinner hours approaching, many of the fans had drifted out of the stadium, not expecting anything much to happen. "Those who made their exit at this stage," wrote Danzig,

> missed one of the most devastating assaults seen at Forest Hills since Don Budge was hammering the amateur fold into submission. It was in a style more reminiscent of Ellsworth Vines than of Budge that the 19-year-old Californian ripped and volleyed his way through five successive games in which Parker got only five points, and the enraptured gallery exploded into riotous cheers as he rifled three service aces across the net in the ninth game.
>
> The delight of the crowd over this comeback was only a feeble whisper, however, compared to the delirium into which it was thrown as Kramer fought his way up again from an 0–3 deficit in the final set. The tension in the stands was so great during the desperately fought struggle from there on that the end of almost every rally brought forth an uproar of approval or dismal groans.
>
> The cheers were predominantly for Kramer, who was making such a game fight under cruel pressure with admirable self-control, even when his backhand was in a woeful slump, although the equally contained Parker compelled sympathy and applause with his careful, resourceful play. The most nerve-wracking game of all was the fifth of this final set. Seven times Kramer was within a point of breaking through before he finally won the game, in which seven of his nine points were won brilliantly at the net or with his ground strokes. Groans, sighs or cheers marked every

finishing stroke and when the Californian finally broke
through with one of his adroit drop volleys the crowd's
reaction would have taken the roof off if the Stadium had a
roof.

The winning of that game was considered to be definitely
the turning point in the match, in which Kramer had blown
alternately cold and hot with a mixture of painfully weak and
irresistibly brilliant tennis—the variety that Vines frequently
provided in his amateur days before he had consolidated his
game. When the Californian went on to break through Parker
again in the seventh from 0–40 for a 4–3 lead, the crowd was
convinced that he was out of danger. But there was still
trouble ahead. Parker was dead game and full of cunning and
concentration, and his attack on Kramer's forehand provoked
five errors in the eighth to make the score 4–all.

The tension was on again. It was anybody's match, and the
question was how would the 19-year-old react to this bitter
set-back against an opponent who was returning apparent
winners with heartbreaking regularity and never making a
tactical error and seldom a manual mistake. The answer that
was furnished stamped Kramer as a youngster who has not
only the walloping shots of a potential champion but the
steady nerves and clear head that are equally essential
attributes. His reaction was to tear after his man with every
gun firing at maximum power.

An amazing backhand passing shot in reply to a kill, a
forehand drive straight down through the narrowest of
openings, and a forehand volley behind his return of service
gave him the vital break, and he ran out the tenth and final
game at 15 as he attacked behind powerful serves and
approach drives that extracted errors from Parker on his
passing shots.

The same afternoon, Don McNeill, who had been efficiently
making his way through the tournament, disposed of Ellwood Cooke
in four sets and would face Kramer in the semis.

On Saturday, in a match marked by Frank Kovacs's clowning,
Midshipman Joe Hunt of the U.S. Naval Academy sent the Californian to the showers and out of the tournament in straight sets, while
Riggs beat Kramer's doubles partner, Ted Schroeder. In the Hunt-
Kovacs match, the tittering of the crowd at Kovacs's comic gestures
finally exasperated the serious midshipman, and he protested to the
umpire in the chair during the third game of the final set. The
umpire, H. LeVan Richards, thought a request for silence from the

crowd would provoke a storm of resentment and asked Hunt to resume play. When the noise from the crowd persisted, Hunt sat down on the baseline, and Kovacs, who had been preparing to serve, sat down on his baseline and made gestures that pantomimed knitting. Finally Kovacs got up and prepared to serve. Hunt rose too, but leaned on his racket until the uproar in the crowd fell still. While Hunt was leaning on his racket with his head down, Kovacs served the ball unnoticed by Hunt. Then he served another one. At this point, the tournament referee, Dr. H. Ellsworth Davenport, walked out onto the court to restore order. After some discussion, Hunt resumed play and immediately broke Kovacs's serve. Then, as even Kovacs's fine backhand buckled under pressure, Hunt ran out the next three games for the match.

In 1943, Hunt won the wartime National Championship, defeating Kramer. Not long after that, a plane he was flying crashed in the Atlantic, and he was gone.

On the same day on which Hunt easily beat Kovacs, Riggs took Ted Schroeder in four sets. Schroeder, with his catlike quickness at the net, was able to win the second set, but his ground strokes lacked the power to dislodge Riggs, who prevailed with his all-court game. Mary Hardwick defeated Pauline Betz to join another Englishwoman, Valerie Scott, in the semis, along with Helen Jacobs and Alice Marble.

Because of the rain delay at the beginning of the tournament, the semis were held on a Monday, but the workday notwithstanding, the stadium was jammed. Don McNeill, hitting his powerful topspinning shots off forehand and backhand, and serving and volleying with authority, had the power to find Kramer's backhand and exploit it. Kramer believes that 1940 was McNeill's best year, the only great year he had as a player, and he says that McNeill's topspin backhand was the equivalent of Bjorn Borg's famous two-hander, Borg's best shot. McNeill went into the finals with a 6–1, 5–7, 6–4, 6–3 victory, but Kramer's performance in this tournament gave strong portents of greatness to come.

In the other semifinal, Riggs beat Joe Hunt in five sets, but he had come down with a case of flu at just about the worst possible moment. "The match between Riggs and Hunt, rivals from their junior days," wrote Danzig,

> came close to being the classic of the championship. It had everything to rivet the big crowd's interest from the start, and in its combined technical skill and the cleverness of the tactical maneuvers, it unquestionably surpassed all other contests of the past week.

Riggs was not quite at his best yesterday. He was a sick man on Friday and was still feeling the effects of his cold, with a bit of temperature, although he felt much improved over Saturday. He made more errors than is his wont, and he didn't have quite as much sting in his shots, or as much spring in his footwork, but when he was in real trouble there was nothing wrong with him.

Hunt has the reputation of being the finest volleyer in the country. He showed it was not undeserved when he played Frank Kovacs on Saturday, and he lived up to it again yesterday. Riggs' endeavor was to keep Hunt from the net and to get there first, if he could. There is never any question of where the midshipman is going to camp. The entire strategy of the battle centered around the forecourt.

In the first set service held until Hunt broke through in the tenth game with four beautiful winning shots, two of them in return of service. In the second, service was of no account at all for the first five games. Riggs' remarkable retrieving of Hunt's volleys was the decisive factor.

In the third set Riggs went ahead at 5–3. But here the midshipman, who had appeared to be tiring, hit into a magnificent streak, bringing roars from the crowd with his passing shots, his explosive smashes and his volleys and ran four games in a row. When Hunt went on to lead at 3–1 and advantage point in the fourth, it looked extremely serious for the champion, but here Riggs lifted his game and there was no interrupting his procession until he led 2–0 in the fifth. Hunt evened it at 2–2.

But Riggs stormed the net, taking it away from Hunt and won the final set 6–4.

So it would be Riggs versus McNeill in the final, along with Alice Marble versus Helen Jacobs. Marble had steamrollered Valerie Scott, and Helen Jacobs had defeated Mary Hardwick, who had beaten the two players thought to pose the greatest threat to Marble, Pauline Betz and Sarah Palfrey. Jacobs was expected to cause few problems for Marble.

The night before the finals, there was a formal dance at the club, the famous players mingling with the members and their guests, the couples moving on the dance floor and like shadows on the veranda outside, the band playing songs of that summer and of summers before that.

> *You are the promised kiss of springtime*
> *That makes the lonely winter seem long.*

> *The last time I saw Paris,*
> *Her heart was warm and gay.*

There was "Deep Purple," "When You Wish Upon a Star" from *Pinocchio,* and "Stairway to the Stars." Overhead the Long Island moon inspected the transitory scene. The prevailing opinion that night was that Riggs would almost certainly beat Don McNeill, but McNeill, just graduated from Kenyon, with his wholesome good looks, blonde hair, and Ivy League manner, was the sentimental favorite, most especially of the young ladies—and after all, everyone said, he had beaten Riggs that summer and played him close in every match. Most important of all, McNeill had been playing tremendous tennis all week, apparently getting better with every match he played, his first serve crashing home and his powerful topspin drives gaining in pace and penetration.

That night couples strolled along the now quiet gravel paths between the grass field courts or even sat together in the dark stadium. You could see the grass clearly under the moon, not green now, but a silvery white, and there was music across the grass and laughter in the dark, poignant because of the half-aware but widespread sense that not only was this season ending, but that soon it would be Ensign Joe Hunt and Lieutenant Don McNeill and Sergeant Frank Parker, and that more things than this tennis season were coming to an end.

You will know that you are reading about a different era when you hear that, in the fifth set against Riggs the next day, Don McNeill "threw" a point when he felt that Riggs had received a bad call. All of the players wore white in those days, sometimes white trousers, and did not look like walking billboards for sports equipment. The writers covering the match noted the sportsmanship of the two players, their decency toward each other and their grace during the many crises of the match.

Riggs, short and walking like a duck, with a high wheezing voice, certainly did not look like a great tennis player, but he was. He possessed a mongooselike speed around the court. He did not have the booming serve of Budge or Kramer, but he had a great, precise, and deceptive serve, and he actually holds the service-ace record in the Forest Hills stadium—against Frank Kovacs in a later professional match. He also had a formidable variety of shots off the ground.

In contrast to the odd-looking Riggs, Don McNeill was gorgeous, sandy-haired and lean, a tennis player out of Central Casting. Unlike the tricky Riggs, Don McNeill disdained most subtleties. From the first shot he simply hit the cover off the ball, blasting it off forehand

and backhand, and following his powerful strokes to the net. He was
not a great volleyer, stroking the volley too much, but his volley was
good enough, and it was usually a mere formality after a powerful
approach shot. Overhead he was devastating.

That morning, after the national anthem and the introductions
and the warm-up, Bobby Riggs began fast. He took the first set at
6–4 and ran up a 5–1 margin in the second, when he held two set
points at 40–15. Then McNeill's powerful drives began to take over,
and he tied the match at 5–all, only to lose it 8–6 and find himself
two sets down. The match had "elements of greatness," in the
opinion of Allison Danzig,

> in the spectacular heights to which both men rose under
> nerve-wracking pressure. Also there was a nobility to the
> spirit with which the trim, persevering McNeill came on after
> he had suffered adversity that might have broken the morale
> of a less self-reliant player. . . . By all rights, the Oklahoman
> should have been crushed in spirit when his thrilling rally
> from 1–5 and 15–40 in the second set came to naught. . . .
> Four times McNeill saved set point, pulling out both the
> seventh and eighth games from 15–40, with his top-spin
> backhand bringing thunderous cheers from the stands. When
> the Oklahoman, after going ahead 6–5 with his swinging
> assault, lost the next three games to be two sets down his
> plight seemed hopeless.
>
> But they come no gamer, and his refusal to accept defeat,
> along with Riggs' failure to hold his game together and keep
> on pressure turned the tide. McNeill showed in the final set
> how brilliant a player he could be when in full cry, and some
> of his interceptions and redemptions, after being run ragged
> by lobs, had the Stadium in a frenzy of delight.
>
> With the score at 4–all and deuce in the final set, McNeill
> made a backhand volley across court to Riggs' forehand side-
> line. The linesman serving there instantly signalled the ball
> as out and then hastily gestured with his hands to indicate that
> the shot was fair. Riggs had turned his head to the advantage
> court and did not know of the change in the decision until
> Umpire Benjamin Dwight called "advantage, McNeill."
>
> The defending champion, who rarely questions a decision,
> turned at the call and then walked back toward the linesman,
> asking him why he had changed his ruling. The official
> maintained that the ball was good and Riggs, without further
> quibbling, accepted the costly decision and lost the next point

and the game as McNeill passed him at the net with a beautiful forehand drive.

In the opening rally of the final game Riggs went forward and had a short high ball to deal with. The ball just barely reached the net and the defender gingerly endeavored to keep from touching the tape as he made his volley. But instantly the umpire announced that his foot had touched the net and he had lost the point. At that critical stage it was a bitter pill to swallow but Riggs took it without arguing.

McNeill, however, apparently did not like to win the point that way even though the ruling was correct, and when he knocked Riggs' next service far out of court the Stadium rang with applause. Such was the spirit in which these two rivals, who have fought each other to exhaustion a half dozen times this year, went at each other.

The final set of this two-hour struggle compares with any of recent years in the intensity of drama that unfolded before the 7,500 spectators in the Stadium of the West Side Tennis Club. . . . The spectators were whole-heartedly, almost rankly, partial to the Oklahoman, and they fairly tore the place apart as he fought his way out of the hole in the final set. The shot of all that brought the house down came after Riggs had been reprieved at the first match point against him in the final game. The champion went to advantage point, and in the next rally he tore for the net behind a strong approach that shot to McNeill's backhand. His sharp cross-court volley, cut down with spin, seemed a sure winner, but McNeill, rushing pell-mell, took the ball on his forehand and whipped it back across court for a passing shot that was as close to the impossible as anything in tennis.

That great stroke so unnerved Riggs that he failed on his lift volley behind his next service, and the match ended as McNeill drove a beautiful backhand return of service at Riggs' feet.

All of the newspapers complimented Riggs for being "gracious in defeat and the loss of his championship, and for the enthusiasm with which he congratulated the victor."

Jack Kramer thinks that Riggs had been weakened by the flu and that this, after his tough semifinal against Joe Hunt, contributed to his loss to McNeill. "Unfortunately," writes Kramer in his memoir, *The Game,*

> Bobby came down with a flu during Forest Hills, and he was all-out to beat Joe Hunt in the semis. I lost to Don McNeill in

another tough semi-final. McNeill was a class guy who had won the French in '39, but basically he had one great year, 1940. It all came together for him that year. He was an attacking ground-stroker, with a lifted high backhand that could mix you up. As a matter of fact, McNeill's backhand was not all that different from Borg's two-hander with all the topspin.

But still Riggs was the best; he won the first set in the finals and got an early break in the second. I think if Bobby could have held that lead for the set he could have swept McNeill, but he got broken back and had to play out to 8–6 to win a set he should have won long ago. It wore him out, and weakened by the flu, Bobby lost 7–5 in the fifth.

Maybe. But McNeill had played inspired tennis all year. As Kramer said, he had won the French championship in 1939, but during 1940, his *annus mirabilis,* he had won the National Clay Court Championship, the Intercollegiate Championship, the Newport, Southampton, and Baltimore tournaments, and had been a finalist at Rye. He thus came to Forest Hills with plenty of momentum, and it may well have been those topspinning drives and his astonishing determination that beat Riggs.

According to Jack Kramer, the big loser may have been Don Budge, who had turned professional. The expectation had been that Riggs would win in 1940, turn professional, and tour with Budge. The loss scrambled those plans, and the promoters turned to Big Bill Tilden, still a great player but no match for Budge at the pinnacle of his powers. Kramer is convinced that Budge would have beaten Riggs badly enough to preclude a postwar Budge-Riggs tour. Instead, Kramer thinks, it would have been Budge-Kramer, with Kramer not yet mature enough to handle the great player. But instead it was Budge-Riggs after the war, with Riggs winning and eliminating Budge as the star attraction. Then it became a Riggs-Kramer tour, with Kramer winning and moving to a position of dominance in the professional tennis scene. If Riggs had beaten McNeill in 1940, Kramer believes, Budge might have been professional champion until 1950. "Don could have beaten Gonzales with his head in '49"

In contrast to the situation in the fiercely contested men's tournament, Alice Marble had completely dominated the women, dismissing Helen Jacobs 6–2, 6–3 in the final. Marble's dominance in 1940 equaled or perhaps even surpassed that of Martina Navratilova in recent years, and their games had a lot in common. Marble was tall and powerful and came to net behind a true American twist service for which her opponents had little answer. No one really believed that either Pauline Betz or Sarah Palfrey, early upset victims, would have fared much better against Marble than Jacobs did.

There is a surprising addition to the Alice Marble story, which the former star, now seventy-two has only recently disclosed. During the war she tried to join one of the various women's services but was refused because of the traces of a bout of tuberculosis at age eighteen. At that point President Roosevelt asked her to join his fitness council and play exhibition matches for the armed forces around the world. Because she would visit many military installations, she required an FBI security check.

"You know," the agent who interviewed her said later, "you shouldn't be doing this at all. You should be working for us instead."

"I'm a tennis player, not a detective," she said, laughing. "Why would you say something like that?"

"You know, it's clear you have a photographic memory."

"Oh, that," said Marble. "I've always had that."

She played some 500 exhibition matches during the war and married a U.S. Army pilot named Joe Crowley. She got pregnant and lost the baby as a result of a car accident. Then Crowley was killed over Germany, and she experienced a period of deep depression. One day a man approached her in a restaurant. Army Intelligence. She agreed to meet with him and other agents in a Brooklyn office. The war was ending; Hitler was finished.

"The Nazis are shipping billions of dollars to Switzerland," the intelligence agent told her.

"I don't see what this could possibly have to do with me," said Marble. "I'm not a spy. I'm a tennis player."

"The banker handling the deal," said the agent, "is named Hans Steinmetz."

Hans Steinmetz. Back before the war, Marble had had a wonderful one-month liaison with the handsome Swiss.

"In his basement," the agent told her, "is a safe with the records we need. It is booby-trapped. But we can teach you to get in. We want you to go to Switzerland and pick up where the two of you left off in 1936. We want you to find a way into that house and photograph those records—no matter what you have to do. One more thing. The Russians are also after them."

Marble agreed to try. They showed her how to operate a tiny infrared camera and how to pick locks. She left for Switzerland, where she easily met Steinmetz, now a very prominent banker, and resuming their affair, moved into his chateau outside Geneva. After an evening of moonlight and champagne, she asked him about the future. Money was no problem, he said, and he even had duplicate records in his basement for added security. The next night they were scheduled to go to a party, but Marble begged off, claiming a headache, and insisted that Steinmetz go alone. It took her two hours to open the safe in the basement and ten minutes to photograph the records she found. She finished well after midnight, whereupon she heard a door slam and Steinmetz calling her. She slipped upstairs and hid behind a door. As soon as she heard Steinmetz descending the stairs to the basement, she ran from the chateau, jumped into her car, and headed for the airport.

As she sped down the twisting mountain road, she saw a set of headlights in her rearview mirror, gaining on her. Halfway to the airport, the pursuing car pulled alongside Marble's car and forced it off the road. When she got out, she was amazed to find herself gazing at the Army Intelligence agent who had recruited her. Greatly relieved, she said, "I've got it."

"Thank God," said the agent. "Let me have it."

"Just as soon as we get out of here," she said.

From within the other car came another man's voice. "Get the film. We haven't got all night."

The agent grabbed the film, and just then another car arrived on the scene. Shots echoed through the mountain valleys. Marble did not see the agent fall because she had already been hit herself. The next day she regained consciousness in a Swiss hospital and learned that the Army Intelligence man had been a double agent who was planning to sell the film to the Russians.

"You were magnificent," she was told, "but I'm afraid you risked your life for nothing. Just before he died, he exposed your film."

But that is where her photographic memory came in. She had seen all of the documents she was photographing. She did not know then, and does not know now, what the names and numbers meant, but she was able to repeat them for the Americans. The American Intelligence men told her to forget them, permanently. She still has the scar of the bullet wound.

That summer of 1940, with the war rolling at us, brought to an end the golden era of tennis begun by the great McLoughlin. There were the shrunken, wartime tournaments and then a brief coda after the war, a kind of silver age dominated by Kramer. Then the big money transformed the game. We have had great players in this later phase—Borg, McEnroe, Lendl, and perhaps Becker—as good as the players of 1940. But the whole atmosphere has changed. In 1940 the players were mostly successful athletes from ordinary backgrounds, but on and around the courts of Wimbledon and West Side, they conformed to the graceful restraints of the gentlemen's code. As we have seen, Don McNeill actually threw a point late in the decisive set of the final round match when he felt Bobby Riggs had been wronged by a call. What a difference we see today. Many of the top players glory in the loutish manners of proles. On and around the courts, they do not rise to better behavior, but sink below the norm. They pout and throw tantrums and make obscene gestures. A sense of humor is in short supply. Their tennis costumes are multicolored advertising layouts. Seldom do they seem to be having much fun. The handshake at the end is a mere residual convention. The crowds at the fine new National Tennis Center have to be seen to be believed. They behave like the crowds at a baseball game or a prizefight—noisy, partisan, vulgar, a complete confusion of genres. At the night matches, many of them are drunk, and when they think there has been a bad call, they do not whistle in the former way; they throw half-full paper cups of beer. Norman Brookes, Don McNeill—where are you?

Willkie

When Wendell Willkie met Stalin in the Kremlin, the Germans held much of Stalingrad, and the Soviet position in the Caucasus was crumbling. Molotov told Willkie that things were at a very dangerous crisis, and Stalin looked drawn and tired. Willkie was FDR's goodwill ambassador and had been touring Soviet schools and factories.

The bearlike Willkie was surprised at how small, even delicate, Stalin looked—not the man of steel depicted in Russian propaganda—and he had a pasty, pockmarked, hard-looking face. His gray shirt was military, and he wore black riding boots over a pair of surprisingly pink whipcord trousers.

Stalin, Willkie later recalled, "pushes aside pleasantries and compliments and is impatient with generalities." He wanted an Allied landing in France, 10,000 American trucks per month, wheat, canned food. He denounced Churchill for "stealing" 152 American planes bound for Russia from a convoy in Scotland, and he attacked Roosevelt for subservience to Churchill. "He asked searching questions," according to Willkie, "each of them loaded like a revolver."

Wendell Willkie remarked to Stalin that he had been much impressed by the Soviet schools he had seen, also the libraries. Willkie joked: "If you continue to educate the Russian people, Mr. Stalin, the first thing you know, you'll educate yourself right out of a job." An oceanic roar of Stalin's laughter swept over the large American, who did not think he had said anything funny.

Willkie's best-seller, *One World,* was ghostwritten by an American Communist and laced with sentimental illusions. In 1944, Tom Dewey ended Willkie's presidential aspirations by trouncing him in the Wisconsin primary. Willkie sometimes talked about running in 1948. He termed both 1944 platforms pitifully inadequate. He speculated about heading a liberal third party, more liberal than either major party. When he died suddenly that year at fifty-two, some people said that this was a tragedy because he had become a statesman with a global vision.

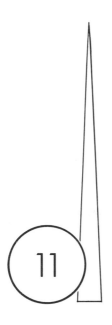

WRITING THE BIG BOOK

11

In 1940, large literary ambitions were in the foreground. The local circulating library was a major fact of life, a product of the Depression. The drugstore at the corner and the cigar store down the street had a couple of large bookcases where you could get *Gone With the Wind, The Grapes of Wrath, You Can't Go Home Again,* and *For Whom the Bell Tolls,* along with *Mrs. Miniver, The Yearling, How Green Was My Valley, Oliver Wiswell,* and John Kennedy's *Why England Slept* for five cents a day. The average price for a best-seller was two dollars, but that was a serious expenditure in 1940.

At the beginning of the year 1940, the big book was John Steinbeck's *Grapes of Wrath,* and 1940 would be a year of big books, of grand ambitions to write the Great American Novel, to make major poetic statements, grand philosophical syntheses, final statements. Along with the best-sellers, we had Edmund Wilson's *To the Finland Station,* about heroic politics; Yeats's *Last Poems,* an astonishing conclusion of an astonishing career; T. S. Eliot's *Idea of a Christian Society;* and George Santayana's *Realm of Spirit,* the fourth volume of his *magnum opus,* an attempt to describe the total human reality. Scott Fitzgerald was writing *The Last Tycoon* in Hollywood. The last tycoon—resonant title. The feeling of final things was in the air.

As the year opened, John Steinbeck was undoubtedly the literary man of the hour. *The Grapes of Wrath* had been the number-one best-seller of 1939. It remained in the top ten during 1940 and was not only popular, but the subject of serious critical acclaim. The movie was named the outstanding picture of the year, beating out Eugene O'Neill's *Long Voyage Home*. Another Steinbeck movie, *Of Mice and Men,* opened in February to enthusiastic reviews and starred Burgess Meredith and Betty Field. "His biographers," wrote Frank Nugent in the *New York Times,* "report that John Steinbeck's pet aversions are Hollywood and New York. Happily the feeling is not reciprocated. Hollywood, which brought his 'Grapes of Wrath' so magnificently to the screen, has been no less reverent toward the strangely dramatic and compassionate tale that Steinbeck called 'Of Mice and Men.' And New York, unless we have miscalculated again, will endorse its film version, at the Roxy, as heartily as it has endorsed the film of the Joads."

Steinbeck adamantly refused to become a public personality. If there had been TV talk shows in 1940, you would not have seen Steinbeck on them. He had grown up in rural Salinas, California, wild and beautiful Monterey county, and had attended Stanford in a desultory way and dropped out. In 1940, he said he hated New York, and his relations with Hollywood were transacted exclusively through his agent. His write-ups stressed the things he did not do.

> John Steinbeck never socked a Parisian gendarme, never
> caught a half-ton tuna and never, never got into a night-club
> brawl. As a matter of fact, he doesn't even go to night clubs.
> But in spite of these literary lapses, he has managed pretty
> well as a writer. "Tortilla Flat," "Of Mice and Men," and
> "The Grapes of Wrath" made him one of the most eagerly
> read and highly rated novelists working in America today.
> Little is known about him—and most of that is conjecture or
> hearsay. There seems to be only one picture of the author
> extant, and that one, accompanying reviews and advertise-
> ments of his books, gives an impression of strength that his
> friends assert is borne out by the man himself. He is
> something more than six feet tall, with the body of an athlete
> rather than that of a man of letters.

The Grapes of Wrath. Its vast popularity and its critical triumph are somewhat difficult to understand today, requiring an effort of the historical imagination to think our way back into the year 1940. It was read as a Depression-protest novel, the saga of the Joad family of dust-bowl Okies who are forced off their land and journey in a dismal caravan to migrant-labor camps in California. Seen in this way, *The Grapes of Wrath* can be read as a period-piece classic of 1930s protest art: how can a fate like this, a fate like the Depression, befall Americans, befall *us?* The novel kindles protest anger, an aesthetic emotion certainly, and demands *action,* explicitly federal—Rooseveltian—action. The federal migrant camps are far superior to the fascistic private ones. But there are strong indications that Steinbeck himself did not see his novel that way. His disgust with his acclaim and with the nature of that acclaim surely reflected his different intention.

The Grapes of Wrath is also a religious novel, a peculiarly American religious novel. It belongs to the tradition of American transcendentalism, which is both a vague and powerful thing in our culture, and its conclusions are not political but religious. Significantly enough, the chief criticism of it at the time was that it had no real conclusion—but it does. That Steinbeck's basic intention was religious should have been apparent from his title and by the name of his Joad family, which is a sort of pun on "Job." Steinbeck was closer to Emerson and Whitman than to the WPA. He *was* protesting the sufferings of the Joads, and he did want political action to ameliorate their lot, but he had more cosmic matters in mind.

Steinbeck seems to have undergone some sort of spiritual transformation during the writing of this book. The origin of the novel was a series of articles Steinbeck wrote for the *San Francisco News* after visiting a number of migrant workers' camps. During 1937 and 1938, he worked on a novel about the migrant workers, which was to be called *L'Affaire Lettuceberg,* and he completed 65,000 words of it. In June 1938, he wrote to his agent and his publisher announcing his decision that the book could not be published. It was written in the bitter and ironic—and *superior*—tones of *In Dubious Battle* and *Of Mice and Men,* and Steinbeck now found it a "bad book," what his father would have called a "smart alec" book. "My whole work and drive," he said, "has been aimed at making people understand each other, and then I deliberately write this book, the aim of which is to cause hatred through partial understanding." He discarded *L'Affaire Lettuceberg* and rewrote the material during the summer of 1938 as *The Grapes of Wrath.*

As applied to this novel, Steinbeck's phrase, "making people understand each other," means much more than merely understanding their motives and emotions. Toward the end of the novel, Tom Joad, who has been purified by suffering and seen the ex-preacher Casy, now a labor organizer, murdered by union busters and has himself killed the murderer, achieves a higher form of consciousness. Tom Joad experiences a transcendent charity.

They sat silent in the coal-black cave of vines. Ma said,
"How'm I gonna know about you? They might kill ya an' I
wouldn' know. They might hurt ya. How'm I gonna know?"

Tom laughed uneasily. "Well, maybe like Casy says, a fella
ain't got a soul of his own, but on'y a piece of a big one—an'
then—"

"Then what, Tom?"

"Then it don' matter. Then I'll be all aroun' in the dark.
I'll be ever'where—wherever you look. Wherever they's a
fight so hungry people can eat, I'll be there. Wherever they's
a cop beatin' up a guy, I'll be there. If Casy knowed, why, I'll
be in the ways guys yell when they're mad an'—I'll be in the
way kids laugh when they're hungry an' they know supper's
ready. An' when our folks eat the stuff they raise an' live in
the houses they build—why, I'll be there. See? God, I'm
talkin' like Casy. Comes of thinkin' about him so much.
Seems like I can see him sometimes."

Steinbeck's intention was to bring the self-contained Joad family
to a Whitman-like sense of brotherhood through suffering. Early in
the novel, Tom Joad, an ex-convict, rebuffs a friendly truck driver:
"Nothin' ain't none of your affair except skinnin' this here bull-bitch
along, and that's the least thing you work at." When ex-preacher
Casy tells him that "they's gonna come a thing that's gonna change
the whole country," Tom Joad treats it as hot air: "I'm still layin' my
dogs down one at a time." Ma Joad is relentlessly centered on her
family, and protecting it is her absolute priority: "All we got is the
family unbroke. Like a bunch of cows when the lobos are ranging,
stick all together. I ain't scared while we're all here, all that's alive,
but I ain't gonna see us bust up." But the Joad family does bust up.
The dog dies on the highway, Grampa dies of a stroke before they get
out of Oklahoma, Granma dies before they reach California farm
country, Rose of Sharon's child is stillborn, and Tom Joad leaves as a
fugitive murderer.

There is something beyond self, however, and beyond the family.
It is understanding, but understanding in a special sense: brotherhood, universal love. Ex-preacher Casy had his post-Christian revelation in a California jail cell. Recalling the inmates of the prison,
he says: "Well, they was nice fellas, ya see. What made 'em bad was
they needed stuff. An' I begin to see, then. It's need that makes all
the trouble."

Of course there is a colossal sentimentality about this view of
reality. Today, anyone riding the New York subway or walking down
an urban street at night would justifiably consider such a view as

The Joad family. Hard times in *The Grapes of Wrath*.

too painful to bear.
it," and Rick Blaine
over it.

Jack Benny in his Maxw

Franklin Roosevelt cheerful at Casablanca. Winston Churchill skeptical.

A tough little English kid, Winston Churchill.

The great tennis player Frank Shields, grandfather of Brooke, is here shown making a movie with an actor whom you might recognize.

The Brown Bomber—you don't want to fight him.

Ernest Hemingway with
Martha Gellhorn at Sun
Valley, where he wrote *For
Whom the Bell Tolls.*

(Kennedy Library)

He may have been the
greatest baseball player of
all time.

Robert Moses decreed. And thus it came to pass.

(King Features)

Mayor Fiorello H. LaGuardia in a tranquil mood.

(Hearst)

The heroic future as seen at the Pan American flying boat terminal at LaGuardia airport.

Zelda adores him.

derisory. The parents of murdered Yale student Bonnie Garland would not buy it, nor would anyone who had absorbed Dostoyevsky, Shakespeare, St. Paul, or Freud. But in 1940 both Steinbeck's readers and his reviewers were ready for the optimism of his message. The men in the California jail "was nice fellas, ya see. What made 'em bad was they needed stuff." Like them, we prisoners of the Depression are nice fellas. The Depression just happened to us. We did not deserve it. And we will surmount it through a sense of human brotherhood, with Tom Joad (and maybe Joe Hill) all around us in the dark. We participate, if we can reach that level of consciousness, in one great soul of which we are individual fragments, the "Manself" Steinbeck speaks of in Chapter 14. Steinbeck was serious about his intense American religious transcendentalism.

In this last connection, it seems important to know that Steinbeck could not write the big novel he planned to do about World War II. He wrote propaganda in support of the war effort. He visited the battle fronts. But he found the actuality of war too disturbing to write about. Tom Joad was not all around in the dark when men were being blown to bits by high-explosive shells.

Rereading *The Grapes of Wrath* a half-century after its appearance is a peculiar experience. On the one hand, there are many passages where you know that Steinbeck is writing as well as any American writer, and you feel the sheer exhilaration of his literary power. Steinbeck's opening chapter, about the drying out of the land, is equal in artistic power to the famous opening chapter of *A Farewell to Arms,* and it is related to and demands comparison with Eliot's *Waste Land:*

> In the water-cut gullies the earth dusted down in dry little
> streams. Gophers and ant lions started small avalanches. And
> as the sharp sun struck day after day, the leaves of the young
> corn became less stiff and erect; they bent in a curve at first,
> and then, as the central ribs of strength grew weak, each leaf
> tilted downward. Then it was June and the sun shone more
> fiercely. The brown lines on the corn leaves widened and
> moved in on the central ribs. The weeds frayed and edged
> back toward their roots. The air was thin and the sky more
> pale; and every day the earth paled.

This is precise writing of mythic power, the death of the earth. And the passage about the tortoise in Chapter 3 is so good that it should be anthologized as prose poetry, the humble and surprising meta-

phor for Steinbeck's optimism. The mean-spirited truck driver
"swerved to hit it," but the sturdy beast lives:

> His front wheel struck the edge of the shell, flipped the turtle
> like a tiddly-wink, spun it like a coin, and rolled it off the
> highway. The truck went back to its course along the right
> side. Lying on its back, the turtle was tight in its shell for a
> long time. But at last its legs waved in the air, reaching for
> something to pull it over. Its front foot caught a piece of
> quartz and little by little the shell pulled over and flopped
> upright.

That tortoise is Depression America, the Joads who will prevail,
Roosevelt who pulled himself to his own feet, the good guys who
will win, and the natural land that will be restored. Within Steinbeck's large optimism, the probability that the truck would have
smashed the tortoise is not admissible.

But Steinbeck can really write, as in his evocation of his native
California:

> The spring is beautiful in California. Valleys in which the
> fruit blossoms are fragrant pink and white waters in a shallow
> sea. Then the first tendrils of the grapes swelling from the
> old gnarled vines cascade down to cover the trunks. The full
> green hills are round and soft as breasts. And on the level
> vegetable lands are the mile-long rows of pale green lettuce
> and the spindly little cauliflowers, the gray-green unearthly
> artichoke plants.

And yet. And yet. The endlessly repeated misfortunes of the Joads
(yes, Jobs) become so relentless that you marvel at the imagination
that could think them up. In the end, the effect is actually comic.
Death, disaster, murder, poverty, floods. Toward the end of the
novel, Rose of Sharon finally gives birth in a railroad boxcar:

> The air was close and fetid with the smell of the birth. Uncle
> John clambered in and held himself upright against the side
> of the car. Mrs. Wainwright left her work and came to Pa.
> She pulled him by the elbow to the side of the car. She picked
> up a lantern and held it over an apple box in the corner. On a
> newspaper lay a blue and shriveled little mummy.

By this point in the Perils of the Joads saga, you recall Oscar Wilde's comment on Dickens's account of the death of Little Nell. You would have to have a heart of stone to read it without laughing.

When *You Can't Go Home Again* appeared that fall, Thomas Wolfe's posthumous novel—he had died of pneumonia at thirty-eight—possessed a powerful psychological appeal. The hero, George Webber, who is transparently Thomas Wolfe, has published a successful novel based on his home town of Libya Hill, Old Catawba (Asheville, North Carolina), and Webber's former neighbors are outraged at this use of them. He literally can't go home again. Wolfe's first novel, *Look Homeward, Angel,* had produced a similar response for him. But the phrase "you can't go home again" had tremendous resonance in the year 1940.

> The phrase had many implications for him. You can't go back
> home to your family, back home to your childhood, back
> home to romantic love, back home to a young man's dreams
> of glory and fame, back home to exile, to escape to Europe
> and some foreign land, back home to lyricism, to singing just
> for singing's sake, back home to aestheticism, to one's
> youthful idea of the "artist" and the all-sufficiency of "art"
> and "beauty" and "love," back home to the ivory tower, back
> home to places in the country, to the cottage in Bermuda,
> away from all the strife and conflict of the world, back home
> to the father you have lost and have been looking for, back
> home to someone who can help you, save you, ease the
> burden for you, back home to the old forms and systems of
> things which once seemed everlasting but which are changing
> all the time—back home to the escapes of Time and Memory.

In 1940 this was powerful stuff. Wolfe's readers knew that there was no going back for America and that there were dark events in the offing. We ourselves were not going home again, but onward into some improbable future.

You Can't Go Home Again begins as George Webber's first novel is about to be published and ends with him visiting Germany in 1936 and becoming aware that something chillingly evil is occurring. The novel contains interesting fictionalized portraits of the great Scribner's editor, Maxwell Perkins (Foxhall Edwards), and Sinclair Lewis (Lloyd McHarg); a vivid evocation of New York society on the eve of the 1929 Crash; an account of Webber-Wolfe's love affair with an older, married Jewish woman named Esther Jack (in real life, Alicia Bernstein); a comic-pathetic account of Webber teaching at the School for Utility Cultures (Wolfe teaching at New York University); and much else. The intention here is on the grand scale, Whitmanesque, "I contain multitudes," as if Wolfe, the 6-foot-6, legendary author, were some sort of whale and had simply opened his mouth and engorged the entire reality of his time.

The novel opens with a fine evocation of the diffuse eroticism of New York:

> As George leaned looking out of his back window a nameless
> happiness welled within him and he shouted over to the
> waitresses in the hospital annex, who were ironing out as
> usual their two pairs of drawers and their flimsy little dresses.
> He heard, as from a great distance, the faint shouts of
> children playing in the streets, and, near at hand, the low
> voices of the people in the houses.

Toward the end of this autobiographical behemoth, Webber visits Germany while the 1936 Olympics are underway, has a love affair with a blonde Valkyrie named Else, sees Hitler rigidly saluting with upraised hand in his open car, and absorbs the pervasive atmosphere of fear, the sense that there are friends whom it may be dangerous to see again, the sense that people just disappear and that it is dangerous to inquire further about them. On the train taking him out of Germany, George Webber sees a rather disagreeable Jewish passenger arrested by the Gestapo—he is smuggling currency out of Germany. His future—and, by implication, ours—is very bleak.

When *You Can't Go Home Again* appeared, its reception varied wildly. One reviewer commented that "the new book is described as 'a novel about a modern who has found himself.' That would seem to be precisely the thing Wolfe was never able to find. According to those who knew him personally, he lived and moved in a state of almost unbroken physical and mental turmoil, bedevilled by ambition, self-pity and an enormous natural gift. Certainly he never found himself in terms of simple English language." On the front page of the September 22 *New York Times Book Review,* J. Donald Adams said the opposite: "This novel, the last work completed by Thomas Wolfe before his death two years ago at the age of 37, makes that event appear even more tragic now than then. . . . The novel which is now published gives me, at least, every reason to believe that had Thomas Wolfe lived he would have been the greatest of all American novelists."

One can indeed say yes, that was certainly the scale of Wolfe's ambition and intention. But, of course, no one today thinks of Wolfe in terms of the potentially greatest of all American novelists. His reputation is virtually nil. He is little read, and his works go unmentioned in literary criticism. A year before Wolfe died, Scott Fitzgerald wrote to him from Hollywood, counseling more attention to form and selectivity, only to receive back from Wolfe a 2,000-word letter telling him to go to hell: "Now you have your way of doing something and I have mine, there are a lot of ways, but you are honestly mistaken in thinking that there is a 'way.' . . . But Flaubert me no Flauberts, Bovary me no Bovarys. Zola me no Zolas."

If *You Can't Go Home Again* had been edited ruthlessly, cut by more than 50 percent, preserving the good things and exorcising the suet, it might still be alive today. There is no doubt that Wolfe himself would have refused such radical editing of his work. He really believed in his "loose and baggy monsters," to use a phrase of Henry James. Wolfe was a virtuoso of unearned significance. Book VII of *You Can't Go Home Again*—Book VII!—consists of a thirty-seven-page—thirty-seven-page!—letter from Webber to his editor in which Webber-Wolfe sets forth his "philosophy of life" and purports to explain why he parted from Maxwell Perkins and Scribner's and went to Harper and Row. J. Donald Adams in the *Times* called it "one of the finest tributes that one human being ever laid at the feet of another." Nonsense. Wolfe left Maxwell Perkins because everyone was saying that Perkins, as the editor of his disorderly and massive manuscripts, was practically the coauthor of Wolfe's novels. Wolfe, telling lies at inordinate length, says that Perkins is too skeptical and conservative for him and his visionary idealism. The proffered "philosophy of life" turns out to be banal and mindless. The Great Enemy—hold your breath—is Greed. Society as we know it must somehow be "completely revised." *Revised!* We are in the stupefying presence of junk.

But just as you are going to fling Wolfe's novel into the fireplace, you also pause in the presence of his mindless but real lyric gift:

> Something has spoken to me in the night, and told me I shall
> die, I know not where, saying: To lose the earth you know, for
> greater knowing; to lose the life you have for greater life; to
> leave the friends you loved, for greater loving; to find a land
> more kind than home, more large than earth—Whereon the
> pillars of this earth are founded, toward which the conscience
> of the world is tending—a wind is rising, and the rivers flow.

Just what all this means is hard to say, but Wolfe did capture a widespread sense that we were rushing toward some dark destiny.

Almost simultaneously with Wolfe's vast novel, there appeared an equally ambitious—indeed, heroic—book that attempted to grasp a vast theme, the essence of history itself. Edmund Wilson's *To the Finland Station* was astringent and intellectual, whereas Wolfe's book was emotional and self-indulgent. It tells the story of Western socialism up to the night of April 16, 1917, when Vladimir Ilyich "Lenin" arrived at the railroad station in Petrograd to take over the Bolshevik faction and oversee the revolution. The grand theme of the book is that man can play a heroic role in discerning and embodying the vast movements of human history. Again, we feel here the powerful presence of the sensibility of 1940, the sense of the possibility of heroic will.

Lenin, "lost himself now in events," seems to have been conscious of himself solely as the agent of historical force. Those who knew him have noted with surprise his complete lack of self-importance. Angelica Balabanova says that she cannot remember when she first met him in exile, but that "externally he seemed the most colorless of all the revolutionary leaders." Nor did the shift from the Zurich library to the dictatorship of the Kremlin release a love of power for its own sake or an impulse to play the great man. Bruce Lockhart, when he saw Lenin after the October revolution, thought "at the first glance" that he

> looked more like a provincial grocer than a leader of men. Yet in those steely eyes there was something that arrested my attention, something in that quizzing, half-contemptuous, half-smiling look which spoke of boundless self-confidence and conscious superiority. . . . The only feature of Lenin's appearance that people do seem to have found striking was his small hazel eyes, which are described as sharp, quick and glittering. These eyes now looked out on Europe through the lens that Marx and Engels had polished, and brought sharply into focus through it the real conflict behind the fumes of battle.

The primal Leninist insight, in Wilson's account, was severely practical. In his pamphlet *What Is to Be Done?*, Lenin had set it forth with stark clarity. The revolution will be carried out under the leadership of the smallest number of people possible, who have devoted their lives to the revolutionary goal. It is easy for the police to attack and demoralize a large organization. But it will be difficult for them to deal with a small and secret staff who will concentrate all the revolutionary planning in their hands, prepare pamphlets, appoint leaders in each town and factory and educational institution. Lenin triumphantly carried through this theory of revolution.

In *To the Finland Station* Edmund Wilson writes about heroic thought and action, but also exhibits his own version of intellectual heroism. The book is brilliantly specific in its details, its sense of time, of place, of personality.* It ranges from Karl Marx's stuffy apartment to the sweeping and intoxicating historical formulations of Hegel. Here is Marx:

> Annenkov has left a vivid description. Marx presented, he says "a type of man all compact of energy, force of character and unshakable conviction—a type who was highly remarkable in his outward appearance as well. With a thick black mane of hair, his hands all covered with hair and his coat buttoned up askew, he gave the impression of a man who had the right and the power to command respect, even though his aspect and behavior might seem to be rather odd. His movements were awkward, but bold and self-assured; his manners violated all the social conventions. But they were proud and slightly contemptuous, and the metallic timbre of his voice was remarkably well adapted to the radical verdicts which he delivered on men and things. He never spoke at all except in judgments that brooked no denial and that were rendered even sharper, and rather disagreeable, by the harsh tone of everything he said."

But Hegel. The sensibility of our time exists at a great remove from that of the young Hegelians early in the nineteenth century who packed his lecture at the University of Berlin. The effect of Hegel's thought was intoxicating, grand in its sweep and authority. Edmund Wilson's book, written during a period of deepening historical crisis, is itself Hegelian in spirit, Hegelian in its will to rise above the chaos of history and glimpse its ultimate order. Here is its intellectual core, put in terms that both echo and cite the great Berlin professor:

> Julius Caesar, says Hegel, for example, did of course fight and conquer his rivals, and destroy the constitution of Rome in order to win his own position of supremacy, but what gave him his importance for the world was the fact that he was performing the necessary feat—only possible through autocratic control—of unifying the Roman Empire.

---

* My own copy of *To the Finland Station,* a first edition, is inscribed in Wilson's hand: "To Anaïs Nin, with the hope of encouraging her to appreciate the concrete, from Edmund Wilson, Sept. 24, 1945."

"It was not then merely his private gain but an unconscious impulse," writes Hegel, "that occasioned the accomplishment of that for which the time was ripe. Such are all great historical men—whose own particular aims involve those large issues which are the will of the World-Spirit. They may be called Heroes, inasmuch as they have derived their purposes and vocation, not from the calm, regular course of things, sanctioned by the existing order; but from a concealed fount—one which has not attained to phenomenal, present existence—from that inner Spirit, still hidden beneath the surface, which, impinging on the outer world as on a shell, bursts it in pieces, because it is another kernel than that which belonged to the shell in question."

To the Finland Station goes back to the beginning of Western socialism and locates that beginning in the eighteenth-century philosopher Vico and his "science" of history.

One day in January of 1824, a young French professor named Jules Michelet, who was teaching philosophy and history, found the name of Giovanni Vico in a translator's note to a book he was reading. The reference to Vico interested him so much that he immediately set out to learn Italian. . . . "I was seized with a frenzy caught from Vico, an incredible intoxication with his great historical principle." And even reading Vico today, we can feel some of Michelet's excitement. It is strange and stirring to find in the *Scienza Nuova* the modern sociological and anthropological mind waking amid the dusts of a provincial school of jurisprudence of the end of the seventeenth century and speaking through the antiquated machinery of a half-scholastic treatise.

Vico had grasped the organic character of human society and viewed history as the product of human forces that could be analyzed scientifically. "Here, before the steady rays of Vico's insight—almost as if we were looking out on the landscape of the Mediterranean itself—we see the fogs that obscure the horizons of the remote reaches of time recede, the cloud shapes of legend lift." Michelet brought Vico's insights and general approach to bear on his own great history of France, culminating in the French Revolution, and it was through Michelet's history that the "scientific" understanding of history entered the European intellectual mainstream.

Wilson's detachment may conceal from the reader, unless attentive, a deep ambiguity about all of this. Suppose there is in fact no "science" of history. Suppose Vico, Michelet, and their many descendants were not only political radicals, but radically *wrong* in their belief that they could discern the "laws" of history and by so doing master the historical process. Edmund Wilson does not write at the highest levels of technical philosophy, but there is a startling case to be made that Marx, who was an extremely able philosopher, willfully did violence to Hegel's metaphysics in the interest of creating a "closed" reality in contrast to Hegel's "open" one. Marx wanted to define God out of reality and make the historical process entirely a matter of man and so-called empirical law. These are deep waters, but as Eric Vogelin analyzes the matter:

> When Marx says that his rational dialectics [of materialism]
> stands Hegelian dialectics on its feet, he does not correctly
> describe what he is doing. Before the actual inversion begins,
> he has done something much more fatal: he has abolished
> Hegel's problem of reality. . . . The Marxian position is not
> anti-Hegelian, it is anti-philosophical; Marx does not put
> Hegel's dialectic on its feet, he refuses to theorize. . . . Did
> Marx know what he was doing? . . . If we return to his early
> work we find that Marx had an excellent understanding of
> Hegel's problem of reality but preferred to ignore it. Marx
> understood Hegel perfectly well. . . . Was Marx being
> intellectually dishonest? As the editor of Marx's early writing
> phrased the matter: "Marx—if we may express ourselves in
> the matter—misunderstood Hegel as-it-were deliberately."
> They do not dare outrightly call Marx an intellectual
> faker. . . . After all, Marx was not a common swindler. . . .
> At the root of the Marxian idea we find the spiritual disease,
> the Gnostic revolt. . . . Marx is demonically closed against
> transcendental reality. . . . Marx knew that he was a god
> creating a world. He did not want to be a creature.

All of this certainly bears on *To the Finland Station*. Wilson wants to believe that his Western socialists, his thinkers and agitators, organizers and leaders, can drive the locomotive of history. Vico, Michelet, Babeuf, Saint-Simon, Fourier, Lassalle, Marx, Engels, Bakunin, Lenin, Trotsky, Stalin. The sweep of the book is heroic, sublime. Two hundred years before Lenin arrived at the Finland Station, Giambattista Vico, writing in a distant corner of Europe, the whole width of the continent away, in asserting that "the social world" was "certainly the work of man," had given birth to the vision, and now in 1917 Lenin stepped forward onto the stage of history, the embodiment of the idea. "The armored car started on, leading a procession from the station. The cars dimmed their lights to bring out the brightness of Lenin's. In this light he could see the workers' guard stretching all along both sides of the road. 'Those,' says Krupskaya, 'who will not have lived through the revolution cannot imagine its grand solemn beauty.'"

But Edmund Wilson is not a true believer. By the time *To the Finland Station* appeared, the great Stalin purge trials had taken place, and Wilson knew very well that they had been rigged, the confessions forced, gross lies promulgated, and tens of thousands murdered. The chill of this awareness is very much present in *To the Finland Station*. "Then the confusions of Marxist morality become more and more obvious in Trotsky as its conceptions are brought into question. . . . Thus such means as lying and killing are morally indifferent in themselves. Both are necessary in time of war, and it depends on which side we want to win whether we approve them or reprobate them." The shadows are deepening. The locomotive of history is careening off the tracks. By the time Wilson's book appeared, Trotsky himself, former commander of the Red Army, had had his skull crushed by an ice ax in Mexico on the orders of Stalin.

Wilson was too intelligent and skeptical not to be aware of the intellectual vulnerability of the whole "scientific" enterprise. His great socialists might stride heroically across the stage of history, History, but "outside the whole immense structure (*Das Kapital*), dark and strong like the old Trier basilica, built by the Romans with brick walls and granite columns, swim the mists and septentrional lights of German metaphysics and mysticism, always ready to leak in through the crevices." Wilson recognizes that the Marxist Dialectic and the Labor Theory of Value are the two central dogmas on which the entire structure rests—and that both are unsound. He sees that the theory of class struggle is based "primarily on psychological assumptions which may or may not be true." Wilson has certainly enjoyed the heroic sweep of the story he tells, but in the end his own eighteenth-century American rationalism cools the whole thing: "it is almost a wonder that Richard Wagner never composed a music-drama on the Dialectic."

Readers of *To the Finland Station* could also read—the two books appeared the same week and were often reviewed together—a remarkable memoir by the British writer Freda Utley. Her story represents a kind of appendix to Wilson's book. The daughter of a wealthy family and herself a socialist, Utley was educated in Switzerland and then attained an M.A. with honors from the London School of Economics. She joined the Labour Party and then the British Communist Party and in 1927 made the pilgrimage to the Soviet Union, where she married Arcadi Berdichevsky, a Russian Jew. Between 1930 and 1936 she held various positions in the Comintern—the Commissariat of Trade, the Commissariat of Light Industry—and in the Communist Academy. Then, though he was a supporter of the Stalin regime, her husband was arrested in 1936 and disappeared into the concentration camp system. The charges were never disclosed, and Utley never saw him again.

In her memoir, Utley paints a grim picture of life in Moscow, even for the privileged elite of the Party. We hear about the ruthless rule of the bureaucracy and the ghastly conditions under which both the industrial workers and the peasantry live. She believes that the system requires the arrest of thousands of people who are guilty of nothing, merely to provide a supply of slave labor. Her special venom, however, is reserved for Western "liberals" who condone everything that happens in the Soviet Union: "had it not been for the chorus of praise which went up from Western 'liberals' Stalin would not have dared to execute thousands and condemn hundreds of thousands—perhaps millions—to the concentration camps without trial." She makes an interesting analysis of the Soviet and the Nazi systems, concluding that they are much alike, though Hitler's is superior within the socialist-totalitarian genre. Icily she says that she reaches this conclusion because she approaches Hitler's Germany "from the East, not from the West."

Edmund Wilson called his book *To the Finland Station,* a poetic and heroic title. With equal appropriateness he could have used Utley's title: *The Dream We Lost.*

In 1940 the three most important American novelists of the time—and the most important as the century draws to a close—were involved with the big book. Hemingway, Fitzgerald, and Faulkner were attempting major statements. When these authors were writing well, no one has written better.

The Hamlet, which appeared that year, may well be Faulkner's best book, though *The Sound and the Fury* and *Light in August* have been the subject of more expert commentary and are probably read in more college courses today. I call *The Hamlet* a "book" rather than a novel because Faulkner is not quite properly called a novelist. He is a bard, a storyteller, all of his immense narrative somehow latent in his mind from the beginning, gestating, coming to birth when he returned to Mississippi after serving in the Royal Air Force. With that fact about Faulkner you begin to understand him. The Royal Air Force, the RAF. Faulkner was a knight of the Old South; his brain was inhabited by it; and his almost limitless narrative is a colossal parable of the disintegration of noble and heroic values.

Faulkner's fiction should really be one big seamless book, his dream of Yoknapatawpha County in northern Mississippi unfolding as he writes, characters appearing and disappearing in the successive books and stories. Faulkner had heard the old stories around Court House Square, over bourbons, from the black cook, in the general store—stories passed on and soaked in legend and corn liquor, stories about the old planter aristocracy, the hill people and the swamp people, the Indians and the peasantry and the black folk. Faulkner had the imaginative power of Dickens. Legend lived. He retold the legends and elaborated on them, infusing them with a new emotional energy and a gift for language that made them larger than life, mythic figures appearing on his pages, figures of good, evil, madness, and heroic endurance. Faulkner's people represent not only the South but also universal experience. "All of his books in the Yoknapatawpha saga," Malcolm Cowley has written, "are part of the same living pattern. It is this pattern, and not the printed volumes in which part of it is recorded, that is Faulkner's real achievement. Its existence helps to explain one feature of his work: that each novel, each long or short story, seems to reveal more than it states explicitly and to have a subject bigger than itself." The great Faulkner subject is the contest between tradition and amoral energy. The great tragedy is that tradition loses, but Faulkner's genius is that he also sees the defeat as comic. In the struggle between the old planters and the old farmers, the old is defeated internally because of codes that prevent them from using the unscrupulous weapons of the upstart Snopeses and the repellent Popeye.

The energies of *The Hamlet* exist at the very center of this saga of a South "unvanquished" in spirit by the Civil War, but rotted from within by some dark failure of nobility or imagination. In *The Hamlet,* the anarchic, poor-white Snopes clan, led by the brilliant and demonic Flem Snopes, bursts through the sides of the rotten Southern barrel and spreads chaos through the land. In *The Hamlet,* Faulkner is certainly at the height of his powers. Who but a great writer could make a love affair between an idiot and a cow, in which the Snopes idiot actually has sexual intercourse with the cow, a lyrical and even moving romance?

> Then he would hear her, coming down the creekside in the
> mist. It would not be after one hour, two hours, three; the
> dawn would be empty, the moment and she would not be,
> then he would hear her and he would lie drenched in the wet
> grass, serene and one and indivisible in joy, listening to her

approach. He would smell her; the whole mist reeked with
her; the same malleate hands of mist which drew along his
prone drenched flanks palped her pearled barrel too and
shaped them both somewhere in immediate time, already
married.

Faulkner's human cow, Eula Varner, is a monster of fecundity, the

incredible length of outrageously curved dangling leg and the
bare section of thigh between dress and stocking top looking
as gigantically and profoundly naked as the dome of an
observatory. . . . He wondered at times in his raging
helplessness how buttocks as constantly subject to the impact
of that much steadily increasing weight could in the mere act
of walking seem actually to shout aloud that rich mind- and
will-sapping softness. . . . [Eula] attended the school from
her eighth year until shortly after Christmas in her fourteenth.
She would undoubtedly have completed that year and very
probably the next one or two, learning nothing, except in
January of that year the school closed. It closed because the
teacher vanished. He disappeared overnight, with no word to
anyone. He neither collected his term's salary nor removed his
meagre and monklike personal effects from the fireless rented
lean-to room in which he had lived for six years.

Eula Varner's fecund sexuality had been too much for him, and he
fled.

The part of Book Four of *The Hamlet* which is also printed
independently as the long story or novella "Spotted Horses" is
certainly one of the finest things Faulkner or anybody else ever
wrote. The demonic Flem Snopes turns up, along with a "Texan"
who must really be from a precinct of Hell, along with a herd of evil,
spotted ponies who are completely uncontrollable and are tied together with barbed wire. Through some sort of mass delusion, the
Yoknapatawphan peasants actually regard these ponies as "bar-
gains" and purchase them with their meager funds. The energies of
Faulkner's narrative prose are overwhelming:

They descended the steps and approached the wagon, at the
tail of which the horses stood in a restive clump, larger than
rabbits and gaudy as parrots, and shackled to one another and
to the wagon itself with sections of barbed wire. Calico-
coated, small-bodied, with delicate legs and pink faces in
which their mismatched eyes rolled wild and subdued, they

huddled, gaudy, motionless and alert, wild as deer, deadly as
rattlesnakes, quiet as doves. The men stood at a respectful
distance, looking at them.

The Texan and Flem are credible devils, Flem with his tiny bow
tie and opaque eyes, the Texan with "his belly fitted neat and as
smooth as a peg into the tight trousers."

> "Them's good, gentle ponies," the stranger said. "Watch
> now." He put the carton back into his pocket and approached
> the horses, his hand extended. The nearest one was standing
> on three legs now. It appeared to be asleep. Its eyelid drooped
> over the cerulean eye; its head was shaped like an ironing
> board. Without even raising the eyelid it flicked its head, the
> yellow teeth cropped. For an instant it and the man appeared
> to be inextricable in one violence. Then they became
> motionless, the stranger's high heels dug into the earth, one
> hand gripping the animal's nostrils, holding the horse's head
> wrenched half around while it breathed in hoarse smothered
> groans. "See?" the stranger said in a panting voice, the veins
> standing white and rigid in his neck and along his jaw. "See?
> All you got to do is handle them a little and work hell out of
> them for a couple of days. Now look out. Give me room back
> there." They gave back a little. The stranger gathered himself
> then sprang away. As he did so, a second horse slashed at his
> back, severing his vest from collar to hem down the back
> exactly as the trick swordsman severs a floating veil with one
> stroke.

One of the great episodes in American fiction must be the one in
which a boy is watching the milling ponies through a knothole,
whereupon the herd explodes, destroys the wooden wall, and leaves
the little boy "unscratched, his eye still leaned to the vanished
knothole." Neither Mrs. Armstid's Christian patience—"He ain't no
more despair than to buy one of them things. And us not but five
dollars away from the poorhouse, he ain't no more despair"—nor
the law itself can contain the demonic energies of Flem Snopes and
the evil ponies. The story or section of the book ends: "'I can't
stand no more,' the old Justice cried. 'I won't. This court's adjourned! Adjourned!'"

That summer and fall everyone was waiting for the big new novel
by Ernest Hemingway. He had been to the Spanish War; his play *The
Fifth Column,* set in war-torn and besieged Madrid, had opened on

Broadway; and he had written the text for a propaganda movie called *The Spanish Earth,* directed by Joris Ivens. The more astute critics awaited the new novel with some wariness. There had been no doubt about the quality of Hemingway's work all through the 1920s, through *A Farewell to Arms* in 1929, but then something strange happened to his art. He published two works of nonfiction, both interesting but rather windy, about bullfighting and about big-game hunting, and he became a public figure with, as Edmund Wilson put it, an "ominous" resemblance to Clark Gable. His closest companions now were not writers, as in the 1920s, but millionaires. He published a volume of good short stories in 1933 and two fine short stories in 1936, one of them, "The Snows of Kilimanjaro," among the best things he ever wrote—but its subject was emotional and artistic bankruptcy, and death. In 1937 he published *To Have and Have Not,* a genuinely bad book.

But when *For Whom the Bell Tolls* appeared in October, Hemingway seemed to have recouped everything—tremendous sales, critical acclaim, all of his old power. "This is the best book Ernest Hemingway has written," proclaimed J. Donald Adams on the front page of the *New York Times Book Review,* "the fullest, the deepest, the truest. It will, I think, be one of the major novels in American literature." Scott Fitzgerald, however, was not so sure. He wrote to Zelda to say that it was not as good as *A Farewell to Arms,* lacking its intensity. He called it Hemingway's *Rebecca,* meaning a good if facile popular novel.

On the surface, and as the book was widely read at the time, the story concerns the adventures of Robert Jordan, who is fighting with loyalist guerrillas in the Guadarrama Mountains. Jordan, an American, is trying to do his part to bring about a Republican victory over the forces of General Franco; he has a love affair, the earth famously moves when he has an orgasm; there are good descriptions of the war scene and of the tensions and demoralization within the guerrilla band; the book ends with Robert Jordan, his leg broken, waiting to be killed by enemy troops.

But below the surface, that is not what the novel really seems to be about. Robert Jordan has actually given up on the Loyalist cause. He has seen the cynicism of the Communists and the general incompetence of the government's armies. Indeed, "progressives" in 1940 were disturbed by this aspect of the novel. The dark undertow of the book involves the death of Jordan's predecessor, Kashkin, whom Jordan has executed in order to prevent his being captured and tortured, the moral disintegration of the guerrilla leader Pablo, previously a great fighter, and Pilar's gypsy forebodings after reading Jordan's palm. In the course of the novel, we are constantly reminded that the enemy is growing stronger and stronger, as is suggested by the increasing presence of planes in the sky and by the slaughter from the air of El Sordo's guerrilla band.

Robert Jordan is really in the Spanish War to die, and the book, like much of Hemingway's fiction, is really about suicide. Jordan's father has committed suicide, and Jordan despises him for the weakness this supposedly showed. But his grandfather had been a guerrilla fighter during the American Civil War. What Jordan does is fuse the two roles. He is a guerrilla fighter like the grandfather, but this is really a cover for his underlying tropism toward death, which is what Pilar sees in his palm. It is notable that at the end Jordan makes no effort to escape with Maria and the others, though it would not have been impossible to splint his broken leg and prop him on a horse.

Hemingway's first story in his major book, *In Our Time* (1925) had been about suicide, with a wounded Indian slicing his own throat with a razor, and suicide is the implicit or explicit subject of some of his most powerful stories. It is the real subject of *For Whom the Bell Tolls,* which was hailed at the time—absurdly, in retrospect—as a progressive, humanitarian epic and evidence of Hemingway's growing political maturity. Its sales, however, were vastly greater than those of any other of his books. It was a Book-of-the-Month Club selection, topped all of the best-seller lists for weeks, and provided the basis for a popular movie starring Gary Cooper and Ingrid Bergman, both of whom became Hemingway cronies.

Scott Fitzgerald had been in Hollywood since the summer of 1937, working as a highly paid but ultimately unsuccessful screenwriter. He had come up from the depths of 1934–36, when he suffered from alcoholism, debt, and despair, and throughout 1940 he was working on a novel about Hollywood in which he intended to make a major statement about America. His last novel, *Tender Is the Night,* had appeared in 1934, and it was filled with Spenglerian gloom about the civilizations of both Europe and America. But in his new novel, he wrote from a quite different perspective. In 1940, with Hitler rampaging in Europe, America looked a lot better to Fitzgerald than it had in the early thirties. He made his hero a Jew, Monroe Stahr, based on the legendary Irving Thalberg. This novel would represent Fitzgerald's great comeback, show that he still could write the big book.

Stahr's first name recalls President James Monroe, author of the Monroe Doctrine, a kind of second American Declaration of Independence. And Stahr, the heroic movie producer, is a star in the Hollywood sense, a major celebrity, but he can also be seen as a star in the American flag, and Fitzgerald wove through the material he completed a set of associations with American presidents, including a visit to Andrew Jackson's Hermitage home. In a note lying between the pages of his unfinished manuscript, he wrote: "I look out on it and I think it is the most beautiful history in the world. It is the history of me and my people. And if I came here yesterday like Sheilah [Graham] I should still think so. It is the history of all aspiration—not just the American dream but the human dream and if I came at the end of it that too is a place in the line of pioneers." Fitzgerald's Monroe Stahr is one of the most impressive Jewish characters in American fiction. Fitzgerald explicitly makes of him an American hero, in implicit defiance of Hitler and the Nazis.

The novel, one of the possible titles of which was *The Last Tycoon,* remains unfinished, none of it in fact in final form. We cannot know whether it would have been the great novel Fitzgerald intended it to be, but his will to greatness was undiminished, and he was writing superbly.

William Butler Yeats died in January 1939 in the south of France, arguably the greatest poet writing in English since Shakespeare, though John Milton and T. S. Eliot have strong claims. Auden wrote the famous elegy: "The day of his death was a dark cold day." The coldness of that January day was more than climatic:

> *In the nightmare of the dark*
> *All the dogs of Europe bark,*
> *And the living nations wait,*
> *Each sequestered in its hate.*

Yeats's volume, *Last Poems,* appeared in May 1940, the product of his seventy-first through seventy-fourth years, acclaimed everywhere as a literary triumph, eloquent, full of a Swiftian, old-man's defiance:

> *Hurrah for revolution and more common shot!*
> *A beggar on horseback lashes a beggar on foot.*
> *Hurrah for revolution and cannon come again!*
> *The beggars have changed places but the lash goes on.*

The old poet was not buying any socialist utopian hopes. And he had had a wild ride.

As a young man, he had been in love to the point of pathology with the beautiful Maude Gonne and had been repeatedly rejected. "Why," he wrote, "should I blame her that she filled my days with

misery?" He tried to marry Maude's daughter, Iseult, and was
turned down. He finally married a woman named George, who, on
their honeymoon, dictated to him while in a trance a complex theory
of history. The great poems poured forth. "I saw a staring virgin
stand / Where holy Dionysius died." Late in life, he had a Steinach
operation in Zurich, which involved the implantation of monkey
sexual glands. Apparently this procedure is a medical fraud, but its
psychological effect was to revive Yeats's sexual powers, and he had
affairs with much younger actresses. His friends referred to him as
the "Gland Old Man." His poetry became more explicitly erotic as
he aged.

And now in 1940 came the great *Last Poems* with their heroic
eloquence:

> *Irish poets learn your trade,*
> *Sing whatever is well-made,*
>   *Scorn the sort now growing up,*
> *All out of shape from toe to top.*

The *Last Poems* ends with his own epitaph as composed by himself:

> *Under bare Ben Bulben's head*
> *In Drumcliff churchyard Yeats is laid*

and then the epitaph:

> *Cast a cold eye*
> *On life, on death.*
>   *Horseman, pass by.*

The aristocratic "horseman" can "pass by" because he knows as his
birthright Yeats's stoic and aristocratic scorn. "All must be cold,"
he had written about tragic art. "The supernatural is present, cold
winds blow across our hands, upon our faces, the thermometer falls,
and because of that we are hated by journalists and groundlings."
With *Last Poems,* the cold curtain falls in Drumcliff churchyard.

But wait. There is a joker in the deck. During the last few weeks
of his life, the poet worked out a list that showed the order of the
poems he desired for the volume. The volume did not end with the
cold horseman epitaph. After Yeats's death, his wife and his publisher organized the volume differently, altering its total meaning.
In 1985 a new edition appeared, reflecting Yeats's own scheme, and
it does not end with the cold epitaph but with the poignant old man's
poem "Politics." Thomas Mann had written solemnly that "in our

time the destiny of man presents its meaning in political terms."
Yeats's final poem rejected this:

> *How can I, that girl standing there,*
> *My attention fix*
> *On Roman or on Russian*
> *Or on Spanish politics?*
> *Yet here's a travelled man that knows*
> *What he talks about,*
> *And there's a politician*
> *That has read and thought,*
> *And maybe what they say is true*
> *Of war and war's alarms,*
> *But O that I were young again*
> *And held her in my arms!*

Placing this poem last in the volume makes an important difference
from Yeats's wife's arrangement—less stern, less stoic, more human
and poignant. It is an attractive modification, but perhaps Mrs.
Yeats was not enthusiastic about the emotions expressed.

Final statements were in the air in 1940, as if in an effort to get it
all down, complete the major work, before the coming deluge. That
fall the great American philosopher George Santayana published the
fourth and concluding volume of his *magnum opus, The Realms of
Being,* called *The Realm of the Spirit.* Though written for the ages,
the great project could also be seen as an act of civilizational
recovery, a sustained effort to recover and preserve a full account of
human nature, at a time when the lights of civilization were being
extinguished in Europe and Asia. It was as if the entire Western
tradition in philosophy was speaking through the former Harvard
professor. "To find anything in literature or philosophy resembling
it," wrote Columbia's Irwin Edman in a review, "one would have to
go a long way back and one would have to reach high; as far back as
St. Bonaventura's *Itinerary to the Mind of God,* and to no less an
elevation. The analysis is subtle and the book is important as a
completion of one of the most arresting and singular systems of
philosophy in our time, though Mr. Santayana is one of the most
orthodoxly human." Santayana, indeed, compared the scale of his
enterprise with Dante:

> It is fundamentally the same subject as that of Dante's *Divine
> Comedy,* treated in critical prose instead of in a magnificent
> biographical and cosmic myth, into which all the fervor and

venom of an unhappy life could be infused with the
tenderness of a pure poet. But if we ask what the vision of
Dante conveys in the end by way of a lesson, I think we may
say it is this: The morphology of spirit, illustrated by great
examples, showing what spirit suffers and what it gains by
existing.

A philosophical atheist, though Catholic in sensibility, Santayana
means by the term "spirit" the human awareness, intellectual light,
but the divine may slip into his system through a certain imprecision
in his use of the term spirit. Sometimes he writes not of spirit but of
the spirit, and in terms that suggest something coherent and even
everlasting. As T. S. Eliot wrote, "There is only the fight to recover
what has been lost / And found and lost again and again; and now
under conditions that seem unpropitious."

That year, T. S. Eliot, along with Yeats one of the great poets
writing in English, tried to look beyond the war and discern what
might be the desirable situation of society in the future. *The Idea of a
Christian Society* appeared in January, and in it Eliot hoped for a
rather hierarchical society grounded in Christian belief. Eliot got
Clement Atlee and the Labour Party instead, but the book did
foreshadow an important Christian revival after the war in which
Eliot himself, C. S. Lewis, and Charles Williams were central
figures.

Richard Wright's *Native Son* appeared that March, widely acclaimed, Book-of-the-Month, Guggenheim Fellowship, "the best
novel yet by a Negro." In the realist tradition, Wright tells the story
of a black named Bigger Thomas, who commits two brutal murders
and ends in the electric chair. Bigger Thomas is meant to represent
black victimization in America. Its real interest, however, lies in
Wright's ability to go beyond the more obvious and familiar social
protest themes and find dark Dostoyevskian depths as he tells his
own story of crime and punishment.

There were many other good books, some of which have lasted in
a minor but authentic way and are more than just period pieces. In
How Green Was My Valley, Richard Llewellyn brought his readers to
a Welsh mining village, still green and serene fifty years ago. A long
street of stone houses climbed steeply up from the collieries, and at
noon on Saturday the women would sit on chairs outside the houses
and wait as their husbands and sons came up the hill from the mines.
The men would toss their week's wages into the white skirts of the
women, bathe, and enjoy a big Saturday dinner. Llewellyn created

the charm of that vanished world in a lyrical narrative that was especially welcome to readers in a darkening present.

Robert Nathan published *A Portrait of Jennie,* about an artist who meets a shy and wistful girl in a misty Central Park twilight. The movie version made Jennifer Jones into a Hollywood star. Jan Struther's *Mrs. Miniver* persuaded readers that the steady British virtues were still intact and might well prevail over fanaticism and madness. *The Beloved Returns* was minor Thomas Mann, but a welcome and moving story of Goethe's reunion in Weimar with his great love, Lotte, whom the poet has not seen for forty-four years. Again, civilized relief from the present was part of the book's appeal.

That summer John F. Kennedy published *Why England Slept,* an analysis of the mistakes that had led to catastrophe, with a foreword by Henry Luce hinting at a future for Kennedy which Luce would play a considerable role in bringing to pass: "In recent months there has been a certain amount of alarm concerning the 'attitude' of the younger generation. If John Kennedy is characteristic of the younger generation—and I believe he is—many of us would be happy to have the destinies of this Republic handed over to his generation at once." *Why England Slept,* along with the later *Profiles in Courage,* helped to create the useful myth that Kennedy was an intellectual and even something of a historian.

In *After Many a Summer Dies the Swan*—beautiful title—Aldous Huxley brilliantly satirized the pretensions and follies of Hollywood. In *Father and Son,* James T. Farrell pursued his endless investigation of Chicago working-class life, now with Danny and Jim, the father going down while the son is coming up. John O'Hara's *Pal Joey* is a down-at-heels nightclub singer who is as complete a stinker as we have seen in fiction. The Broadway version was a big hit. Clare Boothe returned from Europe and published a moving account of the spring before the war, as Europe slid toward chaos, *Europe in the Spring.* At the age of twenty-two, Carson McCullers, a Southern writer, in *The Heart Is a Lonely Hunter* created a remarkable world of grotesques—two deaf-mutes, a ranting drunkard, a Negro lost in his fantasies of equality, fat people, a sensitive young girl—and explored the emotions of this improbable collection with startling skill. Many reviewers and critics believed that a major new talent had appeared on the scene.

As the year drew to an end, Edna St. Vincent Millay, whose best work lay behind her in the 1920s, published a frankly progagandistic book of poetry called *Make Bright the Arrows.* Characteristic is such a poem as "The Old Men of Vichy":

Only the young, who had so much to give,
Gave France their all: the old whose valorous past
(In anecdote not only: in bronze cast)
Might teach a frightened courage how to live.
Wheedled by knaves, from action fugitive,
Sold their sons' hopes to make their porridge last.

Millay's heart was in the right place, but this is rant nevertheless. Alcohol, drugs, and mental instability had probably done their work, though Millay herself at least knew that the 1940 poetry was bad. "I have one thing to give in the service of my country," she wrote to a Vassar friend, "my reputation as a poet. How many more books of propaganda poetry containing as much bad verse as this one does, that reputation can withstand without falling under the weight of it and without becoming irretrievably lost, I do not know—probably not more than one. But I have enlisted for the duration."

But bad poetry can hardly be good propaganda, and one turns gladly from these poems to *A Few Figs From Thistles,* her sonnets, and her other early work to the Millay evoked in an essay by one of her multitude of lovers, Edmund Wilson:

> At the time I was writing this memoir [of Millay], I happened one day, in the country, at Wellfleet on Cape Cod, where I live, to meet my neighbor from Truro, Phyllis Duganne. We talked about Edna Millay, and she told me of a memory she had of seeing her years ago in Greenwich Village running around the corner of Macdougal Street, flushed and laughing "like a nymph," with her hair swinging. Floyd Dell, also laughing, pursued her. Phyllis said she had always remembered it; and I leave this image here at the end to supplement my firsthand impressions—a glimpse of Edna as the fleeing and challenging Daphne of her *Figs From Thistles* poems—from the time I did not know her, when she had first come from Vassar to the Village.

Gehrig

On May 2, 1939, the Yankees were in Detroit when their first baseman, Lou Gehrig, asked manager Joe McCarthy to take him out of the lineup. The Iron Horse had played in 2,130 consecutive games, but he knew that something was seriously wrong. After he handed the lineup card to the umpire. Gehrig went over to the water cooler in the dugout and began to weep. Pitcher Johnny Murphy threw a towel at him to break the mood, but Gehrig just stood there with the towel over his head, weeping. Later, after the game, Gehrig explained that he had had only four hits in his last twenty-five turns at bat. "I haven't been a bit of good to this team since the season started." His reflexes were gone, and so was his coordination.

By November 1940 Gehrig was confined to his chair and unable to walk when columnist John Kieran visited him to talk about football. "It is often forgotten," wrote Kieran,

> that Lou Gehrig was quite a football player before he rose to fame on the diamond as the slugging first baseman of the Yankees and the Iron Horse of the National Pastime. Yes sir, Lou has faded clippings with large headlines to prove that he could carry the ball in his Columbia days. . . . He keeps up with the scoring across the country, but he reserves his loudest rooting for the Columbia Lions and Prof. Lou Little [the Columbia coach].

Kieran found that "except for his underpinning," Gehrig was "as strong and cheerful as ever." He "couldn't get out and run the bases as he did of yore, but as he sits in his chair at home and 'pops off' about football or baseball he gives the same impression of tremendous power and physical energy that he did all his Yankee years."

The two men reminisced about the day he pitched for Columbia against Williams College and lost the game 5–1, even though he struck out seventeen Williams batters. "I think I must have walked every batter I didn't strike out. I could heave the ball in there pretty fast, but I never knew where it was going."

They talked about how he came to play for the Yankees, discovered by Paul Krichell, the Yankee scout who traveled the college circuit. "Paul followed me around," said Gehrig, "and he couldn't make up his mind. He wasn't sure that I could hit a curve. So Ed Barrow sent for Bob Connery to look me over and check with Krichell. Bob saw me in a game against N.Y.U. and they had a good curve-ball pitcher named Carlson. Well, I had a good day against his curve ball. You know how it is. Somedays they seem to be throwing them where you are swinging. Other days. . . ."

"Just think of that big fraud," wrote Kieran, "sitting there and apologizing for having a good day at bat, as if it had been something of an accident, a strange occurrence in his career. If it was, he should spend the remainder of his life offering apologies to the

American League pitchers of the last seventeen years—and the National League pitchers he clubbed in World Series, too."

"Well, anyway," said Gehrig, "I had a good day against Carlson and Connery gave me the okay. And that's how the Yankees came to sign me up."

A little later, Kieran "shoved off and left Buster Lou looking over his big scrapbook of clippings." Less than two years after taking himself out of the Yankee lineup, Lou Gehrig was dead at thirty-eight.

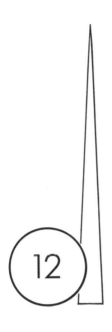

THE JITTERS OF 1940

12

From the beginning of that year, life went on mostly in the old ways. "1940 Born in Wild Revelry," read the headline in the *New York Times,* date January 1. "Good Year for Nation Seen." A crowd estimated at 1,250,000 packed Times Square in 22-degree temperature. The high spirits and good humor of the crowd reminded reporters of the great pre-Depression ticker-tape parades for Pershing and Lindbergh, and, indeed, all the economic indices were pointing up. The horn-honking, bell-ringing throng watched the 300-pound illuminated ball atop the flagpole on the Times building slide slowly down the pole as the final seconds of 1939 elapsed. An electrician, Thomas Ward, studied his watch as the ball descended. At midnight, he threw a switch that turned out the ball's 260 bulbs and another that lit the numbers 1-9-4-0 on the electric signs on each side of the Times Tower. People kissed, shook hands, blew horns, and jitterbugging couples were "getting in the groove" all over Times Square, as well as in the Rainbow Room, the Stork Club, the Roosevelt Grill, and the Grillroom at the Hotel Pennsylvania, where a band called the "Royal Pennsylvanians" helped revelers to welcome the New Year.

The news seemed to be good in the early months of 1940. Virtually every day the newspapers carried stories of amazing Finnish

265

victories over the Soviet hordes, as the white-garbed Finnish ski troops swept silently through arctic forests, and the Russians froze into grotesque postures as they died. About it all, however, there were suggestions of whistling in the dark. In the popular newspapers and magazines, there appeared no serious analyses of the real Finnish military prospects or estimates of the time frame within which the Finns were necessarily operating, determined by the sheer weight of material forces. The Soviet army attacked relentlessly, and stories reported that the rear company of attacking troops were machine-gunned routinely by the officers in charge to indicate to those ahead what awaited them if they faltered.

In February, New York's leading society women held an "Arctic Circle Dinner Dance" at the Coq Rouge for the purpose of aiding the Finns. National sentiment, indeed, was virtually unanimous in support of the Finns. Polls showed upwards of 80 percent support for them, and less than 10 percent for the Russians. At the Arctic Circle Dance, the orchestra platform stood within a simulated log hut, complete with dripping artificial icicles. Skis and snowshoes adorned the walls against a background of cardboard penguins. Mrs. Martin Aigner III was head of the advisory committee. Perhaps the committee thought the Finns had flown in the penguins from the South Pole for some mysterious military reason.

Reported to be looking "marvelously fit after his sojourn in Florida," William T. Tilden had been in New York no more than a few hours before he took command of arrangements for the tennis matches to be held on a Sunday night at Rip's Indoor Courts in the Seventy-first Regiment Armory. The proceeds would go to the Finnish Relief Fund, headed by former President Herbert Hoover. The forty-seven-year-old Tilden was considered by the press to be "the marvel of the athletic world," and everyone said that he was still the best player in the world "for one set." Tilden would play the 1938 champion and the first Grand Slam winner, Don Budge, in the feature match.

The past remained firmly and reassuringly with us. Hoover, who had headed European famine relief two decades earlier, had now come to the rescue again and was in charge of Finnish Relief. He even considered himself to be running for president in 1940, going home again, yes, in one of the great second acts in American life. Tilden, a dominant 1920s personality, who had won his last national championship in 1929 but was trim and aquiline as ever, brought that golden era with him into the present. He would play Don Budge. If Tilden at his peak had not been the greatest player ever to hold a tennis racket, then Budge, at his peak right now, certainly was. The music would always play, the dancers would always dance, and Tilden did his part to make time stand still.

While Budge and Tilden were warming up on the armory court, former president Hoover and his party entered and took their seats in his box. Hoover received a five-minute standing ovation from the tennis crowd, an ovation for his Finnish work, but also a defiant and even angry anti–New Deal ovation from these middle-class and upper-class tennis fans. The Finnish national anthem was followed by "The Star Spangled Banner," and then the great Tilden faced the tall, red-headed Californian.

"Tilden's backhand," wrote Allison Danzig,

> was not quite the marauding weapon of old as he struggled to
> underslice it, but it could be strikingly effective. His forehand
> was nailing the ball to the lines and he was working up
> openings for the volley with a skill and craft that would not
> be denied. But as remarkable as was Tilden's performance, it
> was not good enough to break down an opponent who was
> serving cannonball aces that almost tore the racquet from the
> veteran's hand, and when Budge laid into his backhand there
> was nothing like it in sheer rapacity. The red-haired
> champion never had cause for concern. It was simply a matter
> of time until the punishing pressure of his pace and length
> would undermine Tilden's strength and control, and until that
> time his murderous service was enough to keep Tilden at bay.
> After Tilden had reached five-all, the play turned into a
> procession. But in the final game the Philadelphia veteran
> electrified the crowd as he saved four match points with
> strokes as brilliant as any he had produced in the match.

Budge, who had a right arm as big as your thigh, used specially designed extra-heavy rackets—on the order of Babe Ruth's special bats. Even these he made still heavier with lead strips affixed to he head. He probably hit harder shots, on the average, than anyone who has ever played. Yet Tilden, from the 1920s, could live on the court with him. Things were still intact.

That year Vivien Leigh won the Oscar for her Scarlett O'Hara in *Gone With the Wind,* and Robert Donat won it for his role in *Good-bye, Mr. Chips.* The "ladylike" theme was stressed in the new gowns on display at Saks Fifth Avenue, and the S.S. *Queen Elizabeth,* defying the submarines, sailed from Clydeside to New York on her maiden voyage. Everything was all right, as winter showed signs of giving way to early spring. The Finns would surely hold. The French and British would hold. The French had the largest and best army in the world, and the British had the Royal Navy. These powerful civilized dikes stood between America and the bizarre things that had been going on, and were going on, in Central Europe.

But everything was not all right, and beneath the familiar and reassuring surfaces of life, this dark awareness was general, part of the national nervous system. In the global village, a saber-toothed tiger had escaped from the zoo. There was a polar bear in the flower garden. By 1940, it was not Hitler's territorial ambitions that worried people. Nations always had territorial ambitions. The Kaiser had been hated, but his regime had not come close to awakening the amazement and fear that Hitler's did. It was the nature of Nazi politics, the mentality behind it, that was profoundly disturbing, widely grasped if not known in every detail, frightening to think about.

Take, for example, the way in which Hitler handled the problem of his longtime follower Ernst Röhm, a war veteran and SA "Brownshirt" chief of staff who had been with Hitler in the failed Munich coup of 1922. In January 1933, Röhm's Brownshirt street fighters, who had played such an important role in Hitler's rise to power, numbered some 400,000. By the spring of 1934, he had built this force up to some 4 million. They were fanatically loyal to both Röhm and Hitler, but Hitler regarded this auxiliary army with understandable concern. It earlier had been his own private army, but now he commanded the Reichswehr, the real army. If it could be done, he wanted both.

The insoluble problem was that he and Ernst Röhm had different conceptions of the Nazi revolution. Each understood the term "national socialist" in a different way, Röhm stressing "socialist" and Hitler "national." Röhm was a genuine left socialist and, along with much of the SA, viewed the Nazi revolution as profoundly egalitarian, a sweeping away not only of Jews and profiteers, but of the old classes generally—the wealthy businessmen, the hierarchical army, the great industrialists. That was not what Hitler had in mind. He did not want some sort of proletarian republic. His vision was of a mystical, hierarchical Reich, all components working in harmony, with himself as mystical, even quasi-papal, leader. He did not intend to destroy either the industrialists or the Reichswehr. He needed them to realize his conception of a Greater Reich that would embrace all of Central Europe and the Ukraine.

Ernst Röhm was fanatical enough to challenge Hitler directly. On April 18, 1934, he published the following manifesto: "The Revolution we have made is not a national revolution, but a National *Socialist* Revolution. We would even underline this last word 'Socialist.' The only rampart which exists against reaction is represented by our Assault Groups, for they are the absolute incarnation of the revolutionary idea. The militant in the Brown Shirt from the first day pledged himself to the path of revolution, and he will not deviate by a hairbreadth until our ultimate goal has been achieved." Röhm omitted the customary "Heil Hitler" with which important statements ended. And of course this was flat, open, doctrinal heresy. The Brownshirts were not the "incarnation" of the Nazi revolution. Hitler considered that he himself was precisely that.

At the beginning of June 1934, Hitler met with Röhm for five hours and attempted to return him to political and doctrinal orthodoxy. Röhm was unshakable, the Trotsky of the Nazi movement. He had in effect signed his own death warrant, as Hitler made his own position unmistakably clear. "I am resolved," Hitler told the leader of the Brownshirts, "to repress severely any attempt to overturn the existing order. I will oppose with the sternest energy a second revolutionary wave, for it would bring with it inevitable chaos. Whoever raises his head against the established authority of the State will be severely treated, whatever his position." From Hitler's standpoint, Röhm's movement threatened his rearmament program and the rebuilding of the Reichswehr, both vital to his projected Greater Germany. "The Fuhrer," wrote Winston Churchill, "had to choose between the generals who hated him and the Brownshirt thugs to whom he owed so much. He chose the generals."

When he had decided to put an end to the whole business, Hitler moved with ruthless efficiency. On June 15 he ordered the Reichswehr confined to its barracks and ammunition issued to his own private army, the Blackshirt SS, commanded by Heinrich Himmler. Röhm had called a meeting of all the senior Brownshirts at the town of Bad Wiessee in the Bavarian lake region. Röhm was ill and had gone there for his health. Hitler flew to Munich, sitting silently in the copilot's seat of his plane, resolved to annihilate the plotters. The plane landed in Munich before dawn on June 30. Accompanied by Goebbels and a dozen personal bodyguards, Hitler drove to the Brown House and placed the leaders of the local Brownshirts under arrest. Then he and his bodyguard drove to Bad Wiessee, the procession of automobiles arriving at Röhm's chalet at 7:00 A.M. They arrested the surprised Röhm, returned with him to Munich, and placed him in the same jail cell he and Hitler had shared in 1922.

That afternoon the slaughter of Röhm's followers and suspected followers began throughout Germany. Röhm himself was given a revolver, but he refused to do the decent thing, and after a while the door of his cell was opened, and he was riddled with bullets. In Munich the firing squads of eight had to be relieved from time to time because of the frayed nerves of the executioners. All afternoon the volleys were heard every ten minutes.

Ex-Chancellor Kurt von Schleicher had been imprudent enough to pass the word to the French ambassador in Berlin that Hitler would soon be overthrown. He and his wife, who threw herself in front of him, were both shot in their house. Gregor Strasser, the Nazi ideologue, was arrested and shot. Franz von Papen's private secretary and some of his staff were shot, but Papen himself for some reason was spared. During a span of twenty-four hours, an estimated 7,000 people were shot. On the afternoon of the next day, Hitler decided to call a halt to the slaughter, which was spreading beyond Röhm's Brownshirt followers. To show that he had a sense of limits, Hitler even condemned to death a number of SS Blackshirts who had gone too far in slaughtering their prisoners. The firing squads fell silent during the early hours of July 1.

The news of this bloodbath of course reached the outside world. These events were not taking place in some remote jungle or on the steppes of Asia, but in the heart of civilized Europe. "This massacre," writes Winston Churchill, "however explicable by the hideous forces at work, showed that the new Master of Germany would stop at nothing, and that conditions in Germany bore no resemblance to those of a civilized state. A dictatorship based on terror and reeking with blood confronted the world. . . . I was deeply affected by this episode, and the whole process of German rearmament, of which there was now overwhelming evidence, seemed to me invested with a ruthless, lurid tinge. It glittered and glared."

The Nazis glittered and glared next at Austria. There was a strong Nazi movement in that country and during the summer of 1934 a lot of traffic back and forth between Bavaria and Austria. Toward the end of July, a Nazi courier fell into the hands of the Austrian border guards and was found to be carrying coded material and the complete plans of a Nazi coup against the conservative Dollfuss government. Dollfuss was slow to react, even as the signs of revolt came into the open on July 25. As street fighting broke out in Vienna, a contingent of Nazis forced its way into the chancellery and hit Dollfuss with two revolver bullets. As Dollfuss bled to death in the chancellery, the local Nazis seized the radio station and announced the resignation of the Dollfuss government and the formation of a new government under the Austrian Nazi Anton von Rintelen.

Like Hitler's Munich coup of 1923, however, this shoot-out failed. The army and the police rallied to the support of the decapitated Dollfuss government; President Miklas called for the restoration of order; and Dr. Schuschnigg assumed administrative leadership. The coup had failed, but once again, Americans saw that the Nazi style in politics had much in common with gang warfare in Cicero, Illinois.

Austria would have to wait, but Hitler also introduced a new style of major-power diplomacy. At 10:00 A.M. on the morning of March 7, 1936, German Foreign Minister Konstantin von Neurath summoned the British, French, Belgian, and Italian ambassadors to the Wilhelmstrasse and proposed to them a twenty-five-year agreement. Both sides of the Rhine would be demilitarized; there would be an agreed-upon limitation of all armaments and nonaggression pacts negotiated throughout Eastern Europe. Two hours later, Hitler addressed the Reichstag, announcing that he was reoccupying and militarizing the Rhineland, and even as he spoke, German armed columns were pouring across the boundaries. It was a bold, intuitively based gamble, since German rearmament had not given his armed forces anything like the power to resist the French if they decided to contest the lunge. The Reichswehr units would have been annihilated and Hitler humiliated, perhaps driven from power. But no one wanted war, and the British and French swallowed Hitler's annexation.

Though Germany had twice the population of France, the prudent professionals on the General Staff warned the Führer that the Reichswehr could not be expected to match the French army before 1943 and that it might take fifteen years to build up the German navy to its former strength on the high seas. But Hitler had the vision to see the military and political possibilities of a revolutionary new weapon: air power. He saw that a formidable air arm could be created much more quickly than conventional divisions and battleships, and indeed, the infrastructure for German air power had long been in place. Germany was full of glider and sports-planes enthusiasts, and the factories were prepared to pour out fighter aircraft. Air power was an appropriate strategic tactic for a revolutionary and still relatively have-not state. It was hard to monitor or measure, and it was relatively cheap. The Nazis pushed energetically ahead to develop in the Luftwaffe the best air force in the world, and it would be a principal component of the *blitzkrieg*. Politically, air power was extremely useful for a regime based upon terror. The psychological threat of air attacks on London and Paris would strengthen the desire for peace at just about any price.

Two years passed between Hitler's seizure of the Rhineland in March 1936 and the liquidation of Austrian independence in March 1938. The same smash-and-grab style of politics was on view again. The Austrians had modest frontier defenses—nothing like the heavy Czech fortifications—and Hitler ridiculed them while bullying the

Austrian chancellor, Dr. Schuschnigg, into taking into his cabinet the leaders of the newly legalized Nazi Party. Hitler summoned Schuschnigg to Berchtesgaden along with Guido Schmidt, the Austrian foreign minister. Dr. Schuschnigg made a record of the following dialogue:

Hitler: *I only need to give an order, and overnight all the ridiculous scarecrows on the frontier will vanish. You don't really believe that you could hold me up for half an hour? Who knows— perhaps I shall be suddenly overnight in Vienna: like a spring storm. Then you will really experience something. I would willingly spare the Austrians this; it will cost many victims. After the troops will follow the SA and the Legion! No one will be able to hinder their vengeance, not even myself. Do you want to turn Austria into another Spain? All this I would like if possible to avoid.*

Schuschnigg: *I will obtain the necessary information and put a stop to the building of any defense works on the German frontier. Naturally I realize that you can march into Austria, but, Mr. Chancellor, whether we wish it or not, that would lead to the shedding of blood. We are not alone in the world. That probably means war.*

Hitler: *That is very easy to say at this moment as we sit here in club armchairs, but behind it all there lies a sum of suffering and blood. Will you take the responsibility for that, Herr Schuschnigg? Don't believe that anyone in the world will hinder me in my decisions! Italy? I am quite clear with Mussolini: with Italy I am on the closest possible terms. England? England will not lift a finger for Austria. . . . And France? Well, two years ago when we marched into the Rhineland with a handful of battalions—at that moment I risked a great deal. If France had marched then we should have been forced to withdraw. . . . But for France it is now too late!*

This cordial conversation took place at eleven in the morning. After a formal lunch, the Austrian statesmen were summoned into a small adjoining room, where Joachim von Ribbentrop and Franz von Papen handed them a written ultimatum. The Nazi Seyss-Inquart was to be appointed to the Austrian cabinet as minister of security, in charge of the police. There was to be a general amnesty for all Austrian Nazis in detention. The Austrian Nazi party would become part of a new government, the Fatherland Front. After this ultimatum had been delivered, Hitler received the Austrians. "I repeat to you, this is the very last chance. Within three days, I expect the execution of this agreement." Hitler meanwhile ordered the implementation of "Operation Otto," the invasion of Austria. In doubt, however, was the attitude of Italy, whose geopolitical interest had indicated an independent Austria. The Austrians, the British, and the French had hoped for support from Mussolini, but the Duce had been outraged by the sanctions imposed by the British and French over his seizure of Ethiopia. Mussolini crossed his Rubicon, moving from courted player in balance-of-power politics to partner of Hitler.

The terrorist pressure on Austria mounted. Hermann Göring dictated a message over the telephone to the Austrian Nazi Seyss-Inquart. He scribbled it on a note pad and delivered it to Schuschnigg: "The situation can only be saved if the Chancellor resigns immediately and if within two hours Dr. Seyss-Inquart is nominated Chancellor. If nothing is done within this period the German invasion of Austria will follow." Abandoned by Italy, offered nothing by England and France, the Austrians crumbled, and Hitler anticipated a triumphal return to his native land. To his fury and astonishment, it fizzled. The new German equipment broke down. For the night of March 12, the Nazi party in Vienna had planned a torchlight parade to welcome the Führer, but he did not arrive. The German columns had broken down near his home town of Linz. Defects had appeared in the motorized artillery. Tanks were backed up for miles. Hitler was caught in a military traffic jam. Enraged, he ordered that the light tanks, which worked, be extricated from the mess and mobilized for his entry into Vienna the next morning. Appearances were saved; the crowds in the streets waved Nazi flags; and Hitler declared the end of the Austrian Republic and the incorporation of Austria into the German Reich.

Neville Chamberlain succeeded the ailing and bewildered prime minister, Stanley Baldwin, on May 28, 1937. He was a clearheaded and efficient administrator. By the end of 1937, Chamberlain was identified in England with the return of a modest prosperity, with personal integrity, and a commonsense approach to public policy. He was the obvious and overwhelming popular choice to succeed Stanley Baldwin as prime minister. Winston Churchill, who saw Chamberlain's foreign policies as tragic at the time, nevertheless, and writing retrospectively at the nadir of Chamberlain's reputation, respects him in a mixed sort of way. In contrast to Stanley Baldwin, Neville Chamberlain was

alert, businesslike, opinionated and self-confident in a very
high degree. . . . Instead of a vague but none the less deep-
seated intuition, we now had a narrow, sharp-edged efficiency
within the limits of the policy in which he believed. Both as
Chancellor of the Exchequer and as Prime Minister he kept
the tightest and most rigid control upon military expenditure. . . . His all-pervading hope was to go down to history
as the great peacemaker, and for this he was to strive
continually in the teeth of facts, and face great risks for
himself and his country. Unhappily he ran into tides the force
of which he would not measure, and met hurricanes from
which he did not flinch, but with which he could not cope.

Chamberlain, an admirable statesman in a peaceful era, had the
misfortune to be on a collision course with a genuinely radical
personality, Adolf Hitler, who was capable of thoughts that could
never even occur to Neville Chamberlain. It was because of Chamberlain's very strengths, his normality and decency, that Hitler was
able to surround him in terms of power politics and made him the
sucker of Munich. The reason Hitler bested Chamberlain at Munich
was that in support of his vision of a Greater Reich stretching to the
Ukraine, he was willing to threaten an unthinkable European war,
while Chamberlain, pursuing a peace which not only he, but virtually unanimous feeling in England and France desired, could go
no further in accommodating Hitler than adjustments in the Continental balance of power.

Chamberlain's policies could have succeeded with the correct
military backup. Against Hitler, England could have mobilized the
combined power of France, the Soviet Union, and, perhaps even
Italy. But in pursuit of that kind of power politics against Hitler,
England itself would have to go into high war production, build up
an air force, perhaps introduce conscription. When Chamberlain's
foreign secretary, Anthony Eden, confronted the prime minister
with the facts and figures of the German military buildup, Chamberlain told him to go home and take an aspirin. Eden soon resigned. Chamberlain would go to Munich during the Czech crisis
militarily and politically naked, the leader of a nation paralyzed by
memories of the slaughters at Passchendaele and Verdun. When
Chamberlain looked across the table into those peculiar blue eyes of
Hitler, the English had only about one hundred antiaircraft guns.
The Hurricanes and Spitfires were only beginning to be produced.
When Chamberlain considered his own cards, they had nothing on
them.

While the German columns were advancing into Austria, Hitler accompanied them in an automobile with General von Halder. Hitler turned to him and said, "This will be very inconvenient to the Czechs." A light bulb went on in General von Halder's mind. He knew that Hitler was not talking about an invasion of Czechoslovakia from the south. That was nonsense. The only railroad into Czechoslovakia, through Linz, could be put out of business in an hour. The mountain passes could not be forced. Hitler was thinking in much broader terms. He meant that, with the conquest of Austria, the Czechs were out of business politically. The British and French had not gone to war over the Rhineland, and they were not going to war over Austria. The concrete was hardening on the Siegfried Line facing France, and no French politician would risk another Verdun there. Hitler's factories were pouring out military aircraft. It would be "inconvenient" for the Czechs indeed.

On May 28, 1938, Hitler called a meeting of his chiefs of staff and ordered them to prepare to attack Czechoslovakia. He met with resistance. The generals were prudent and skeptical. The French had, on paper at least, a heavy numerical advantage in the west. It would require all of Germany's thirty-five divisions to break the Czech fortress line in their northern regions. The Czechs had 2.5 million men mobilized and, in the Skoda works, the best armaments industry after Krupp. To the German generals, a war with Czechoslovakia, given Germany's nakedness against the French and complete uncertainty about subsequent Russian moves in the east, seemed to go beyond the bounds of reason. Hitler brushed all of this aside. "I will decide," he told Marshal Keitel, "to take action against Czechoslovakia only if I am firmly convinced, as in the case of the de-militarized zone [the Rhineland] and the entry into Austria, that France will not march and that therefore England will not intervene."

In pursuit of a European peace, Neville Chamberlain threw away the Czechs, not only their freedom and national independence, but more materially, their fortress line in the north, their Skoda works, their large modern army of thirty divisions. The argument at the time was that northern Czechoslovakia, the Sudetenland, was ethnically German and that German aspirations had to be accommodated. And so they were. But Chamberlain threw away the balance of power in Central Europe and, in the name of peace, made it possible for Hitler eventually to attack France.

During the Czech crisis, Chamberlain flew to Germany three times to try to deal with Hitler. He was treated with alternating charm and bullying. At the final meeting, the negotiations lasted until the small hours of the morning, exhausting the will of the

emotionally normal statesmen, Chamberlain of England and
Daladier of France, facing Hitler and Mussolini. The agreement was
signed at 2:00 A.M. and communicated to the Czechs. The Sudetenland and its fortress line was to be evacuated. An "international
commission" was to determine the "final frontiers." In fact, Czechoslovakia was finished as a nation. Hungary seized part of its
territory. Poland, playing the jackal, seized more, not aware that
Poland itself was next.

When he flew back from Munich after signing the agreement with
Hitler, Neville Chamberlain landed at the Heston airport. An assembly of politicians and a large and enthusiastic crowd welcomed
him. He waved the joint declaration with Hitler's signature on it. At
10 Downing Street in London, he waved the piece of paper again to
cheering thousands in the streets. He said: "I believe it is peace for
our time." His phrase echoed, perhaps unconsciously, the phrase in
the Anglican liturgy, the prayer for "peace in our time, O Lord."
Chamberlain, a successful man of conventional intelligence, did not
understand that Hitler regarded this document as purely tactical, a
collection of ink and paper atoms whirling in a void, a void that
would be given shape by Hitler's personal will.

Mussolini had cracked earlier, unable to understand or pursue his
and Italy's interest. A cold-blooded, balance-of-power decision
would have made Mussolini resist—by force of arms, if necessary—
Hitler's seizure of Austria. When Mussolini failed this power-poli-
tics test, he destined himself and his mistress for that meat hook in
Milan. Hitler spoke on the phone to his emissary to the Duce,
Prince Philip von Hessen:

Hessen:	*I have just come back from the Palazzo Venezia. The Duce accepted the whole thing in a very friendly manner. He sends you his regards. He had been informed from Austria; von Schusch-nigg gave him the news. He had then said it [Italian intervention] would be a complete im-possibility; it would be a bluff; such a thing could not be done. So he [Schuschnigg] was told that it was unfortunately arranged thus, and it could not be changed any more. Then Mussolini said that Austria would be immaterial to him.*
Hitler:	*Then please tell Mussolini I will never forget him for this.*
Hessen:	*Yes.*
Hitler:	*Never, never, never, whatever happens. I am still ready to make a quite different agreement with him.*

Hessen: *Yes, I told him that too.*

Hitler: *As soon as the Austrian affair has been settled I shall be ready to go with him through thick and thin; nothing matters.*

Hessen: *Yes, my Führer.*

Hitler: *Listen. I will make any agreement—I am no longer in fear of the terrible position which would have existed militarily in case we had become involved in a conflict. You may tell him that I do thank him ever so much; never, never shall I forget that.*

Hessen: *Yes, my Führer.*

Hitler: *I will never forget it, whatever may happen. If he should ever need any help or be in any danger he can be convinced that I shall stick to him whatever might happen, even if the whole world were against him.*

Hessen: *Yes, my Führer.*

Hitler never forgot the Duce's loyalty at this climactic moment over Austria. He would rescue Mussolini again and again—in Greece, in Yugoslovia, in the deserts of North Africa, and finally, with a romantic glider operation, in northern Italy. Hitler finally despised him, but he would always pay his political debts to the Duce.

Hitler's thoughts in 1939 moved relentlessly eastward, and German diplomacy began to menace Poland. In conversations with Ribbentrop, the Polish ambassador asked about the Lithuanian port of Memel, which was ethnically German. Two days later, Poland received its answer. German troops landed and seized Memel. Hitler was demanding an end to the "Polish Corridor," which split Prussia off from the main body of the Reich and gave Poland its only access to the sea at the port of Danzig.

Amidst this maelstrom, Prime Minister Neville Chamberlain did an astonishing thing. From the start, his "appeasement" policy had possessed a certain internal intellectual coherence. If the rationale was never fully spelled out, it was nevertheless discernible. Give Hitler the Rhineland and then turn him east. That seemed to be what he wanted anyway, East Europe and the Ukraine. Give him Austria. Give him Czechoslovakia. Let him fight Stalin. Hungary and Rumania were already in his camp anyway. The logic of this policy meant give him Poland too.

But all of a sudden, Neville Chamberlain "guaranteed" Poland. By this time, Chamberlain had assumed complete control of foreign policy, though Lord Halifax was officially foreign secretary, and on March 17, 1939, Chamberlain made a momentous speech in Birmingham in the midst of the escalating Polish crisis. Chamberlain, of course, was under excruciating political pressure to do something about the Hitlerian depredations, but Hitler, who thought that he had understood British foreign policy, must have thought that he was now dealing with a madman.

Chamberlain began by denouncing Hitler for a breach of faith about the Munich agreement. He recited the assurances Hitler had given him. "This is the last territorial claim which I have to make in Europe." "I shall not be interested in the Czech state any more, and I can guarantee it. We don't want any more Czechs." The prime minister continued: "I am convinced that after Munich the great majority of the British people shared my honest desire that that policy should be carried further, but today I share their disappointment, their indignation, that these hopes have been so wantonly shattered. . . . Is this a step in the direction of an attempt to dominate the world by force?" The period of accommodation with Hitler was at an end. On March 31, Chamberlain addressed Parliament: "In the event of any action which clearly threatened Polish independence and which the Polish Government accordingly considered it vital to resist with their national forces, His Majesty's Government would feel themselves bound at once to lend the Polish Government all support in their power. They have given the Polish Government an assurance to this effect. I may add that the French Government have authorized me to make it plain that they stand in the same position in this matter as do His Majesty's Government."

Thus Chamberlain guaranteed Poland. The Polish government considered Poland a modern military power, but it was not. England and France, because of geography, could do nothing for the Poles except threaten warfare against Germany from the west. Chamberlain's guarantees made sense only if the Red Army could be brought to bear against Hitler in the east, and the Poles would never agree to an alliance with Russia and the Red Army on Polish soil. According to French Premier Paul Reynaud, the Polish attitude was: "With the Germans we risk losing our liberty; with the Russians our soul."

Three years later in the Kremlin, after a good deal of vodka, Stalin gave Winston Churchill his own version of those weeks when Europe slid toward war. "We formed the impression," Stalin said, "that the British and French governments were not resolved to go to war if Poland were attacked, but that they hoped the diplomatic lineup of Britain, France and Russia would deter Hitler. We were sure it would not." Stalin said that he had inquired how many

divisions the French could send against Hitler. The answer was
"about a hundred." He had asked how many the English would field.
The answer was "two, and two more later." Stalin repeated the
words to Churchill: "Two, and two more later." He indicated that in
1939 he believed that in London he was dealing with fools or cynics.
How many divisions would the Soviets have to put into the field if
they went to war with Hitler? Stalin said, "Three hundred."

He decided to sign a nonaggression pact with Hitler, seize a piece
of Poland, and leave the British and French to their own devices.
Both Hitler and Stalin were aware that the pact was merely a
temporary expedient. Stalin hoped that Germany might be weaker
after a year or two of war in the west. Hitler, pursuing his strategy of
"one at a time," would swallow Poland and deal with Stalin later.
What Stalin got out of his pact with Hitler was a deployment of the
German army farther from his own borders. In the event, when
Hitler decided to attack Russia, it took his panzer divisions about
three days to smash through the Polish territory that Stalin had
gained in 1939.

Hitler threw the switch on August 31, issuing his "Directive
Number One for the Conduct of the War":

1. Now that all the political possibilities of
   disposing by peaceful means of a situation on the
   Eastern frontier which is intolerable for Germany
   are exhausted, I have determined on a solution by
   force.

2. The attack on Poland is to be carried out in
   accordance with the preparation made. . . . The
   date of the attack, September 1, 1939. Time of
   attack—04.45. [The Führer inserted this dawn
   attack time in red pencil.]

3. In the West it is important that the responsibility
   for the opening of hostilities should rest
   unequivocally with England and France. At first
   purely local action should be taken against
   insignificant frontier violations.

Thus, on point number three, Hitler did not take the Western democracies seriously in a military sense. He and Stalin were in perfect
analytical agreement. England would commit two divisions, and two
more later.

William L. Shirer graduated from an Iowa college and went to Paris in 1925 as a foreign correspondent for Colonel McCormick's Chicago *Tribune*. He reported from Paris and also from Vienna, and he covered the fighting in Afghanistan and Gandhi's movement in India. At the end of the summer of 1934, he was stationed in Berlin, where he reported on the rise of Hitler and the seizure of Austria and Czechoslovakia and then the outbreak of general war. By the time of the Austrian crisis, Shirer had been hired by CBS Radio, and he watched the Nazi takeover in Vienna. To avoid the German censorship, he decided to try to fly to London, where his friend Ed Murrow was the CBS man, and broadcast from there directly to New York.

When he arrived at the airport outside Vienna, he found that the Gestapo had seized it and that only Luftwaffe planes were operating. A black-coated SS officer shouted at him that no civilian planes were taking off. He tried British Airways anyway and was informed that all flights were overbooked, mostly, it turned out, by frightened Jews. No Jews were flying to Berlin, and Shirer managed to get a seat on a Lufthansa flight. An Austrian police official told Shirer that the Gestapo had seized the Austrian chancellor, Kurt von Schuschnigg, an authoritarian conservative. He would spend the next seven years in the Dachau concentration camp, where he was joined by—among others—Léon Blum, the former French premier; Dr. Hjalmar Horace Greeley Schact, Hitler's financial wizard; Prince Philip von Hessen; and Pastor Martin Niemöller.

Shirer's Lufthansa flight at last was cleared out of Vienna, and he made it to Tempelhof Airport in Berlin, where he got a seat on a Dutch airlines flight to London. At Tempelhof, he picked up a copy of the *Völkischer Beobachter,* which had a three-inch headline: "GERMAN AUSTRIA SAVED FROM CHAOS." The story described "Red disorders" in the streets of Vienna, "fighting, shooting, pillage." It said that Seyss-Inquart, the Austrian Nazi leader, had telegraphed Hitler, asking him to send in troops to protect the Austrians from "armed Socialists and Communists." Shirer had been in Vienna and had witnessed no such disorders. He assumed, correctly, that the telegram had been faked in Berlin.

Shirer wrote the script for his broadcast on the plane to London, and when he reached Croydon, he phoned the BBC studio. CBS had arranged for him to go on the air for fifteen minutes at 6:30 P.M. New York time, 11:30 P.M. London time. At the BBC studio in London, Shirer nervously watched the minute hand on the clock circle to 11:30, and over the feedback from New York, he heard the CBS announcer introduce him: "A little more than twenty-four hours ago, Nazi troops passed over the border into Austria. . . . At the time of the invasion yesterday, William L. Shirer, Columbia's Central European Director, was in Vienna. This afternoon he flew to London to bring you an uncensored, eyewitness account of the move. . . . *We take you now to London.*"

The next day, a Sunday, Shirer and Murrow put together from London the first world-news roundup, with correspondents reporting from London, Vienna, Paris, and Rome. At 1:00 A.M. London time, 8:00 P.M. New York time, Shirer sat in the studio at Broadcasting House and listened through his earphones as the calm, smooth voice of Bob Trout introduced him in New York: "To bring you the picture of Europe tonight Columbia now presents a special broadcast with pickups direct from London, from Paris and such other European capitals as have communication channels available. . . . Columbia begins its radio tour of Europe's capitals with a transoceanic pickup from London. *We take you now to London.*"

Shirer spoke briefly, expressing the view that the Chamberlain government would do little besides issue a protest over Hitler's seizure of Austria. Ellen Wilkinson, a British M.P., came on to say that "the British are annoyed at Hitler. But no one in Britain wants to go to war." Edgar L. Mowrer came in from Paris and wondered whether people would now understand that Hitler stood for "brutal, naked force." Shirer began to think that this news roundup might be the start of something new in radio.

He covered the German smash through the Low Countries and into France for CBS, and he beat the print journalists on June 20 when Hitler dictated terms to the French in Marshall Foch's old railroad car in the forest of Compiègne, where the Germans had surrendered in 1918. "It was a perfectly lovely summer day," he later wrote

> A warm June sun beat down on the stately trees, elms, oaks, cypresses and pines, casting pleasant shadows on the wooded avenues that led out from the little circular clearing. In the middle of it stood the old *wagon-lit* of Marshall Foch. . . . Precisely at 3:15 P.M., by my watch, I watched the dictator and his minions arrive in a caravan of black Mercedeses and alight in front of the French monument to Alsace-Lorraine. I noted down their dress: Hitler in a double-breasted gray military uniform (in contrast to the brown Nazi party uniform he had always worn until the war came); Göring, by the grace of the Führer the only field marshall of the Reich, in a special, fancy sky blue uniform of the Luftwaffe, fiddling with his marshal's baton. . . . [Hitler's face] was grave, solemn, yet brimming with revenge. There was also in it, as

in his springy step, a note of the triumphant conqueror, the
defier of the world. There was something else . . . a sort of
scornful inner joy at being present at this great reversal of
fate—a reversal he himself had wrought.

By the spring of 1940, America moved grudgingly toward arma-
ment, the president calling for an air force of 50,000 planes, an
army of 10 million men, and a two-ocean navy. Suddenly it was
reported that virtually the entire U.S. fleet was to be stationed
indefinitely at Pearl Harbor and would conduct maneuvers in the
Pacific. "The most important series of war games ever held by
American forces," wrote Hanson Baldwin in the *New York Times,*
"have recently been completed, are going on, or will be held later in
the year. The recently announced corps and army maneuvers of
70,000 regular army—the largest peacetime concentration in our
history to be held in May in Texas and Louisiana and the participa-
tion of about 180 ships and 350 planes of the United States Fleet in
far-flung Pacific exercises during April and May will be the largest
and most important of a series of exercises which during 1940 will
be more ambitious and more impressive than ever before."

How did it sound in America, as Europe went to war again? If you
were home from school with the flu and lying in bed, you heard it
all over your small, brown plastic radio. "We are here at the Gare du
Nord in Paris. French soldiers in uniform are arriving on bicycles.
They are carrying their rifles. Their officers are assembling them in
regimental formations. The French troops are arriving from all over
France. They own their own uniforms and they have their own rifles.
France is going to war. . . ."

In the east, it would be the year of the tank and, above all, of the
Stuka dive-bomber. The Stuka was a formidable psychological
weapon, utterly terrifying to the uninitiated. It was painted black. It
had bent, gull wings. The Nazis equipped it with a siren that
screamed as it dove. On the "March of Time" newsreels between the
feature films on a Saturday afternoon, you could see the Stukas
devastating the Poles. There were columns of people in carts and
overcoats fleeing the Stukas along country roads. The Polish army
was charging on horseback, cavalry charges, being wiped out. The
Stuka helped break the French army in 1940, scattering them as
they retreated, an undisciplined military horde.

But the Stuka, screaming as it dove, was a military fraud. Its top
speed was 125 miles per hour. It had nonretractible landing gear.
The next year, when Air Marshal Hermann Göring threw his air
force against England in 1940, being a Stuka pilot was a suicide

mission, and the Germans withdrew the plane. Hitler was not dealing with Poles now. He was dealing with England, a serious enterprise after all. Hitler did not know that the British had designed the best military plane in the world, the Spitfire. This plane has to be seen to be appreciated. It is the last, great propellor-driven plane, and it approaches the later jets in some of its performance features. It goes 200 miles an hour (poor Stuka!). It gathers speed fast, with a growling sound, and soon the engines scream. Within forty seconds, a Spitfire can jump off its grassy English aerodrome.

The Royal Air Force said no, Hitler could not control the Channel. Without that twenty-mile strip of strategic water, Hitler, at the pinnacle of his personal and political career, could not control the world. But the ferocity of the *blitzkrieg* had startled the world. Military analysts in the newspapers and magazines discussed the question of whether it was even possible to resist the onslaught of the panzers, and the consensus was not reassuring: *Maybe*. A terrible power had been released in the center of Europe, apparently sweeping all before it.

As catastrophe loomed, the words of the great poet W. H. Auden expressed an emotional gloom that was indeed widespread:

> *I sit in one of the dives*
> *On Fifty-second Street*
> *Uncertain and afraid*
> *As the clever hopes expire*
> *Of a low dishonest decade.*

The Ivy League kids liked those dives on Fifty-second Street— jazz joints with booze and strippers, blue with smoke and noise, and filled with the frantic awareness that we were probably going over the falls.

On the day his troops crossed the Polish frontier, Hitler ordered the liquidation of the old and incurably ill in all German hospitals. They were given lethal injections. He wanted these useless human beings eliminated on principle, and he also knew that he would need those hospital beds for his soldiers. A short time later, Heinrich Himmler made a fine moral distinction in the official SS newspaper, the *Schwarz Korps*. Because of the need for manpower, German women were encouraged to have children, even out of wedlock. But "Don Juanism" was by no means permitted. "German women are no free game. Within the elite guard care has been taken to see that respect for the German woman and mother remains the supreme law of a manly and chivalrous attitude toward life, if necessary by force. And we shall take care that this matter-of-course moral standard obtains the force of law outside our narrower confines as well—a law that does away with the seducer." To underline Himmler's point, a man who had seduced a girl who then committed suicide was condemned and shot.

In 1940, the totalitarian mentality possessed an icy quality, a chill that was felt across the Atlantic and across the American continent. In 1914, what lay ahead was unknown. Perhaps the war would be over by Christmas. By the end of 1940, everyone knew how bad it was going to be.

The Jackal

On May 17, 1940, President Roosevelt wrote to him: "Reports reaching me from many sources, to the effect that you may be contemplating early entry into the war, have given me great concern." The president said that a further extension of the fighting could lead to the "destruction of millions of lives and the best of what we call liberty and culture of civilization." Nevertheless, Mussolini, in awe of his ally Hitler's lightning conquests and pushed by newspaper editorials and mobs of demonstrating Italian fascisti—but against the advice of his generals—abandoned even the pretense of neutrality. "Italy," he replied four days later, "is and intends to remain allied with Germany and Italy cannot remain absent at a moment in which the fate of Europe is at stake." He believed that Hitler would quickly subdue the British and consolidate the continent of Europe and that if Italy remained out of the war, it would have little to say about the future of Europe. Also, after Hitler had seized Austria, the panzers were on his borders, and Italy had become a military satellite.

On June 10, Italian forces swarmed across the French border. Mussolini announced to cheering crowds below his trademark balcony: "We take the field against the plutocratic and reactionary democracies who have blocked the march and frequently plotted against the existence of the Italian people." Mussolini was committing suicide in at least two respects. His own death followed directly from the decision to invade France, and his reputation went into the garbage can of history—he became a laughingstock. In a powerful address, dripping with aristocratic hauteur, Roosevelt referred to the Italian invasion of France as "the hand that held the dagger has stuck it into the back of its neighbor."

The Duce's Black Arrow Division had fought well in the Spanish War, and the Italians had defeated the Ethiopians without much trouble, but even the demoralized and crumbling French border army was too much for them. The Italians were stopped cold at the border. Much worse followed. Mussolini had a flashy Mediterranean fleet, very fast moving, impressive in the newsreels. The movies did not show that its armor was too thin. The British navy sank it in an afternoon. There was no *mare nostrum*. The Italian armies reeled backward in North Africa and had to be rescued by General Rommel and the Afrika Korps. As it was, tens of thousands of Italians surrendered to the British, forming immense, snakelike columns in the desert. Mussolini seized Albania and invaded Greece, but the Greeks, marching in white skirts and with pompoms on their shoes, routed his army and would have thrown it back into the Adriatic in a fascist Dunkirk if Hitler had not rescued him again by smashing Yugoslavia and Greece. Mussolini had plunged into war with inadequate firepower. As the much more skeptical Francisco Franco realized, it was not clear that England would be defeated. Spain stayed out.

Mussolini has become such an object of derision and contempt that it is now all but impossible to accept the undoubted fact that he was once one of the most admired leaders in Europe. His 1922 blackshirt march on Rome brought to an end a period of political deadlock and leftist riot. His domestic achievements were substantial. Roland Sarti, a Marxist historian, sums them up objectively in a recent monograph: "Under Fascist rule, Italy underwent rapid capitalist development, with the electrification of the whole country, the blossoming of the automobile and silk industries, the creation of an up-to-date banking system, the prospering of agriculture, the reclaiming of substantial agricultural areas through the draining of the marshlands, the construction of a considerable network of highways, etc. Italy's rapid progress after World War I . . . would have been unimaginable without the social processes begun during the Fascist period." Mussolini's power never achieved anything approaching the totalitarian coordination of Hitler and Stalin and was probably even milder than Franco's rule in Spain. There was repression, the administering of doses of castor oil, but no Gulags and Belsens or Cambodian-style slaughter. The social philosopher, Ernest van den Haag, belonged to the underground resistance against Mussolini and was even shot while fleeing a police raid. Today he says that, knowing what he knows now, he would probably not have been in the resistance.

Mussolini was probably better read than any other national leader of his time. A former editor of the newspaper *Popolo d' Italia,* he was entirely familiar with the works of Marx, Spengler, Sorel, Bergson, William James, Pareto and LeBon. Vilfredo Pareto, with his theory of elites, was probably the most profound intellectual influence on him. Mussolini's leadership made even proletarians take some pride in being Italian, and his addresses, broadcast across the Atlantic, were listened to with respect in American-Italian households. In his classic study of Italian Fascism published in 1935, Herbert Finer remarks that Mussolini "reads assiduously, with a wider range than a professor." He corresponded with Shaw, Freud, Pareto, Sorel. John Gunther viewed him as "the only modern ruler who can genuinely be termed an intellectual." Churchill considered him a "really great man." Austen Chamberlain, British foreign secretary from 1924 to 1929, wrote: "The more one knows the Italian prime minister, the more one appreciates him and loves him." American admirers included Andrew Mellon, secretary of the treasury under three presidents, several American ambassadors, and James Farley. Hugh Johnson of the National Recovery Administration spoke on one occasion of the "shining name" of Mussolini. President Roosevelt, writing to the ambassador in Rome, confided that "I am much interested and deeply impressed by what he has accomplished."

Mussolini stood 5 feet 6 inches and had a massive, handsome head. After an interview in the middle 1920s, Ernest Hemingway wrote in the newspapers that Mussolini had "nigger's eyes," by which remarkable formulation Hemingway meant that they were dark and perhaps shifty. Mussolini liked to interrupt his working day several times with sexual intercourse, often standing up and in his uniform, a very rapid performance.

When he foolishly invaded France on June 10, 1940, Mussolini insured that he would be run over by history. A few years later, fleeing northward as the German front crumbled in Italy, he and his mistress, Clara Petacci, were seized by Communist partisans and, on the orders of Communist boss Palmiro Togliatti, machine-gunned, as La Clara at the last moment threw herself between Mussolini and the bullets. Then the bodies were mutilated and hung by the feet in the Piazzale Loreto in Milan, upside-down being traditionally the most ignominious position, the equivalent since the Renaissance or even before of the Roman crucifixion.

His story may perhaps be said, in Samuel Johnson's words, to "point a moral, and adorn a tale"—illustrating the catastrophic results of a single error in judgment, his invasion of France in 1940—the dismal fate of an overreacher. But it would be fitting, rather, to let his great admirer, Ezra Pound, have the last word here:

> *The enormous tragedy of the dream in the peasant's*
> *bent shoulders*
> *Manes! Manes was tanned and stuffed,*
> *Thus Ben and Clara* a Milano
> *by the heels at Milano*
> *That maggots shd / eat the dead bullock.*

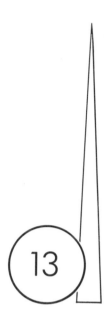

REMEMBER
JOE DIMAGGIO

13

The way to Ebbets Field from Queens in 1940 was to get on the IRT elevated that ran along Roosevelt Avenue, clang along through Sunnyside to Queens Plaza, change over to the BMT, which ran over the bridge to Brooklyn—you could see the battleships, symbols of American power, in the Navy Yard below—and then on into Brooklyn and finally Flatbush. In front of Ebbets Field, you walked across a wide plaza covered with trolley tracks and trolleys bringing people to the game, the trolleys clanging, bumping, sparking from their masts along the trolley wires, with bells that clanged when the trolley was about to start up. It was said that the name Dodgers derived from the Brooklyn Trolley Dodgers of some distant day. Then, with the rest of the crowd, you surged into the stadium's rotunda, across the tile floor with its blue, crossed-bat motif, bought a ticket, then through the turnstile and up the stairs and ramps to the entrance to the seats.

The first glimpse of the diamond was always overwhelming in its greenness and transported you instantly out of urban America with its asphalt and auto horns and into a manicured, green slice of pastoral America, a kind of dream of the preindustrial origins of the republic. Baseball, even now, is somehow always the old days. Its uniforms with their three-quarter-length pants and gaiters are self-consciously archaic. Football uniforms and tennis costumes have changed far more than those baseball uniforms. Baseball moves at an old-fashioned leisurely pace, the only major team sport that is not ruled by the clock. Baseball's rhythms are slow rural rhythms, prolonging the twenty minutes of action into a three-hour crawl, including the ritual of the seventh-inning stretch. In some games, the outfielders could safely take naps. Baseball is pervaded with archaic ritual from the earlier republic, the players chewing tobacco as if this were still the day of the brass spitoon, the manager arguing with the ump even though he never wins the argument, the dugout keeping up a constant stage-chatter in some unintelligible argot. The players themselves, especially in 1940, seem to have stepped out of America's past. Indeed, over 60 percent of them have actually come from the rural South. They have names like Dixie Walker, Pee Wee Reese (the Little Colonel), Enos "Country" Slaughter, Mort and Walker Cooper, Kirby Higbe, Whitlow Wyatt. In 1940, people were not self-conscious about ethnicity. Even as Joe Louis was alliteratively called the Brown Bomber, Hank Greenberg, the home-run hitter of the Detroit Tigers, was widely referred to as the Jolting Jew.

The Brooklyn Dodgers of 1940 were the most exciting team in the major leagues, full of a sense of coming possibility. During the early and middle 1930s, they had been clowns, notable for having fly balls drop on the skulls of outfielders and having three base runners end up together on third base. Larry MacPhail put an end to all that. Out in Cincinnati, MacPhail, a tempestuous character and general manager of the Reds, had been feuding with the owner. In 1936 he quit. At that point, the Dodgers were hopelessly mired in the second division; attendance was way down; and the assets were in the hands of a bank, the Brooklyn Trust Company. MacPhail was recommended to the Dodger ownership by St. Louis general manager Branch Rickey, known as the Mahatma, and Commissioner Ford Frick. MacPhail signed on as general manager of the Dodgers for the 1938 season and changed everything.

The special atmosphere he was able to create through his theatrical genius in Ebbets Field was made possible by the nature of the stadium and by its location. It had first opened for the 1913 season and, with a capacity of 32,000, was in 1938 the smallest stadium in the National League. Sometimes, against all of the fire laws, this swelled to 36,000, with people filling the aisles and hanging from girders. The small and crowded stadium created a special intimacy and cohesion among the fans, and between the fans and the players. From the front rows you could see the players a few feet away, read their expressions, hear them shout, see whether they were tired. When MacPhail made the team a serious pennant contender, it became a special focus of local Brooklyn pride. About half the seats in Ebbets Field were estimated to be filled by people who walked to the stadium from their homes. These fans knew each other, came all summer to the ball park, or listened to Red Barber's play-by-play on radios at the job.

The Dodgers players themselves were familiar local figures. Between batting practice in late morning and game time, they would take a half-hour off and clatter across the street for a beer at a local tavern. On days off, they would be down at the beach in Rockaway, often throwing a football. Even as pennant contenders in 1940, the Dodgers were known as "Dem Bums," reminiscent of an earlier era when they really did play like bums. According to sports legend, a vociferously disappointed Dodgers fan during the early 1930s would scream at the team, "Ya bum, youse bums, ya bums," and even when three runners were no longer meeting at third base, the name stuck. Willard Mullin, the great *New York Herald Tribune* cartoonist, created a caricature Bum as the symbol of the team, a pear-shaped hobo with flopping soles, loose lips, and a ragged hat. The symbol of the Bum, even in 1940, had a poetic truth. The characteristic of the 1940 Dodgers fan was that he desperately wanted the pennant and the World Series but had no real confidence that he would get them. In his heart, he felt that the Yankees would.

In 1938, the Brooklyn Trust Company gave MacPhail an open checkbook, and the impresario was off and running. He had Ebbets Field repainted and redecorated. He installed lights for night baseball, a daring innovation. He hired Babe Ruth as a first-base coach and hired Red Barber away from Cincinnati to give New York its only daily baseball broadcasting. He created Ladies' Day and the Knot-Hole Gang—twenty-five-cent seats for kids, building a future constituency. He paid Olympic star Jesse Owens $4,000 for a pregame, sprinting exhibition and hired Gladys Gooding to play a pipe organ installed behind first base. For the first night game in history, 38,748 fans—far over the legal limit—jammed the stadium to see Johnny Vander Meer of Cincinnati pitch his second successive no-hitter. People told each other that "anything can happen at Ebbets Field."

Everyone knew Hilda Chester, a large and loud woman who brought a cowbell to the games, along with a sign proclaiming "Hilda Is Here." Tex Rickard ran the public address system and was loved for his malapropisms: "A little boy has been found lost." "Will the fans along the railing in left field please remove their clothes." The so-called Dodger Sym-Phony consisted of a bunch of horn blowers and drum beaters with little musical ability, a bunch of Italians from the Williamsburg section of Brooklyn. At first they were pursued through the stands by police, but they soon became an expected feature of the show, with seats reserved for them by MacPhail. When an umpire made a suspect call against the Dodgers, the Sym-Phony played "Three Blind Mice." When an enemy player struck out, they would play "The Worms Crawl In, the Worms Crawl Out," and they would musically follow him back to his dejected seat in the dugout, waiting for him to plant his defeated posterior on the bench. At that point the Sym-Phony would hit the big bass drum—BANG. The strikeout victims often played a kind of game with the musicians, dawdling around before being seated, going to the water cooler, but the Sym-Phony had an eagle eye, and when they finally sat down, it would be BANG.

The atmosphere in the tiny old stadium reached a pitch of frenzy when the hated New York Giants—whose manager, Bill Terry, had once asked "Is Brooklyn still in the league?"—came to town. The bull pen for the visiting team was down in the left-field corner, and during a Giants game the frenzied Brooklyn fans would shower the opposing athletes with tomatoes, hot-dog rolls, rotten eggs, and verbal insults. The Dodger third baseman was a wizard fielder named Cookie Lavagetto, and one fan repeatedly screamed "Cooooooooookie" during the games. She became famous as the "Cookie Monster."

Leo Durocher, the Dodgers manager in 1940, was the perfect choice—MacPhail's—for that time and place. He also played expertly at shortstop and was a ferocious competitor, though not much of a batter. His nose-to-nose arguments with umpires like George Magerkurth made him a hero to the Brooklyn fans. Leo "The Lip" Durocher was always kicking dirt at an umpire's blue trousers and getting thrown out of the game. He would shortly reappear in the stands, dressed in one of his fancy suits, and receive thunderous applause. His own philosophy was eloquently summed up when he said, "Nice guys finish last."

The Dodgers and their fanatical supporters had reason to feel cautiously optimistic in the spring of 1940. In 1938, MacPhail's first year, they had finished seventh, but attendance had doubled. In 1939, Durocher's first year, they had finished third. Of course, the Dodger fan in the spring of 1940 had no right to the serene self-confidence of the Yankee fan uptown, who had every expectation that the Yankees would win a fifth consecutive World Series that year. After all, they had not only won the last four World Series but had won nine World Series games in a row. In outfielders Joe DiMaggio, George Selkirk, Tommy Henrich, and the apelike Charlie "King Kong" Keller, they had the best outfield in baseball, a home-run machine. Bill Dickey, catcher, was a giant player who also generated home runs. The infield was superb, with Red Rolfe at third, Frankie Crosetti at short, and Joe Gordon at second. The pitching was formidable. Only at first base could the Dodgers claim an edge over the Yankees. You could argue that Dolph Camilli, with his clothesline home runs and skillful glove, was superior to Babe Dahlgren.

But the Dodgers had an edge nowhere else. Before the season opened, 67 of 77 baseball writers picked the Yankees to win the pennant and the series. On April 6, John Drebinger of the *New York Times* foresaw another championship for the Yankees: "Incredible as it may sound, the Yankees, world champions for four years in a row, never appeared more formidable on the eve of a championship race than they do now. Infield, outfield, pitching, catching, hitting power and reserve strength: in fact, wherever one looks one sees an accomplished performer in an amazingly efficient machine. There is no single weak point. It seems as if the champions, put on their mettle by cries of 'Stop the Yanks' and 'The Red Sox can do it,' are more determined than ever to smash another American League pennant race to smithereens." "Marse" Joe McCarthy, the Yankee manager, acknowledged that a fifth consecutive pennant would be against the law of averages, but he told the press that the Yankees were a team that defied the law of averages. "We are," he said, "going to the post as well equipped as we have ever been."

But the Dodgers were no longer "Dem Bums" either, and while Larry MacPhail had more than a touch of P. T. Barnum in him, he also was serious about building a championship team in Brooklyn. During 1939 he had made important moves, getting Dixie Walker from the Tigers, Whitlow Wyatt from Milwaukee, and Hugh Casey from Memphis. In 1939 attendance had doubled to more than one million.

On opening day, Cleveland's twenty-one-year-old phenomenon pitched the only opening-day no-hitter in history against the White Sox. Feller deserved his headlines. Calling his column "A Really Great Feller," sportswriter John Kieran recalled:

> It was in 1937 that the Giants, swinging northward with the Indians on an exhibition tour, first caught sight of Bob Feller in action. Dare-devil Dick Bartell, lead-off man for the Giants that day at Vicksburg, Miss., took a cut at the first ball and hit it hard. It wasn't a safe hit. Daredevil Dick was thrown out at first. But he had hit the ball squarely. A few minutes later when the Giants were in the field—it didn't take

Feller long to put them there—Bartell was hit on the head by a bad bounce and retired to nurse his injury. He didn't have to face Feller again that day. But those who did face Feller had no luck during the innings that he pitched. The Giants made only one gesture that looked like a rally. Somebody eagerly accepted a base on balls. That evening the awed Giants were discussing Feller, and Bartell filed a minority report. Feller wasn't so much by the Bartell account. Mungo and others were faster. Bartell would take a chance with Feller any day. He did in later days. In the series he came up something like sixteen times against Feller. As it is vaguely remembered, he struck out twelve times and didn't get the ball out of the infield on his other attempts at bat.

Kieran goes on to talk about a Cleveland–St. Louis game:

Lippy Leo Durocher was in that game in a Cardinal uniform. On demand Lippy Leo will give an impersonation of himself as he acted against the phenomenon from an Iowa farm. He never saw the first two strikes; he merely got wind of them. But he was determined that he wasn't going to stand there and take it. He would go down swinging. So he started to swing as Feller started his windup. He swung. He didn't have the faintest idea where the ball was. He heard a loud crack and, when he looked around, the catcher had it and the umpire was barking "Strike three—he's out." That suited Leo down to the ground. He didn't want to hit. He just wanted to get away from there without being hit. Feller was a little wild in those early efforts. He still has some occasional trouble in getting the ball over the plate. But when he gets it over the plate, the batters have greater trouble in getting it away from there. He's a marvel, and there's no better time to realize it than right now, so that everybody can enjoy it as he goes along to glory.

Feller certainly was a marvel, and he deserved his opening-day headlines in 1940, but soon all eyes were on the Dodgers, who came off the starting line with a tremendous burst and won nine games in a row, including a no-hit victory over Cincinnati pitched by Tex Carleton. Nine games in a row! Brooklyn was gripped by pennant fever. So was MacPhail. He traded with St. Louis for Joe "Ducky" Medwick—"Ducky" because of his waddle—an outfielder who had won the triple batting crown in 1937 with a .332 average. MacPhail told the newspapers: "We may go broke trying to pay for this fellow, but he is the man we wanted, and he is the player needed to give us a pennant contending club." With an outfield of Dixie Walker, Pete Reiser, and Joe Medwick, Brooklyn certainly was in the race. In 1940, Pee Wee Reese joined the Dodgers, a potential superstar at shortstop, and Durocher began putting Reese in the lineup instead of himself; Reese was superb on defense and a much better batter than Durocher.

Then both Reese and Medwick were beaned. On June 1, while playing against the Cubs in Chicago, Reese was hit on the head by a pitcher named Jack Mooty. He spent three weeks in the hospital, and although he then returned to the lineup, those three weeks had been lost.

Medwick's beaning seems more sinister. He had been acquired by MacPhail from St. Louis. The first time his former team came to Brooklyn, Durocher and Medwick traded insults with a St. Louis pitcher named Bob Bowman in an elevator. Bowman allegedly stalked out of the elevator saying something about "taking care of" the two Dodgers. That afternoon at Ebbets Field, Bowman, on the mound, got into serious trouble at the onset as the first three Dodgers hit safely and two runs crossed the plate. Maybe Bowman was still smarting from the elevator incident, and his present treatment by the Dodger batters could hardly have sweetened his temper, but when Medwick, batting at cleanup fourth, stepped to the plate, Bowman's first pitch was a fastball that bounced off Medwick's skull. The Dodger fell on his back, unconscious, with his feet in the air. As pandemonium broke loose in the stands and the Dodgers emerged from their dugout and advanced menacingly on the Cardinals, Medwick was carried from the field on a stretcher. Somehow the umpires managed to keep the two teams separated, and the Cardinals went on to win 7–2, but Bowman had to sneak out of Brooklyn under the protection of two plainclothes detectives. Future mayor William O'Dwyer, then Brooklyn district attorney, looked into possible criminal charges against Bowman.

Despite their torrid start, the Dodgers soon found themselves in a tough three-team race with the Giants and Cincinnati, with the lead frequently changing hands. There is little doubt that the injuries to Reese and Medwick, though the two players did return to action, cost them some momentum. At midseason, Brooklyn had six players on the All-Star Team—Durocher, Lavagetto, Medwick, Phelps, Wyatt, and Coscarart—and was surely a strong contender at last.

But on July 7, further disasters overtook the Dodgers during the first game of a double header in Boston. "Disaster overwhelmed the Dodgers today," reported the *Times*.

> They not only dropped a double-header to the Bees
> 1–0 and 2–1, but lost their star first-baseman, Dolph Camilli,

for an indefinite period and fell into second place behind the victorious Reds in the National League. In the third inning of the first game Camilli collided with Buddy Hassett and was unconscious for nearly five minutes. Later he walked from the field and was taken to St. Elizabeth's Hospital. . . . Hassett dragged a bunt down the first-base line, and both Camilli and Wyatt went after the ball. Wyatt apparently pushed Dolph accidentally and Hassett crashed into Camilli as Dolph fell across the foul line with the ball. . . . Hassett, Boston first-sacker, was also knocked out and had to leave the game.

By midsummer the joys of spring had very much faded for the Dodgers. "Leo Durocher's once devastating Dodgers were warbling 'The St. Louis Blues' at twilight yesterday, and well they might. Playing baseball and running the bases with shocking ineptitude, they dropped a double-header to the Cardinals at Ebbets Field 4– 2 and 6– 3. A constant chorus of Bronx cheers from 14,563 paying rooters dinned in the Dodgers' ears as they went nine games behind the Reds and only three and a half ahead of the Giants. The double downfall ran the Brooklyn losing streak to a new high for the season, six games."

Disaster followed upon disaster. On July 23, the Reds took a doubleheader at Ebbets Field and extended their lead to seven games. Coscarart was spiked at second base by Frank McCormick and badly injured, and the two teams met in the middle of the field in a slugfest. Not long after that, in a losing effort in Philadelphia, Pee Wee Reese broke a bone in his foot sliding into second base and was carried off the field, out for the season. "The Dodgers' cup of woe was filled to the brim yesterday," said the *Times*. In fact the pennant race was as good as over, with Cincinnati clinching its victory in mid-September with a lead of twelve games over the fading Dodgers, a victory march shadowed, oddly, when catcher Willard Hershberger committed suicide by cutting his throat in a hotel room. Earlier, when his roommate asked him whether he would be going to the ballpark, Hershberger replied that he would be a little late.

In contrast to the Dodgers, who began the 1940 season with those nine straight victories and then faded in the second half of the season, the Yankees started dismally and then came on with a rush in the second half. Picked by almost everyone to win the pennant and loaded with talent, they began by playing ragged ball and soon found themselves tied with the White Sox in the American League cellar. By August 9 they were playing no better than .500. A portent of things to come—they lost on opening day in Philadelphia. DiMaggio sat out the first part of the season with an ankle injury and returned on May 7, but the Yankees suffered their fourth straight loss that day anyway.

DiMaggio, however, was the team leader, and when he returned to full effectiveness and began to nail the ball as before, the Yankees began to move up in the standings. "If you saw him play," wrote sportswriter Jimmy Cannon, "you'll never forget him. No one ran with such unhurried grace. His gifts as an athlete were marvellous because they were subdued. Here was an outfielder who followed a fly ball with a deft serenity as though his progress had been plotted by a choreographer concerned only with the defeat of awkwardness."

The climactic rush for the pennant began in the middle of August, and headlines like the following became regular reading: "Yankees Down Indians for 5th straight. DiMaggio Smashes No. 27." John Drebinger wrote in the *Times:*

> The spectacular dash of the Yankees that may yet bring that elusive fifth straight American League pennant to New York is still moving irresistibly forward. It swept the Indians down to defeat for the second successive afternoon at the Stadium yesterday and sent a Ladies' Day crowd of 22,051 shrieking jubilantly out of the arena as the now fully aroused Bronx Bombers, inspired by Joe DiMaggio's twenty-seventh home run of the campaign, flattened Ossie Vitt's faltering front-runners 5–3. As a consequence, Marse Joe McCarthy's thundering juggernaut scored its twelfth victory in the last fourteen games, extended its winning streak to five triumphs in a row and whittled the once almost insurmountable lead of the Indians to a matter of seven lengths. The Indians are four games in front of the Tigers.

August 30: "Yanks Win Two, 2nd in 13th, And Gain Game on Indians. DiMaggio 3-Run Pinch Homer Ties Nightcap in the Ninth." John Drebinger:

> Only a game fish, they say, swims against the tide, but yesterday it seemed that the Yankees, continuing their electrifying dash for a fifth straight pennant, practically thrashed all the water out of the stream as they sank the Browns in both ends of a double header at the Stadium. The opening engagement the Bombers won 10–3, their entire output of runs crashing home in the sixth inning to give Marius Russo, their youthful left-hander, his eleventh mound triumph of the year against eleven defeats. But that wasn't a

match to what had 7,865 hardy onlookers roaring themselves
a deep purple as Manager Joe McCarthy's champions came on
twice to tie the nightcap and finally win it in the thirteenth,
6–5. With the Yanks trailing Eldon Auker by three runs in the
ninth they saw Joe DiMaggio hobble to the plate as pinch-
hitter for Babe Dahlgren and with two aboard the bases bang
the ball into the right-field stand for his twenty-eighth homer
of the year. That deadlocked the battle at four-all.

On May 27 of that year, the great DiMaggio had been presented
with the Golden Laurel of Sports award, the ceremony taking place
in the Court of Sports at the New York World's Fair. The award went
to the best athlete of the year and was based upon DiMaggio's
performance during 1939. The recipient for 1938 had been Don
Budge, the first grand-slam winner in the history of tennis.

At the Golden Laurel ceremonies, DiMaggio was characteristically immaculate in a dark blue, double-breasted suit. Since he
had started making money in baseball, he had taken pride in his
appearance and had even been named by the Custom Tailors Guild
of America as number eight among the ten best-dressed men in
America, joining Joseph E. Davies, special aide to Secretary of State
Cordell Hull and later ambassador to the Soviet Union; Paul White-
man, the orchestra leader; Paul V. McNutt, the Social Security
administrator and presidential aspirant; John Gregg, president of the
Gregg Shorthand Publishing Company; William Rhinelander Stewart of New York; and Dr. James Bryant Conant, president of Harvard. DiMaggio was presented with the award by Julian W. Curtis,
an octogenarian who had been on the Yale crew of 1878.

DiMaggio had come far and fast from his humble roots in California. He was born on November 25, 1914, in Martinez, the eighth of
nine children. His father, a Sicilian, had come to America in 1902,
made his way to the Coast, and continued his trade as a crab
fisherman with modest success. While DiMaggio was still a young
child, the family moved to the North Beach neighborhood of San
Francisco, occupying a ground floor apartment near Fisherman's
Wharf. North Beach was a self-enclosed Italian community with its
Catholic church, boys' club, playgrounds, and a high school named
for Galileo, which DiMaggio attended. Neither his father, Giuseppe,
nor his mother, Rosalie, spoke English.

As a boy DiMaggio rejected the life of a fisherman, disappointing
his father. He hated the smells and was subject to seasickness. Much
later, living in San Francisco in retirement, he liked to sail his forty-
foot yacht, but only on calm days. Rather than go out with his father
and brothers on the crab boat, DiMaggio worked at odd jobs for

pocket money and played pickup and Boys' Club League baseball. He began playing baseball when he was ten, and by the time he was sixteen, had earned a local reputation as a batter and agile fielder. The managers of independent teams in the region began to approach him.

At seventeen he dropped out of Galileo High School and took a job in an orange-juice factory. His older brother, Vince, by this time had become a good, semipro baseball player and in 1932 signed a contract to play for the San Francisco Seals in the tough Pacific Coast League. Vince advised the Seals to take a look at his kid brother, and Joe played in a few games for them during 1932. In 1933, his first full season, he was so good that Vince DiMaggio became expendable, and the Seals let him go.

During that 1933 season, DiMaggio was nothing short of spectacular. Giving a preview of his great 1941 hitting streak for the Yankees, he set a Pacific Coast League record which still stands by hitting safely in 61 consecutive games. He hit 28 home runs and finished the season with a .340 average. He made impossible plays in the outfield.

The Yankees knew about DiMaggio, but general manager Ed Barrow balked at the $75,000 price tag the Seals had on him. Still, the retirement of Babe Ruth had left a big hole in the Yankee picture, and Barrow knew he needed to fill it. Finally Barrow made a deal. DiMaggio would come to New York in return for $25,000 plus four players, but would have to remain with the Seals through the 1935 season. He did, finishing with a startling .398 average, 34 home runs, and an unprecedented total of 456 bases. Was he a greater hitter than Babe Ruth? New York wanted to know. "It was the best deal I ever made," Barrow recalled later. DiMaggio would begin the 1936 season as the most publicized, most eagerly awaited rookie in Yankee history. When the season got under way, people did not have long to wait for some answers.

On June 24 in Chicago, with his batting average .360, he hit two home runs in one inning and added two doubles to that feat. That season DiMaggio was a major factor in the Yankees' American League pennant. Against the National League New York Giants, DiMaggio had a great series. He batted .346, got nine hits, including three doubles, and drove in three Yankee runs. They took the series 4–2.

For the second game of the series, at the Polo Grounds, President Roosevelt threw out the first ball and stayed for the entire game. On the last out, the Giants' Hank Leiber hit a towering drive that chased DiMaggio 500 feet from the plate and between the two flights of stairs that led to the clubhouse. Instead of dashing up the steps to the clubhouse, however, he had the natural tact to remain standing where he was while the president left the stadium. As FDR was driven in his open limousine toward the centerfield exit gates, he passed DiMaggio and, amid the cheers of the crowd, saluted him. After the Giants lost the series, their manager, Bill Terry, sat in the clubhouse reflecting on the series. "I've always heard," said Terry, "that one player could make the difference between a losing team and a winner and I never believed it. Now I know it's true." That is how good DiMaggio was in his first season as a Yankee.

With the $35,000 he made as a rookie, he opened a family restaurant business on Fisherman's Wharf and bought his parents a new home in North Beach. He also received for his excellent performance the key to the city of San Francisco.

The rest, as they say, is history. DiMaggio's relations with the Yankee management and New York fans were periodically strained by his demands for sizable salary increases and delays over signing his contract, but that was only a footnote to a universal admiration for his ability. DiMaggio's manner was also a problem for some of the players, who considered him, variously, aloof, cold, uncommunicative, arrogant. The truth is that he was a provincial young man from North Beach who felt at ease only with his large family. "Fame irritated DiMaggio," wrote Jimmy Cannon.

> He is one of the loneliest men I've ever met and usually he
> moved through crowds. The flattery most men enjoy
> embarrasses him. I've spent most of my adult life in the
> newspaper business. Joe DiMaggio is the shyest public man I
> met. The great outfielder has been my friend since he broke
> in with the Yankees in 1936. I made the first road trip he took
> as a big leaguer. Since then I've spent vacations with him and
> we've loafed together in a lot of towns. I don't know him well
> although I've killed a lot of time in his company. I doubt if
> anyone fully understands his lonely character. He is more a
> spectator than a participant in any group. He is concealed and
> withdrawn.

DiMaggio regarded himself with an accurate and sometimes critical eye. When he performed at a level less than his idea of perfection, he reacted with cold fury. He was not sociable. "I don't want to be dined," he once said, "because I have done nothing to be dined about. Besides, I'm a ballplayer. I have my career in front of me. I cannot affort to stay out late and I can't neglect my diet. If I decline invitations, I hope my friends will realize the situation I'm in and not feel that I'm putting on a high hat or going Hollywood or Broadway."

But if he had what some regarded as personal limitations, his talent was unlimited. He also communicated a sense of great personal dignity in a professional game that was often raucous and rowdy. He may have been the greatest baseball player of all time, a judgment which Ernest Hemingway appears to have shared. In *The Old Man and the Sea* (1952), the old fisherman, Santiago, a baseball fan, is discussing the current season with the young boy Manolin. "The Yankees cannot lose," he says. Manolin fears "the Indians of Cleveland." But Santiago knows: "Have faith in the Yankees my son. Think of the great DiMaggio."

In 1940, the Yankees could not quite do it because they had such a wretched start, but coming out of the cellar, they showed that they were the best team in the league, and they turned the pennant race into a breathtaking duel with Cleveland and Detroit. On September 11, they won the opening game of a doubleheader against Cleveland, defeating the formidable Feller 3–1. Pitcher Ernie Bonham kept the Indians off the bases for the last six innings. John Drebinger: "With a magnificent spurt that defied the taunts and lemon tossings of an irate crowd of 33,471, the Yankees moved briefly into first place today when they tripped the Indians in the first game of the afternoon's doubleheader 3–1, beating Bob Feller behind their own rookie star Ernie Bonham." The Yankees were out of first place later that afternoon when they lost to Cleveland 5–3 and were showered with lemons and boos.

Successive headlines reflect the closeness and the intensity of the race that year. "Yankees Tighten Flag Race by Crushing Tigers 16–7." "Yanks Pennant Hopes Fade After Rout By Tigers; Indians Shut Out Red Sox." "Double Setback Halts Yank Pennant Dash; Tigers Yield First Place." Cleveland had moved into first place after taking a doubleheader in Philadelphia. In the first game, Feller yielded two hits. "Yanks Crushed By Browns; Indians Divide; Lead By Half Game as Tigers Win." "Yanks Win Two, Stay in the Race." "Tigers Clinch Pennant By Blanking Indians; Feller's 3-Hitter in Vain." "Indians Hold Second Place, Yanks Third as Season Closes." Thus Cleveland ended up one game out, the Yankees two games out in one of the closest races on record.

So it would be Detroit against Cincinnati in the 1940 World Series. The Tigers had two .340 hitters in home-run champion Hank Greenberg and the young outfielder Barney McCosky. The powerful Rudy York was at first base, the skilled Charlie Gehringer at second, Dick Bartell at short, Pinky Higgins at third. Their pitching staff included Schoolboy Rowe, Tommy Bridges, and the burly, irrepressible Bobo Newsom, so called because he called everyone "Bobo."

Bucky Walters and Paul Derringer led the Cincinnati pitching staff. Both had won twenty games during the regular season. The Reds had only two sluggers, Frank McCormick and catcher Ernie Lombardi. At times during the series it looked as if the surprising Detroit team was going to blast the Reds off the field, but they hung on to defeat Detroit in seven games. Detroit's capture of the American League pennant was voted by sportswriters that December as the second most surprising sports event of the year, the first being Dartmouth's fifth-down upset of mighty Cornell.

But wait till next year. The Dodgers added Kirby Higbe to their pitching roster after a deal with Philadelphia and then catcher Mickey Owen from the Cards; both were major additions to Dodger strength. DiMaggio won the American League batting championship with a .352, and he would be back. The Dodger management was worried about the effect the military draft would have on their team, which had an unusual number of bachelors. In fact, it would be a subway series between the Dodgers and the Yankees next year. Ace catcher Mickey Owen would drop that third strike. . . . But that is another year and another story, and a few weeks later the Japanese bombed Pearl Harbor and America was at war.

Anthropologists have said that sports is the real religion of America, and though that is an exaggeration, there is still much truth in it. For sports is indeed about both death and immortality, which are the central concerns of religion as well. About all athletics there exists a kind of double focus. The players on the field are always young, and year after year there in the stadium the game is always going on, as if time stood still. From that perspective, the stadium stands outside of time, and the ever-recurring game has intimations of immortality about it. The bands will always play, the crowds will always roar, the young will always strive.

But from another perspective, sports are about mortality. Defeat is a kind of death, irretrievable once the last out has been made or the last second run out on the clock, and we see how the players handle this death, well or badly. If we attend closely to the players, we see them enact a kind of death before our eyes. Their once-enormous skills decay and desert them, and they die a first death before the ultimate death we all share with them. DiMaggio's legs will betray him, Pete Reiser will run into the centerfield wall too often, Joe Louis will stagger around the ring and lose. And so sports are a deeply moving and deeply serious thing, a metaphor for life itself. Homer, Virgil, and Aristotle knew that, even if most contemporary professors do not.

The Man Who Knew Everything

Everyone assumed that large chunks were going to fall out of the familiar sky. Versailles, in 1919, was only a breather, and scores would be settled sooner rather than later. It was, as T. S. Eliot wrote in "East Coker," *"l'entre deux guerres."* "O dark dark dark," he wrote. "They all go into the dark." "Things fall apart," Yeats wrote in 1921, "the center cannot hold; / Mere anarchy is loosed upon the world, / The blood-dimmed tide is loosed." In 1939, from the perspective of one of the dives on Fifty-second Street, Auden looked back, "uncertain and afraid / As the clever hopes expire / Of a low dishonest decade."

Arnold Toynbee, Winchester and Balliol—what he called an "old-fashioned education in Greek and Latin classics"—struggled to believe that history made some sense and was not merely the cockroach nightmare of Kafka. The skies were falling on the dreaming spires of Arnold's and Newman's and Toynbee's Oxford, "steeped in sentiment as she lies, spreading her gardens to the moonlight, and whispering from her towers the last enchantments of the Middle Ages." Toynbee read Thucydides—in the original Greek of course—and the book struck him with the force of revelation. The defeat of Athens. Athens! The whole thing had happened then too—catastrophe, Belgium, the mud of the Somme, Verdun, disaster, the Peloponnesian War, and Alcibiades alive in the streets of the old gray city of London.

Toynbee came into the possession of an illumination that carried him beyond the chaos of the period between the wars. He would apply the pattern he saw in Thucydides to all of human history, soar beyond the ghastly particulars to the heights of generality and certainty. In the structured patterns of Toynbee's cycles, the wars of the twentieth century actually made sense, part of the great cycles of challenge and response that carry civilization to higher levels of cognition and creativity, decline hinging on to renewal. The philosophers of Ionia gazed into Toynbee's eyes. There had existed twenty-six civilizations. Toynbee could read Babylonian stone tablets—in the original of course. The declining phase of each civilization consisted of discernible phases: the breakdown, the disintegration, the dissolution. The breakdown of Egyptian civilization occurred in the sixteenth century before Christ. The dissolution came in the fifth century *anno Domini*. China lay "petrified" for a thousand years.

But a civilization could be renewed (his word was "transfigured") by a creative elite, just the sort of elite Oxford was supposed to produce. A civilization could move to a higher plane of spirituality, incorporate the spiritual insights of diverse cultures, the city of man moving toward the city of God. The pattern of history dictates the too-familiar process—the spread of sin and especially sensuality, vulgarization, violence, and philosophical confusion. Thucydides had seen it all. It had happened in Sumeria too. "If we now extend our synoptic view of the Sinic, Orthodox Christian and Western renaissance of a classical language and literature to embrace the whole course of each of these three movements from beginning to end, we shall notice that the Sinic and Orthodox Christian renaissances resemble each other, but differ from the Western renaissance in two respects." If you knew enough, history made sense.

Yes, beyond the meaninglessness of flux, there was a great pattern. The Logos could be discerned in History. God is with us after all. "We may and must pray," wrote Arnold Toynbee, "that a reprieve which God has granted to our society once will not be refused if we ask for it once again in a contrite spirit and with a broken heart."

His first six volumes were published between 1934 and 1939. In Volume XII, he made some modifications and answered his critics.

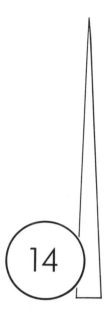

14

Things could be done. "Macadam gun-gray as the tunny's belt, / Leaping from Far Rockaway to the Golden Gate," wrote the visionary poet Hart Crane. By the time he wrote those lines, the visionary park and highway planner Robert Moses was making it happen. One of Moses' major highways in the year 1940 was the Southern State Parkway on Long Island. The ten-year-old boy sped along it of a weekend, his father driving the second-hand 1936 Buick that had been Simonized to a mirrorlike shine, going along the Southern State to Moses' Jones Beach, about an hour out from Queens on the southern shore of Long Island, the farms and grassland of central Long Island spinning away outside the windows of the car.

In those days, architects and city planners came from other cities, from other countries, to view Jones Beach. It had been begun by Moses with strong support from Governor Al Smith and finished in 1929 under Governor Franklin Roosevelt. It grew larger and more popular all through the years of the Great Depression, an embodiment in brick and stone and intricate planning of the fact that American creativity was still alive, and it provided a model for other cities and for the world.

For this was not just another beach. It was something genuinely new. Prior to Jones Beach, you had beaches attached to amusement parks, places like Coney Island, Asbury Park, and Atlantic City, which had a raucous and raunchy charm. The beach there was an adjunct to roller coasters, merry-go-rounds, throw the ball and win a dolly, guess your weight, and the smells of beer and hot dogs. Or you had vacant and almost deserted stretches of sand where people put up tents, and maybe there were some wooden shacks that were called bathhouses, just a place to change into your suit. Jones Beach resembled neither traditional beach.

At the end of the Southern State Parkway, the 1936 Buick arrived at the beach. As you approached, you could see in the distance a tall, Italian-style campanile, which turned out to be the water tower. At one point along the parkway, Stetsoned state police stopped the car, saluted, and handed out a card on which the Rules were neatly printed. No littering. No roadside picnicking. The policeman saluted the driver of the departing car. Violations drew summonses which became famous for their severity. At the beach, there were huge parking lots for the thousands of New Yorkers escaping the heat and crowding of a New York summer. And then the bathhouses. Bathhouses! Their low and sweeping lines were the subject of articles in architectural journals. No one had ever before conceived of bathhouses like these, punctuated with restaurants, chair and umbrella concessions, first-aid office, diaper-changing rooms.

Jones Beach was an organically conceived work of art, an architectural poem born in the mind of Robert Moses. You kept discovering new thematic elements and variations on familiar themes, all connected with the central nautical theme. The railing along the boardwalk was a ship's rail. The drinking fountains were operated by a miniature ship's wheel. The trash baskets were housed in what looked like ship's funnels. The flagpoles had crow's nests and were festooned with multicolored signal flags. The paved walks had mosaics of compasses and maps. Even the recreation provided along the boardwalks was evocative of life aboard an ocean liner: shuffleboard, quoits, Ping-Pong, deck tennis. On the miniature golf course, every hole included some reminder of the sea—a rusty anchor, an old keel, a rum keg.

Everywhere you saw, in concrete, in the ironwork of the directional signs, in mosaic, the central symbol of Jones Beach, the ubiquitous gray sea horse. All Jones Beach employees were uniformed as sailors. The lower ranks wore sailor suits and sailor caps, their superiors officer uniforms complete with gold braid. Each brass button was adorned, of course, with a sea horse.

The whole place was immaculate, like a good ship. A carelessly discarded match or cigarette butt was picked up by a clean-cut college boy in a sailor suit and deposited in one of the ship's funnel trash barrels. It was very much the point of this demonstration that the college boy did not use one of those sticks with a pin in it to pick up the trash, but *bent over* and picked it up. A spiked stick would indicate that Jones Beach expected people to litter. The bent-over youth in his sailor suit demonstrated the opposite and constituted a silent rebuke to the miscreant visitor. Indeed, every twenty mintues or so a bugle call sounded over the public address system, and a voice "thanked" the people for keeping Jones Beach clean. And they did. A reprobate would hustle his empty Budweiser can to one of the trash cans. Luncheon material was neatly disposed of.

Jones Beach, indeed, was one of the finest flowers of the progressive, reformist sensibility in America. It not only provided recreation for the urban masses, it provided *healthy* recreation: the word "wholesome" pervaded its press write-ups. But even beyond that, it aimed to "improve" them, make them neater and more respectful of each other and of both property and nature. This was not Coney Island. This was the way things really should be according to the progressive sensibility—rational, tasteful, healthy, convenient, and uplifting—the individual invited to achieve his best self and take a quiet pride in this momentous civic achievement.

Jones Beach was written up in the authoritative *Architectural Forum:* "Usually a public institution of any kind in this country has been the occasion for especially dull architecture and walls of cheerless dimension which invite only the scribbling of small obscenities. But Mr. Moses, being essentially a romanticist, has revived the handicraft spirit in his designers, with the result that the equipment at Jones Beach exhibits irrelevant and endearing good spirits. The architecture has the great virtue of being scaled down to the size of a good time." The term "irrelevant" as used here by the *Architectural Forum* bears some reflection. It is architecturally ideological. It means that sea horses are "irrelevant" to swimming at the beach, not "functional" as the reigning ideology would demand. But the ideology of Jones Beach was not functional but perfectionist. Indeed, from a perfectionist perspective, the gray sea horses are highly functional. As an English journalist commented, "This is the finest seashore playground ever given the public anywhere in the world."

The whole thing, and a very great deal more, was conceived by a Yale graduate of the class of 1909, Robert Moses, a wellborn, highly intelligent New Yorker, with good political and social connections and imbued from an early age with the traditions of civil idealism and good government that flowed from Lincoln Steffens, Jacob Riis, Ida Tarbell, and Teddy Roosevelt. At Yale, the intense and dark-eyed young man wrote poems about beauty and the beauty of truth for the *Yale Literary Magazine*. Electric with energy, he participated in everything, including the varsity swimming team, and throughout his life was partial to aquatic pursuits. In late night bull sessions, he spoke passionately of a career in public service.

After Yale he took a Ph.D. at Oxford and wrote a lucid, hard-edged dissertation on the British civil service. Returning to New York, he struck his friends as burning with ideas. They recalled that Moses would go on walking tours of New York, emitting a cascade of ideas about improving the city. He wanted to refurbish a decaying Central Park and include shelters so that mothers could change diapers without going all the way home. He envisioned better traffic flow, highways, and bridges. He wanted an apolitical civil service, based entirely upon merit, independent of the fetid crooks of Tammany and the machine. When he made his arguments before the Board of Estimate or the Good Government organization, his mastery of the facts was always formidable, his tone businesslike and reasonable. Brought into the reforming administration of Mayor John Purroy Mitchel in 1914, Moses experienced temporary setbacks in achieving his goals, but his instinct for political power in New York City and New York State was virtually infallible over the years, and a strong case can be made that Robert Moses's career had more influence on the lives of more citizens than that of any president of the United States during this century.

Among his burning ideas was one of irrefutable validity. New York's crowded population was bursting the seams, hungering for a walk in the woods, a swim in the sea, but it was devilishly difficult for people of the inner city to get from the canyons of the city to open land or water. You could drive over the Queensboro Bridge and then for miles and hours along the existing roads of Long Island. Among the millionaires' estates along the North Shore, there were few segments of the shoreline that were not marked "Private." The roads out along the South Shore among the potato farms were primitive. The only way to get from Manhattan to New Jersey or Staten Island was the ferry. Moses understood the sense of suffocation, and one answer to it, he saw, was Long Island.

During the early 1920s, Moses and his wife Mary had visited friends in the town of Babylon on Long Island's South Shore, and he began to incorporate the entire region into his gestating vision. Here, only thirty miles from Manhattan, was a virtually deserted paradise, the haunt of a few fishermen who plied Great South Bay. Moses bought a motorboat which he called the *Bob* and began exploring the bay and its tributaries. He spent hours talking with old fishermen, sounding their memories regarding local history, and he found old books and maps in the Babylon town library that filled in some of the blanks. He was particularly drawn to a long sand-barrier beach about five miles off the southern shore of Long Island, hard to pinpoint on the old maps because, year after year, the sea kept reshaping it and shifting its position. He found that "Fire Island," the section farthest east, was really a corruption of the eighteenth-century name "Five Islands," that territory then being divided by inlets—pirate lairs—which no longer existed.

In the old books in the Babylon library, Moses learned about a Major Thomas Jones who had fought for King William at the Battle of the Boyne in 1690 and had been rewarded for his services with a king's commission as a "privateer," which meant that he was permitted under English law to operate as a pirate, except with respect to English ships. Privateer Jones amassed a fortune through such pillage. In 1695, for a barrel of cider, he purchased from the local Indians thousands of acres along the South Shore of Long Island, populated the place with his pirate crews, went into whaling, built a magnificent mansion, and married a beautiful woman with the remarkable name of Freelove Townsend.

In the early 1920s, nothing much had changed on Jones Beach since Pirate Jones, Jones the Whaler, had strolled there with Freelove Townsend. When Robert Moses beached his motorboat on the wet sand and stepped ashore, there were no human beings in view, only miles of gleaming white sand stretching into the distance, dunes and windswept scrub grass, and a splendid variety of beach birds, sandpipers, gulls, herons. Moses was no lover of unspoiled nature. When he looked at the deserted sand strip, his mind was full of parks and pavilions, of fresh air and recreation for the masses, not nature in the raw but, in the eighteenth-century phrase, nature methodized, not wilderness but parks in the tradition of Lord Burlington and Capability Brown. Moses was the greatest landscape architect in twentieth-century America.

At his cottage in Babylon, Moses pored over maps of Long Island. It seemed possible to draw a straight line for a parkway that mostly traversed South Shore water-supply property. Such land would not need to be purchased or condemned by the state. His mind moved beyond the as-yet-unbuilt Jones Beach to other park and beach possibilities along the South Shore, to deserted promontories, empty meadows, scrub grass, and empty coves. It moved as well to Long Island's North Shore and was not fazed by the gigantic problems that would loom there: the North Shore was dominated by millionaires, men of vast wealth and formidable political power, people with names like Pratt, Phipps, Vanderbilt, Whitney, and Morgan, whose green acres and private golf clubs crouched behind walls of stone and brick. Moses's imagination extended beyond Long Island to places like Troy, Utica, Albany. He drew up a *State Park Plan for New York,* which was unusual not so much for the large bond plan it proposed—$15 million—as for the philosophy behind it. Moses was not proposing a traditional conservation plan, buying land to keep it pristine, but a plan for recreation and permanent improvement, along with a major highway development that would allow people to get to the parks and beaches.

Moses sold a skeptical Governor Al Smith on the idea. Together they visited a barren and wintry South Shore, and Moses conjured up for the governor his sweeping vision of beaches and parks and parkways, and families at picnic tables in the leafy shade or reclining on the best beaches in the world. Brought into the magic circle of Moses's vision, the tough but honest and idealistic governor signed on. The Smith organization pushed the $15-million bond issue through the state legislature.

During the summer of 1923, Moses went on long walking tours around Long Island, taking endless notes. He tramped along the shores of the island, across potato fields, past shuttered and fenced estates and through the scrub pine. Jones Beach would be only the beginning. In Hampton Bays he discovered miles of vacant beach. On the North Shore, he discerned the great beach potentiality of Sunken Meadow. The potato farmers and Wall Street magnates who chatted with the thin, sad-eyed man had not the slightest idea that he had serious designs on their land.

Moses's restless mind kept enlarging the whole idea. He wanted state parks, not only at Jones Beach but on Fire Island as well, and along the South Shore at Montauk Point and Hampton Bays. On the North Shore, he wanted beaches at Sunken Meadow, Wildwood, Lloyd Neck, and Orient Point. He wanted, in the center of the island, parks on the Belmont and Yoakum estates. He envisioned two great parkways, the Southern State and the Northern State, with a connecting link between them, 124 miles of parkway—not just good roads, but roads landscaped like a private garden, parks in themselves, so that even as people headed for one of the beaches, they would be driving through parks.

Governor Al Smith, a cigar-smoking product of the city, had very little interest in the outdoors, but Moses' conception of doing magnificent things for the ordinary people of the state appealed to him, and he himself became enthusiastic about beaches and green spaces and families together in the wholesome outdoors. He invited Moses to head up the whole project and made him president of the Long Island State

Park Commission. Moses proceeded to draft innocuous-looking legislation which, when read closely and correctly understood, gave him the power to acquire the land he neded, even against the wishes of its owners. If they would not sell at a negotiated price, Moses had the power to have the land condemned by the state and seized.

A typical incident. A Brooklyn-born farmer named John Jacob Rasweiller had a farm in Malverne on property scheduled for Moses's Southern State Parkway. Robert Caro quotes his son, P. G. Rasweiller, in his fine book about Moses: "The farm was going good. Then Moses came one day. He introduced himself as 'I'm Robert Moses, representing the State of New York. We're going to put a parkway through this section of Long Island.' He was very polite, very diplomatic, at first. But when he saw my father wasn't going to sell, he stood up in our kitchen and he said: 'You know, Mr. Rasweiller, the state is all-supreme when it comes to a condemning procedure. If we want your land, we can take it.'" The next day a Moses engineer walked onto the farm and set up his surveying instruments. Asked whether they had court papers to thus trespass, the engineer and his assistants said they did not. Rasweiller got his shotgun and ordered them off. Moses immediately called for the state police. The state police arrived and told the engineering team, "You can't go on this man's land without papers." Rasweiller went to court, and Moses was forced to pay him more per acre than he had first offered, but the best acreage on the farm went to the parkway.

Nor was wealth and power up on the North Shore any guarantee of tranquility. During the summer of 1924, the Vanderbilts, Pratts, Whitneys, and the rest noticed a curious phenomenon. Surveying teams appeared outside their gates and began setting up their equipment, pointing their little telescopes at the great houses themselves. When servants were sent out to inquire, they returned with the astounding information that the surveyors were laying out the route for a new parkway. Moses did not win all of his legal and political battles on the North Shore, but backed by Smith, he won most of them. "A Few Rich Golfers Blocking Plans for a State Park" read a typical *New York Times* headline. In a bruising, legal-political battle, Moses was forced to put an eleven-mile kink in his parkway to protect some choice Wheatley Hills property, but the Northern State Parkway progressed relentlessly eastward.

During the summer of 1926, Moses invited several of the best architects in the nation out to the vacant sands of Jones Beach. They included landscape architect Gilmore Clarke, who had designed the new Bronx River Parkway, and Harvey Corbett, architect, among much else, of Rockefeller Center, as well as numerous Long Island mansions. It quickly became evident to the small group of men who accompanied Moses that what he had in mind was no ordinary beach. Pointing here and there and drawing on the back of an envelope, Moses indicated where the bathhouses would be, the connecting roads, the swimming pools and boardwalks, the parking lots. His bathhouses were to have 10,000 lockers apiece. There would be swimming pools with platform diving facilities and another beach on the bay side of the sand strip. There would be solaria and restaurants with colored umbrellas. Nurseries for children. Games areas. Green grass and foliage and flowers on the sandbar. This would not be "public building" in the traditional pedestrian manner, but light, airy, brilliant, inventive, something to raise the spirits.

Moses wanted a focal point for Jones Beach, something visible from a distance that said "Jones Beach" to the approaching motorists. He decided upon the water tower. This would certainly not be the usual metal tank upon four metal stilts, but something striking. Harvey Corbett suggested an Italian campanile and began to describe several varieties. Moses chose one resembling the campanile in Venice, and it came to pass.

He rejected the first set of designs submitted to him for the bathhouses and selected the designs of an unknown young architect named Herbert Magoon. These called for one long, low, sweeping structure of brick, stone, and green tinted glass. The austerity of the design when seen from a distance gave way to an unexpected richness of detail as you approached. Another bathhouse of stone and brick was more playful, Moorish in its effects. Another resembled a medieval castle. Moses himself chose the material to be used from samples shown to him. One basic element would be Ohio sandstone, gray with undertones of gray and blue, a kind of stone sister to the sea itself. The brick he wanted he saw on the facade of the Barbizon Hotel on East Sixty-third Street in Manhattan. When the architects objected that these were both among the most expensive building materials available, Moses did not hesitate. They were the most appropriate for the project, and he would have them.

Moses became a relentless force in the state, disposing of millions of dollars in contracts, employing a vast work force. By the fall of 1928, the watershed properties along the Merrick Road had been filled with bathhouses, baseball fields, picnic tables, and bridle paths. There were lakes, floats, diving boards. Heckscher State Park contained miles of motor road and bridle paths, ball fields and bathhouses containing thousands of lockers. More of the same appeared at Sunken Meadow, Wildwood, Orient Beach, Montauk Point. Thousands of lockers became available at Valley Stream.

Moses had particularly strong support from the *New York Times* and the *Herald Tribune*, but his treatment by the press as a whole was encomiastic. Adjectives like "fearless," "brilliant," "persistent," "tall," and "muscular" festooned the write-ups about Moses in the newspapers.

Moses preserved the historic battlefields at Saratoga, Oriskany, and Fort Stanton. He purchased parkland on Whiteface Mountain. During the the summer of 1928, he expanded the few, scattered, state parklands to over 2.2 million acres and had commenced linking them to a state highway system. He bought large tracts of land in the Lake George region and mapped out plans for a park system there.

To Moses's growing power and startling achievements the political backing of Governor Al Smith was indispensable. In 1928, with Smith's successor, Franklin Roosevelt, who hated Moses, the equation was rather different. Roosevelt had been necessary to Smith's statewide career as the Tammany politician from the fourth ward rose to the governor's mansion and reached for the presidency of the United States. The Catholic politician needed the support of a prominent Protestant; the man from the sidewalks of New York needed an upstater; the poorly educated, self-made man needed the trappings of respectable backing. Roosevelt solved these problems for Smith: the Harvard graduate, the Episcopalian, the squire of Hyde Park in Dutchess County, the relative of Theodore Roosevelt, secretary of the navy under Wilson, Roosevelt was perfect. He and Smith formed a close political alliance, though they were not close friends, and Roosevelt was uncomfortable with Smith's cronies at the Tiger Room in the Biltmore.

Smith's circle, in turn, regarded Roosevelt as a lightweight in politics, an amateur, who knew little about state issues and less about the realities of practical politics. At the 1920 Democratic convention, Roosevelt, still lithe and athletic, had seconded Smith's token nomination in a ringing speech. At the 1924 convention, now terribly crippled by polio, Roosevelt, nevertheless, was Smith's floor manager and, struggling to the podium with his leg braces and crutches, delivered the great "happy warrior" speech in nomination of Smith. The speech was entirely the work of a Smith aide named Joseph Proskauer and is connected with an amusing bit of political arcana. When Proskauer showed Roosevelt the speech, Roosevelt read it and refused to deliver it. He felt that it would be ridiculous to use Wordsworth's "happy warrior" line. It was too "poetic for a bunch of politicians." After some acrimony back and forth, the Smith camp told Roosevelt that he would either give that speech or no speech. He gave it, and it marked an important step toward his eventual nomination eight years later.

Under the Smith administration in Albany, Roosevelt, as chairman of the Taconic State Park Commission, clashed repeatedly with Moses in his capacity as president of the Long Island Park Commission, with the governor settling all disputes, usually in favor of Moses, who was the better political infighter. In 1928, Smith finally won the Democratic nomination, with Roosevelt again his floor manager, and he and his strategists decided that they needed Roosevelt to run for the New York governorship in order to help the Smith candidacy with upstate farmers and Protestants. Roosevelt, still weakened by the polio, tried to escape by traveling to Warm Springs and genuinely did not want to run, but Smith reached him by telephone and prevailed upon him to run for the good of the party.

On November 6, 1928, Smith went down with 87 electoral votes, losing even New York, to Hoover's 444, but despite the Republican landslide, Roosevelt won the governorship by a narrow margin and became a key man in the Democrats' future. Moses no doubt looked on this turn of events with some dismay. The governor now was Roosevelt, a man who seemed to hate him and for whom he had no intellectual respect.

There then transpired a peculiar—indeed, opaque—episode in the history of politics. Smith generously offered to give the new governor any aid and advice he could, sent repeated messages to the capitol, and hung around Albany waiting to be called. No call came from Roosevelt. When he offered advice on the inaugural address, he was rebuffed. When he asked Roosevelt to retain the services of Moses, Roosevelt was noncommittal and soon indicated to Moses that he was stripping him of the only state office he had the power to take away from him, secretary of state. Roosevelt gave it to boss Ed Flynn of the Bronx.

Roosevelt's dislike of Moses was open, and Moses's contempt for Roosevelt was also unconcealed. His acid comments about Roosevelt, a "pretty poor excuse for a man," as well as his derision about Eleanor's looks and voice, probably got back to the Roosevelt circle. But for Roosevelt's callous treatment of Smith, biographers and historians have not come up with a persuasive explanation. No doubt Roosevelt wanted to appear to be his own man. No doubt he knew that many around Smith considered his intellectual ability negligible. He was certainly planning to run for the presidency in 1932, and Smith was potentially a rival. But none of this explains the rudeness, which amounted to cruelty. Robert Sherwood has spoken of a side of Roosevelt that was "petty" and "vindictive." The historian Oscar Handlin writes that "Roosevelt was never at his best in getting rid of people who were no longer useful to him." There is speculation that

Roosevelt, in power now, simply took a cruel, if petty, pleasure in letting Smith know it.

But Roosevelt had a bitter lesson coming, a lesson that he could not indulge what may have been the special malice of a cripple, even a presidential cripple. In early 1935, Roosevelt tried to pressure LaGuardia to fire Moses by having his secretary of the interior, Harold Ickes, threaten to cut off federal funds New York needed. LaGuardia stalled, but Moses went public. Instantly, as if the lights had suddenly been turned on in a dark room, Ickes and Roosevelt stood exposed as corruptly wielding the power of the federal treasury in pursuit of a personal vendetta. "There are certain facts that should be known to the public," announced Moses to the press. It was obvious that special Order 129 restricting funds had been formulated by the White House for the sole purpose of levering him out of his job, even though Ickes himself was on the record as considering him "honest and competent." The reason for the vendetta was that "I . . . was not sufficiently friendly to the administration." The American people deserved to know what was happening. "The federal appropriations for public works and work relief are the funds of all the people of the country. . . . If personal or political considerations are to govern the expenditure of public works and work relief money, this fact should be known to the public."

Roosevelt found himself caught in a firestorm of public fury. The newspaper editorials were savage. The *Herald Tribune:* "If Mayor LaGuardia allows one of the ablest of his public servants to be dismissed by a Washington official, without shadow of cause, through a secret ukase so extraordinary and so contemptible that the official himself is ashamed publicly to admit it, then it seems to us that Mr. LaGuardia might as well resign his Mayorality right now." The *American* abandoned complete sentences: "Bureaucracy! Patronage! Politics! If the order stands it will be a lasting stain on the record of the Administration." The *New York Times* threw its ordinary gray caution to the winds: "If he [LaGuardia] has the backbone of a lamprey, he will stand by Bob Moses, right through to that Judgment Day which he is himself so fond of evoking." The good-government organizations flocked to the Moses ramparts, issuing thunderous pronunciamentos: the Long Island Chamber of Commerce, the Conference on Port Development of the City of New York, the Park Association of New York City, the City Club, the Bronx Board of Trade, the New York Board of Trade and the Merchants' Association of Sheepshead Bay, the Elmhurst Community Council, the Jackson Heights Taxpayers' Association, the North Woodside Community Organization, the Astoria Property Owners' Association, the Madison Manor Civic Association, the Atlantic

Business Mens' and Taxpayers' Association, the Automobile Club of New York, the Corona Community Council, and the New York Chapter of the American Institute of Architects.

The press smoked Roosevelt out. *New York Times* headline: "President Aware of Order on Moses." Everyone now knew that the president was not only "aware," but that he had issued the order himself. Delegations from 147 civic, business, and social organizations met in protest in the auditorium of the State Chamber of Commerce Building on Liberty Street. The Letters-to-the-Editor pages were deluged. The White House was inundated with indignant mail, and Roosevelt's advisers and old friends turned against him. Congress began to consider formal investigation of the matter. Powerful reform elements in New York politics let it be known that they were commissioning a legal analysis of Order 129; their lawyers soon arrived at the conclusion that the order was "an arbitrary and capricious fiat without any authority in law" and a breach of "governmental morality." Roosevelt asked an old friend and associate, Joseph Price, whether the president of the United States was not "entitled to one personal grudge." Replied Price, "No."

Al Smith's revenge was particularly sweet. He bided his time in his office on the thirty-second floor of the Empire State Building and let the pressure on Roosevelt boil up. Then he called in reporters and issued a magisterial statement: "Over ten years ago, Bob Moses was talking to me about a single unified plan for park and highway development for the state." He praised Moses's conduct of the plan. He said that it would be ridiculous not to permit him to complete it. He characterized Order 129 as "narrow, political and vindictive." With a straight face he said that he could "not believe that the president could be a party to it."

The very next day, according to Ickes, the president concluded that "a retreat was in order." Roosevelt dictated a letter to be signed by Ickes to the effect that Order 129 was not meant to be "retroactive." The letter was falsely dated to indicate that it had been written the day before Al Smith's detonation. Later, recalling the Moses affair in a letter to a friend, Ickes wrote: "There can be no doubt of the porcupinish disposition of Moses. And is he clever! . . . He put it all over President Roosevelt and me in that squabble."

The opening ceremonies of the Triborough Bridge took place on July 11, 1936. Ickes initially was invited only as a "general spectator," though his personal appeals finally got him a "special invitation." Roosevelt himself at first declined to attend, until it was brought home to him that he could not politically afford to pass up an event like this in a presidential election year. Roosevelt stipulated, however, that he not be introduced by Moses, and LaGuardia agreed to introduce the president. At a meeting in the mayor's office, Moses showed LaGuardia the timetable for the ceremonies. Roosevelt was scheduled to speak for five minutes. LaGuardia pounded his fist on his desk and said this was ridiculous. Moses was conciliatory. He gave Roosevelt six minutes.

During those Depression years, paradoxically, LaGuardia and Moses created in New York and also across the nation a sense of civic possibility and optimism that has never been recaptured. The diminutive Little Flower, whose feet dangled in the air when he sat in his swivel chair, who often looked at visitors to his office through a cage of his fingers, and was famous for his shock of black hair and his huge Stetson, was ubiquitous all over the city. He rode on fire engines and in police-motorcycle sidecars. He would appear at precinct stations and lead police door-breaking raids on malefactors. One freezing morning he appeared at dawn at the Municipal Market, and to a police bugle call mounted a flatbed truck: he declared war on gangsters in the artichoke business. He relentlessly attacked "tin horn" gamblers and warned housewives away from the "racket" of Grade A milk. He slashed thousands of political appointees from the city rolls and balanced the budget. He read the Sunday comics over the radio for the kids: "And now, seeee, there is this character Flattop. . . ."

What old New Yorkers remember today is how clean things were. In memory, the streets glistened, and no one even thought of throwing garbage out of a window or spraying subways with spray-can graffiti. An intellectual New Yorker and a splendid writer, Lionel Abel, remembers it this way:

> Once the WPA jobs were opened to the unemployed, real
> change came over the city. The breadlines disappeared, and
> that was very important because of the psychological effect
> the lines had. And then the WPA workers went into the parks
> and streets and cleaned and polished and decorated them so
> that this city of New York, with all its millions, among whom
> so many were certainly ill-housed and shabbily dressed, was
> suddenly spic-and-span, swept from one end to the other, its
> piles of trash removed. New York was, I think, during this
> period, a model city with respect to the cleanliness of its
> streets and parks and the expeditious disposal of its waste—
> not all of the city to be sure, but yet at the height of the
> Depression, for the most part, it looked better than it has ever
> looked since. Much as been written against the WPA projects,
> about the waste of government money on jobs poorly
> performed or simply not attended to, and no doubt some of

the criticism has point. But in fact, the WPA workers did a great deal for the beauty and cleanliness of this city, whose features, so begrimed today, were well cared for at that time. Maybe the WPA workers were overpaid for what they did. Many of them worked only part of the time, and no doubt then it was easier to keep the city proper. But the WPA workers did more than keep the city clean; they also decorated it. Artists from the Artists' Project, among whom were painters like Arshile Gorky, Willem de Kooning, Philip Evergood, and Philip Guston, painted murals in banks and government buildings. Malraux had said that no one wants to look at an art work in a sea of blood. The artists were helping the government by their work, saying, there can't possibly be a sea of blood here, for look, here are works of art.

LaGuardia and Moses often clashed in screaming matches in the mayor's City Hall office. Privately Moses referred to the mayor as "that wop son of a bitch" and "that dago bastard." But at the most important level, both men were idealists about the city and its possibilities. They complemented and deeply respected one another. Moses needed LaGuardia's political support. LaGuardia basked in the glow of Moses's civic accomplishments, and Moses made sure that LaGuardia was present and received full credit for the opening of every new park, bridge, tennis court, highway, swimming pool, or housing project. For major opening ceremonies, Moses staged gala events, with military bands and massed ranks of uniformed police and state troopers, as the Little Flower trotted along in an "inspection."

Moses opened playgrounds at a breathtaking rate: 60 in 1934, 71 in 1935, 72 in 1936, 52 in 1937. Bathhouse facilities arose at Jacob Riis Park in Rockaway. They have fallen into sad disrepair today. Other beach parks arose at Orchard, Fort Tryon, Pelham Bay. Under Moses's administration, they remained immaculate.

The old Yale swimmer built gigantic new neighborhood swimming pools, and *Fortune* magazine called 1936 the "swimming pool year," as Moses opened one per week that summer. These pools were 330 feet long and 165 feet wide—enormous. They had subsidiary pools at each end, a wading pool for tots and a deep-water pool for platform diving, facilities for the masses better than Yale's. Roosevelt's aide, Harry Hopkins, called the pool in Astoria, Queens, the "finest pool in all the world." Moses staged the openings at night so the underwater lighting would be more spectacular as Olympic stars swam in the big pool and dived from the high platform.

Moses named the playground at Williamsburg Bridge Plaza the "Fiorello H. LaGuardia Playground" and cracked that the best thing about it was the name. The year 1940 was the first year of operation for the Bronx-Whitestone Bridge, and 6,317,489 vehicles passed through its tollbooths.

In his book, *The Power Broker,* a masterful study of Robert Moses, Robert Caro makes a number of severe criticisms of the master builder. He shows that Moses was ruthless and arrogant, power hungry, that he tore down neighborhoods and expropriated property, that he may have discriminated against the poor and the black in keeping railroads away from Jones Beach and elsewhere, that many of his smaller New York playgrounds lack the imaginative flair of his favorite earlier projects. Mr. Caro reminds us that Moses insisted that he was not Jewish, an insistence that enraged many Jewish groups but certainly did not cost him the support of the *New York Times* or the powerful New York Jewish establishment. Moses's position was that Judaism was a religion in the same sense as Christianity and that he was not religious. LaGuardia was Italian and Jewish by extraction, but he was not a Catholic. Bob Moses was Jewish by extraction, but not by religion. He was a Yalie, a New Yorker, and an American.

Moses, as Mr. Caro shows, surely had his faults, but on Mr. Caro's own showing, his positive accomplishments, in the end, disinterested and for the good of his New York and national community, render his mistakes and personal faults insignificant—all the more so from our present perspective, when, for example, New York's Westway replacement for Moses's own West Side Highway was stalled for a decade by courts, bureaucrats, and squabbling politicians and then finally abandoned. New York's Senator Daniel Patrick Moynihan summed up the situation in a recent interview: "There is a kind of stasis that is beginning to settle into our public life. We cannot reach decisions. Central Park could not be conceivably built today as it was when there was enough power in Tammany Hall to make the decision. Four and a half years after they dug the first spade of earth for the new IRT, Commodore Vanderbilt rode the length of it in his private subway car. They laid the cornerstone of the Empire State Building on St. Patrick's Day in 1930, and it was up in fifteen months. We don't have that capacity. I worry that we're fearful that we won't be as good as the people who came before us."

Asked what those earlier people possessed that we now do not, Senator Moynihan replied: "Confidence. It comes to that." Perhaps Robert Moses would not have prevailed over the inertial and politically contradictory forces that defeated the great Westway project, but no one should bet on it.

In retrospect, Robert Moses, striding out of the Depression years on a wave of achievement and civic purpose, may be seen to have much in common with those other great figures of the period, much in common with his grinning enemy, Franklin Roosevelt, with Joe DiMaggio and Albert Einstein and Joe Louis, Mayor LaGuardia and Don Budge, champions all, certainly, but all expressive too of an intact will, which was part of the culture of 1940, and of a national buoyancy that rose above economic catastrophe and achieved excellence.

At the End

He was forty-four and had proved that there are second acts in American lives. The previous year he had hired young Frances Kroll to be his secretary in Hollywood. He did not want anyone who was working for the movie studios; he wanted his new novel to be composed in secrecy. Frances was "unprepared for the poetic, handsome face. I had expected him to be older. The faded blonde hair and pale skin were signs of middle age or illness. The eyes were very blue and inquiring. He nodded in greeting—a funny little gesture, as if he were doffing a hat except that he wasn't wearing one." Sheilah Graham remembers his habit of tilting his head to one side when asking a tricky or arch question.

By 1940, he had almost conquered his destructive binges— "benders," in the slang of that time. He tippled steadily, with a gin bottle always in his desk drawer at MGM, but MGM thought he was worth $1,500 a week in 1940 money. Gloria Swanson recalled that "if you sat in a room with him, he'd give you the feeling that somewhere around the corner something exciting was gonna happen. He was warm and wonderful and producers were in awe of him."

David Niven was starring in a movie called *Raffles* but had been called to duty with the British army. The script was bad. Scott hero-worshipped Niven, a man of great charm, tall, lean, and elegant, who was going off, perhaps to die. He fixed up the script for $1,200.

Scott thought that *Tender is the Night,* published five years earlier, was a much greater book than Steinbeck's *Grapes of Wrath,* which was a best-seller that year, and a greater book than Hemingway's *For Whom the Bell Tolls,* another best-seller. He wondered, tentatively, whether clever people thought so too. But, a professional, and hard at the core, he knew he was right.

It was late in the fall of 1940 before Scott was able to give full attention to *The Last Tycoon,* but he moved forward so quickly that it was obvious that he had thought the major themes through. "We established a routine," recalls his young secretary. "He turned out pages and I typed—first in triple-spaced drafts giving him ample room for making corrections, then re-typing in double-space and then, likely as not, another retyping for the 'first' draft."

Tender Is the Night had been full of Spenglerian doom, the going-down of the West, a civilization rotten at the core. Dick Diver had said goodbye to all of his ancestors. In *The Last Tycoon,* however, with the darkest of clouds looming across the Atlantic, Fitzgerald's estimate of the situation was different, and he felt that America was different.

He was a social anti-Semite from Princeton, also antiblack, but something changed in him, and he made his hero a Jew. With Hitler looming over the continent of Europe, Fitzgerald was glad of Roosevelt's reelection, telegraphing his secretary:

> SLEEPING LATE STOP STUFF ON DINING ROOM TABLE HOORAY FOR ROOSEVELT.

The "stuff" was manuscript *Last Tycoon.*

A few weeks later, at the end of November 1940, Fitzgerald experienced an attack of dizziness while in Schwab's drugstore on Sunset Boulevard in Hollywood. His doctor ordered him to bed, where he was able to write for a couple of hours a day on a piece of board. Frances Kroll remembers her last glimpse of him alive. "I was going to my car; he was going on to Schwab's Drug Store on Sunset Boulevard, just a couple of blocks away. He was wearing a dark topcoat and a gray homburg hat. As we kept pace, I looked over at him and was chilled by his image, like a shadowy figure in an old photograph. His outfit and pallor were alien to the style and warmth of Southern California—as if he were not at home here, had just stepped off and was dressed to leave on the next train."

Fitzgerald believed that he was making a good recovery from his heart attack. On December 13, he wrote to his wife Zelda, then in a mental hospital, that "the novel is about three-quarters through and I think I can go on till January 12 without doing any stories or going back to the studio. . . . The cardiogram shows that my heart is repairing itself but it will be a gradual process that will take some months. It is odd that the heart is one of the organs that does repair itself."

His heart was not repairing itself. In her last memoir of Fitzgerald, Sheilah Graham remembers that during the night of December 19–

20 he slept restlessly, getting up to pace the floor. He was worrying about the last chapter of *The Last Tycoon*. "It's the chapter. I can't make it hang together." Graham, a newspaper columnist, left in the morning to interview Spencer Tracy. When she returned to the apartment, Fitzgerald was joyful. "I've been able to fix it," he said. "Baby, this book will be good." They decided to celebrate with dinner at Lyman's, a restaurant on Hollywood Boulevard, and then see a preview of a movie starring Melvyn Douglas and Rosalind Russell, *This Thing Called Love*. When the lights went on and they started back up the aisle of the theater, Fitzgerald stumbled and held her arm. As they drove home, he told her, "I had the same dizziness as that time in Schwab's."

The next morning he slept late, dressing around noon. They planned to eat some sandwiches Sheilah Graham had bought at a local delicatessen. She recalls:

> I settled into the sofa with a biography of Beethoven. To reinforce the book, I asked Scott if it was alright for me to play the *Eroica* on the record player. . . . Scott smiled and sank into the dark green armchair with the latest *Princeton Alumni Weekly*, focusing on an article about Princeton. A few minutes later, Scott stood up and said, "I want something sweet, I'm going to Schwab's for some ice cream."
>
> "But the doctor is coming soon," I reminded him. "I'm sure he'll have some good news about your heart. Will a Hershey bar do?" I went to the drawer in my bedroom where I had put it for later munching and gave it to Scott. He savored it slowly while, as I found out later, writing down the nicknames of football heroes of his class opposite their names in the magazine. We both looked up at the same time and smiled at each other while he licked his fingers and then we settled back to the reading. A few minutes later, while the *Eroica* shrilled its prophecy, I half saw Scott jump to his feet and clutch the mantlepiece as though to steady himself. He would often stand up suddenly when he had an idea for some writing. Or was it the dizziness again? Before I could reach him, he fell to the floor, spread-eagled on his back. His eyes were closed and he was breathing heavily.

Miss Graham tried to pour some brandy between his clenched teeth, but by the time the doctor arrived, he was dead.

Eileen West's watch stopped at 2:55 the next afternoon. December 22, 1940, the instant she was killed. Nathanael West had written *Miss Lonelyhearts*, *The Day of the Locust*, and much else, along with many movie scripts, but he had always been a lousy driver, dangerous. They were driving north along Route 111 in his station wagon, heading for Highway 80 and El Centro. The other driver saw the station wagon from the highway. It did not stop at the intersection. West's body lay on the highway for twenty-five minutes before the police got there. Friends thought that he had been preoccupied with his knowledge of Scott's death the day before: he had been Scott's closest friend in Hollywood. Both bodies were cared for at Pierce Brothers Mortuary. A day of the locust.

ENVOI

On December 8, 1941, President Franklin Roosevelt addressed a joint session of Congress to declare war against the empire of Japan. As the president entered the packed chamber, he was greeted by a cataract of cheers, applause, and even rebel yells. Solemnly, and with the ringing precision of that Roosevelt articulation, he delivered what many considered to be the best piece of brief oratory since Lincoln's Gettysburg Address:

> Yesterday, December 7, 1941—a date which will live in infamy—the United States of America was suddenly and deliberately attacked by naval and air forces of the Empire of Japan.
>
> The United States was at peace with that nation and, at the solicitation of Japan, was still in conversation with its Government and its Emperor looking toward the maintenance of peace in the Pacific. Indeed, one hour after Japanese air squadrons had commenced bombing in Oahu, the Japanese Ambassador to the United States and his colleague delivered to the Secretary of State a formal reply to a recent American message. While this reply stated that it seemed useless to continue the existing diplomatic negotiations, it contained no threat or hint of war or armed attack.
>
> It will be recorded that the distance of Hawaii from Japan makes it obvious that the attack was deliberately planned many days or even weeks ago. During the intervening time the Japanese Government has deliberately sought to deceive the United States by false statements and expressions of hope for continued peace.
>
> The attack yesterday on the Hawaiian Islands has caused severe damage to American naval and military forces. Very many American lives have been lost. In addition, American ships have been reported torpedoed on the high seas between San Francisco and Honolulu.
>
> Yesterday the Japanese Government also launched an attack against Malaya.
>
> Last night Japanese forces attacked Hong Kong.

323

Last night Japanese forces attacked Guam.

Last night Japanese forces attacked the Philippine Islands.

Last night the Japanese attacked Wake Island.

This morning the Japanese attacked Midway Island.

Japan has, therefore, undertaken a surprise offensive extending throughout the Pacific area. The facts of yesterday speak for themselves. The people of the United States have already formed their opinions and well understand the implications to the very life and safety of our nation.

As Commander-in-Chief of the Army and Navy I have directed that all measures be taken for our defense.

Always will we remember the character of the onslaught against us.

No matter how long it may take us to overcome this premeditated invasion, the American people in their righteous might will win through to absolute victory.

I believe I interpret the will of Congress and of the people when I assert that we will not only defend ourselves to the uttermost but will make very certain that this form of treachery shall never endanger us again.

Hostilities exist. There is no blinking at the fact that our people, our territory, and our interests are in grave danger.

With confidence in our armed forces—with the unbounded determination of our people—we will gain the inevitable triumph—so help us God.

I ask that Congress declare that since the unprovoked and dastardly attack by Japan on Sunday, December seventh, [1941], a state of war has existed between the United States and the Japanese Empire.

The United States was entering a global conflict to the rhythms of a vast industrial machine suddenly come to life after a decade of somnolence, but it would be an industrial machine far greater than the one that had sputtered to paralysis in 1929. With a federal mechanism put in place by the New Deal to manage a global war, and with American forces in action all over the world, commitments were being forged which would determine the scope of the American empire for the rest of the century. The last year of the old America, secure in its isolation, the last year of those lazy summers and provincial slumbers, that last year, 1940, had now vanished like the morning mist. Things would never be the same again. In the phrase of Yeats, a terrible beauty had been born.

SELECTED BIBLIOGRAPHY

In writing this account of the year 1940, extensive use was made of the pertinent periodical literature, e.g., *Time, Life,* the *New York Times* and other newspapers. In addition, the following books, among others, proved valuable.

Barbour, Alan G. *Humphrey Bogart* (Pyramid, N.Y., 1973).

Bergreen, Laurence. *James Agee: A Life* (E. P. Dutton, N.Y., 1984).

Berlin, Isaiah. *Personal Impressions* (Viking, N.Y., 1980).

Blaik, Earl. *The Red Blaik Story* (Arlington House, New Rochelle, N.Y., 1974).

Breiting, Richard. *Hitler* (John Day, N.Y., 1971).

Brendon, Piers. *Winston Churchill* (Harper and Row, N.Y., 1984).

Cannon, Jimmy. *Nobody Asked Me, But* (Holt, Rinehart and Winston, N.Y., 1978).

Caro, Robert. *The Power Broker* (Knopf, N.Y., 1974).

Collier, Richard. *1940: The Avalanche* (Dial Press, N.Y., 1979).

De Gregorio, George. *Joe DiMaggio* (Stein and Day, N.Y., 1981).

French, Warren. *John Steinbeck* (Twayne, N.Y., 1975).

Gallagher, Hugh Gregory. *FDR's Splendid Deception* (Dodd Mead, N.Y., 1985).

Grobman, Alex and Devid Landes, eds. *Genocide* (Simon Wiesenthal, Los Angeles, 1983).

Harrison, Helen A. et al. *Dawn of a New Day: The New York World's Fair 1939-40* (New York University Press, N.Y., 1980).

Joes, Anthony James. *Mussolini* (Franklin Watts, N.Y., 1982).

Kramer, Jack. *The Game* (Putnam, N.Y., 1979).

Leamer, Laurence. *As Time Goes By: The Life of Ingrid Bergman* (Harper and Row, N.Y. 1986).

Lloyd, Ann. *Movies of the Forties* (Orbis, London, 1982).

Loomis, Vincent, with Jeffrey Ethell. *Amelia Earhart: The Final Story* (Random House, N.Y., 1985).

Lord, Walter. *The Miracle of Dunkirk* (Viking, New York, 1982).

Louis, Joe. *My Life* (Harcourt Brace Jovanovich, New York, 1978).

Mead, Chris. *Champion: Joe Louis, Black Hero in White America* (Scribner's, N.Y., 1985).

Morgan, Ted. *FDR: A Biography* (Simon and Schuster, N.Y., 1986).

Neal, Steve. *Dark Horse: A Biography of Wendell Willkie* (Doubleday, N.Y., 1984).

Pegler, Westbrook. *'Taint Right* (Doubleday Doran, Garden City, 1936).

Rice, Damon. *Seasons Past* (Praeger, N.Y., 1976).

Romasco, Albert U. *The Politics of Recovery* (Oxford University Press, N.Y., 1983).

Segal, Ronald. *Leon Trotsky* (Pantheon Books, N.Y., 1979).

Shields, William X. *Bigger Than Life: A Biography of Francis X. Shields* (Freundlich, N.Y., 1986).

Snow, Richard. *Coney Island* (Brightwaters Press, N.Y., 1984).

Strait, Raymond and Leif Henie. *Queen of Ice, Queen of Shadow* (Stein and Day, N.Y., 1985).

Taylor, John Russell. *Strangers in Paradise* (Holt, Rinehart and Winston, N.Y., 1985).

Toland, John. *Adolf Hitler* (Random House, N.Y., 1976).

INDEX